Praise for *Border and Rule*

"In Walia's expert hands, the planet's sprawling borderlands are exposed as capitalism's gaping wounds, filled with escalating terror and torment as whiteness ferociously seeks to defend its imagined boundaries. This is ⸺ of unsparing truth and dazzling ambition, providing read⸺ with ⸺ led intellectual ammunition to confront the ⸺ rmous contribution to our movements."

of *On Fire*

"I was haunted and agitated by this ⸺ larion call for radical action. Harsha Walia of ⸺ of the violences of forced migration, borders, imperialis. ⸺ capitalism. The case studies presented in this book weave a quilt that provides us with needed knowledge to confront current problems that demand an organized collective response. The ideas in this book will linger long after you've put it down."

—Mariame Kaba, founder and director of Project NIA

"This indispensable, deeply researched, and beautifully written book is the first and most in-depth global analysis of borders and immigration, wars and displacement, and imperialism and Western white nationalism. Always with her ear to the ground and paying close attention to the people whose lives are wrecked or lost, Walia demands action and offers real solutions."

—Roxanne Dunbar-Ortiz, author of *Not "A Nation of Immigrants"* and *An Indigenous Peoples' History of the United States*.

"Harsha Walia's deeply thoughtful and well-written book makes creative connections that other writers have preferred to ignore. It offers a lucid, insightful survey of the most difficult political issues that we face."

—Paul Gilroy, author of *The Black Atlantic*

"In this exceptional book, Harsha Walia takes us on a stunning and terrifying tour of the Great Wall of Capitalism, the border killing zone where viral fascism feeds on the bodies of the poor and persecuted."

—Mike Davis, author of *The Monster at Our Door* and coauthor of *No One Is Illegal*

"*Border and Rule* provides a kaleidoscopic exposé, painstaking analysis, and damning indictment of the border regimes that are generating and fueling anti-migrant brutality and state violence on an international scale. Harsha Walia is relentless in drilling into, detailing, and cataloguing the array of processes, players, policies, and ideologies that uphold systems of border imperialism—while simultaneously mapping out for us an understanding of how we can disrupt and dismantle them."

—Justin Akers Chacón, author of *Radicals in the Barrio* and coauthor of *No One Is Illegal*

"Building on the thesis of her seminal book *Undoing Border Imperialism*, Harsha Walia's incisive voice in *Border and Rule*—equally rigorously theoretical and lovingly community-minded—refuses to allow our struggles and organizing to exist in vacuums. From anti-Black police murders and carcerality, to the fortressing of borders across Indigenous lands, to the fabricated migrant crises, to the exploitations of their labor, and to the racial nationalisms and legal structures that drive these violences, Walia's latest book provides an international cartography of the crisis of global neoliberalism. It is a stunning and horrific elucidation of Ayesha Siddiqi's line that 'Every border implies the violence of its maintenance.' But the narrative Walia deftly weaves is the polar opposite of alarmist political nihilism: it is a clarion call for our solidarities to always transcend the physical and ideological boundaries drawn by empire. This is not simply a book about violence, it is also a book about the potential for care and for freedom."   **—Zoé Samudzi**, coauthor of *As Black Resistance*

"Timely and topical, *Border and Rule* will be of interest to scholars, activists, and general readers. Walia connects variants of ethnonationalism across borders and illustrates how a world order predicated on aggression and displacement harms the most vulnerable among us, a category that includes a significant portion of the global population. Her analysis presents clear and compelling evidence that our current trajectory is unsustainable and offers cogent solutions trained on justice for the victims of endless war and colonial accumulation."
      —Steven Salaita, author of *Inter/Nationalism* and *Uncivil Rites*

"Harsha Walia's *Border and Rule* forwards a clear and incisive analysis of the multiple crises facing migrants today amidst the rise of racist nationalisms globally. Her work highlights the entanglements between global capitalism, imperialism, and past and present dynamics of Indigenous genocide and anti-Black governance that are at the heart of the border regime. *Border and Rule* is a must-read, sure to become a classic, for those of us concerned with building a world premised on freedom of movement, against and beyond the logics of the nation-state."
      —Robyn Maynard, author of *Policing Black Lives*

"Read Harsha Walia and your understanding of the world will shift. This book is a comprehensive demolition of the borders that divide us and a deft takedown of the myth of the nation. Through a range of case studies, Walia reveals overarching patterns of exclusion and exploitation, crisscrossing the globe to make a brave, deeply learned, and utterly convincing call for radical solidarity. With cries of 'build a wall' ringing out and ethnonationalism gaining steam, Walia's critical intervention couldn't be better timed."   **—Astra Taylor**, author of *Democracy May Not Exist, but We'll Miss It When It's Gone*

"Confused about how we got to this point? Harsha Walia explains clearly and concisely the multiple forces causing global poverty and displacement—and the resistance and organizing around the world. Walia provides a historical analysis of policies that have cut down people's well-being and driven poverty, violence, terror, and mass migration, and highlights the myriad forms of resistance and organizing that are all too often invisibilized. An excellent explanation of borders, migration, and the exploitative systems that produce both." —**Victoria Law**, author of *Resistance Behind Bars*

"Harsha Walia's decades of visionary leadership in border abolition and migrant justice work, along with her relentless intellectual rigor, is apparent in this immensely important book, arriving right when we need it most. As governments lock down borders, mobilizations against policing reach new peaks, economic crisis worsens, and climate change accelerates, we desperately need this book if we hope to build a nuanced analysis of what we are facing and what kinds of transformation are necessary. Walia deftly exposes the inadequacy of liberal responses to the current crises, paving the way for a deeper understanding of the conditions we are facing and meaningful avenues for resistance. Walia's deeply researched, crystal-clear text creates a robust toolbox for comprehending the current crises and assessing resistance strategies. This book is invaluable right now, a must-read for anyone working to dismantle prisons and borders, and to end poverty and war."
— **Dean Spade**, author of *Mutual Aid: Building Solidarity During this Crisis (and the Next)*

"As communities and social movements scramble to respond to the threat of a globalized far-right against the apocalyptic backdrop of a global pandemic and impending ecological disaster, Harsha Walia's *Border and Rule* reminds us of how we got here. With clinical precision, Walia unravels the genealogies and histories of border militarization, incarceration, and imperialism, laying bare the webs of domination and exploitation that threaten the poor and vulnerable everywhere, from those incarcerated in Australia's offshore immigration camps to the victims of drone warfare in Yemen. As we struggle with the cruel symptoms of a global disease—incarceration, exploitation, occupation, colonialism, environmental collapse—Walia picks this web apart, exposing the ways in which these crises interlock and overlap. It is a stark but necessary blueprint to understand. This book is also full of hope. It bears witness to the struggles of those who have survived and continue to resist in spite of merciless repression—the Indigenous, the enslaved, the exploited, the dispossessed, and the undocumented. It is an urgent and revolutionary call to action that invites us to revisit the problem so that we may dream and fight harder for the world we want." —**Aamer Rahman**, comedian with *Fear of a Brown Planet*

"We know that borders are violence. We know that violence numbs our collective imagination. We know that imagination is a muscle that must be exercised daily to prevent atrophy. This book is the workout. *Border and Rule* works us. With rigor, precision, and care, Harsha Walia pushes us beyond false solutions, rainbow imperialisms, and exclusionary projections. What a privilege to think with her, to build movement muscle for a world free of borders." —**Shailja Patel**, author of *Migritude*

"Every once in a while there comes a book that makes you never see the world the same way again. Harsha Walia's *Border and Rule* is such a book. Incisive and rigorously researched, Walia lays bare the border apparatus like no other: its bloody history based on colonial dispossession, Indigenous genocides, anti-Black enslavement, and its contemporary function of maintaining—with militarized enforcement of divisions—a racialized global system of subjugation and exploitation rife with criminal inequalities and ecological catastrophes. *Border and Rule* is the most important reframing of borders and their enforcement apparatus that I have ever read. It demonstrates that the border is not a passive wall but an expansive omnipresent regime and that there is no "border crisis" but a displacement crisis. I will be turning to its pages again and again, not only for its analysis but also for its inspiration. Indeed, Walia strips borders of their pretense and justifications in such a powerful way, that after finishing the book it feels like we can tear down the walls, and all they represent, with our bare hands."

—**Todd Miller**, author of *Empire of Borders* and *Border Patrol Nation*

Border & Rule

*Global Migration, Capitalism,
and the Rise of Racist Nationalism*

HARSHA WALIA

Haymarket Books
Chicago, Illinois

Published in 2021 by
Haymarket Books
P.O. Box 180165
Chicago, IL 60618
773-583-7884
www.haymarketbooks.org
info@haymarketbooks.org

ISBN: 978-1-64259-269-6

Distributed to the trade in the US through Consortium Book Sales and Distribution (www.cbsd.com) and internationally through Ingram Publisher Services International (www.ingramcontent.com).

This book was published with the generous support of Lannan Foundation and Wallace Action Fund.

Special discounts are available for bulk purchases by organizations and institutions. Please call 773-583-7884 or email info@haymarketbooks.org for more information.

Cover design by Rachel Cohen.

Printed in Canada by union labor.

Library of Congress Cataloging-in-Publication data is available.

10 9 8 7 6 5 4

for Stella August (Nuu-chah-nulth Nation)
for Sheung Leung (Popo 婆婆 Sue)
for Beatrice Starr (Heiltsuk Nation)

beloved elder matriarchs
in the Downtown Eastside, a borderland of sorts

Contents

Acknowledgments

Like all endeavors toward liberation, this book is a collective effort.

Haymarket Books has skillfully shepherded this book and welcomed me into their legendary house of publishing. Thank you to Anthony Arnove, Ashley Smith, Róisín Davis, Jim Plank, Charlotte Heltai, Ida Audeh, and everyone on the team who believed in this book. Nisha Bolsey, in particular, responded to all my rookie questions about publishing, and her warm encouragement despite my lack of academic or institutional affiliation, and generous flexibility with timelines and word counts, were pivotal in this book coming to fruition. Compañera Naomi Klein also offered invaluable guidance and advice. I am utterly thrilled and humbled that the genius of Robin Kelley, whose prolific scholarly work and uncompromising political commitment has been one of my foremost inspirations, is part of this book, and that Nick Estes, one of our generation's most politically grounded and profound thinkers in this corner of the world, has offered an afterword. I remain eternally grateful to comrades Robin and Nick for giving so freely of their revolutionary, internationalist spirit to think and write alongside.

I am blessed this book has been guided by the intellectual and ethical rigor of Tamara K. Nopper, offering shape to my arguments and challenging me to think deeper with her razor-sharp insights and probing questions at this book's inception. Tamara's scholarly work has long influenced me, and working with her was a dream come true. Will Tavlin was a diligent fact-checker, curbing my enthusiasm for hyperbole in every sentence (ha!). Mehtab Chhina's excitement for the research was contagious, and I am thankful for his assistance in transcribing troves of material and indulging my nerdy rabbit holes. In the middle of the pandemic and with their own lives turned upside down, Adam Hanieh, Syed Hussan, Anja Kanngieser, Jenna Loyd, David Moffette, and Dawn Paley gave so generously of their time to read and offer thoughtful comments. My biggest debt is to Stefanie Gude, a patient friend and exacting editor who deserves any and all praise for this book's clarity and coherence. This manuscript was a pile of word vomit until Stef's fairy pen and gentle magic touched it.

I am grateful to Nassim Elbardouh and Sozan Savehilaghi, who read through and heard me stumble through the worst parts of this book, and offered their unqualified support and constructive engagement. These angels are two of the most inquisitive futurists, and their feminist friendship and loyal sisterhood has grown me in the best ways possible. Harjap Grewal is the most loving co-parent and my biggest critic, and our political debates have sharpened my analysis and argumentation. Our comradeship is both rocky and my rock, this life's strangest and greatest gift. My radiant daughter, Avnika, has been my most steady source of encouragement, and her faith in my ability to produce a useful book ("just say borders are bad") and be a decent mother is sunshine on the gloomiest and loneliest of days. I cannot remember life before the gaggle of babies and kids around me, and their relentless antics and unconditional affection springs a deep hope. May we make the world worthy of their trust.

Everything I have written has been said before. The citations trace an inheritance of intellectual labor by brilliant writers, and the book also draws heavily from the innumerable conversations and collaborations with hundreds of community members and organizers over the years. Movement organizing spaces, and kinship networks within them, have always been my primary teacher. Thank you to those comrades named above as well as Adriana Paz Ramirez, Alaina John, Alejandra López Bravo, Alejandro Zuluaga, Alex Hundert, Alex Mah, Arthur Manuel, Audrey Huntley, Audrey Siegl, Avi Lewis, Ayendri Perera, Benita Bunjun, Binish Ahmed, Bridget Tolley, Carmen Aguirre, Carol Muree Martin, Cassie Sutherland, Cease Wyss, Cecilia Point, Cecily Nicholson, Chanelle Gallant, Chauncey Carr, Chin Banerjee, Chris Dixon, Clayton Thomas-Muller, Colleen Cardinal, Cynthia Dewi Oka, Daisy Chen, Dana Olwan, Dustin Johnson, Ellen Gabriel, Erica Violet Lee, Eriel Tchekwie Deranger, Faria Kamal, Fariah Chowdhury, Fathima Cader, Fatima Jaffer, Freda Huson, Glen Coulthard, Gord Hill, Gurpreet Singh, Hari Alluri, Hari Sharma, Hubie, Irene Billy, Irina Ceric, Ivan Drury, Jaggi Singh, Janice Billy, Jen Meunier, Jen Wickham, Jessica Danforth, Jorge Salazar, Kanahus Manuel, Karen Cocq, Karla Lottini, Kat Norris, Khalilah Alwani, Kiko Montilla,

Khelsilem, Kirpa Kaur, Konstantin Kilibarda, Jerilyn Webster, Laibar Singh, Leah Lakshmi Piepzna-Samarasinha, Lee Maracle, Leila Darwish, Lena Mc-Farlane, Liisa Schofield, Lily Shinde, Lindsay Bomberry, Mac Scott, Magin Payet Scudalleri, Mel Bazil, Melina Laboucan-Massimo, Melissa Elliott, Mike Gouldhawke, Molly Wickham, Mostafah Henaway, Myrna Cranmer, Naava Smolash, Nandita Sharma, Nanky Rai, Natalie Knight, Nazila Bettache, Nora Butler Burke, Omar Chu, Parker Johnson, Parul Sehgal, Philippa Ryan, Proma Tagore, Rachna Singh, Ray Bobb, Rita Wong, Robyn Maynard, Ros Salvador, Rosina Kazi, Ruby Smith Díaz, Rup Sidhu, Sacheen, Sadhu Binning, Samir Shaheen-Hussain, Samira Sud, Sara Kendall, Sean Devlin, Setareh Moham-madi, Shadrach Kabango, Shameem Akhtar, Sharmarke Mohamed, Sharmeen Khan, Shireen Soofi, Shiri Pasternak, Skundaal, Smogelgem, Stan Kupfer-schmidt, Suzanne Patles, Teresa Diewert, TJ Tupechka, Tracey Jastinder Mann, Wayde Compton, Wolverine, Yogi Acharya, Zainab Amadahy, and many others for all that they have taught me. The ecosystem of resistance is an inherently collectivist one, and my acknowledgments here are as much an expression of personal gratitude as they are an affirmation of the interdependencies of labor and genealogies of movement knowledge produced together.

The Downtown Eastside has been a spiritual and political home, and women and elders in the neighborhood, whom I will not name to preserve their anonymity and safety, have extended me their trust, respect, and teachings, which will live with me forever. Their precise and unflinching ability to discern the truth of the world, and their daily practices of nurturing care, courage, and coexistence are actualizations of true liberation. My praxis has also evolved and continues to transform as a result of generative critiques and direct challenges. Though hard to swallow, most have been necessary, and this work is part of my meditation on interrogating my complicities (as a cisgendered savarna non-Black immigrant-settler with a managerial-class job in the NPIC on stolen lands) and stretching my political analysis and ethical commitments. My material privileges are built atop the unceded jurisdictions of Musqueam, Squamish, and Tsleil-Waututh nations and, in continuities of oppression, also the extracted lands, exploited labor, and expendable lives of many others locally and globally. This book is in service to dismantling the violences we are bound up in and to imagining relations and worlds anew.

Foreword

I write these words amid a global pandemic. The twenty-four-hour news cycle is saturated with images of suffering and death as well as a parade of healthcare professionals recruited to share stories from the front lines or impart expert opinion. These workers are often South Asian, Latinx, Caribbean, Filipino, and African American, many presumably immigrants or children of immigrants. They are the battle-worn troops at war, not only with this new virulent strain of coronavirus, but with a privatized, corporate healthcare system and public policies that continue to put profit before people. And they continue to risk their lives in an increasingly xenophobic and racist political culture.

The Covid-19 crisis, therefore, lays bare an even larger theater of war—one that the mainstream media largely ignores. The US government has accelerated border closings, imposed more barriers to asylum seekers, and expanded immigrant detention. Laws protecting workers are being shunned, and retail and warehouse workers for Amazon and Instacart, gig workers, and laborers in the meatpacking industry fight for their lives as infection rates rise exponentially. Indian country has become the latest coronavirus epicenter in the US, thanks largely to the federal government's continued legacy of neglect. Prisoners and prison staff are the most vulnerable, with 80 percent of the prisoners at Ohio's Marion Correctional Institution testing positive for the virus. We have seen a spike in anti-Asian racism provoked by the myth that "Chinese" are carriers. Cases of domestic violence have also spiked, as many women have been forced to choose between homelessness and "sheltering in place" with abusive partners. Meanwhile, armed white militias have begun to show up at rallies and on the steps of state capitols, defying social distancing measures. After years of watching footage of unarmed Black people beaten and killed by police for walking, loitering, running, standing in front of their homes, showing insufficient deference, protecting their kids, or being a kid, these scenes of white men brandishing AR-15s in the face of police and government officials and evading jail, injury, or death begs incredulity.

Harsha Walia's incisive and prescient book, *Border and Rule*, could not have been timelier. She reminds us that these wars are not new. This global pandemic is just the latest manifestation of capitalism's five-hundred-year war on the earth by means of land enclosure, dispossession, occupation, extraction, exploitation, commodification, consumption, destruction, pollution, immiseration, and oppressive forms of governance. It is war on the people in the form of military violence, executed in the name of "security"—securing resources, borders, life, and "liberty" against dictators, terrorists, and communists. As a consequence, most of the earth's inhabitants face unprecedented levels of displacement, detention, debt, precarity, poverty, and premature death. The past decade bore witness to insurgencies against this global war regime and its neoliberal ideology in the form of Occupy, the Arab Spring, anti-austerity protests, the defense of Latin America's Bolivarian revolutions, and resistance to racialized state violence everywhere. But we have also seen a resurgence of racist nationalism, misogyny, femicide, and authoritarian regimes *elected* into power.

What do we make of our current condition? If you want answers, read this book. If you believe the culprit is Donald Trump and his crew and that all we need is a return to the good old days of Clinton/Obama/Biden, *definitely read this book*. Harsha Walia doesn't peddle easy solutions or liberal bromides. She has a knack for going to the root of our planetary crises and explaining how we arrived here, and what to do about it. Those of us who have been reading and following her for years expect nothing less. She is not only one of North America's most brilliant thinkers, but also an organizer who has devoted her life to fighting racial capitalism, colonialism, militarism, xenophobia, patriarchy, and defending the rights of migrants, Indigenous people, women, and the unhoused.

This book is a shock to the system. The evidence she marshals of mass detention, state-sanctioned violence, the suspension of democracy, the commodification of care and goods we need to live, and the global scale of authoritarianism will certainly shock anyone out of complacency and disrupt easy explanations for the refugee crisis. *Border and Rule* is also a kind of epistemic shock to the oft-repeated mantra that the US and Canada are "nations of immigrants." Critics of Trump and his regime's draconian immigration policies persistently invoke this mantra, insisting that building walls and criminalizing hardworking people seeking opportunity is inconsistent with our values as descendants of immigrants. Besides erasing Indigenous and Black people, and ignoring the fact that all modern democracies were founded as ethnonational and/or racial states where exclusion and xenophobia were commonplace, the "nation of immigrants" paradigm implies that the original dream driving (European) settlement was a dream of freedom for all but simply unfulfilled. Walia exposes this story for what it is: a lie. The US, Canada, and Australia were not the creation of hardworking, plucky pioneers seeking a better, more democratic life for all but, rather, the product of the violence of capitalist expansion and racial ideology, armed settlers backed by joint stock companies, a colonial state apparatus, and capital in the form of kidnapped labor.

Walia attends to the history of settler colonialism and its racist, patriarchal, and nationalist foundations, but she also understands the moment we're in now and where we might be headed if we don't fight back. The resurgence of right-wing nationalism, whether under Trump, Bolsonaro, Modi, Orbán, or Duterte, is not history repeating itself. It is not the fascism of the 1930s redux, nor does it mark the end of neoliberalism. Rather, it represents both a continuation of neoliberal logic and a new historic bloc comprising extreme right-wing fundamentalists, corporate interests, and a portion of disaffected working people to form a new authoritarian, neofascist movement ruled by fear but still governed by neoliberal reason. Vestiges of a welfare state are replaced by an expanded military-police state tasked with protecting "national interests," defending borders, creating conditions favorable to capital (no matter the cost to health, the environment, or the most vulnerable people), and privatizing wealth while socializing risk. As long as the nation-state is understood to be a corporation and therefore *owned*, ownership also takes on a domestic quality. Nationalist discourse is about protecting the home front, and the nation is cast as a home in need of security in an unstable world.

For Walia, nationalism, capitalism, and its neoliberal push for privatization, and the concomitant demonization of the Other—the stranger, the minority, the migrant—constitute the real security threat. Granting and protecting liberal rights for all is simply not enough. We need to overturn this system, we need *revolution*. Walia is not afraid of that word, nor does she underestimate what is required to build genuine and effective international solidarity. The power of a global working class, she reveals, is masked by the very category of the im/migrant. She demonstrates that the migrant is not a thing, an object, or even an identity. The migrant is a historically contingent, relational category imposed by the state. It is a category that uses difference (often race) to determine the rights and privileges of citizenship, facilitate labor segmentation, ensure a vast army of casualized labor, and empower the state to use deportation to remove dangerous, unwanted, or deviant sections of the working class. The category of im/migrant has been essential in forming the nation-state and national identity; constructing borders and a security regime to define and police those borders; and reproducing ideologies justifying inclusion, exclusion, and outright criminalization.

Racist nationalism has long regarded the "immigrant," alongside the domestic poor, as an environmental threat. Walia reveals how the threat of climate catastrophe is used as justification for ethnic cleansing, freeing capitalism from any responsibility for a warming planet, wildfires, and massive inequality. Liberals, she points out, are complicit in creating and maintaining modern-day eco-apartheid. They look to corporations as saviors by promoting cap and trade, natural gas, and "clean coal" as alternatives, and they regard the climate refugee as a problem to be treated as any other humanitarian crisis—with relief, shelters, and temporary aid.

As long as we treat migrant, displaced labor as dependent wards of philanthropic largesse, we won't see them for what they are: the very heart of a global labor force whose movements are linked to war, capital flows, policies imposed by states and international financial/economic bodies, racist and patriarchal security regimes, and the struggles of working people on every side of every border. The liberal claim that this "nation of immigrants" must simply live up to its creed of inclusion, fix our broken immigration system by rationalizing the process of documentation, naturalization, and citizen-making, masks the historical and structural forces that produce the migrant, giving way to false dichotomies (e.g., immigrants *compete* with "American" labor). And perhaps most importantly, it masks their power—the power to end human suffering and save the planet.

In other words, what we usually call "immigrant" struggles are indisputably labor struggles or *class struggles*. It is no accident that anti-immigrant laws and so-called criminal syndicalism and anti-sedition laws were often considered one and the same. During the first half of the twentieth century in the US, socialists, anarchists, communists, and trade unionists were frequently targeted for deportation. And this is why organizations such as the Industrial Workers of the World (IWW) insisted that all working people resist deportations on the principle that an injury to one is an injury to all. Walia compels us to shift our perspective, to take a longer and broader view of the struggle not as immigrant rights or the immigrant problem, but as a global struggle against capital and empire under a thoroughly racist and patriarchal system.

No one is excluded. No one is illegal. She is clear about what is to be done: "Exclusionary projections of who belongs and who has the right to life upholds ruling-class and right-wing nationalism, thus breaking internationalist solidarity and entrenching global apartheid. A political and economic system that treats land as a commodity, Indigenous people as overburden, race as a principle of social organization, women's caretaking as worthless, workers as exploitable, climate refugees as expendable, and the entire planet as a sacrifice zone must be dismantled."

Robin D. G. Kelley
May Day, 2020

Introduction

"But how can you say gentrifiers aren't welcome when you believe no one is illegal?" asked a caller to a conservative radio talk show on which I appeared, against my better judgment. Discussing an anti-gentrification rally planned by women in Vancouver's Downtown Eastside, one of the poorest neighborhoods in Canada, I was outlining the lived experiences of escalating displacement, homelessness, and police violence when a caller hopped on and referenced my migrant justice organizing against detentions and deportations. I was being baited, of course, but the question nagged at me for months. Anti-gentrification struggles push back against the forces of racial capitalism and the entitlement of those seeking to solidify their power, as they profit from and police neighborhoods already under siege. Confronting gentrification is about opposing those who represent and reproduce structural and spatial injustice, not about preventing the movement of oppressed people seeking safety and dignity. People *do* move into the Downtown Eastside every day, in search of better services, hoping to secure social housing, care for their aging family, and knit kinship networks in a vibrant oasis of low-income residents, Indigenous matriarchs, Chinese Canadian seniors, artists, drug users, sex workers, and cacophonous dissidents. Migrants and refugees have much more in common with these humble residents than they do with rapacious hipster colonists.

While the caller was blatant and opportunistic in conflating gentrifiers with migrants and, conversely, anti-gentrifiers with border agents, the conclusion was unsurprising. Even though bordering and gentrifying regimes work to hoard wealth, displace people, and police racial segregation, the popular characterization of migrants and refugees as "foreign invaders" turns the border into a purportedly anticolonial architecture. The border, however, is less

1

about a politics of movement per se and is better understood as a key method of imperial state formation, hierarchical social ordering, labor control, and xenophobic nationalism.

Following Vivek Shraya, who raises the compelling question "Why is my humanity only seen or cared about when I share the ways in which I have been victimized and violated?" this book refuses anthropological consumption.[1] Numerous stories and photographs circulate about dead migrants and refugees attempting to cross the Mediterranean Sea, the Pacific Ocean, the Rio Grande, and the Sahara and Sonoran Deserts. Media images of the drowning deaths of toddlers Alan Kurdi and Angie Valeria went viral to invoke shock and sympathy, yet the same media outlets depict the world's remaining seventy million refugees as swarms, floods, invaders. One refugee may summon pity, but large groups are painted as a threat. Instead of romanticizing migrants and refugees as either poor victims or heroic survivors, totalizing their experiences, I turn our gaze away from varied subjectivities to the systems of power that create migrants yet criminalize migration. Classifications such as "migrant" or "refugee" don't represent unified social groups so much as they symbolize *state-regulated* relations of governance and difference.

I have previously theorized "border imperialism" to depict the processes "by which the violences and precarities of displacement and migration are structurally created as well as maintained," including through imperial subjugation, criminalization of migration, racialized hierarchy of citizenship, and state-mediated exploitation of labor.[2] While *Undoing Border Imperialism* is a contribution to movement organizing, this book is a modest endeavor to more deeply interrogate the formation and function of borders as a spatial and material power structure. Borders are an ordering regime, both assembling and assembled through racial-capitalist accumulation and colonial relations. By looking at various jurisdictions around the world, I also intend to break through methodological nationalism—specifically US exceptionalism—and unearth transnational trends. Many on the left believe the cruelties of US immigration policy are homegrown and then exported, when, in fact, most repressive technologies of border rule are perfected elsewhere. *Border and Rule: Global Migration, Capitalism, and the Rise of Racist Nationalism* examines a number of seemingly disparate geographies with shared logics of border formation—displacing, immobilizing, criminalizing, exploiting, and expelling migrants and refugees—to divide the international working class and consolidate imperial, racial-capitalist, state, ruling-class, and far-right nationalist rule.

Conservatives and liberals alike conceive of US immigration policy as an issue of domestic reform to be managed by the state. Language such as "migrant crisis," and the often-corresponding "migrant invasion," is a pretext to shore up further border securitization and repressive practices of detention and deportation. Such representations depict migrants and refugees as the *cause* of an *imagined* crisis at the border, when, in fact, mass migration is the *outcome* of the *actual* crises of capitalism, conquest, and climate change. The border crisis, as I argue in the first part, is more accurately described as crises of displacement and immobility, preventing both the freedom to stay and the freedom to move. American liberals may demand an end to excessive violence against Latinx migrants and refugees, exemplified in their opposition to concentration camps or family separation, but they rarely locate immigration and border policies within broader systemic forces. A long arc of dirty colonial coups, capitalist trade agreements extracting land and labor, climate change, and enforced oppression is the primary driver of displacement from Mexico and Central America. Migration is a predictable consequence of these displacements, yet today the US is fortifying its border against the very people impacted by its own policies. Analyzing the border as part of historic and contemporary imperial relations, hence the term "border imperialism," forces a shift from notions of charity and humanitarianism to restitution, reparations, and responsibility.

From the US–Mexico border's early formation—entangled in the terrors of territorial expansion, Indigenous genocide, anti-Black enslavement, and racialized expulsion—to the more recent hemispheric war on drugs and the global war on terror, the first two chapters detail how bipartisan US immigration policy is a linchpin in synchronous domestic and global warfare. US border rule reveals seamless relations between the carceral administration of genocide and slavery at home and imperial counterinsurgency abroad, domestic neoliberal policies of welfare retrenchment and foreign policies of capitalist trade, and local and global regimes of race. This is unmistakable in the deployment of US Border Patrol Tactical Unit (BORTAC) to train border guards in Iraq and Guatemala, while engaging in SWAT-style operations to grab protestors off the streets of Portland in unmarked vehicles at the height of Black-led uprisings against police violence in 2020. This synergy between the local and global is also evident in President Donald Trump's proposal to classify all irregular, economic migrants as "enemy combatants" and incarcerate them at Guantánamo Bay.[3] The pattern of constructing migrants as enemy aliens emerges worldwide, examined in chapter 3. Mainstream narratives of a "global migration crisis" depict migrants as threats without implicating the crises of forced dispossession, deprivation, and displacement. Capitalist dispossession and imperialist subordination manufacture bordered regimes of export processing zones in Bangladesh, land enclosures in Mozambique, and militarized settler occupation in Palestine. Border crises are, therefore, not merely domestic issues to be managed through policy reform. They must, instead, be placed within globalized asymmetries of power—inscribed by race, caste, class, gender, sexuality, ability, and nationality—creating migration and constricting mobility.

Border panics blasted in newspaper headlines take migrant "illegality" for granted, and the criminalization of migration is the focus of part 2. Displaced people become "illegal" because of multiplying technologies acting as a wall to migration, including visa restrictions, safe third country agreements, offshore detention, deportation, interdiction, militarization of maritime space, and an empire of externalization, detailed in chapter 4. Such state restrictions force people to undertake irregular, and often fatal, migration journeys. Erik Prince, operator of the world's largest mercenary training facility and the dirty Blackwater business spanning from Iraq to New Orleans, is now peddling the idea of a public–private partnership via the burgeoning border security industry to further militarize the Mediterranean, already the world's deadliest border.[4] While corporate elites and politicians outdo one another to see who can build the tallest wall as an edifice to xenophobic nationalism and state sovereignty, borders are actually elastic. I explain how borders function through four primary modes of governance beyond walls: exclusion, territorial diffusion, commodified inclusion, and discursive control.

Most maps do not conceptualize the shifting cartography of borders. Bordering regimes are increasingly layered with drone surveillance, interception of migrant boats, security controls, and boots on the ground far beyond territorial limits. This is illustrated by White Australia's exported geography of offshore detention, turning resource colonies into penal ones, surveyed in chapter 5, and Fortress Europe's externalization of border security across waterscapes, charted in chapter 6. US, Australian, and European subordination of Central America, Oceania, Africa, and the Middle East compels countries in these regions to accept external checkpoints, offshore detention, migration prevention campaigns, and expelled deportees as conditions of trade and aid agreements. Countries in these regions including Libya, Mali, Mexico, Nauru, Niger, Papua New Guinea, Turkey, and Sudan have become the new frontiers of border militarization. These countries are further dispossessed of their resources and their lands are now being used to build externalized infrastructures of migration control under racial imperial management. Imperialism is already a root cause of global migration, and now the management of global migration through outsourcing is also becoming a means of preserving imperial relations. Migrants and refugees, meanwhile, become bargaining chips for authoritarians like Recep Tayyip Erdoğan in Turkey and General Mohamed Hamdan Dagalo (Hemedti) in Sudan. To economic dependency, climate debt, and military domination, as theorized by movement giants like Walter Rodney and Edward Said, we can also add the soft power of immigration diplomacy as a central pillar in the maintenance of our colonial present.

We are told that immigration policy is about law and order, not racial exclusion in an allegedly post-racial society. But there is no objective fact of migrant illegality; as Catherine Dauvergne maintains, "Illegal migration is a product of migration law. Without legal prohibition, there is no illegality."[5] While borders are hierarchically organized and permeable for white expats, a handpicked immigrant diaspora, and the rich investor class, they form a fortress against the millions in the "deportspora," who are shut out, immobilized, and expelled.[6] The global turn toward deportation and detention as the central means of immigration enforcement is attendant to the rise of neoliberalism. The consolidation of spatial carcerality through prisons and borders correlates with wealth concentration, dismantling of public services, and the simultaneous manufacturing and disciplining of surplus populations. Contemporary Black-led abolitionist uprisings in response to the cold-blooded police murders of George Floyd, Breonna Taylor, Ahmaud Arbery, and countless others expose the crisis of legitimacy for the state, capitalism, and carceral regimes. Police, prisons, and borders operate through a shared logic of immobilization, containing oppressed communities under racial capitalism. Notably, the word "mob," a criminalizing vocabulary used to link large groups of poor, racialized people to social disorder, including in inner cities and at the border, derives from the word "mobility."[7] Even as explicitly racist prohibitions on people of certain races or national origins have been removed from most states' immigration policies in an era of alleged "color blindness," mobility continues to be restricted and contained along color, class, and caste lines. Discourses of climate security, which merge the climate crisis with the migration crisis to entrench eco-apartheid, escalate this immobilization. Amid apocalyptic invocations of the climate, austerity, and migration crises, European Commission president-elect Ursula von der Leyen, for example, suggested renaming the migration policy portfolio "Protecting Our European Way of Life."[8]

Furthermore, regardless of actual legal immigration status, racialized others are cast as cultural outsiders in shallow and essentializing multicultural discourses. Borders and the notions of belonging they engender are not simply demarcated by towering walls experienced equally by all; they rely on and reproduce racism within the spaces they establish. A vicious cycle has developed: legal routes to migration—family sponsorship, asylum claims, and permanent residency—are limited, thus increasing irregular border crossings, which in turn become a centerpiece of dog-whistle politics about "illegals" and "too many immigrants" to justify further racist migration controls. Finally, state-centric taxonomies like "unauthorized arrival" and "asylum seeker" are only possible because of a prevailing assumption of the border as a legitimate institution of governance. Even liberals arguing for more humane immigration policies presuppose the border is natural without explaining who it serves or how it functions. Nicholas De Genova probes, "If there were no borders, there would be no migration—only mobility."[9] Most ironic, the migration crisis is declared a *new* crisis with *Western* countries positioned as its victims, even though for four centuries nearly eighty million Europeans became settler-colonists across the Americas and Oceania, while four million indentured laborers from Asia were scattered across the globe and the transatlantic slave trade kidnapped and enslaved fifteen million Africans. Colonialism, genocide, slavery, and indentureship are not only conveniently erased as continuities of violence in current invocations of a migration crisis, but are also the *very* conditions of possibility for the West's preciously guarded imperial sovereignty.

Borders are not fixed or static lines; they are productive regimes concurrently generated by and producing social relations of dominance. In addition to migration being a consequence of empire, capitalism, climate catastrophe, and oppressive hierarchies, contemporary migration is *itself* a mode of global governance, capital accumulation, and gendered racial class formation. Radhika Mongia writes, "The very development of the nation-state occurred, in part, to control mobility along the axis of the nation/race," which we see in the early organization of passports to regulate movement within the British empire, foreshadowing the modern state.[10] Contrary to common analysis, borders being simultaneously monetized and militarized—open to capital but closed to people—are not contradictory juxtapositions. The free flow of capital *requires* precarious labor, which is shaped by borders through immobility. International talk of "managed migration" and a concerted shift toward "temporary labor migration" in high-income countries unambiguously proves this requirement. Insourced labor from labor migration programs and outsourced labor in free trade zones represent flip sides of the same coin. This is a bifurcation and segmentation of the global labor force, made precarious through bordering practices.

Part 3 of the book details the function and expansion of temporary labor migration. One of the five key features of temporary labor migration programs, described in chapter 7, is the legal tying of immigration status to employment. This turns migrant workers into a state-sanctioned pool of unfree, indentured laborers. The state differentiates these workers as *migrant* laborers, whose labor power is first captured by the border and then manipulated and exploited by the employer. Impoverishment is a consequence, not a coincidence, of capitalism. Temporary labor migration is a crucial method of accumulation, helping to facilitate the holding of more than $9.1 trillion of global wealth by 2,200 billionaires, while the world's poorest 3.8 billion people hold $1.4 trillion.[11] Migrant workers are kept compliant through threats of termination and deportation, dangled in tandem as union-busting mechanisms, thus revealing the crucial connection between their migration status and precarious labor position. The commodified inclusion of migrant workers is "in a continuum with exclusion, rather than in opposition to it," as border controls channel irregular migration into temporary labor migration.[12]

As the current phase of advanced capitalism, neoliberal globalization facilitates the movement of capital and militaries but restricts the mobility of impoverished racialized people *unless* they agree to inclusion as migrant workers with deflated labor power and no legal or social citizenship. We must not mistake this commodified inclusion for free migration. Migrant worker programs are carceral regimes, where many workers have their identification confiscated, are held captive in their place of employment, and are traded between employers like goods. Thus, like those of undocumented and irregular migrants and refugees, the experiences of legally authorized migrant workers are foundationally organized through immobility.

Migrant worker programs shape and are shaped by racial capitalism, where land and labor are appropriated but people are disenfranchised. Coming from Mexico and Ghana, for example, indebted farmers and peasants, displaced from their own lands and livelihoods by capitalist trade liberalization, become bonded laborers for agribusinesses in the US and Italy. Because these distinctly racialized migrant workers are categorized as "foreigners," a material and ideological differentiation is produced between them and citizens. This distinction further conjoins race to the nation-state, buttresses racialized and nationalized working-class identities, and exacerbates the legally constructed and state-sanctioned vulnerability of migrant workers. Migrant workers are segregated from citizen workers in a divergent labor pool and are unable to access labor protections or public services. They typically cannot bring their families and, in the case of domestic workers, perform the gendered labor of caring for others' families while forcibly separated from their own. This gendered racism is not secondary to, but rather is constitutive of, bordering practices, especially given the connection between feminization of labor, poverty, and migration. There is nothing inherently low-skill or low-wage about domestic work, but it is intentionally devalued by the workings of gendered racism through capitalism and bordered care chains.

While migrant workers are temporary, temporary migration is permanent. Temporary migration has become a modality central to state formation, citizenship regulation, labor segmentation within national labor markets, and segregated social ordering. I investigate the kafala system in the Gulf Cooperation Council countries in chapter 8 and the Temporary Foreign Worker Program in Canada in chapter 9. I chose these two programs because while the kafala is habitually dissected and condemned, Canada's program is labeled the "Rolls Royce" of labor migration. The far-right Alternative für Deutschland party, for instance, calls for German immigration policy to be based on the Canadian model.[13] Instead of using a liberal dichotomy to position one program as "modern-day slavery" and the other as a "best practice," I suggest both are perfected systems of labor discipline and racialized exclusion. The misogynist criminal charge of absconding in the Gulf countries and the ableist issue of medical deportation in Canada provide two of the most striking examples of migrant workers' commodification and expendability. Worldwide, as we witness escalating anti-immigrant xenophobia, fearmongering about racial demographic change, and panics about job losses due to austerity, border imperialism produces migrant workers as a pool of cheapened and disposable labor without disturbing the racial social order. Labor migration thus shapes the state and capital's ability to coerce labor and manage citizenship, dovetailing perfectly into racist nationalisms.

In summary, border imperialism produces mass displacement, while immobilizing migrants through oppressive technologies that prohibit and criminalize free migration, alongside policies expanding indentured migrant labor pools, all entwined in reactionary nationalisms, the focus of part 4. In chapter 10, I trace the connection between anti-immigrant racial violence and mounting right-wing racist nationalisms. Although far-right murders are often characterized as acts of "lone wolves," a coordinated network of groups and governments, especially in the US, Israel, India, the Philippines, Brazil, and across Europe, are escalating fascistic hatred against both migrants and subjugated citizens. I explore how they mobilize the interlocking ideologies of ethnonationalism, penal populism, welfare nationalism, and imperial gendered racism, operating together to solidify the relationship between the state, capitalism, and racism.

Racial citizenship is a universal motivating factor for far-right voters. Anti-migrant xenophobia is mapped onto enduring racial warfare against Indigenous, Dalit, Black, Muslim, Roma, and Latinx communities, as well as social warfare against rural peasant and urban poor communities. This architecture of racist nationalism, scaffolded by xenophobia against migrants, is most evident in the unfolding crisis of statelessness. I sketch the practices of turning already-subjugated citizens into stateless noncitizens in their own countries of birth in India, Myanmar, Dominican Republic, and the Arab Gulf region. These mass disenfranchisements maintain a hierarchical social order by ensconcing exclusionary racial citizenship and are as vital to producing racist nationalism as anti-migrant xenophobia itself.

Right-wing demagogues are making rising populist appeals about "foreigners" stealing *our* jobs, draining *our* services, ruining *our* environment, infecting *our* neighborhoods, and tainting *our* values. This rhetoric deflects responsibility from the underlying systems producing mass inequality, impoverishment, and misery by conveniently scapegoating "foreigners." Right-wing populist appeals uproot class struggle from capital accumulation and elite control and, instead, overlay it with entitled and exclusionary projections of who rightfully constitutes the nation-state. Anti-immigrant sentiments underwrite this demographic racism and supplement reactionary nationalism. This manifests in working-class struggles animated by race and nationality or eco-fascist trends in environmental movements, described in chapter 11. But right-wing nationalism—pitting whites against racialized people, migrant workers against unionized workers, refugees against citizens, the West against the rest—is a ruling-class ideology. It breaks internationalist solidarity, lowers the wage floor for all workers, and maintains extractivism and exclusion in a warming world. Right-wing nationalism purports to defend the working class but is vehemently anticommunist.

The politics of fear is a distracting cover for inequality and is a material basis for the disenfranchisement of racialized communities and exploitation of racialized workers. White supremacy within the working class is not simply misdirected rage about economic anxiety, nor is gendered racism extricable from class formation. Interpellations such as "white working class" or "national working class" exist at the expense of *all* working people, especially racialized immigrant women workers who comprise the working-class majority. Racialized women are overrepresented in the underpaid care sector, currently a front line in the struggle for a new green economy and whose value as an essential service socially reproducing life is crystal clear during the Covid-19 pandemic. Nurses, cleaners, teachers, domestic workers, grocery clerks, service workers, single mothers, and land defenders leading political struggles during the pandemic, and well before it, trenchantly assert that inequality is a product of austerity *and* also of differences made through nationality, race, gender, sexuality, and ability, which are co-constituents of class relations. As interdependent and interwoven societies, our fiercely internationalist struggle is not against "foreigners" but against any oppressors.

State responses to the global Covid-19 pandemic have blown off the lid on border and rule practices and exposed the fault lines in our societies. "Corona is the virus, capitalism is the pandemic," rings out loudly as millions of people endure devastating job losses, appallingly inadequate healthcare, collapsed social safety nets, cruel evictions and foreclosures, and fatal working conditions from grocery stores to meatpacking factories. As Whitney N. Laster Pirtle articulates, "[R]acial capitalism is a fundamental cause of the racial and socioeconomic inequities within the novel coronavirus pandemic."[14] While the right-wing "anti-lockdown" movement is a palpable refraction of the settler-colonial logic of frontier freedom, the most under-protected are the most overpoliced by the overlapping racial-capitalist state forces of, as Ruth Wilson Gilmore depicts it, organized abandonment alongside organized violence.[15] Refugees and migrants are bearing a disproportionate distribution of risk and violence. Despite no directive from the World Health Organization to do so, and in violation of the legal principle of non-refoulement forbidding states from returning a person to a country where they may face persecution, a staggering fifty-seven countries have shut their borders to people seeking safety.[16]

The pandemic, like every global crisis before it, provides a perfect excuse to hasten in the vision of securitized borders and usher states of emergency into permanency. The government of Malta abandoned several boats carrying refugees and migrants in the Mediterranean, claiming it was too overwhelmed by the pandemic. In one instance, Malta ignored distress calls from passengers on a boat filling up with water. Maltese officials let the boat drift for five days, during which time seven people died of dehydration and another seven people were presumed dead from drowning. Then the Maltese government clandestinely and illegally paid private vessel operators to forcibly return the boat to Libya.[17] Similarly, Italy blocked ships carrying refugees rescued in the Mediterranean from entering its ports, Bangladesh and Malaysia refused to dock trawlers with five hundred Rohingya refugees stranded at sea for months, and Hungary indefinitely suspended admission of all migrants and refugees along its border with Serbia by alleging a connection between the virus and "illegal immigration."[18]

The global health crisis also provides a pretext for further internalization of the border, with policing of the pandemic escalating the carceral containment and immobilization of migrants and refugees within states. Governments continue to incarcerate migrants and refugees in horribly overcrowded and filthy detention centers, and refugee camps and housing centers are locked down with orders imposing severe restrictions on movement. Syrian refugees in Lebanon, for example, are subjected to discriminatory restrictions, such as lengthier curfews that do not apply to Lebanese citizens, and are threatened with revocation of their identity documents for any violations.[19] African migrants in Guangzhou, China, are being subjected to mandatory testing, arbitrary quarantine, mass surveillance, forced evictions, and prohibitions on entering hospitals, stores, and restaurants.[20]

Elsewhere, police checks to enforce public health orders are a funnel for immigration enforcement, and migrants are increasingly terrified to enter highly surveilled public spaces, including when requiring access to healthcare, out of fear of being turned over to immigration authorities. In one operation in Malaysia, under the guise of preventing the spread of the virus, 586 migrants were arbitrarily rounded up and forced into immigration detention.[21] Homeless migrants and refugees are particularly impacted by the structural distribution of vulnerability. Unable to meaningfully shelter in place, they are among the most at risk of contracting the virus, while also subject to heavy state enforcement. More than three thousand homeless migrants and refugees on the outskirts of Paris live in overcrowded tent encampments within which physical distancing is not feasible. In March 2020, approximately seven hundred homeless migrants in the Aubervilliers encampment were evicted by police, who cited a risk to public health and enforcement of a national lockdown.[22] Platitudes such as "We are all in this together" are obnoxious in the face of such glaring inequality and hierarchies of rights to safety, dignity, and well-being.

While the pandemic has resulted in bans on most cross-border movement, including the essential movement of refugees seeking safety, deportation flights are violently expelling people *out* and exporting the virus to countries with weaker health and sanitation systems. In April 2020, nearly one-fifth of all known coronavirus cases in Guatemala were deportees from the US.[23] Meanwhile, parallel flights bringing migrant workers *in* remain a high priority for racial-capitalist state interests. Workers in the US agricultural and food industry have been categorized as an "essential" group of workers during the pandemic. Even though almost all other immigration and refugee processing has been brought to a halt, H-2A migrant farmworker visas are being churned out to maintain a steady supply of cheapened labor for food supply chains. Government officials are also seeking to reduce wage rates for migrant farmworkers in a relief measure for agribusinesses.[24] Though the commodities migrant farmworkers produce are deemed essential, the workers themselves are underpaid and disposable, unprotected and deportable—revealing not a contradiction but rather a *central* function of border imperialist rule. Millions of migrant and undocumented workers across the country endure impoverishment and lethal work conditions in overcrowded and unsanitary farms, meatpacking plants, and grocery stores. Without valid social security numbers, many are ineligible for federal relief stimulus checks or adequate health insurance,[25] trapped in the American dream of choosing to sell one's labor for a wage under deadly conditions or death by unemployment and destitution. Meanwhile, the US billionaire class has experienced a wealth surge of $434 billion during the coronavirus pandemic.[26]

The horrific exploitation of migrant and undocumented workers and the cruel expulsion of migrants and refugees is justified through dehumanizing far-right rhetoric scapegoating racialized bodies as "infectious" and "diseased." Trump referred to coronavirus as "the Chinese virus," ignoring the web of capitalist industrial food production extending from China to the US; he also linked the need for a border wall to the threat of disease transmission from migrants.[27] Trump's racist fearmongering echoes a long and xenophobic history of vilifying Irish, African, and Asian people for outbreaks of cholera, Ebola, and SARS. In March 2020, the US Centers for Disease Control and Prevention issued a sweeping order suspending the entry of noncitizens from countries where an outbreak of a communicable disease exists and justifying the immediate deportation of migrants and refugees at the border on public health grounds.[28] Characterizing the US nation-state as a vulnerable and pure body to be protected from foreign contagions is offensive, particularly as migrants experience deadly and dangerous conditions that leave them more susceptible to contracting the virus; ahistoric, given that European settlers introduced diseases to the US and used biological warfare to commit genocide against Indigenous people; and untrue, since the initial spread of the coronavirus is more closely associated with luxury and business travel by the upper classes of rich countries than the movements of migrants and refugees.[29]

The spread of the novel coronavirus across borders unearths another truth: flattening the curve requires flattening all inequality. To keep any one of us safe, we must keep every single one of us safe. Yet most discussions about immigration tend to emphasize seemingly neutral and technocratic questions of quotas and legality. Liberal centrism tries to convince us the best solution to right-wing revanchism and its entanglements with anti-migrant xenophobia is a superficial antiracism, exemplified through the refrains of "racism is bad" and "hate is a virus." Liberal antiracist analysis, obsessed with superficial representation and flag-waving, purposefully fails to interrogate the material structures upending racism. Instead, we are offered the shallow politics of humanitarianism, such as "Welcome refugees," or liberal multiculturalism proclaiming "We are all from somewhere," or commodifying platitudes such as "Immigrants build our economy." Such moralizing discourses emphasize generosity toward "good" immigrants and refugees, for whom "buying power, respectability, assimilation, and nationalism are the price of welcome" into neoliberal citizenship.[30] People from the professional class, proximate to the dominant race and caste, cisheteronormative, and without criminal records are selected and welcomed as an act of benevolence to serve racial-capitalist political economies.

In the face of the far right's overt racism, liberal centrists defend a hollow multiculturalism, even though its essentialized framings of culture animate racial violence. Liberal multiculturalists and racist nationals share an assumption that racialized communities are "bearers of difference,"[31] and, as such, state multiculturalism is organized to subtend, not dismantle, racial power. Sara Ahmed explains, "Strangers are not simply those we do not recognise but those we recognise as strangers."[32] While liberalism may challenge negative stereotypes attributed to the "stranger," it still assumes and imbues meaning in this recognition of immigrants *as* strangers. The categorization of immigrants as strangers and outsiders, whether tolerated through commodified inclusion or marked for exclusion, consolidates racial state governance.

Our movements must refuse *both* the vicious far right and the banal liberal center. Status-quo liberalism upholding neoliberal capitalism is interwoven with right-wing nationalism inflected by class, race, caste, gender, sexuality, ability, and citizenship. Both anti-refugee xenophobia and liberal gestures of charity fail to challenge the root causes of displacement and colonial-capitalist complicity in order to maintain global asymmetries of power. Racist ethnonationalism and liberal multiculturalism both serve to uphold racial regimes through a social organization of difference. A proclamation like "Immigrants steal our jobs," and its rejoinder, "Our economy needs immigrants" treats immigrants as commodities to be traded in capitalist markets and discarded if deemed defective. Migrant justice must not endorse categories of desirable or undesirable, expectations of gratitude or assimilation, gestures of charitable humanitarianism, tropes of migrating to modernity, the commodification of labor to benefit capital accumulation, or state borders and other carceral regimes as legitimate institutions of governance.

A prevailing assumption, even among some progressives, is that while blatant immigration restrictions are racist, *too much* immigration would "taint" cultural values and "flood" labor markets. This is apparent in the founding of Aufstehen, a German leftist organization opposed to open border policies, as well as the surge of Blue Labour during and after the 2019 UK election calling for "conservative socialism" in opposition to Jeremy Corbyn's migration platform. But borders do not protect labor; the border is a bundle of relations and mode of governance acting as a spatial fix for capital to segment labor and buffer against the retrenchment of universal social programs. Simply put, borders manufacture divisions within the international working class. Borders are exploited by the class-conscious ruling class through outsourcing and insourcing to weaken collective bargaining rights and working-class resistance to transnational capital and its austerity measures. The social, political, and economic conditions simultaneously cultivated and weaponized by the far right can only be confronted by a radical and unabashed internationalist left.

Finally, we cannot allow the state and elites to become the arbiters of migration and, in doing so, to characterize migration as a crisis while hypocritically presenting themselves as the victims *of* migrants. Ghassan Hage observes that colonial domination is necessarily shaped through imagined victimhood: "A feeling of being besieged by the very people whom one is actually colonising."[33] Millionaire Jason Buzi has proposed one of the most offensive solutions to the global migrant and refugee crisis, pioneering "Refugee Nation," a scheme to relocate the world's displaced people to one island state. Framed as a human-itarian gesture, Buzi argues it is "a country which any refugee, from anywhere in the world, can call home."[34] Buzi's ideas are vague, including building a new island in international waters or buying an island-state like Dominica, but he is certain English would be the national language and everyone would be trained to work with no welfare handouts. Harry Minas correctly calls it a "hair-brained idea" and "analogous to not long ago when we used to have leper colonies."[35]

There are other similarly wonky ideas. A billionaire wants to buy an island from Italy or Greece on which to stash refugees away, an architect wants to build a new city-state on the Tunisian Plateau, and two academics have proposed a network called Refugia. These proposals share a desire to isolate migrants and refugees, perfect for our current system of global apartheid, where displaced people are racially ordered and segregated as superfluous, capitalist techno-solutionism pretends to solve what it has created by trading in a market of dispossessions, imperial states spuriously claim to care about refugees without sullying their own heavily guarded sovereignty, and elite humanitarianism is positioned as more pragmatic than meaningful justice.

Instead, migrants and refugees—a constitutive outside to bordering regimes whose journeys are largely an accounting of debts, reparations, and redistribution long due—must be the authorities of our own emancipatory movements. In 2018, as many as 164 land defenders were killed protecting their land from invasive industries like mining, logging, and agribusiness.[36] The same year, border controls killed 4,780 people worldwide.[37] Freedom is always in excess of capitalist economies, hierarchical orderings, and bordered sovereignties; the freedom to stay and the freedom to move are thus intertwined, and the most urgent and ethical responses to the asymmetries of power generating mass displacement and immobility today.

PART 1

Displacement Crisis, Not Border Crisis

CHAPTER 1

Historic Entanglements of US Border Formation

The history of the US border is one of nearly unimaginable terror and grief, land theft, ethnic cleansing, forced marches, concentrated resettlement, war, torture, and rape.

—Greg Grandin, "American Extremism
Has Always Flowed from the Border"

In the summer of 2019, a photo of Óscar Alberto Martínez Ramírez and his toddler Angie Valeria went viral. The child had her tiny arm wrapped across her father's back, as both lay facedown, dead, in the murky waters of the Rio Grande. That same summer, the world also watched in horror as images poured in of children in cages, bodies crammed on floors flooded with sewage, and families torn apart at the border. These images captured the cruelty of President Donald Trump's restrictive and punitive immigration policies. The Refugee and Immigrant Center for Education and Legal Services (RAICES) reported from the Texas border: "Hundreds of migrants are locked up in what are akin to disaster relief camps the day after an earthquake. Families are cramped together, porta-potties and mylar blankets are strewn across an industrial wasteland. Cleaning facilities appear non-existent and families are forced to wait outside throughout the day in sweltering heat."[1] At least seven children died in US immigration custody in 2019, and thirty-three adults died in Immigration and Customs Enforcement (ICE) custody between 2017 and 2019.[2] When sixteen-year-old Carlos Gregorio Hernandez Vasquez contracted a dangerous flu while in Border Patrol custody in Texas, he was not taken to a hospital but quarantined in a cell instead. Carlos died in a pool of blood on May 19, 2019.

A record 69,550 migrant children were incarcerated in the US in 2019, more children separated from their families and detained than in any other country on the planet.[3] This mass caging was the culmination of Trump's abominable "zero-tolerance" policy mandating criminal prosecutions of all migrants, including families, for irregular border crossings. Since July 2017, as many as 5,400 children have been separated from their caregivers at the border and detained, 89 percent of whom were from Guatemala and Honduras, and at least 207 were babies under the age of five.[4] Young children have described devastating symptoms, like "every heartbeat hurts" or "I can't feel my heart."[5] Beatriz, a young Maya girl, was beaten with the metal end of a belt while in custody at a child migrant shelter; she sustained bruises on her legs and a scar on her back. Her father, Jairo, was tricked into signing deportation documents and deported without her. By the time Beatriz was reunited with her family, she could no longer speak her language and was unable to communicate with her mother.[6]

In addition to the zero-tolerance policy, Trump instituted a Muslim ban, issued an executive order to expand detention and expedite deportations, authorized greater local powers in immigration enforcement, and increased funding for thousands of additional miles of the border wall. He capped refugee admissions at the lowest level in decades, reserving spots for Iraqis and Afghans loyal to US war efforts. He also implemented new rules making it more difficult for refugees to establish "credible fear" and restricted asylum claims for women fleeing gendered violence. Furthermore, Trump attempted to cancel the Deferred Action for Childhood Arrivals (DACA) program impacting seven hundred thousand undocumented youth and ordered an end to Temporary Protected Status (TPS) for people from El Salvador, Haiti, Nicaragua, and Sudan. In 2020, weaponizing the coronavirus crisis, he issued an executive order to curb immigration green cards for permanent residents and implemented new border regulations so all migrants and refugees, including unaccompanied minors, crossing the US–Mexico border irregularly could be turned back. This unprecedented policy authorized an expedited deportation process, averaging ninety-six minutes, and over ten thousand migrants and refugees were summarily expelled from the border within the first eighteen days of its implementation.[7] Between March and May 2020, only two people were able to exercise their right to seek asylum at the US–Mexico border.[8]

Even though most of these orders have been challenged in court and some even blocked, they have created a chilling effect in racialized communities and emboldened white supremacists. After Trump's election, reported hate crimes increased by 17 percent, and by 2019 as many as 216 militia groups were active in the US.[9] For the first time in its history, the Department of Homeland Security (DHS) was forced to admit that white nationalism is a major domestic threat, especially after the armed United Constitutional Patriots militia kidnapped and illegally detained hundreds of migrants at gunpoint in 2019.[10] State-sanctioned white nationalism has also intensified. The Department of Homeland Security Appropriations Act, signed in 2018, was the largest border enforcement and immigration budget in history. Receiving a whopping $23.7 billion for Customs and Border Protection (CBP) and ICE, DHS became the country's largest enforcement agency, with a budget 6,000 percent larger than in 1980.[11]

While Trump's overtly malicious and cumulative policies of separating families, caging children, banning Muslims, building the border wall, and overturning minimal protections for refugees and undocumented migrants has garnered international condemnation, US immigration enforcement has been routine and bipartisan practice for over two centuries. Liberal lawmakers and their supporters may critique the overt, racist treatment of migrants under Trump's reign, but they too naturalize the border's existence and uphold the state's right to exclude migrants through border rule. It is essential, however, that we ask how and why the border is made. US bordering practices traverse many land and maritime jurisdictions, and the US border is externalized far beyond territorial limits; this is explored further in chapters 2 and 4. This chapter conceptualizes the formation of the US–Mexico border through the historic entanglements of war and expansion into Mexico, frontier fascism and Indigenous genocide, enslavement and control of Black people, and the racialized exclusion and expulsion of those deemed undesirable. The US–Mexico border must be understood not only as a racist weapon to exclude migrants and refugees, but as foundationally organized through, and hence inseparable from, imperialist expansion, Indigenous elimination, and anti-Black enslavement. US–Mexico border rule intersects with global and domestic forms of warfare, positioned as a linchpin in the concurrent processes of expansion, elimination, and enslavement, thus solidifying the white settler power of racial exclusion and migrant expulsion.

We see the rhythms of these overlapping histories reverberate at Oklahoma's Fort Sill army base, a former prison where hundreds of Chiricahua people including Geronimo were incarcerated, then a World War II internment camp for seven hundred Japanese Americans, and subsequently a detention center holding thousands of migrant children under President Barack Obama. Fort Sill made headlines again when Trump also considered using it as a detention facility for children. In response, the base became a site of regular protests bringing together Indigenous people, Japanese Americans, and Latinx community members, drawing connections between their experiences of forced family separation. In early 2019, DHS also floated the possibility of detaining migrant children at Guantánamo Bay, America's first overseas naval base.[12] This omnipotent symbol of US imperialism in Cuba is maintained by thousands of Jamaican and Filipinx migrant workers employed in construction, cleaning, and cooking. The gulag is a legal black hole, where thousands of Haitian refugees were detained in the 1980s and 1990s and a thousand Muslim detainees from thirty-five countries were imprisoned and tortured at the height of the war on terror. Lisa Lowe reminds us that "settler seizure and native removal, slavery and racial dispossession, and racialized expropriation of many kinds are imbricated processes, not sequential events; they are ongoing and continuous in our contemporary moment."[13]

Conquest as Border Formation

We may wish to rearticulate our understanding of white supremacy by not assuming that it is enacted in a single fashion; rather, white supremacy is constituted by separate and distinct, but still interrelated, logics.
—Andrea Smith, "Indigeneity, Settler Colonialism, White Supremacy"

Interrogating the formation of the US–Mexico border exposes the moorings of the US as a settler, slaveholding, expansionist, and exclusionary state. The southern border has been particularly pivotal in the ideology of manifest destiny, a tenet of territorial expansionism wherein northern and southern US states found common ground in the belief that God had ordained frontier wars.[14] Frontier fascism was most forcefully enacted by President Andrew Jackson, whose bloody reign from 1829 to 1837 included massacring Indigenous people and expanding slavery. Jackson also attempted to negotiate with the Mexican government for the purchase of Texas, while tacitly supporting the flow of white Anglo-American settlers into the region to mount a revolt. During the 1830s, Mexico's decision to outlaw slavery and refuse Anglo-settler immigration from the southern US fueled a white secessionist Texian movement. In 1837, Jackson officially recognized the independent Republic of Texas, where Texians affirmed slavery and free Black people required special permission to live.[15] The US annexation of the Republic of Texas as a slave state in 1845 was followed by a full-blown US military invasion of Mexico and debt manipulation by President James Polk, eventually resulting in the forced annexation of half of Mexico through the imposition of the Treaty of Guadalupe Hidalgo in 1848.

The treaty forced Mexico to drop any claims to Texas and authorized the US to capture land comprising all or part of present-day Arizona, California, Colorado, Nevada, New Mexico, Utah, and Wyoming. In total, the US seized more than 525,000 square miles of territory in Mexico, shifting the border south, and rendering Mexicans living in what was now the US "a conquered people."[16] An Anglo-American racial order of conquest was enforced. Mexicans in the captured territories were given the hollow option of US citizenship, while enduring systemic racial discrimination and segregation as alien citizens.[17] Indigenous lands were seized, and sovereign nations, including the Comanche, Apache, Seri, Coahuilteca, and Kiowa, were forcibly assimilated into the US nation-state. Enslaved Black people were subject to the Fugitive Slave Act, while all Black people continued to be denied citizenship, a pillar of white supremacy in the expanding slavery frontier.

Most mainstream analyses of US immigration ignore this history of border and state formation, even as it continues to animate US imperial ambitions and racial-capitalist rule. Roxanne Dunbar-Ortiz argues that the liberal narrative of a "nation of immigrants" is grossly inaccurate, erasing the violence of conquests and borders upon Mexican, Indigenous, Black, and colonized communities to produce the sanitized myth of a melting pot.[18] In contrast to the inaccurate framing "We are a nation of immigrants," the more subversive chant "We did not cross the border, the border crossed us" destabilizes the southern border by interrogating the assumption of "migrant" on seized lands and exposing the hypocrisy of colonizers calling people "illegals." Subjugated communities, particularly Indigenous and Black (importantly, not mutually exclusive), are often folded into the liberal narrative of "racial minorities." Further, Indigenous decolonial and Black abolition struggles are largely seen as disconnected from the immigrant rights movement, except in identifying shared struggles against racism. However, the war on migrants does not exist separate from or simply parallel to anti-Indigenous and anti-Black violence. Early US bordering practices were, in fact, conceived of as a method of eliminating Indigenous people and controlling Black people, and US border imperialism is structurally bound up in these genocides.

Border Formation through Indigenous Elimination

No one is illegal on stolen land except those who stole it.
—Red Nation, "The Red Deal: Indigenous Action to Save Our Earth"

The US not only expanded beyond its borders to build its empire but was founded *as* a genocidal empire upon Indigenous nations. Originating from a series of papal bulls in the late 1400s, the Doctrine of Discovery declared that any and all lands uninhabited by Christians could be claimed. This colonial doctrine of conquest formed the socio-political justification for the dispossession of Indigenous lands and jurisdiction, and it was formalized in law in the 1823 unanimous Supreme Court decision *Johnson v. McIntosh*, wherein Chief Justice John Marshall wrote that "the principle of discovery gave European nations an absolute right to New World lands."[19] Within a few years of the decision, Jackson enacted the Indian Removal Act of 1830, forcing fifty thousand Indigenous people to relocate west of the Mississippi River to a specifically designated "Indian territory." The militarily enforced process violently displaced eighteen thousand Cherokee and killed another four thousand, while opening twenty-five million acres of ethnically cleansed land to white settlement and cotton plantation slavery. An economy of dispossession was solidified, rooted in colonization and racial subordination to turn both land and people into property. This racialized economy of dispossession is described by scholars as "the multiple and intertwined genealogies of racialized property, subjection, and expropriation through which capitalism and colonialism take shape historically."[20]

The Trail of Tears, as it came to be known, was but one part of the Indian Wars, marked by thousands of forced relocations and massacres by the US military and state-led militias, as Anglo-American settlement pushed violently westward and southward. Spanning two hundred years and continuing into the present day, extermination campaigns have been supplemented by a system of elimination that includes apartheid confinement on reservations; biological warfare and starvation; child kidnapping and forced assimilation in boarding schools; epidemics of missing and murdered women and two-spirit people; criminalization through the Court of Indian Offenses; control through the Bureau of Indian Affairs and imposition of tribal council governance; incarceration of Indigenous resisters; and evolving colonial technologies of land theft including the Homestead Act, the Dawes Act, and the Bureau of Land Management's expropriation of millions of acres of land. Dispossession is gendered, and, as Leanne Betasamosake Simpson puts forward, land loss is enacted by attacking Indigenous nations through targeted violence against women and two-spirit people.[21] Body sovereignty is intimately connected to land sovereignty, and 80 percent of Indigenous women in the US today experience violence, 97 percent of which is committed by non-Indigenous people.[22] Patrick Wolfe articulates this totality of settler-colonial invasion as "a structure, rather than an event," where "expropriation continues as a foundational characteristic of settler-colonial society."[23]

Immigration and citizenship have been specifically weaponized to further the genocidal elimination of Indigenous political and social formations. Under the 1887 Dawes Act, for example, Indigenous people could become US citizens only if they agreed to live on individual plots of land, carved from the US government's confiscation and violent partitioning of tribal lands. Forcing Indigenous people to relinquish collective land title and assimilate into the capitalist economy of the white settler state, citizenship was thus dependent on the legal regime of private property. Then, in 1924, the Indian Citizenship Act imposed US citizenship on Indigenous people.[24] In the same year, the Johnson-Reed Immigration Act imposed national origins quotas based on existing census numbers, drastically limiting especially Jewish and Slavic immigration from southern and eastern Europe. The purpose of this act was to maintain a white settler polity favoring settlement from northern and western Europe. The act additionally extended a prohibition on all Asian immigration and effectively excluded those from other non-European countries on the basis of racial undesirability.[25] This restrictionist immigration policy, actively constructing national identity through race and racial difference, also prohibited the migration of Indigenous people from Canada to the US. This happened shortly after Crees and Chippewas from Canada and Yaquis from Mexico crossed into the US in the late nineteenth and early twentieth centuries and launched political battles for federal tribal recognition to challenge the US state's subjugation of them as "foreign Indians" and deportable "illegal immigrants."[26]

The normalization of settler colonialism evades settler occupation as a method of imperialism and, instead, tries to produce Indigenous people as domesticated citizens of the US. Theories of domestication and claims to Indigenous lands, explains Dunbar-Ortiz, "obliterate the present and presence of Indigenous nations struggling for their liberation from states of colonialism."[27] The characterization of Indigenous people as a domesticated US "racial and ethnic minority group" not only omits the inherently anti-imperialist nature of Indigenous struggles, but also homogenizes a multiplicity of Indigenous nations into a pan-Indigenous identity and undermines Indigenous understandings of treaties as international diplomacy. Audra Simpson critiques the ways in which Indigeneity has become legible within liberal frameworks of "minorization" and "culture," rather than analyzed as diverse and distinct jurisdictions captured by the "political project of dispossession and containment."[28]

The dichotomy between "domestic minorities" and "foreign subjects" further unravels with the knowledge that the eliminationist Indian Wars laid the foundation for conquest abroad, becoming the template for genocidal warfare in Hawaii, Puerto Rico, Guam, and the Philippines. Laleh Khalili emphasizes, "[W]hat was learnt in the Indian wars became the necessary, if unwritten, manual for subsequent overseas asymmetric warfare."[29] This continues into our present era; for example, the high-profile US operation to capture and kill Osama bin Laden was named "Geronimo." As noted by Maggie Blackhawk, "The last three administrations have pointed to the Indian Wars as precedent to justify executive action in the war on terrorism."[30] Within this context, George Manuel coined the term "Fourth World" to expand the analysis of the Third World's subject position to include Indigenous struggles that are geographically but not conceptually of the First World.[31]

Today, while continuing to affirm their own distinct and diverse political and social orders, Indigenous people remain occupied subjects of US empire. Many urban Indigenous people provocatively refer to themselves as refugees displaced from their homelands. The representation of Indigenous people in inner-city homeless populations is, after all, a crisis of colonial dispossession and displacement scaffolded by settler property relations under racial capitalism. Meanwhile, according to Nick Estes, "A quarter of adults alive today in the US are direct descendants of those who profited from Homestead Act's legacy of exclusive, racialized property ownership and economic mobility, a legacy that categorically excluded Black, Indigenous and other nonwhite people."[32] Jodi Byrd uses the term "arrivants," borrowing from Kamau Brathwaite, to refer to racialized diasporic people in settler societies displaced by colonial and imperial acts of violence and thus differently positioned, though not necessarily innocent, within settler colonialism.[33] Present-day immigration, alongside and atop settler colonialism, is bound up in the complicities of empire and its incessant negation of Indigenous sovereignty.

A further obfuscation of the relationship between Indigeneity and US border rule takes place when contemporary immigration issues are relegated to the realm of domestic policy and further siloed as a homogenizing Latinx issue, obscuring the specific context of Indigenous dispossession and displacement across the Americas. For instance, the crushing poverty and horrific violence Central Americans are fleeing are most acute for Indigenous people. In Honduras, 88 percent of Indigenous and Afro-Indigenous children are impoverished compared to 10 percent of all children, while 74 percent of Indigenous people in Guatemala are impoverished compared to 56 percent of the general population.[34] A large proportion of Central American migrants and a growing share of Mexican migrants to the US are Indigenous people colonized by the Spanish, captured by Mexico and Central American nation-states, subsumed into a pan-Latinx and mestizx identity, and criminalized through the imposition of borders on Abya Yala. Derived from Guna cosmology, Abya Yala refers to the whole continent of the Americas and transhemispheric Indigenous relations.[35] As Maya Kaqchikel writer Silvia Raquec Cum tells it, "From the perspective of Indigenous peoples, migration has always existed as a form of exchange and communication within the dynamics and life of our communities. We have seen how the United States began to build its borders and divide towns, creating physical and ideological barriers, and how, in spite of this, people still continued to migrate."[36]

Shannon Speed argues that the particular vulnerability of Indigenous women migrants is structural, with their migration representing a transit between Latin American and Anglo-American settler state structures both built on Indigenous elimination, including the brutal impacts of neoliberalism, militarization, and inequities generated by race and gender.[37] Jakelin Amei Rosmery Caal Maquin, a seven-year-old Q'eqchi' Maya girl who died in US Border Patrol custody in 2018, for example, came from territories destroyed by the cumulative impacts of Spanish colonial invasion, genocidal massacres during the civil war targeting Q'eqchi' communities, large biofuel and sugar plantations displacing Indigenous livelihoods, and now one of the areas in Guatemala most vulnerable to climate change. Claudia Patricia Gómez González, a twenty-year-old shot in the head by US Border Patrol in 2018, was also Maya. Claudia left her village in May 2018, hoping to find work to pay for a university accounting degree, but was killed within three weeks of beginning her journey.[38] Her father, Gilberto Gómez, worked as an undocumented migrant in the US after the horrors of the civil war and was deported shortly before his daughter attempted her own journey. He has now filed a lawsuit against the US government for her wrongful death. "It's a year since my daughter was killed and I want the same thing now as I did then: justice," Gómez told media.[39] The chant of "No borders on stolen land" ringing in protests elucidates a prescient anticolonial analysis when considering the disproportionate displacements and migrations of Indigenous people today.

Anti-Black Controls and Border Politics

Pre-occupation with Black movement was central to the colonies and what would become American democracy.
—Benjamin Ndugga-Kabuye and Tia Oso
(Black Alliance for Just Immigration), "Forged in Struggle:
How Migration, Resistance and Decolonization Shape
Black Identities and Liberation Movements in North America"

Immigration restrictions are described by Iyko Day as "Jim Crow in a transnational context," whereby "immigration policy not only determined entry into the nation but could legally bar an immigrant from naturalizing, voting, owning, and transferring property, and working."[40] The criminalization of migration today is not analogous to but has been inescapably structured through the legal trafficking of millions of Africans during the slave trade, the policing and regulation of Blackness as constitutive of white supremacy and racial capitalism, and the anti-Black production of vagrancy and alienness within the nation-state. Contemporary immigration enforcement and border controls draw heavily from the foundational terror of anti-Black violence, particularly the regulation of Black movement, as evidenced in the borrowing of both a structural logic of racial control and a punitive legal architecture. Similarly, the current protections of legal citizenship on which many immigrants in the US rely, such as birthright citizenship for their children, originate in Black struggles to defend the constitutional principle of birthright. Especially after the despicably racist Dred Scott Supreme Court decision in 1856, upholding the denial of US citizenship to Black people, Black movements forced the ratification of the Fourteenth Amendment in 1868.[41]

Rinaldo Walcott and Idil Abdillahi emphasize that the entire politics of migration is embedded in anti-Black racial logics. "Movements that we now call migration are founded in anti-blackness, taking their logic from transatlantic slavery," they write.[42] Indeed, the architecture of US border controls derives from anti-Black technologies regulating mobility. Shortly after the imposition of the Treaty of Guadalupe Hidalgo and as part of the Compromise of 1850 between northern and southern states after the conquest of territories in Mexico, the passage of the 1850 Fugitive Slave Act allowed slaveholders to kidnap and capture Black people they claimed had escaped to the professed free states. Slave catchers and authorities would kidnap and transport Black people across state borders. After the annexation of Texas, slave owners in the state also formed militias to patrol the US–Mexico border to prevent Black people from escaping to Mexico. The border militias swelled their ranks from slave patrols and would conduct cross-border raids in the South in the quest to capture Black people. Robyn Maynard and Simone Browne put forward that similar racial technologies of spatial control were used in the North, such as "birch certificates" (or "certificates of freedom") issued by the British in the late 1700s, effectively operating as passports to scrutinize Black movement and prevent enslaved Africans from escaping to Canada.[43] Maynard argues, "[T]he global positioning of Black life as enslaveable placed Black migrants in a structural position that differs from other migrants of color."[44]

These early laws and militias regulating and punishing Black movement constitute a foundational continuity of immigration enforcement today. Roberto Lovato claims that the contemporary design of racist immigration enforcement developed from these anti-Black practices of spatial control. Specifically, Lovato argues the federal ICE Agreements of Cooperation in Communities to Enhance Safety and Security (ACCESS) program, authorizing states to deputize local law enforcement to pursue and arrest undocumented migrants, is based on the Fugitive Slave Act.[45] Philip Kretsedemas similarly contends the socioeconomic order of white rule established through state-level Jim Crow laws was later emulated in the devolution of federal immigration enforcement policy to the state level.[46] This devolution to state and local law enforcement not only mimics the design of anti-Black laws but also disproportionately impacts Black migrants, who are most likely to be profiled by local police and law enforcement officers and then turned over to immigration authorities. I discuss this further in chapter 2.

As the abolitionist movement grew in the early and mid-1800s, the weaponization of the border to control Black people took on a dual function. In addition to border militias ensuring enslaved Black people remained within the US, there were calls and plans, for example by the notorious American Colonization Society, for the mass deportation of non-enslaved Black people out of the US to Liberia and Sierra Leone. So-called free states like California, Illinois, Indiana, and Oregon, fearing an influx of Black people, also began codifying prohibitions on interstate Black migration in their constitutions, all of which occurred during the antebellum period and foreshadowed federal immigration exclusion.[47] Shortly thereafter, beginning in 1865, the postbellum Black Codes were enacted across southern states and became a de facto system of re-enslavement. Under the Black Codes, convict leasing was enforced through forced penal labor and debt peonage, surveillance was intensified through vagrancy laws, curfews and pass systems were implemented, and additional restrictions were placed on interstate Black migration. Saidiya Hartman observes how vagrancy statutes to contain Black emancipation maintained a continuity "from slave to servant, from servant to vagrant, from domestic to prisoner, from idler to convict and felon," thus codifying the criminalization of free mobility through the racial logic of anti-Blackness.[48]

The criminalization of the presumed idleness and unemployment of Black people as "vagrancy" was a critical weapon to coerce Black people to sign exploitative labor contracts. This form of Black bodily dispossession encompassed yet completely exceeded the rubric of labor; as Frank Wilderson emphatically states, "[T]he point is we were never meant to be workers; in other words, capital/white supremacy's dream did not envision us as being incorporated or incorporative."[49] Coerced labor as a result of the Black Codes, and racialized surveillance and enforcement of work in coal mines, plantations, and lumber camps, including the frequent requirement of residency on former slaveowners' properties, anticipated the distinctly carceral bracero program with Mexico and the Caribbean migrant worker program (see part 3). After the Civil War, the KKK was also formally established, and during and after the Reconstruction era, white terror included extrajudicial violence and around ten thousand lynchings.[50] Zoé Samudzi writes of the white witnessing of lynching as "a reinscription of white supremacy: a reification of the boundary between the white self and the black 'others' through a passive bystander witnessing and the enforcement of race through public violence."[51] Anti-Black racial torture as a form of white supremacist public spectacle became a blueprint for border vigilantes, the Nazis, and for state torture at Guantánamo Bay, Abu Ghraib, and the Metropolitan Detention Center.

More recently, the workings of anti-Black warfare through mass displacement and carceral immobility were laid bare by the disaster of Hurricane Katrina. Black homes were most vulnerable to the storm, Black people were criminalized during the storm, and Black neighborhoods were abandoned by recovery efforts after the storm. Seventy-three percent of the eight hundred thousand dislocated people were Black residents, who then saw their neighborhoods policed and landscapes privatized, leaving most people permanently displaced.[52] This era also saw the expansion of immigration enforcement through the war on drugs and war on terror. The war on drugs frames migrants as criminals and the war on terror frames them as security threats, both of which are a priori dependent on the anti-Black warfare of the prison industrial complex and the mass detention of Haitian refugees, described in chapter 2. Fred Moten, drawing on Cedric Robinson, depicts the position of Black people in the US as one of an "eternal internal alien."[53]

Today, Black migrants and refugees face the brunt of anti-migrant criminalization with the triple threat of stop-and-frisk policing, convictions and incarceration stemming from the war on drugs, and subsequent deportation. As explained by the Black Alliance for Just Immigration (BAJI), "Black people are far more likely than any other population to be arrested, convicted and imprisoned in the US criminal enforcement system—the system upon which immigration enforcement increasingly relies."[54] Combined with the overall increase in convictions for drug offenses and the imposition of mandatory minimums, Black migrants are twice as likely to be detained due to a criminal conviction.[55] According to BAJI, even though Black immigrants make up 7.2 percent of the total undocumented population, more than 20 percent of all migrants in deportation proceedings due to criminal convictions are Black people.[56] Jamila Osman legitimately indicts: "In an era where the word intersectionality has entered the public lexicon, the immigrant rights movement has failed at it. It is the deeply pervasive nature of anti-black racism that erases the existence of black migrants."[57] Most recently, just under half of the countries targeted by Trump's Muslim ban are African, including Eritrea, Nigeria, Somalia, Sudan, and Tanzania, thus controlling the movement of hundreds of millions of Africans. The "afterlife of slavery," as Hartman pens, means "black lives are still imperiled and devalued by a racial calculus and a political arithmetic that were entrenched centuries ago. This is the afterlife of slavery—skewed life chances, limited access to health and education, premature death, incarceration, and impoverishment."[58]

State Formation through White Supremacy

Border formation through the distinct but interrelated processes of expansion, elimination, and enslavement imposed a white polity, and racial exclusion and migrant expulsion further solidified the white racial state. While Anglo-European settlers were welcomed, actually encouraged as part of the settler-colonial project to eliminate Indigenous jurisdiction, immigrants racialized as non-white faced marginalization. The distinction between settler citizenship and illegalized immigration was key to racial population politics. Racist citizenship can be traced to the first citizenship law, the Naturalization Act of 1790, which conferred citizenship on "any alien, being a free white person." Similarly, the first federal immigration laws merged race-based exclusion with criminalization of sex work and drug prohibition in the imperial "yellow peril" era of the late 1800s. The Page Act and the Chinese Exclusion Act fused white, working-class sentiments against Chinese "coolie labor" with white, middle-class moral panics about Chinese "uncleanliness," "prostitution," and "opium dens" to ban Chinese laborers. Anti-Chinese sentiment was further sexualized by claims of both heterosexual luring of white women by Chinese men and the gendering of Chinese men as effeminate or gay. Chinese immigrants, as opposed to white settlers, were treated as suspicious agents of war, which, in turn, represented settler possession "as a form of protection rather than conquest."[59] As Nikhil Pal Singh documents, in 1889 the US Supreme Court upheld Chinese exclusion on the basis that "foreigners of a different race" were "potentially dangerous to peace and security."[60] Similarly, the criminalization of poverty through vagrancy laws deporting the poor, especially single women migrants deemed to be promiscuous, attacks on labor unionism through the expulsion of communists and anarchists dating back to the Palmer Raids, maintenance of a cisheteronormative sexual order through sodomy laws and bars on queer migrants, and medical examination as a basis for excluding disabled migrants were all integral to constructing narratives of productive citizens versus deviant others. The border was thus a central modality for state formation, hierarchical social ordering, and population control through exclusions and expulsions.

White power has shaped state formation and border controls, particularly in Texas and California. In Texas, the paramilitary militia Texas Rangers was initiated through violent attacks on the mighty Indigenous Comanches and mass executions to clear the frontier for Anglo-American settlement.[61] Kelly Lytle Hernández writes that the Texas Rangers "battled Indigenous groups for dominance in the region, chased down runaway slaves who struck for freedom deep within Mexico, and settled scores with anyone who challenged the Anglo-American project in Texas."[62] After the Treaty of Guadalupe Hidalgo and the advent of the railroad brought in more settlers to both sides of the Rio Grande, land was mass-appropriated from Tejanx (Mexicans in Texas). State officials, the army, and Texas Rangers enforced these land grabs with brute force. Within a decade, and in just two counties, 187,000 acres of land were expropriated from Tejanx for Anglo-settler ranchers.[63]

During the decade-long Mexican Revolution that began in 1910 against the dictatorship of Porfirio Díaz and the landowning oligarchy, Anglo settlers were terrified the uprising would spread into Texas and result in the re-appropriation of property they now claimed. In the middle of the revolution, President Woodrow Wilson deployed 130,000 National Guardsmen and 30,000 troops along the border, the largest concentration of state forces since the Civil War.[64] Texas Rangers and armed forces were also deployed in the Lower Rio Grande Valley to patrol the borderlands and suppress revolutionary actions. Vigilantes and state officials acted in concert using sheer force to enforce a color bar in the labor force and terrorize Mexicans and Mexican Americans through beatings, torture, shootings, and mass decapitations. Thousands of Mexican Americans were killed during La Matanza (the period of massacres) and in the Porvenir Massacre of 1919, fifteen men and boys were executed, their corpses left to rot.

Formed in 1924, the US Border Patrol's first generation of agents was recruited from the ranks of the Texas Rangers and Klansmen, laying the ground for the culture of racism, militarism, and violence still prevalent in the agency. Today's migrant killings by border agents in the borderlands and the tens of thousands of apprehensions at the Texas–Mexico border are a continuity of the Anglo-settler violence permeating the heart of Texas. We also see it in the use of violent terminology like "tonks," referring to border crossers; the word is derived from the sound border agents' flashlights supposedly make when hitting migrants over the head. Organized vigilantes capturing Black people, paramilitaries hunting Indigenous people, and militias apprehending migrants laid the foundation for our irredeemable modern-day police and border forces.

At California's inception as a state, white settler violence also instantly structured its bordering practices, beginning with two dozen state-funded militia expeditions authorized to kill Indigenous people.[65] Justin Akers Chacón and Mike Davis argue that the first US border formation predated the Treaty of Guadalupe Hidalgo and actually took place in California during the years of genocidal conquest.[66] Vigilantes inspired by these militia expeditions killed 6,460 Indigenous people beginning in 1846, and 100,000 Indigenous people were later killed during the California Gold Rush.[67] Throughout the height of the gold rush, hundreds of Mexicans, including miners, were also lynched by vigilante mobs.[68] During the subsequent period of economic decline, state-backed vigilante forces relentlessly waged lethal attacks on immigrant workers. Anti-Chinese race riots and massacres, including the 1871 massacre where white vigilantes killed 10 percent of all Chinese people in Los Angeles, the formation of the Japanese and Korean Exclusion League, and the KKK's "Swat a Jap" campaign were all expressions of "Keep California white" efforts to consolidate white settler imperial jurisdiction and citizenship.[69]

Pressure for racial exclusion by white power vigilantes subsequently led to a California law prohibiting the employment of Chinese workers (bluntly titled An Act to Protect Free White Labor against Competition with Chinese Coolie Labor), the federal Page Act prohibiting East Asian "coolie labor" and Chinese women deemed to be sex workers, and the federal Chinese Exclusion Act banning all Chinese laborers. After the passage of the Chinese Exclusion Act, armed watchmen on horseback, alongside the Texas Rangers, patrolled the southern border from California to Texas and the northern US–Canadian border to prevent Chinese migration. Authorized by the Bureau of Immigration and calling themselves "Chinese catchers," they became a de facto border patrol until its official formation in 1924.[70] That same year, the Johnson-Reed Immigration Act was passed; spurred on by a national march of forty thousand Klansmen demanding immigration restriction, it barred all Asian immigration and imposed a national origins quota.[71] Alexis Goldstein summarizes: "In a terrifying feedback loop, vigilantism both pressured politicians to pass oppressive federal policy, and then, once the discrimination was law, even more violent vigilantism followed."[72] White entitlement remained a bedrock of California, as the state later led the country in race-science eugenics and narratives of "inferior immigrants," and twenty thousand women were sterilized in state institutions between the 1920s and 1950s.[73] More recently, racist rhetoric about "illegals" culminated in punitive policies such as Proposition 187, a ballot initiative in 1994 to deny undocumented migrants access to most California state services and impose a screening and reporting system based on immigration status. Though many parts of the law were found to be unconstitutional, Proposition 187 had a chilling effect and created a precedent for an avalanche of reactionary state-level immigration policies across the country over the next two decades.

While the early anti-immigrant vigilante mobs in California were often made up of white working men, they were primarily organized and funded by capitalist interests to break class solidarity and protect agricultural grower profits. The Industrial Workers of the World (IWW), which emphasized solidarity with migrant Chinese, Filipinx, and Japanese farmworkers, was consistently attacked over the course of three decades by the anticommunist American Protective League and the white supremacist KKK operating in the state. In one incident, over one hundred vigilantes attacked three hundred IWW members and their families and submerged young children in cauldrons of boiling coffee.[74] Under the aegis of the Growers and Shippers' Protective League, the Imperial Valley Anti-Communist Association was created in 1934 to tag unionization drives on the farms and fields as "a red menace."[75] At the time, close to seventy thousand Mexican, Black, and Filipinx workers in the Cannery and Agricultural Workers' Industrial Union were staging almost fifty different workplace walkouts, including the historic cotton strike, during which twelve thousand mostly Mexican cotton pickers walked off the fields and shut down three hundred square miles of production.[76] These strikers faced farmer-organized and state-deputized vigilante beatings, arson of their labor camps, arrests, and murder.

As the Great Depression set in, the Placita raid in Los Angeles and the nationwide deportation of between 1 and 1.8 million Mexicans and Mexican Americans (60 percent of them US citizens) broke working-class unity, and racial expulsion emerged as a jingoist solution.[77] Nearly 20 percent of the entire Mexican population in the US was deported, a move described by Mae Ngai as "a racial expulsion program exceeded in scale only by the Native American removals of the nineteenth century."[78] The foundations of anti-immigrant terrorism and anti-labor red-baiting were laid in tandem. Not coincidentally, in order to control Mexican mobility and labor, the Department of Labor oversaw the US Border Patrol from its inception until World War II, when the department's role shifted to overseeing the advent of the bracero program. Border enforcement thus became entrenched as a key method for labor regulation and racial-capitalist accumulation, detailed in part 3.

Indeed, capitalism has always required the social differentiation and hierarchization of race. Cedric Robinson theorized the linkage between racialized expropriation and capitalist plunder as "racial capitalism" to make clear that the social differentiation of race is not a secondary outcome of capitalism but, rather, the racial expropriation of land, labor, and life is innately constitutive of capitalism.[79] Capitalism is based on private ownership of property and production, expropriation and exploitation to guarantee accumulation, and market profit over human or ecological needs. Capitalism does not produce a universal relation of waged labor; capitalism actually requires and reproduces the racial hierarchies that underpin all the processes of territorial expansion, dispossession, enslavement, ownership, proletarianization, surveillance, and border rule. Capitalist plunder is, therefore, inextricable from racial dispossession and the unequal expropriation structuring state and social formation.

Conclusion

Even today, the work of the US Border Patrol extends beyond immigration enforcement. The entanglements of border formation in imperial expansion, anti-Black enslavement, and Indigenous elimination are mirrored in our contemporary moment with border agents patrolling alongside the military in Iraq and Afghanistan, policing Black neighborhoods in the aftermath of Hurricane Katrina, repressing Indigenous water protectors at Standing Rock, and using counterinsurgency tactics, including the snatching of protestors in Portland in July 2020, to suppress uprisings across the US after the cold-blooded police murder of George Floyd. War veterans, in fact, comprise one-third of Border Patrol agents.[80] This is not a coincidence; there is a homology to domestic and foreign conquest. The formation of the US–Mexico border and immigration as a race-making regime cannot be analyzed outside the reciprocal processes of empire building and genocidal violence. Singh explains, "The United States developed its forms of democratic politics and capitalist economics from processes of imperial expansion, colonial dispossession, and racial domination."[81]

As migrant children are separated from their families at the border, communities within the US also endure family separation through the web of child protective services and prison incarceration. Indigenous children are removed into foster care at a rate 2.7 times greater than their representation in the general population, and Black families are torn apart by prison incarceration 50 percent more often than white families.[82] Hernández writes, "This tangle of alienated citizens and criminalized immigrants is a deeply historical construct that reaches up from the unfinished abolition struggle of the 19th century and across the 20th century experience with race and inequity to define today's caste of felons and illegal immigrants."[83] Framing immigration restrictions as solely "anti-migrant racism" ignores the ways in which immigration policy is foundationally constituted through and intertwined in anti-Indigenous, anti-Black, and imperialist warfare to consolidate the US as a nation-state and empire.

The links between empire, race making, and the border are perhaps best symbolized in the construction of the border wall itself: wire mesh recycled from a Japanese-American internment camp, repurposed Air Force landing strips and ground sensors from the Vietnam War, and Elbit Systems' "virtual wall" surveillance technology field-proven on Israel's apartheid wall. By excavating mutual histories and interlocking logics, we replace narrow frameworks of immigration with a more expansive analysis, illuminating the border as a tool of population management and racial ordering that is at once domestic and global. Radhika Mongia observes, "The modern economy of migration, grounded in race and imperialism, is fundamental to the creation of a geopolitical space dominated by the nation-state."[84] The next chapter explores how the US border regime was consolidated at the turn of the twenty-first century, within a constellation of imperial interventions, neoliberal capital flows, policies of carceral containment, and migration controls.

CHAPTER 2

US Wars Abroad, Wars at Home

I will not
dance to your war
drum. I will
not lend my soul nor
my bones to your war
drum. I will
not dance to your
beating. I know that beat.
It is lifeless. I know
intimately that skin
you are hitting.

—Suheir Hammad, "What I Will"

In 2014, a hunger strike and protest by mostly Mexican and Central American detainees resounded through Tacoma's Northwest Detention Center, which is run by the private prison company GEO Group. Seven hundred detainees faced threats of forced feedings and denial of their asylum cases as a result of their political action, but they pushed forward their demands for better conditions and release on bond. "Without a bond," they collectively wrote, "we spend months, even one-to-two years locked up without knowing what's going to happen to us and our families and without being able to economically support our families."[1] The US has the world's largest immigration incarceration system and, contrary to the myth of being overburdened by generosity, accepts

38

less than 1 percent of the world's displaced population. More important than this disgracefully low percentage, however, is the question of US reparations and responsibility for displacement and migration. US politicians preoccupied with border fortification hypocritically violate the borders of the places they bomb, mine, and pollute.

Hondurans, El Salvadorans, and Guatemalans make up the fastest-growing proportion of people crossing into the US. Over the past decade, migration from these countries has increased fivefold.[2] The US Border Patrol apprehended 432,838 adults and children between October 2018 and July 2019, with families from these countries constituting 92 percent of all family-unit border apprehensions.[3] These perilous migrations, generating white anxieties about the border, are portrayed by liberal media as "not our problem" and stemming from "over there." However, these migrations from "over there" *are* "our problem" because they are inextricable from displacements created by US dirty wars backing death squads and the counterinsurgency terror of the neoliberal war on drugs. The US border crisis is thus more accurately described as a crisis of displacement generated by US policies. Frequent media coverage of migrants fleeing MS-13 gang violence, for example, rarely explains that the street gang formed among marginalized Salvadoran refugee youth incarcerated in the US, many of whom were later deported, eventually becoming a more organized syndicate under Ernesto Deras, a former Salvadoran special forces member trained by the US Green Berets.[4]

This chapter chronologically explicates how immigration exclusion over the past five decades, from the war on drugs to the war on terror, correlates with global dispossessions caused by US empire and voracious capitalism, as well as with domestic forms of warfare, including neoliberalism, prison and detention expansion, and welfare retrenchment—all underwritten by racialized and gendered hierarchies. Faced with multiple crises beginning in the 1960s, including a deep recession, military defeat in Vietnam, and an enormous wave of social protests and strikes, the US ruling class set out to restore US capitalism and empire. They did so by adopting and exporting neoliberalism, rolling back social movement gains by normalizing carceral governance, and reimposing imperial supremacy beginning with genocidal wars in Central America and culminating in the global war on terror. Consequently, a growing number of people were displaced and then contained by the US through its expanding border imperialist regimes across maritime space with Haiti and at the land border with Mexico. US immigration policies were not only parallel to but a *fulcrum* between domestic and global warfare. Repressive border policies served as a thread braiding together social warfare, mass destabilization and displacement, capitalist extraction, and militarized carceral control, both at home and abroad.

War on Drugs: Criminalization, Crackdowns, and Counterinsurgency

> *It is possible for prison walls*
> *To disappear,*
> *For the cell to become a distant land*
> *Without frontiers.*
>
> —Mahmoud Darwish, "The Prison Cell"

President Richard Nixon's government was the first iteration of the US ruling class's drive to expand neoliberal carceral governance. In the 1960s and 1970s, Nixon's southern strategy, expansion of the war in Vietnam, and operations at the border converged. The southern strategy was Nixon's successful transformation of large portions of the white working class into Republican voters by exploiting their racial hostility toward Black communities. The jargon of a "culture of poverty" and "law and order" began to be employed in order to deflect attention from Black resistance and hundreds of labor strikes responding to socioeconomic inequity. "Welfare queens" and "ghetto predators" were some of the pathologizing, gendered, sexualized, anti-Black stereotypes that took hold of the public consciousness despite declining crime rates. Naomi Murakawa explains: "The US did not confront a crime problem that was then racialized; it confronted a race problem that was then criminalized."[5] Drawing on the post-Reconstruction legacy of criminalizing Black freedom, detailed in chapter 1, new prisons were built, police were introduced into public schools and housing, and Black and low-income racialized neighborhoods became war zones occupied by law enforcement forces. Thus began the evolution of the prison industrial complex as we now know it.

The prison industrial complex emerged as an ordering and bordering regime, a central technology of gendered racial confinement and mobility control. As Angela Davis and Gina Dent observe, "We continue to find that the prison is itself a border. This analysis has come from prisoners, who name the distinction between the 'free world' and the space behind the walls of the prison."[6] The association of Blackness with both crime and welfare benefits concomitantly legitimized policies that grew the carceral state while shrinking the welfare state. At a civilian level, the rise of a new era of white power movements alongside anticommunist groups was not a coincidence; white supremacists portrayed communism as a ruse of class equality masquerading for racial equality. The World Anti-Communist League, founded in 1966, is illustrative, bringing together white power movements and anticommunists to support the Vietnam War, Rhodesian independence, and an end to civil rights legislation.

The border was drawn into this web of criminalization. In 1969, Operation Intercept was a crackdown on the "marijuana problem," with Nixon exaggerating claims of drug smuggling and alleging 80 percent of marijuana in the US came from Mexico.[7] Led by Joe Arpaio, Intercept followed the 1964 termination of the bracero program, which had brought millions of Mexican workers into the US, and the implementation of the Immigration and Nationality Act of 1965, which repealed national origins quotas but limited Mexican immigration through provisions capping legal immigration from the Western Hemisphere. As a result of these two changes implemented in 1964 and 1965, within a decade almost all migration from Mexico was deliberately made illegal, and Congress established a magistrate court system to prosecute, detain, and deport Mexican migrants.[8] Additional amendments to the Immigration and Nationality Act to further restrict Mexican immigration were passed in 1976, 1978, and 1980, and the number of Mexicans arrested for unlawful entry between 1965 and 1986 jumped from 55,000 to 1.5 million—an astounding 3,000 percent increase—at the same time that Black incarceration rates were skyrocketing.[9] While Intercept itself was brief, the militarized operation foretold the relationship between border crackdowns and the drug war across Latin America. Today, the war on drugs remains tied to migration control, with US initiatives training Mexican border guards and militarizing the landscape while enforcing austerity.[10] For his part, Arpaio went on to become "America's toughest sheriff" in Arizona's Maricopa County between 1993 and 2017. As sheriff, he staged chain-gang parades of detainees, deputized an armed 3,000-person volunteer posse, and installed checkpoints in Latinx neighborhoods to turn undocumented residents over to Immigration and Customs Enforcement (ICE) for deportation. The Border Patrol Explorer Program was also launched in 1973 under Nixon's reign, training teenagers in militarized border patrol tactics and indoctrinating them into racism.

President Ronald Reagan officially announced the beginning of the war on drugs in 1982, again using implicit racial appeals to white voters as a means of advancing racial-capitalist governance. He responded to economic crisis with his Thatcher-inspired Reaganomics of welfare retrenchment, capital gains tax reduction, and neoliberal deregulation. As an advanced phase of racial capitalism concocted by the notorious Chicago school, neoliberalism is characterized by deregulation of financial and trade markets, privatization of public assets and institutions, social service cuts, protection of private property and corporate profits, an ideology of individualism and competition, and enhanced enforcement to coerce labor while policing impoverishment. Whereas neoliberalism is typically understood through the lens of laissez-faire state economics, David Harvey argues it is a comprehensive political project to weaken the power of labor and expand institutional networks of capital accumulation.[11]

Impoverishment and unemployment generated through neoliberalism in the 1980s was masked by the explosion of the prison industrial complex, itself bolstered by a race-baiting media spectacle about an alleged crack epidemic. This justified a radical transformation of the criminal justice system geared toward drug prosecutions. Furthermore, a "culture of poverty" narrative profiling Black families was accompanied by a broken windows model of policing that linked poor Black communities to disorder. Police officers justified broken windows policing by arguing that enforcing laws against low-level, poverty-related, and property-related offenses, such as street vending or graffiti, prevented serious violent crime. Jordan Camp and Christina Heatherton, however, more aptly describe broken windows policing as the political expression of neoliberalism in urban areas, sustained through racism to consolidate the carceral state and regulate space for capital.[12] Incarcerating the crisis of inequality by advancing the war on drugs as a primary method of neoliberal regulation has had shattering consequences. Drug offense convictions stemming from the war on drugs account for the largest increase in the federal prison population, with 7.3 million people in prisons or some form of correctional control by 2010, and crowning the US with the ignoble honor of having the world's highest incarceration rate.[13]

The war on drugs also became yet another tool in the ongoing production and policing of race within racial capitalism. By 2014, Black people represented one-third of the prison population and were five times more likely to be incarcerated than white people.[14] Women also made up an increasing share of drug-related incarcerations. Victoria Law reports that the gendered and racialized retreat of the welfare state alongside the criminalization of nonviolent offenses led to a 2,800 percent increase in the number of female prisoners, especially Black women, between 1970 and 2001.[15] Provisions in both Reagan's Immigration Reform and Control Act of 1986 and the Anti–Drug Abuse Act of the same year targeted racialized immigrants through the creation of a new category of "aggravated felony" for noncitizens, including legal permanent residents. In the aftermath of these laws, the deportations of people with criminal convictions increased 1,300 percent.[16]

Reagan fused the vocabulary of the war on drugs, especially with respect to narco-trafficking, with his unabashed anticommunism to usher in a brutally violent period of counterinsurgency in Central America. In Guatemala, Reagan trained and backed rampaging military death squads that committed genocide, including massacres, rapes, disappearances, kidnapping, and torture, against two hundred thousand Maya during the civil war. As Don Tiburcio painfully describes, "The shoes, the belts, were piled two meters high and wide, you could see the traces of people who had been killed there. They tied me up and left me sitting in the blood."[17] Reagan also illegally sold arms and trained the right-wing Contra mercenaries against the communist Sandinistas, described by Noam Chomsky as a "large-scale terrorist war against Nicaragua, combined with economic warfare that was even more lethal."[18] As part of this war and also to curb Honduran dissent, the US installed military bases and thousands of soldiers in Honduras. The CIA-backed Battalion 316 used the Argentinian model of "eliminating subversives" to kidnap and kill hundreds of Honduran dissidents, student leaders, unionists, journalists, and communists, and then dump their bodies into unmarked graves.[19]

In El Salvador, Reagan's policy of wiping out communism took shape as a war against the Farabundo Martí National Liberation Front (FMLN). The US provided six billion dollars' worth of military aid and training to death squads to crush the communist, peasant, and Indigenous cadres of the FMLN.[20] This included support for the US-trained Atlacatl Battalion, responsible for the El Mozote massacre of twelve hundred civilians in just one operation. By the end of the civil war, seventy-five thousand El Salvadorans were dead. Reagan rallied domestic support for these interventions by linking three platforms: defeat of leftist guerillas and communism in Central America, stopping narco-traffickers at the source, and preventing waves of refugees from flooding the US (people who were actually escaping the US's dirty wars). In this way, the politics of migration merged with the war on drugs at home and the reproduction of imperialism abroad. In 1984, less than 3 percent of Guatemalan and Salvadoran refugees were accepted in the US.[21]

Reagan's dirty wars during the Cold War era were not exceptional moments; they were preceded by an unbroken line of US interventions in Central America guided by the Monroe Doctrine, whereby the US claimed the entire hemisphere to be within its sphere of influence. In the early 1900s, a US coup installed Manuel Bonilla in Honduras. Bonilla ensured a windfall for the monopoly interests of the United Fruit Company (now Chiquita), which deforested thousands of acres of land, exploited mestizo and Afro-Indigenous Garifuna plantation workers, and maintained Honduras in a state of dependency as the region's leading banana exporter for a century. In 1932, pressured by US companies and local landed oligarchs operating vast coffee plantations in El Salvador, the US government deployed the navy to support Maximiliano Hernández Martínez's military government in quashing a peasant rebellion led by Farabundo Martí. In Guatemala, the CIA and President Dwight Eisenhower orchestrated a coup against Jacobo Árbenz in 1954 and installed a military regime to reverse Árbenz's agrarian reform and land redistribution. The 1980s launch of the war on drugs provided a pretext to further this imperialist agenda.

In the wake of Reagan's genocidal wars in Central America, a leftist, faith-based sanctuary movement emerged to sponsor and shelter refugees in the 1980s. On the right, a group of CIA-funded Vietnam War veterans, known as the Civilian Material Assistance (CMA), supplied funds and arms to the Contra death squads precipitating the Iran-Contra scandal. CMA also organized armed vigilante patrols to harass sanctuary movement activists, and held migrants crossing the border hostage at gunpoint.[22] Pandering to such interests, Reagan declared that "our borders are out of control" and ordered the first stretch of border fencing, increased border patrol funding by 130 percent, and doubled the size of the US Border Patrol, which operated with impunity.[23] Border Patrol agents detained migrants in ice boxes, threw them off cliffs, and raped young girls. Reagan also launched Operation Camarena, which shut down ports of entry, and passed the Military Cooperation with Law Enforcement Agencies Act in 1981 to increase police and military collaboration in drug interdiction and authorize military equipment transfers to interior forces. Border enforcement, therefore, served as a fulcrum between domestic policy and overseas militarism. The border was reanimated as a frontier—drug trafficking and national security coalesced with irregular migration—and solidified the crime-drugs-terrorism nexus still in existence. This police and military assemblage birthed by the war on drugs reconstituted urban areas as a kind of borderlands, as Jennifer Correa and James Thomas document, territorializing space through policing and consequently collapsing interior policing and border enforcement agendas.[24] Stuart Schrader similarly argues that interior policing became increasingly militarized, and his work reveals that techniques came to be shared between local law enforcement and global counterinsurgency units when CIA-led interventions sent police and border patrol overseas to repress rebellions and advance policing techniques.[25]

The war on drugs still maintains US geostrategic and capitalist control over Central America, fueling dispossession and displacement. In 2009, while still in his pajamas, President José Manuel Zelaya in Honduras was ousted by a military coup led by a general trained at the US-based School of the Americas (SOA, now known as Western Hemisphere Institute for Security Cooperation), where sixty-four thousand Latin American military and elite counterinsurgency forces have trained. In Zelaya's place, successive narco-governments favorable to a neoliberal agenda of special economic zones and corporate plunder have been installed. Present-day counterinsurgency operations are layered with the paramilitarized landscape of the war on drugs and the $1.2 billion Central American Regional Security Initiative.[26] Dawn Paley asserts, "The war on drugs is a long-term fix to capitalism's woes, combining terror with policymaking in a seasoned neoliberal mix, cracking open social worlds and territories once unavailable to globalized capitalism."[27] Today, all three countries have some of the world's highest disappearance, homicide, and femicide rates. Lenca Indigenous land defender Berta Cáceres was assassinated in Honduras in 2016 by military hitmen trained at SOA, and Honduras was the deadliest country in the world for land defenders in 2017.[28] Thus, within and across borders and over several decades, the war on drugs has accelerated Cold War geopolitics, escalated border militarization, grown the neoliberal carceral state, and dismantled the welfare state—and, in doing so, revealed their symbiosis.

Detention and Globalized Racial Violence

Internal racial regimes can no longer be treated as incidental to global processes.

— Clyde Woods, "'Sittin' on Top of the World':
The Challenges of Blues and Hip Hop Geography"

The exponential growth of the prison industrial complex and border militarization during the war on drugs coincided with the expansion of the US immigration detention system. The interdiction and detention of Haitian refugees during the 1980s and 1990s laid the groundwork for the US onshore and offshore immigration detention system in place today. Immigration detention is a race-making regime, synchronized through the intertwined dynamics of global imperialism and domestic warfare. During the Cold War, imperial domination of Haitians on the island and domestic carceral governance against Haitian refugees were in a reciprocal relationship; economic and military interventions abroad combined with exclusions at the border, consolidating what Denise Ferreira da Silva calls "the global idea of race."[29] The interdiction and detention of Haitian refugees also solidified US bordering practices against the Caribbean. Though the US–Caribbean maritime border receives less attention than the US–Mexico borderlands, the interdiction and detention of Haitian refugees preceded most onshore policies of mass detention and illustrates the multiplication of US bordering practices across spaces.

US maritime bordering in the 1980s and 1990s is situated within the longer arc of imperialism and enslavement in Haiti. European imperialism caused the near-complete extermination of Taíno Arawaks on Hispaniola in the 1500s, and Saint-Domingue emerged as France's most lucrative colony, with one of the largest enslaved populations violently forced to produce coffee and sugar. In his opus, *The Black Jacobins*, C. L. R. James places the Saint-Domingue slave uprising alongside the French Revolution, and for James, race, class, and imperialism were necessarily interrelated.[30] Even after Haiti's successful revolution, creating the first independent Black republic, France extorted $40 billion dollars (in today's terms) to compensate slave colonialists.[31] Debt manipulation was perpetuated through US banks, including National City Bank, which Peter Hudson notes was "the largest and the most important imperial financier in the United States," as well as US-owned companies like the Haitian American Sugar Company and the National Railroad Company.[32] Together they stole gold from Haiti's national reserves, pushed a thirty-million-dollar loan, pressed for a return to racial slavery through the ruthless corvée forced labor system, and precipitated a US military occupation. During the 1915–34 occupation by the US, fifteen thousand Haitians were killed, Haiti's legislature was dissolved, and a new constitution friendlier to US investment interests was instituted. Just two corporations compelled Haiti to concede 1.5 million acres of land, and dozens of sugar and banana plantations extracted land and labor.[33] As W. E. B. Du Bois famously asserted, "The United States is at war with Haiti."

From the 1950s onward, the US staged numerous coups and installed regimes sympathetic to preserving its interests in Haiti. The despotic regimes of

François Duvalier and his son, Jean-Claude Duvalier, killed tens of thousands of Haitians, imprisoned even more in the dreaded Fort Dimanche torture camp, and fueled a massive exodus of refugees, yet were propped up by the US for nearly three decades as counterpoints to communist Cuba. The Duvalier regimes also sanctioned the forcible restructuring of Haiti's economy by tying US aid to buying US imports. And in 2004, the US, France, and Canada staged a second coup against Jean-Bertrand Aristide and his pro-poor Lavalas party. Since then Haiti has been under US-backed presidencies and de facto UN Stabilization Mission in Haiti (MINUSTAH) rule. Jean Saint-Vil remarks, "Since the 2004 coup, Haiti has had puppet 'governments' put in place to shield from accountability the international puppet masters who are really running the show."[34] These puppet governments are open to neoliberalism and US exports, including the dumping of subsidized "Miami Rice" into Haitian markets, impoverishing millions of local farmers, while over twenty billion dollars' worth of minerals are mined and exported by mainly Canadian and US corporations.[35] The US has also pushed free trade and export-processing zones, maintaining Haitian factory workers as the lowest paid in the entire Western Hemisphere. In the middle of the coronavirus crisis, thousands of garment workers, left without wages for a month during a government-ordered shutdown, desperately returned to work for a pittance in overcrowded garment factories in the US-funded Caracol Industrial Park zone in northern Haiti.[36]

The long shadow of attempts to subjugate Haiti provides the context for Haitian mass migration and ensuing mass expulsion from the US in the 1980s. During the Cold War, Haitian refugees fleeing US destabilization were detained and deported, while Vietnamese refugees characterized as fleeing despotic communist People's Army and Viet Cong forces were rescued and welcomed, thus revealing the geopolitics of the refugee order. By the end of 1980, after 3.8 million people were brutally killed in the Vietnam War, four hundred thousand refugees from Vietnam, Cambodia, and Laos were resettled in the US.[37] Wealthy, white, anti-Castro Cubans were also openly welcomed, and most Cuban refugees were allowed to remain once they reached US soil, with the notable exception of those who were Afro-Cuban, working-class, and/or sex workers. Haitian refugees, however, were characterized as "economic migrants" and detained indefinitely upon arrival. Virtually all Haitian asylum claims were rejected, while the Haitian Program expedited their deportation. A new detention policy was implemented in 1981, and nearly half of all Haitian refugees were detained at the Krome detention center for almost a year.[38] Solidifying the

US maritime border, Reagan also announced an interdiction policy returning all boats transporting Haitians to Port-au-Prince. Those on boats that did make it through were subjected to immediate detention, forewarning today's detention center expansion. Border and immigration budgets more than doubled during that decade, and Attorney General William French Smith did not mince words: "Detention of aliens seeking asylum was necessary to discourage people like the Haitians from setting sail in the first place."[39]

These practices continued into the 1990s, with the opening of Guantánamo to detain intercepted Haitian refugees fleeing the 1991 coup against President Aristide and, within the first year of Guantánamo's operation, the US intercepted 37,000 Haitians, detained over 14,000, and deported most.[40] Only 300 Haitians had their asylum claims accepted, and 250 of them remained detained based on their HIV status in an "HIV prison camp," spatializing the intersections of white supremacist, cisheteronormative, and ableist epidemiology. Haitian detainees revolted throughout the 1980s and 1990s, including staging hunger strikes and a Krome prison break of nearly a hundred people, soon recaptured.[41] On New Year's Eve in 1992, 159 Haitian women and men, constituting two-thirds of the entire Krome population, went on hunger strike to protest their indefinite detention.[42] One year later, detainees at Guantánamo began a hunger strike to protest their prolonged detention. The bipartisan turn toward long-term incarceration for immigration violations, detention as a tool of deterrence, and militarized boat interdictions—all thoroughly entrenched in policy today—are rooted in US policing of Caribbean maritime space and these anti-Black, red scare, criminalizing responses to Haitians fleeing US imperialism. As Jenna Loyd and Alison Mountz argue, the "US Cold War response to these Caribbean migrations established the legal and institutional basis for today's migration-detention and border-deterrence regime."[43]

Neoliberal Impoverishment, Border Militarization, and Carceral Governance

The correlation between racist immigration exclusion and overseas geostrategic interests became even starker in the late 1990s, as border militarization accompanied the North American Free Trade Agreement (NAFTA), the world's largest free trade agreement. While free trade agreements (FTAs) are considered a new phenomenon, they perpetuate the pattern pioneered by the British East India Company of using trade to establish and subordinate markets for the benefit of imperial ruling class interests. Today, FTAs are a staple of globalized capitalism—four hundred new trade agreements were negotiated around the world between 1995 and 2016.[44] Current US trade agreements in the Americas are an extension of the Monroe Doctrine accelerating capitalist capture and colonial control. Under agreements such as NAFTA, the United States–Colombia Trade Promotion Agreement (COTPA) and the Dominican Republic–Central America–United States Free Trade Agreement (US-CAFTA-DR), industries and services are privatized, capital flow and investment are deregulated, resources are commodified for export, export processing zones are expanded, and corporate property rights are protected. These agreements hollow out public social safety infrastructure, while resulting in the large-scale destruction of peasant, rural, and Indigenous livelihoods.

US-CAFTA-DR, for instance, inundates local markets with US agricultural products, harming peasant livelihoods, and it augments construction of development infrastructure through rural communities. It also accelerates land grabs for resource extraction through mining, oil drilling, and biofuel production, which Maya K'iche' leader Aura Lolita Chávez Ixcaquic describes as a colonial invasion of Indigenous lands: "The macroeconomic and neoliberal model creates laws to open the doors to multinational companies to invade our territories without consulting with or providing information to us."[45] Another tenet of FTAs is investor–state arbitration allowing corporations to pursue compensation for restriction of future profit by environmental or health regulatory regimes. Globally, Latin American and Caribbean countries are among the most affected by such arbitrations. Investors have won 70 percent of their cases against these countries, forcing them to cough up twenty billion dollars for corporate coffers.[46] This corporate banditry benefits the ruling class, with preemptive bailouts guaranteeing economic certainty for investment and entrenching the imperial property relation.

The ground for NAFTA was laid in the 1960s, when Mexico launched the Border Industrialization Program to decrease unemployment and social unrest among returned braceros. The strategy gave rise to an export-oriented manufacturing sector with multinational subsidiaries benefiting from duty-free imports of raw materials and equipment. Maquiladoras (border assembly plants) produced everything from televisions to vehicle parts in bordered zones of transnational capital investment and union-free labor. In the 1970s and 1980s, the Mexican economy was further subordinated to the US, World Bank, and IMF through loans and structural adjustment programs, resulting in massive deregulation of state enterprises and 70 percent of capital goods production income going to mainly US corporations.[47] This capitalist economy accelerated with NAFTA prying open domestic industries in Mexico to a global regime of production. In addition to the US annexation of northern Mexico and US efforts to thwart the Mexican Revolution, described in chapter 1, NAFTA was yet another act by the US ruling class, in alliance with the Mexican oligarchy, to dominate Mexico's politics and economy.

Despite spurious claims that the trade agreement's benefits would "trickle down" to Mexicans, over 1.3 million Mexican farmers were pushed into bankruptcy within the first decade of NAFTA.[48] US-based Union Pacific, in collaboration with the wealthy Mexican Larrea family, bought out the national railway, leaving tens of thousands of railway workers jobless. The wage gap between jobs in the US and Mexico widened, and real Mexican wages grew by just 2.3 percent.[49] Fifty-five million Mexicans lived below the poverty line, with women experiencing the highest loss of real earnings.[50] The number of people in primary subsistence economies such as agriculture, fishing, and forestry fell from 8.2 million in 1991 to 6.1 million in 2006.[51] US corn exports, on the other hand, increased by 323 percent within NAFTA's first decade, and by 2016, 65 percent of corn was being imported.[52]

The rhetoric of free trade masked deeply unfair trade practices. NAFTA removed Mexican tariffs on subsidized US meat and agricultural exports, flooding the market with genetically modified cash crops like corn, which impoverished local farmers and threatened Indigenous food sovereignty. Maize is sacred in Indigenous communities; as Aldo Gonzalez describes, "Native seeds are a very important part of our culture. The pyramids may have been destroyed, but a handful of maize seed is the legacy we can leave to our children and grandchildren."[53] The decimation of thousands of varieties of native corn is a form of gendered genocidal violence, disproportionately impacting Indigenous matriarchal cultures and the livelihoods of Indigenous women harvesters. To add insult to injury, NAFTA prohibited Mexican price supports. The Mexican government liquidated state-owned CONASUPO stores and eliminated tortilla subsidies supporting 1.2 million families.[54] With CONASUPO's elimination came price control elimination, leading to a spike in the price of tortillas, and strengthened market cartels like Cargill.

NAFTA also forced numerous amendments to the Mexican constitution, including the abolition of Article 27, enshrined since the revolutionary 1917 constitution, which for decades had affirmed national control over resources and protected communal land redistribution through ejidos. NAFTA opened communal Indigenous and peasant landholdings to fee-simple private ownership, and later reforms sanctioned land seizures for debt collection. Indebted farmers lost their lands, including to US agribusinesses and multinational mining interests. By 2014, as much as 20 percent of land in Mexico was designated for mining interests, 70 percent of which is owned by mainly US and Canadian mining giants.[55] "The international companies are robbing us. They take our lands, our forests, and our mines," describes Indigenous feminist Reyna Cruz López.[56]

The cumulative impacts of NAFTA led to a crisis of displacement. Millions of Indigenous people, farmers, peasants, and ejidatarios from rural areas were dispossessed and then proletarianized into low-wage factory and farm work. Employment in the maquiladora industry exploded by 86 percent within the first five years of NAFTA and, exemplifying the growing feminization of precarious work worldwide, 85 percent of the workforce was women.[57] Maquila border towns were also key sites in the drug war, fueling a crisis of femicide in cities like Ciudad Juárez that continues today. By the year 2000, more than 1.6 million workers toiled in four thousand maquiladoras, 90 percent of which were US-owned, and set the de facto wage floor for manufacturing across the continent.[58] Seven hundred thousand jobs, particularly unionized manufacturing ones, were lost in the US, with Black workers in Detroit hit especially hard.[59] Kate Bronfenbrenner has found that 10 percent of employers in the US threatened to move operations to Mexico in response to union drives.[60] As William Robinson notes, "National trade statistics conceal the transnational essence of the new global economy, and with it, the transnational class relations behind much contemporary international political dynamics."[61]

The day that NAFTA passed, the Zapatistas declared the agreement "a death sentence to the Indigenous ethnicities of Mexico," rising up in armed rebellion and spurring the rise of the global justice movement of the late 1990s. Indeed, since NAFTA's implementation, tens of thousands of migrants from Mexico are Indigenous Maya, Mixtec, and Zapotec.[62] Before NAFTA, Indigenous people made up 7 percent of migrants from Mexico, but a decade later, they constituted 29 percent.[63] Overall, there were 4.5 million Mexican migrants in the US in 1990, a figure that nearly tripled by 2008 to 12.67 million, including 7 million undocumented migrants.[64] This displacement crisis was a foreseen, rather than an unintended, consequence. Though President Bill Clinton declared that NAFTA would mean "less illegal immigration because more Mexicans will be able to support their children by staying home," Congress's own Commission for the Study of International Migration and Cooperative Economic Development warned that NAFTA would create human suffering.[65]

As Clinton was signing NAFTA to ensure the movement of capital and goods, the US Army Corps of Engineers was fencing the border to interdict the movement of people. US Border Patrol also grew, tripling in size, to become the second-largest enforcement agency at the time.[66] Several operations—Hold the Line in Texas, Gatekeeper in California, and Safeguard in Arizona—militarized the border under the "tough on immigration" strategy of prevention through deterrence, officially implemented by US Border Patrol in 1994. Within six years of funneling migration toward the more dangerous Sonoran Desert, Arizona uplands, and southern Texas brush, border deaths from hypothermia, dehydration, drowning, and heat stroke increased by 509 percent.[67] As the Coalición de Derechos Humanos describes it, "Border crossers now enter the US through remote rural areas, fanning out across the backcountry region north of the border and carving a complex web of trail systems through mountain passes, rolling hills, desolate plains, and dense brushlands."[68] Since 1996, the total number of border deaths—what could more accurately be labeled as premeditated border killings—is estimated at eight thousand, with thousands more disappeared.[69]

The Clinton years normalized the most severe consequences of border militarization and mass detention, evident in border operations targeting "illegal" immigrants, alongside laws expanding the category of "criminal alien." Rhetoric of "productive" and "legal" immigrants, with the simultaneous demonization of "criminal" and "illegal" immigrants, became the cornerstone of the Democratic Party's immigration platform for the next two decades. Building on Reagan's legislation, Clinton passed the Antiterrorism and Effective Death Penalty Act of 1996 and the Illegal Immigration Reform and Immigrant Responsibility Act of the same year. These acts expanded the category of aggravated felony convictions and widened the net for detention and deportation of legal permanent residents with minor convictions stemming from stop-and-frisk policing and the war on drugs. The laws also implemented expedited removal (fast-tracked deportation proceedings with limited judicial oversight), imposed criminal penalties for unauthorized entry and reentry, and made detention and deportation retroactively mandatory for certain criminal convictions.[70] Within six years, detentions tripled, with the number of female detainees quadrupling.[71] Deportations shot up by 37 percent after the passage of these laws, averaging 150,000 annually.[72] Tanya Maria Golash-Boza argues that mass deportation, normalized since the passage of these 1996 laws, is a form of racial governance enforced through expulsion of surplus labor.[73] The convergence of "tough on crime" and "tough on immigration" sustains racialized control, while also ensuring a compliant labor force through the containment of surplus labor that exists alongside the outsourcing of maquiladora labor and the insourcing of migrant labor. Mass incarceration and mass deportation within neoliberalism thus serve as key techniques of conterminous social and labor control.

Clinton's punitive 1994 Violent Crime Control and Law Enforcement Act and 1996 Personal Responsibility and Work Opportunity Reconciliation Act intensified neoliberal impoverishment by linking race, immigration, welfare, and criminal law regimes. The Personal Responsibility and Work Opportunity Reconciliation Act excluded many new permanent residents from accessing welfare, barred people with drug convictions from accessing benefits, and slashed welfare for citizens, especially teenage mothers. Social assistance benefits were eliminated for 60 percent of US families.[74] By 2014, the poverty rate for households headed by Black women was 45.6 percent.[75] As the number of people receiving welfare dropped by 6.5 million, low-income racialized families were increasingly surveilled through the Violent Crime Control and Law Enforcement Act, and, under the rhetoric of the war on crime, the incarceration of women increased by 108 percent.[76] The 1994 "tough on crime" laws expanded police and prisons, and mandated harsher sentences, including the death penalty. Like in the war on drugs, the war on crime removed poverty from socioeconomic conditions and placed it onto the plane of "culture." The criminalization of poverty was racialized and gendered, targeting Black and Puerto Rican women with false claims of welfare fraud, tropes of sexual promiscuity and laziness, and the liberal grammar of meritocracy and hard work. Michelle Alexander draws the links between forced impoverishment and incarceration, noting, "During Clinton's tenure, Washington slashed funding for public housing by $17 billion (a reduction of 61 percent) and boosted corrections by $19 billion (an increase of 171 percent)."[77] The neoliberal turn of the 1990s was, therefore, marked by a number of contiguous and correlative forces, including NAFTA's economic liberalization targeting Indigenous lands and union jobs, the beginning of fatal border militarization coupled with the deportation of legal residents, erosion of public services and social assistance most severely impacting Black households, and an explosion in incarceration to manage the racialization and feminization of poverty.

Preemptive Wars of Terror

Alabanza. When the war began, from Manhattan and Kabul
two constellations of smoke rose and drifted to each other,
mingling in icy air, and one said with an Afghan tongue:
Teach me to dance. We have no music here.
And the other said with a Spanish tongue:
I will teach you. Music is all we have.
　　　　　—Martín Espada, "Alabanza: In Praise of Local 100"

In early October 2001, Ansar Mahmood photographed the Hudson River bluffs in New York. Unbeknownst to him, this landscape included a water treatment plant. The FBI arrested the 27-year-old Pakistani pizza delivery worker on suspicions of a terrorist plot to contaminate the water supply. He was cleared of those charges but then charged with harboring illegal aliens because he helped his friends with expired visas obtain housing. He remained incarcerated for years before being deported to Pakistan in 2005. Mahmood was one of thousands caught in the post 9/11 dragnet of expanded police powers, indefinite incarceration of noncitizens, immigration crackdowns, PATRIOT Act investigations, no-fly lists, secret trials, extraordinary rendition, torture, and counterterrorism programs of surveillance—all justified through the racist "us versus them" rhetoric of the war on terror. Juan Cole quips: "White terrorists are random events, like tornadoes. Other terrorists are long-running conspiracies. White terrorists are never called 'white.' But other terrorists are given ethnic affiliations."[78]

The National Security Entry-Exit Registration System (NSEERS) was introduced in 2002, requiring all men who were nationals of two dozen mostly Muslim-majority countries to submit to registration, fingerprinting, and interrogation. Eighty thousand men were forced to register, and more than 16,600 faced detention or deportation.[79] NSEERS, the PATRIOT Act, and the Absconder Apprehension Initiative disproportionately impacted Pakistani men, who comprised 40 percent of those detained under these initiatives.[80] Thirty percent of Brooklyn's entire "Little Pakistan" neighborhood was deported or felt compelled to self-deport.[81] In 2006, the Federal Bureau of Prisons created a secretive regime of prison units designed to isolate prisoners they claimed to be high-risk terrorists. Those incarcerated, 60 percent of whom were Muslim, were severely restricted from using the phone and banned from any physical contact with loved ones and even other prisoners.[82]

"Foreign alien" and "terrorist" became synonymous, and immigration crackdowns served as the front line of war on terror efforts. In 2003, the Department of Homeland Security (DHS) was created with a budget of $9.1 billion, explicitly positioning immigration policy as a national security issue. DHS merged twenty-two federal agencies, including Border Patrol and the Immigration and Naturalization Service, and took control of the newly minted ICE. The Real ID Act granted sweeping powers to DHS to waive dozens of laws impeding border wall construction, including environmental protection laws, and the Secure Fence Act later approved billions of funding dollars for walling. Detention industry profits soared, and the head of the Wackenhut private security company didn't hesitate in expressing enthusiasm: "As a result of the terrorist attacks in the United States in September we can expect federal agencies to have urgent needs to increase current offender capacity if certain antiterrorism and homeland security legislation is passed."[83]

As an extension of earlier imperial wars, including the war on drugs, the war on terror took shape through concurrent global and domestic warfare and solidified the US as an empire that is at once domestic and global. The never-ending war on terror, more accurately described as a war *of* terror, seamlessly integrated domestic immigration policy into overseas military operations. Private contractors making a killing through war contracts were also granted billions of dollars to build the virtual wall and catch "immigrant terrorists" with their promises of infallible high-tech drone surveillance and infrared technology. Unmanned aerial vehicles were first tested on the US–Mexico border before use in drone attacks on Yemen and Pakistan, and Customs and Border Protection (CBP) and the Department of Defense acquired the largest drone fleets of all state agencies.[84] Thus boomeranged the war at home and the war abroad.

Depictions of domestic and foreign threats merged, and the war on terror represented Muslims everywhere as an enemy other. Nadine Naber and Junaid Rana write, "Especially since 9/11, and under the name of the War on Terror, by constructing an enemy of the state as porous and boundless, as anywhere and everywhere, the US justifies waging war against diverse people and regions all lumped together as 'Muslims.'"[85] The relationship between the surveillance, infiltration, entrapment, detention, and deportation of Muslims within the US and the military occupations, air strikes, torture chambers at black sites, and interrogation of citizens of Muslim-majority countries abroad positions Islamophobia as a globalized imperial racism. President George W. Bush peddled it as such: "We are aggressively pursuing the agents of terror around the world, and we are aggressively strengthening our protections here at home," coupling the military industrial complex with the security state.[86] In the first few months after 9/11, as many as 1,200 Afghans were killed in US aerial bombardments, as 1,200 South Asian and Arab Muslims were detained in the US.[87] The war on terror authorized this preemptive war abroad and preemptive incarceration at home, both underwritten by a racially ordered and legally sanctioned presumption of guilt aimed at Muslims.

Preemptive war abroad transformed the modalities of US imperialism. While not new—the US has staged coups for decades and Clinton invoked the doctrine in attacks on Sudan in 1998—preemption became the norm, a carte blanche for permanent wars and overt rather than covert use of force to compel regime change, therefore preserving US hegemony and a unipolar world order. In the war on terror's early days, a feminist facade portrayed military intervention in Afghanistan as a humanitarian cause to rescue women from Muslim misogynists. The Revolutionary Association of the Women of Afghanistan firmly reject the Orientalist justification for the occupation of their country as being prompted by the need to "save" Afghan women from the Taliban (a group that was actually nurtured by the US during the 1980s): "The US invaded Afghanistan under the pretext of 'women rights' but the only thing it brought on our women in the past eighteen years is violence, murder, sexual violence, suicide and self-immolation, and other misfortunes."[88] Intervention in Afghanistan rarely receives media attention anymore, even though civilians killed by US-backed forces and air strikes in Afghanistan in 2019 outnumbered those killed by the Taliban or ISIS.[89] In the same year, 62 percent of US commandos deployed abroad were in the Middle East.[90]

In Iraq, at least 2.4 million people have been killed since the US-led invasion in 2003, and babies in Fallujah have birth defects rates nearly eleven times higher than normal.[91] "Collateral damage" became the justification for this gratuitous death and injury, and "reconstruction" the cover for looting the country's oil reserves. Likewise, declaring African oil to be an American strategic interest and fabricating a terrorist sleeper cell network in the Sahel region, Bush established the US Africa Command (AFRICOM), subsequently expanded under Obama.[92] AFRICOM is now the most active US military command based on number of combat operations, with missions in fifty African countries employing 7,200 personnel.[93] US forces are operating in 70 percent of countries worldwide, and nearly eight hundred US military bases dot the world map. This translates as preemptive and permanent interventions waged by the US in eighty countries, at a cost of $6.4 trillion, and contributing to the colossal crisis of twenty-one million displaced people in Afghanistan, Iraq, Pakistan, and Syria alone.[94] The US-led war on terror is thus global in scope and backed by NATO, Israel, and India, who collectively animate imperial racism and imperialist geopolitics through the convenient and catch-all refrain of preemptively "fighting Jihadi terrorism."

Preemptive war at home evolved into a similarly permanent and omnipresent structure of control and reinforced the same racial logics. The post-9/11 mass roundups and registrations morphed into Countering Violent Extremism (CVE) programs. Based on the racist premise that Muslims are the main perpetrators of terrorism, CVE programs have sought out teachers, faith leaders, social workers, and family members to become informants monitoring the political beliefs and behaviors of young Black and brown Muslims. In parallel, heightened surveillance also enveloped Indigenous people, Black people, and anti-imperialist dissidents. Audra Simpson documents how the war on terror escalated colonial anxieties about Indigenous people. New biometric status cards were issued, armed border guards were posted on Indigenous reserves straddling the US–Canada border, and Indigenous mobility across both US borders was further criminalized.[95] Furthermore, the FBI listed "Black identity extremists" as a domestic terror threat and Assata Shakur as one of the FBI's most wanted terrorists, reconfiguring its earlier Counterintelligence Program (COINTELPRO) into the web of counterterrorism to subvert Black liberation movements. Palestinian leaders in the US, like Rasmea Odeh and Sami Al-Arian, were targeted for detention and deportation, and revolutionaries affiliated with Hamas and the Popular Front for the Liberation of Palestine were characterized as terrorists. Five US citizens who are Muslim, known as the Holy Land Five, were prosecuted and incarcerated for their charity work in the occupied West Bank and Gaza Strip. The International Civil Liberties Monitoring Group notes, "There are few countries today in which citizens and their civil society organizations are not severely affected by the encroachment of the national security state, and the use of 'anti-terrorism' to repress dissent and political opposition."[96]

Noncitizens, overwhelmingly Latinx and Caribbean, were targeted through the war on terror's merging of immigration and security through three enforcement priorities. First, the DHS and Department of Justice launched Operation Streamline in 2005, adopting a "zero-tolerance" approach of criminally charging all people crossing the border irregularly. The classification of migrants entering without authorization as "criminal aliens" resulted in assembly-line prosecutions (sometimes lasting less than a minute), incarceration in private prisons with detention-bed mandates requiring the filling of at least thirty-four thousand detention beds across the country every day, and mass expulsions from the borderlands. [97] "Illegal Reentry" became the most common federal charge,[98] and the increasing procedural overlap between criminal and immigration proceedings led legal scholars to develop the term "crimmigration law."

Second, local authorities were granted greater immigration enforcement powers through Section 287(g) agreements. Under these agreements, the DHS deputized local police and law enforcement officers to perform the enforcement functions of federal immigration agents. This increased collaboration between local officers and federal immigration authorities, and ramped up interior enforcement with checkpoints and raids, disproportionately impacted Afro-Latinx and Afro-Caribbean migrants. Hundreds of new anti-immigration laws were also passed at the state level, including legislation denying state-level benefits and authorizing local police to arrest undocumented residents. Arizona's SB 1070, the most fascistic example, required people to carry immigration identity documentation and mandated local law enforcement to conduct immigration checks.

Third, Bush launched the Secure Communities initiative, turbocharged by Obama. Under Secure Communities, one thousand local law enforcement jurisdictions were linked to ICE and FBI databases, nearly doubling deportation rates under a "catch and return" mandate.[99] The overall prosecution rate for immigration offenses quadrupled through these three enforcement priorities, with one year seeing 360,000 removals, mostly of undocumented residents on unauthorized entry or reentry charges and legal permanent residents with minor criminal offenses.[100] Approximately two million people were deported during the Bush presidency.[101] Vigilantism also soared, with groups like the Minutemen patrolling the border and turning migrants over to border agents. Referring to themselves as "white Martin Luther Kings," the Minutemen boasted 12,000 members and 140 branches.[102] The group's founder, Jim Gilchrist, even ran as a third-party candidate in a California district with the endorsement of the border patrol union.

Following in Bush's footsteps, Obama spent billions securing the border, and under his reign, border and immigration enforcement budgets began to outpace the budgets of all other federal law enforcement agencies combined.[103]

Todd Miller summarizes the massive expansion of immigration and border enforcement under Obama, preceding the horrors of Trump: "Before setting foot in the White House, Trump had a border arsenal unprecedented in US history. This included 650 miles of walls and barriers, approximately 60,000 CBP and 20,000 ICE agents, and enforcement systems that included some of the most sophisticated technology on the market."[104] Obama ordered more than one thousand troops to the border before signing legislation to increase the number of border patrol agents and expand the border's virtual border surveillance systems. After a surge of 68,541 unaccompanied children were apprehended at the border in 2014, Obama also laid the foundation for punishing migrant families. He implemented policies incarcerating families, including children, which then escalated to forced family separation under Trump.[105] In fact, several of the photographs of children in cages claiming to showcase the horror of Trump's presidency were actually taken during the Obama years.

Obama earned the moniker of "deporter-in-chief" for overseeing three million deportations, which he accomplished by weaponizing "good immigrants" against "bad immigrants." Before introducing protections for eligible undocumented youth and their families under Deferred Action for Childhood Arrivals (DACA), Obama signaled his intention to increase enforcement: "Felons, not families. Criminals, not children. Gang members, not a mom who's working hard to provide for her kids." His enforcement priorities became deportations of noncitizens with criminal records and formal removal proceedings for irregular migration. By 2014, half of all federal criminal arrests were immigration related.[106] In late 2019, Obama's former vice president and 2020 presidential hopeful, Joe Biden, evaded questions by immigration activists about Obama's horrific deportation legacy and, in a tried, tested, and tired centrist response, deflected by blustering, "You should vote for Trump."[107]

In the frenzy of denouncing Trump, the liberal establishment is rehabilitating the abhorrent legacies of Bush and Obama. Trump is, irrefutably, a barefaced white supremacist who called Mexicans "rapists," referred to African countries as "shitholes," referred to the coronavirus as the "Chinese virus," and ran 2,200 Facebook ads about "immigrant invasions."[108] His response to the migrant caravan from Central America was to allege that "criminals and unknown Middle Easterners are mixed in" and then dispatch armed troops to the border. But we must not forget that Bush and Obama are also war criminals and laid the political foundations for the ascendance of Trump. They are responsible for waging deadly warfare in dozens of countries, operating an archipelago of secretive black sites, torturing and sexually assaulting prisoners from Abu Ghraib to Guantánamo Bay, expanding immigration detention and deportation, and laying the basis for a strengthened military-security state that simultaneously creates imperialist displacement while criminalizing subjugated citizens and immigrants alike through imperial racial logics.

Trump's initial Muslim ban suspended entry into the US for ninety days for citizens of Iran, Iraq, Libya, Somalia, Sudan, Syria, and Yemen, seven Muslim-majority nations. These were the same countries the US had already either bombed or imposed sanctions on. Under Nobel Peace Prize winner Obama, the US dropped 26,171 bombs—an average of three bombs every hour—mostly through air strikes and drone warfare on Syria, Iraq, Afghanistan, Libya, Yemen, Somalia, and Pakistan in the year prior to the ban.[109] The ban was thus implemented against those whose attempted migration was a recourse from the ravages of US military occupations imposing control and cracking open markets. Rather than debating whether conservative or centrist politicians are worse, border imperialism—as a systemic, analytic framework—conceptualizes US immigration exclusion within capital extraction, imperial destabilization, carceral governance, and gendered racial warfare, all concurrently generating domestic and global circuits of power.

CHAPTER 3

Dispossession, Deprivation, Displacement:

Reframing the Global Migration Crisis

upaly was one of thousands of workers hesitant to go to work on April 24, 2013, in the Rana Plaza building in Bangladesh's Dhaka District. Employed in a garment factory, she and other workers were uncomfortable with deep cracks in the walls of the dilapidated building. A government safety inspector had ordered an evacuation a day earlier, but the manager tried to convince employees it was safe and threatened to withhold wages from anyone who refused to work.[1] A few hours later, the Rana Plaza building collapsed. Rupaly and others were miraculously rescued from the rubble of the eight-story building, amid piles of bright cloth, but 1,130 garment workers were killed.

This mass industrial homicide shook the world. Responsibility was initially placed on smaller local suppliers until it was revealed they were contracted by brand giants like Joe Fresh, Zara, Walmart, and Benetton. More than 5,500 garment factories in Bangladesh employ 4.2 million workers generating 82 percent of the country's export revenue.[2] Most garments are sold in European and North American markets, making Bangladesh one of the world's leading ready-made garment exporters. Eighty-five percent of the workers are women, who work under horrendous labor conditions, including working up to sixteen hours a day, sewing at a dizzying rate of hundreds of clothing pieces per worker, earning less than minimum wage, enduring routine intimidation and killing of union leaders, and working in shoddily maintained death traps lacking ventilation and exposed to open electrical wires.[3] More than 500 garment workers died in factory fires in the country between 2006 and 2012, including the Tazreen Fashions factory fire that killed at least 112 workers.[4]

Many garment factories operate in Bangladesh's export processing zones (EPZs), free trade zones specializing in manufactured goods for export with tax and rent incentives, suspension of national labor and environmental laws, and elimination of customs duties. In World Bank jargon, an EPZ "specializes in manufacturing for export to more advanced market economies by offering exporters duty-free imports, a favorable business environment, few regulatory restrictions, and a minimum of red tape."[5] EPZs are governed by the Bangladesh Export Processing Zone Authority, implementing its own laws geared toward investors. The authority's website displays a flashing banner reading "Bonanza for Investors" and an exaltation of the executive chairman, who is a military officer. Unionization is prohibited in the zones and a specialized policing unit, the newly minted Industrial Police force, suppresses any worker mobilizations. Like capitalist trade agreements, EPZs generate mass impoverishment and displacement within and across borders.

From the preceding exploration of the entanglements of US immigration policy, I now zoom out to explore the root causes generating a global crisis of migration. Migrants and refugees don't just appear at our borders; they are produced by systemic forces. The imperial ruling class overcame the economic crisis of the 1970s by restructuring economies within their advanced capitalist countries and also forcing open lands for capitalist investment and exploiting cheap labor internationally, thus intensifying a global crisis of neoliberal impoverishment and displacement. I reframe the global migration crisis as a dual crisis of displacement and immobility organized through capitalist dispossession and imperialist power. State borders keeping migrants out are but one method of bordering; EPZs, debt and property relations, and land enclosures are also neoliberal and neocolonial bordering regimes that manufacture dispossession and operate through immobility. Here, a focus on Bangladesh serves to illustrate the connection between the spatial reorganization of racial class relations and large-scale dispossession, deprivation, and displacement. The discussion on Bangladesh is followed by brief snapshots of settler occupations, land grabs, and climate catastrophe generating displacement around the world.

Export Processing Zones as Extranational Zones

The division of labor among nations is that some specialize in winning and others in losing.

—Eduardo Galeano, *Open Veins of Latin America:*
Five Centuries of the Pillage of a Continent

EPZs are internal bordering regimes of free capital flows and wage suppression—a capitalist haven of neoliberalism. Like maquiladoras at the US–Mexico border, the full throttle of neoliberal privatization and union busting in EPZs is evident in the very configuration of an EPZ as an *extranational* bordered area. EPZs are outside the bounds of even minimal national labor protections, thereby furthering labor force segmentation. These bordering regimes work to multiply extranational neoliberal enclaves, both internalized and externalized, and cement the relationship between dispossession and exploitation. Women make up 90 percent of the millions of exploited workers in these zones worldwide.[6] The feminization of cheapened labor is not a coincidence; as Lisa Duggan writes, neoliberalism "organizes material and political life in terms of race, gender, and sexuality as well as economic class and nationality, or ethnicity and religion."[7] EPZs provide multinational corporations with free license to dictate labor, environmental, tax, and financial regulations in countries like Bangladesh pulled into the global chain of commodity production. The garment industry doesn't simply benefit from lax regulations in EPZs; they actively lobby to maintain these profitable conditions. Approximately 10 percent of members of parliament in 2013 were also garment industry owners, and Bangladeshi law is inked by these industry magnates.[8]

Bangladesh's oldest EPZ is also one of the oldest in the world. Established in 1983 by the World Bank, the Chittagong zone was advertised on the international market as having the world's cheapest labor. As a result, the number of garment factories in Bangladesh's EPZs grew exponentially. Almost three thousand new garment factories were built between 1980 and 2000.[9] Under the military rule of Hussain Muhammad Ershad, Bangladesh was also one of the first countries subjected to a World Bank and IMF structural adjustment program. The IMF is a predatory loan shark forcing conditions of market liberalization and state austerity as preconditions to receiving a loan, and using debt as a disciplinary mechanism to reorganize economies into bordered sites of resource extraction and labor exploitation. The neoliberal and neocolonial imposition of these structural adjustment programs became known as "debt dictatorship," with developing economies forced to accept severe austerity packages that stripped away social safety measures while increasing capitalist investment and trade tariffs. Naomi Klein summarizes this prescription of the Washington Consensus as "Want to save your country? Sell it off."[10] For the more than seventy countries across the Global South and former Eastern bloc trapped in these neoliberal programs, structural adjustment has been synonymous with increased interest rates, currency devaluation, elimination of state subsidies for domestic industries and essential services, deregulation, export-oriented markets, and swelling poverty rates.[11]

A mantra of neoliberal deregulation is the privatization of profit and socialization of risk. While increasing subsidies for private enterprises and the gluttonous elite, austerity is a bludgeon against public services. Public institutions, such as energy utilities, food rations, healthcare, education, and childcare, are transformed into privatized commodities. In turn, the costs of social reproduction are further externalized onto women as unwaged work in the private domain of the home. By 2003, the total debt accumulated by developing countries reached $2.3 trillion, while trickle-up wealth concentration meant just twenty-six of the world's richest billionaires owned as much wealth as half of the entire world by 2018.[12] A clear correlation exists between nauseating wealth, erosion of public services, and exploitation of the world's majority. Tricontinental Institute has found iPhone workers in China, for example, are twenty-five times more exploited today than textile workers in nineteenth-century England.[13] While the World Bank and IMF are post–World War II institutions, and neoliberalism is considered the latest phase in capitalist globalization, the old globalized plantation economy reverberates through export orientation, imperial class monopolies, intense work surveillance, and extreme hierarchies of race, class, and gender.

Displacement by Starvation Wages and Rising Seas

Migration is increasingly the joker in the globalization pack.
—Stuart Hall, "Cosmopolitan Promises, Multicultural Cities"

Three decades of structural adjustment in Bangladesh have reversed the nationalization of jute, textile, and energy production; slashed public funding, especially to healthcare and education; introduced land reforms geared toward privatization; and imposed capitalist investment and export schemes.[14] Rural and coastal communities are forced into monoculture rice production and shrimp farming geared for export, while agribusinesses profit from cheap land leases. Proletarianized workers form a growing reserve army of labor and are driven into industrial production in EPZs, where capitalist interests can guarantee higher profits from the value created by workers. Women, in particular, are pushed into garment factories, largely due to the cumulative, gendered impacts of structural adjustment: destruction of communal land-based livelihoods, transformation of a small-farm agrarian economy into intensive monocultural production, and farmer debts accumulated through land grabs and agribusiness privatization.

Like the free trade agreements described in chapter 2, the dictatorship of debt through structural adjustment imposed upon Bangladesh has trickled down intensely upon farmers, peasants, and Indigenous communities. Tayyab Mahmud argues that expansion of debt is as essential to neoliberalism as privatization and financialization in order to immobilize and impose precarity on the workforce.[15] David Harvey goes further: "Creation of indebtedness from within the financial system becomes a persistent driver of further accumulation."[16] Harvey's assertion is illustrative, given the rapid expansion of microcredit initiatives, such as the Grameen Bank, across Bangladesh. In 2015, twenty-nine million people in Bangladesh had microcredit loans.[17] Offering small loans to borrowers, microcredit lenders often charge exorbitant interest rates and require almost instant repayment, thus creating a cycle of debt. First-time borrowers, particularly women, are ensnared in formal contractual obligations to repay, propelling neoliberal financialization, dispossession of assets, exploitative wage-labor markets, and risky and desperate measures, such as organ sales, to pay off debt.[18] Dispossession and debt also work together to expand the system of bonded labor and intensify the dispossession of Indigenous communities. Like Indigenous communities under NAFTA, Indigenous Pahari communities in the Chittagong Hill Tracts have lost land at alarming rates, as World Bank–funded development projects take over communally cultivated forests and hills. Many Paharis have become landless bonded laborers to agribusinesses and landholding Bengalis. In this heavily militarized region, bonded labor remains a strategic tool of displacement and immobility in a web of counterinsurgency, land dispossession, and debt discipline.

Climate change is also spurring migration toward urban areas. A low-lying floodplain on the world's largest river delta, Bangladesh is one of the countries most impacted by climate change, despite being one of the least responsible for emissions. A three-foot rise in sea levels would submerge one-fifth of the country.[19] One in three Bangladeshi children is at risk from climate disasters and, according to one estimate, one in seven people in the country will be displaced by climate change by 2050.[20] This is projected to be one of the world's biggest climate displacements. Weather disasters and riverbank erosion have already displaced 6.5 million people and destroyed hundreds of thousands of hectares of crops.[21] Farmer Shites Das told the media: "We have no fertility of land like in the past. This has happened because of climate change."[22]

Adding to this alarming climate reality is the particular vulnerability of the one million Rohingya refugees who fled Myanmar and now live in Bangladesh. The Kutupalong-Balukhali refugee camp in Cox's Bazar District is the world's largest refugee camp, home to more than seven hundred thousand refugees.[23] Built on a slope, the area is highly vulnerable to a catastrophic cyclone, landslide, or flooding. Terrifying plans now exist to relocate refugees from Cox's Bazar to the isolated and cyclone-prone silt island of Bhasan Char, creating a floating detention center on the verge of total submersion by a high tide. People in Bangladesh, whether peasants or refugees, are susceptible to climate catastrophe not simply because of geography but also because neoliberal development has altered the country's ecology. Extreme disasters like floods and landslides are magnified by the slow devastation of deforestation and salinity intrusion caused by imposed monocultural rice production and shrimp farming, causing indebted farmers to lose even more land and unaffordable food imports to skyrocket.

Two thousand people move to the capital city daily, and the International Organization for Migration (IOM) estimates that 70 percent are fleeing environmental shock.[24] Saleemul Huq explains, "Dhaka is filled with people who fled their village because it was swallowed by the sea or the rivers."[25] Since 1995, more than 2.8 million workers have flooded the garment industry, itself toxic and polluting.[26] There is a disproportionate feminization of the labor force; for every new male worker arriving, there are three times as many new women workers, their unfree labor solidifying capitalism.[27] The twinned forces of land dispossession and labor exploitation thus come full circle to generate extreme impoverishment and precarity. In the middle of the coronavirus pandemic, dozens of global fashion brands canceled their orders, including for clothes already sewn, creating ripple effects for over 2.26 million garment workers abruptly abandoned by the corporate industry and lurched further into poverty.[28]

In urban areas like Dhaka, dubbed the world's most crowded city, slum fires in densely packed and inflammable dwellings are a common occurrence.

A single blazing fire in 2019 destroyed fifteen thousand homes and displaced over fifty thousand people.[29] Just as hundreds of garment workers are scorched in factory fires, thousands of slum residents—many of whom work in garment factories—are engulfed by slum fires, sometimes acts of arson committed by developers seeking to clear land. Financial speculation in land and housing has, on the one hand, concentrated poverty into slums and, on the other hand, bulldozed those very neighborhoods when seeking new frontiers to colonize and capitalize. One billion residents inhabit slums worldwide, estimated to reach three billion by 2030.[30] While the poor are thrust into such slums, the global real estate market sits at $217 trillion, constituting 60 percent of global assets and catering a life of luxury to the middle and ruling classes.[31] Gita Dewan Verma illustrates this connection: "The root cause of urban slumming seems to lie not in urban poverty but in urban wealth."[32]

Real estate capital accumulation is yet another means of dispossession. It operates through the nexus of land capture and commodification, appropriation of the means of living, zoning deregulation, and police protection of private property. Often expressed in the colonial language of "barren land" and "frontier," this private property relation spatially segregates the wealthy from the impoverished, illustrated by gated communities situated alongside slums and ghettos. Urban planning is dictated by developers, local tax schemes, rent extraction regulations, bylaws criminalizing poverty and street economies, and gentrification turning monuments to culture into towers of glass. Neil Smith articulates: "Gentrification has become a strategy within globalization itself; the effort to create a global city is the effort to attract capital and tourists."[33] Like EPZs bifurcating labor power, this racialized class ordering reorganizes urban space and displaces poor people by commodifying "dead capital" land that poor people live on but do not own as private property.

As people pour into dense urban areas, others flee starvation wages and rising seas to work abroad in one of the world's largest emigrations; in just one year, seven million people left Bangladesh.[34] As Adam Hanieh remarks, "We need to situate migration as an internal feature of how capitalism actually functions at the global scale—a movement of people that is relentlessly generated by the movement of capital, and which, in turn, is constitutive of the concrete forms of capitalism itself."[35] In the Arab Gulf countries, Bangladeshi workers arrive under contract labor migration schemes characterized by indentured labor, low wages, and lack of permanent immigration status, discussed in chapter 8. For those who are crossing borders without documented status, there is the omnipresent threat of immigration enforcement. At the US border, for example, Bangladesh was among the top twelve countries of origin of people caught up in border patrol apprehensions in 2017.[36] If they are lucky enough to make it across, migrants experience severe poverty under racial capitalism. Thirty-one percent of Bangladeshis in New York City live in poverty and face barriers to equitable employment, housing, and education, while enduring labor exploitation and gendered racial profiling.[37]

Bangladeshi workers were at the forefront of a strike at JFK airport against Trump's Muslim ban. The New York Taxi Workers Alliance—a 21,000-member union comprising predominantly South Asian workers—slammed the "hatred spewed from the bully pulpit,"[38] arguing that the ban left taxi drivers, who are already twenty times more likely to be murdered on the job, more vulnerable to hate crimes in a climate of heightened Islamophobia.[39] New York-based Bangladeshi taxi driver Ahmed Sharif, for instance, was stabbed in the neck by passenger Michael Enright, who asked if Sharif was Muslim before slashing him. In 2018, as many as 3,793 Bangladeshi workers died overseas, mostly from work-related injuries.[40] The same year, a series of worker actions took place against the garment industry in Bangladesh, resulting in charges against 3,000 workers and terminations of 11,600 workers in one hundred garment manufacturing units.[41] Across from Rana Plaza, a memorial has been erected. In stark contrast to the edifice of greed that is every sweatshop, this monument is two calloused fists raised high, holding a hammer and sickle.

Global Dispossession through Land Grabs and Climate Change

The total number of migrants worldwide has reached 272 million, 3.5 percent of the world's population, of which 70.8 million are forcibly displaced people.[42] More than half of all refugees tracked by the United Nations High Commissioner for Refugees (UNHCR) are from Syria, Afghanistan, and South Sudan. Despite the constant border panics blasted by Western media, 95 percent of forcibly displaced people remain internally displaced or in refugee camps in neighboring countries. Just three countries—Turkey, Pakistan, and Uganda—are home to 6.3 million refugees, mostly living in refugee camps or surrounding areas. Refugee camps and encampments warehousing refugees are engineered as bordered areas of containment and abandonment with an endless extraction of time.[43] Jennifer Hyndman and Wenona Giles note that less than 1 percent of refugees living in camps around the world find a permanent home, and the rest, over half of whom are under the age of eighteen, are "caught in a web where they lack permanent legal status, experience restricted livelihoods in their place of temporary refuge, and are unable to return home."[44]

For the vast majority of displaced people, migration is not an option. Spatialized systemic *immobility* maintains the cruelties of racial imperial management and political inequality. Palestinians, for example, are considered the world's most protracted refugee population; the United Nations Relief and Works Agency serves 5.5 million Palestinians in refugee camps. This can be traced back to 1948, when heavily armed Zionist paramilitaries conquered Palestine. In what became known as al-Nakba (the catastrophe), more than four hundred villages were destroyed and 750,000 people were expelled from their lands or fled from war zones and were denied permission to return, thus becoming refugees.[45] Israel initially encompassed 78 percent of Palestinian territory, captured through military might as well as legal technologies of land seizure like the Absentees' Property Law and Land Acquisition Law. As Noura Erakat observes, "War doesn't necessarily take the shape of missiles and ground troops."[46] Occupations of the West Bank and Gaza Strip in 1967 usurped more land, with daily life in this warscape consisting of torture, assassinations, humiliation at checkpoints, curfews, sieges, incarceration, home demolitions, economic deprivation, and construction of settlements. Israel's colonization of Palestinians has become interlaced with violence against African refugees and immigrants and Asian migrant workers in Israel, who are also characterized as "demographic threats" and "infiltrators" and subjected to labor exploitation, sterilization, and deportation. Israel is now a leader in the global security industry, boasting the largest number of surveillance companies per capita and a battle-tested security-military apparatus. The US pours an annual $3.8 billion of military aid into Israel and the Jewish National Fund expropriates land through private investment, while the apartheid wall is one of the world's most securitized barriers and seven million Palestinian refugees are denied the right to return to their homes.[47] Israeli settler expansion is thus contingent upon the militarized occupation and immobility of Palestinians within Palestine and containment within surrounding refugee camps.

While many media stories about migration feature the fate of millions of refugees fleeing political upheaval, mass displacement produced by the terror of imposed neoliberalism and the catastrophes of climate change are less visible. Like the neoliberal projects and flooding disasters unfolding in Bangladesh, a pattern has emerged from thousands of other structural adjustment programs. World Bank–funded development projects displaced at least 3.4 million people between 2004 and 2013 through land grabs, fueling a vortex of dispossession and displacement.[48] Land grabs epitomize the bordering regime of land enclosures, a violent form of accumulation conjoining the triad of capitalist extraction, colonial dispossession, and ecological degradation.

In 1985, the World Bank granted India a $450 million loan for the construction of the Sardar Sarovar dam, a much-touted development scheme to produce hydroelectricity and increase irrigation for food production. It would, however, submerge thirty-seven thousand hectares of land and displace three hundred thousand mostly Adivasi people in 245 villages. Considering the associated development, including highways and a canal system, more than one million people have been impacted.[49] As construction began on the dam, villages began to sink. Ratan, a resident, told the media: "I lost all my belongings and firewood. When the officials came, all they could see was water and they said no village had been there."[50] A major grassroots resistance against the dam, with near-death hunger strikes and long marches, pressured the World Bank to implement its first independent commission on any of its projects. Deputy Chairman of the Morse Commission Thomas Berger concluded: "Tribal people will make up the majority of the people ousted by the construction of the Sardar Sarovar dam. Most of these tribal people live in the forests, raise crops, and graze cattle. Usually they have no formal title to the land, even though they may have lived there for generations, they are called 'encroachers.'"[51] The World Bank was forced to withdraw in 1993, marking its first-ever admission of defeat.

Even though the project stalled for some time following the revocation of dam financing, Prime Minister Narendra Modi inaugurated the dam on his birthday in 2017, delivering a death sentence to surrounding communities. Around the world, large dam construction has displaced between forty and eighty million people over six decades, turning thousands of Indigenous and peasant communities into "dam refugees."[52] Dams are a potent symbol of capitalist development: towering emblems of modernization, a testament of mankind conquering and reshaping waterscapes, and a literal trickle-up—an uphill flow—to guarantee water benefits to the wealthy, while dispossessing those whose livelihoods rely on river ecologies.

The World Bank has also financed land grabs across Africa through its private sector arm, the International Finance Corporation. Eleven of these projects, including in Ethiopia, Gabon, and Guinea, have grabbed seven hundred thousand hectares of land.[53] The 2008 crisis of global food costs resulted in a spike in land grabbing, with agribusiness capturing and clearing land for cash crops alongside commodity supply chains like mineral extraction. One study pegs the scale of land grabbing in twenty-eight countries around the world at twenty-seven million hectares, impacting the livelihoods of twelve million people.[54] Land grabs by the agribusiness sector alone have furtively amassed 2 percent of the world's remaining arable land, since 45 percent of the world's agricultural land is now degraded.[55] To add insult to injury, climate-destroying, thieving agribusinesses are subsidized at a rate of one million dollars per minute.[56]

The African continent is the world's most targeted region for large-scale land acquisitions, the site of close to half of all land grabs by agribusiness.[57] In Gabon, according to Marc Ona Essangui, this has enabled "a massive expansion of industrial palm oil, which threatens our food security and the ecological balance of Congo Basin's ancient rainforests."[58] Nearly sixty million hectares of land was approved for allocation in Africa in one year alone,[59] with the US, China, India, Japan, Qatar, Saudi Arabia, the United Arab Emirates, and European countries leading the way in expropriating land, while Cameroon, Democratic Republic of the Congo, Ethiopia, Gabon, Kenya, Madagascar, Malawi, Mali, Mozambique, Senegal, Sudan, Tanzania, and Zambia have been among the most impacted by speculative investment, cash crops, mining and energy extraction, and biofuel production. Biofuels, touted as a green alternative to fossil fuels, are driving European thirst for African land in the rush to meet minimum biofuel use mandates and renewable fuel targets. Land grabbing in today's warming world is intensifying through greenwashed colonialism. Scholars characterize these land grabs as "green grabs," the process of appropriating land for environmental agendas such as conservation, biocarbon sequestration, and biofuel production.[60] The transition to a fossil-free economy, without actually reducing resource dependency in the substrate of our lives, is also fueling mining invasions to extract cobalt, coltan, and rare earth minerals. As the African People's Land Grab Declaration states, "African leaders give foreign countries and companies the most productive land and forcefully remove us, Africans, from our lands. With our ancestral lands taken away, we become refugees in our own land."[61]

Financialization of land through land grabs devastates local food production, impoverishes and displaces farmers, removes land from customary property tenure, distorts social ecosystems embedded in land, and erodes women's access to lands held in common. Such land dispossession generates property relations; as Saskia Sassen writes, these are "accelerated histories and geographies in the making."[62] Women are not only disproportionally impacted, but neoliberal accumulation *itself* structures gendered relations. This can be traced back to the imposition of a colonial gendered ideology, which Amina Mama depicts as "European chauvinistic constructions of femininity and a marginalizing ideology of domesticity" impacting the status of African women.[63] Despite neoliberal poverty reduction schemes, like microcredit, geared toward rural women's entry into formal land registration mechanisms and wage-labor markets, Lyn Ossome contends that neoliberal land regimes exacerbate African women's dispossession from land by foreclosing customary kinship-based land use as a political process. Ossome maintains: "Arguments that favor formalization of customary land rights expose motives that are less in the interest of women's tenure security and more inclined toward supporting commercial interests in land."[64] Silvia Federici similarly demonstrates that capitalist extraction, enclosures of land, and forced entry into labor markets result in the cumulative attrition of women's socioeconomic relations and consequently intensify gendered violence.[65]

It is not surprising, then, that women form the forefront of movements against land grabbing. Women-led leadership defeated ProSavana, a Japan-Brazil-Mozambique project in the Nacala Corridor targeting thirty-five million hectares of land for export-based soybean, cotton, and maize, and slated to be the largest land grab on the African continent. Although Mozambique has some of the world's strongest protections for peasants and small-scale farmers, including legal rights to customary occupancy, farmers, fishers, and pastoralists all feared being bribed off their lands and losing their livelihoods. The No to ProSavana campaign, a Mozambique-based coalition strengthened by peasant movements in Brazil and Japan, managed to indefinitely stall the project and forced Japanese and Brazilian investors to withdraw. Mozambique's National Union of Peasants chairperson Ana Paula Tuacale declared, "We shall continue mobilizing for a world where we have an equitable distribution of our wealth, particularly in our country, without exclusion, and where social justice is a reality."[66]

Land dispossession is further exacerbated by climate change, which is propelling the fastest-growing displacement crisis, from submerging islands and drought-dried deserts to raging fires and supercharged hurricanes. In recognition of mounting climate displacement, an unprecedented (though not legally binding) ruling by the UN Human Rights Committee in 2019 determined that countries cannot deport people who have sought asylum for climate-related threats violating the right to life.[67] Climate disasters displace an average of 25.3 million people annually—one person every one to two seconds—representing an astounding 86 percent of all internal displacement.[68] In 2016, new displacements caused by climate disasters outnumbered new displacements as a result of persecution by a ratio of three to one.[69] By 2050, an estimated 143 million people will be displaced in just three regions, with projections for global climate displacement ranging as high as one billion people.[70]

Acute weather disasters are compounded by longer-term dispossession caused by desertification, soil erosion, monocropping, ocean acidification, pollution, and strip mining. Indonesia is moving its capital city as Jakarta sinks, Canada is clear-cutting one million acres of boreal forest on Indigenous lands every year for toilet paper and tar sands production, 85 percent of Shanghai's rivers are undrinkable because toxic waste is dumped into them by multinational corporations and manufacturing factories, and powerful states scramble over oil and gas resources under melting Arctic ice caps.[71] Extreme drought and crop failures contributed to the Syrian civil war, which then led to one of the world's largest refugee displacements. Displacements from Central America are similarly aggravated by climate change in the "dry corridor" of Guatemala, Honduras, El Salvador, Nicaragua, Costa Rica, and Panama. El Salvador and Guatemala are among the fifteen countries most at risk from environmental disaster, despite contributing the least to climate change.[72] US-based industries have polluted our world with seven hundred times more emissions than the entire Northern Triangle of Central America, and the overall ecological debt owed to poor countries by rich ones is estimated at forty-seven trillion dollars.[73] The dry corridor is now experiencing drought, storms, landslides, floods, and extreme weather events driven by global warming. The average temperature has increased by 0.5°C (0.9°F), altering El Niño–Southern Oscillation circulation patterns and creating supercharged hurricanes. Climate volatility also impacts the agricultural sector, comprising one-third of the jobs in Guatemala, Honduras, and El Salvador.[74] Rural and Indigenous farmers growing coffee, sugarcane, rice, beans, and maize are facing crop losses, and successive droughts between 2014 and 2018 impacted over 2.5 million people in the region.[75] Meanwhile, multinationals like Coca-Cola suck out and pollute whatever little water supply remains.

The Sahel region is another climate hotspot experiencing record droughts, floods, land degradation, and famine from temperatures rising 1.5 times higher than the global average.[76] Ibrahim Thiaw describes the Sahel as "one of the most vulnerable regions to climate change" with the "largest number of people disproportionately affected by global warming."[77] Lake Chad has shrunk by 90 percent and 80 percent of land in the region is degraded, thus rendering cultivatable land for herders and farmers scarce and leaving thirty-three million people in the Sahel food insecure.[78] This has propelled the displacement of four million people and metastasized armed conflict in the region, such as Boko Haram violence.[79] Climate change is an accelerant for all displacements, or, in US military jargon, a "threat multiplier." But displaced refugees—least responsible for and with the fewest resources to adapt to climate variations—face militarized borders in our warming world. Europe is combating migration from the Sahel through the Africa-Frontex Intelligence Community and border externalization, described in part 2.

The UN's refugee convention does not recognize economic or climate displacement. Those fleeing the wars of capitalism are characterized as "bogus refugees" and denied protection. Those escaping climate calamities also find no refuge. Ioane Teitiota from Kiribati applied for asylum in New Zealand in 2013 as the world's first climate refugee. "I'm the same as people who are fleeing war. Those who are afraid of dying, it's the same as me," he pleaded, as his case was dismissed and he was deported.[80] For Teitiota and millions of others, our era's migration crisis is not marked by human mobility but rather the reality of mass displacement and immobility, produced by the multifarious and interwoven systems of globalized capitalism, imperialism, and climate catastrophe.

PART 2

"Illegals" and "Undesirables":

The Criminalization of Migration

CHAPTER 4

Bordering Regimes

There was a wall. It did not look important. It was built of uncut rocks roughly mortared; an adult could look right over it, and even a child could climb it. Where it crossed the roadway, instead of having a gate it degenerated into mere geometry, a line, an idea of a boundary. But the idea was real. It was important. For seven generations there had been nothing in the world more important than that wall.

—Ursula K. Le Guin, *The Dispossessed*

Early one morning in April 2002, Bennett Patricio was run over and dragged for one hundred feet by a border patrol car on Tohono O'odham lands. The teenager's ribs were broken and his skull crushed. The Tohono O'odham Legislative Council condemned Patricio's death as a state killing and the reckless endangerment by border patrol vehicles as a violation of Tohono O'odham sovereignty. The 1853 Gadsden Purchase fissured Tohono O'odham with an artificial border into what is now southern Arizona in the US and northern Sonora in Mexico. Sixty-two miles of the US–Mexico border run through Tohono O'odham lands and an army of US border agents regularly patrol on the reservation. Agents have also beaten, pepper sprayed, and shot Tohono O'odham people, while drones buzz overhead and surveillance cameras track and capture migrants. In 2013, close to eleven thousand migrants were apprehended in Tohono O'odham.[1] Others were dying in the scorching desert; an average of seventy bodies have been found on reservation lands each year.[2] US Customs and Border Protection

(CBP) has contracted Israel's largest private arms company, Elbit Systems, to construct ten surveillance towers, making Tohono O'odham one of the most militarized communities in the US.[3]

When President Donald Trump announced he would build a border wall through Arizona, the vice chairperson of the Tohono O'odham Nation, Verlon Jose, responded, "Over my dead body will a wall be built."[4] The Tohono O'odham battle against the wall conjoins the Indian Wars and border security policies; as Tohono O'odham member Ofelia Rivas puts it, "It will be in my backyard—the wall, and all its political policies along with it."[5] A border wall would cause irreversible ecological damage, disrupt animal migrations, block Tohono O'odham pilgrimages to sacred sites and ceremonies, and separate families on both sides of the border. Blasting for the wall at Organ Pipe Cactus National Monument, home to Tohono O'odham burial sites, was immediately denounced as a desecration by Indigenous leaders. In response to Trump's increased walling and surveillance, the Tohono O'odham released a video titled "There Is No O'odham Word for Wall."

As towering as they are, walls are not impenetrable. Every day they are jumped, subverted, crossed. And despite our emphasis on the spectacle of walls, there are multiple dimensions to border governance. This chapter describes and explores four border governance strategies: exclusion, territorial diffusion, commodified inclusion, and discursive control. These border governance strategies solidify racism, a power structure constructing racial differences and hierarchies, and described by Ruth Wilson Gilmore as "the state-sanctioned or extralegal production and exploitation of group-differentiated vulnerability to premature death."[6] Borders are not fixed lines or passive objects simply demarcating territory; borders are productive regimes both generated by and reproducing racialized social relations, further imbued by gender, sexuality, class, ability, and nationality. Extrapolating from Gilmore, Jasbir Puar suggests that debilitation is a state of being causing slow death that is endemic to capitalist and imperialist plunder. In contrast to neoliberal framings of disability as exceptional or symptomatic, debility is the quotidian, racialized biopolitics of "working and warring."[7] Border governance is at the nexus of working and warring, exclusion and extraction, and thus produces bodies "deemed available for injury" and perpetual debilitation as a form of racial class control.[8]

Four Border Governance Strategies

To survive the Borderlands
you must live sin fronteras
Be a crossroads.
　　　　—Gloria Anzaldúa, *Borderlands / La Frontera: The New Mestiza*

Exclusion

The first strategy of border governance is an exclusion strategy to contain and expel using walls, detention centers, and deportations. Governance through exclusion works to fortify territorial control, solidify a racialized nationalist identity, and criminalize migrants and refugees as "undesirables" and "trespassers." Mass detention and deportation, and the violent scenes accompanying them such as militarized raids and roundups, are intended to punish, intimidate, and deter. However, migrant illegality is not an objective fact; people become illegalized—are *made* illegal—because of state restrictions on entering or remaining without legal authorization. Pathways to becoming a legal permanent resident are shrinking around the world, with visa entry impositions, asylum claim rejections, removal of citizenship as a birthright, limits on family reunification, and stripping of residency for dubious security and criminal offenses. As a result, the number of people crossing borders irregularly is rising. The law constructs illegality, while racism constructs the illegal. The largest nationality of visa overstays in the US in 2017 was not a Latin American one—even though Latinx migrants and refugees constitute the vast majority of detainees—but actually ninety-two thousand Canadians.[9] Together, Canadians and Europeans represent almost one-half of all US immigration overstay violations but are rarely detained.[10] Illegality and race are inseparable constructions, and "laws appearing race neutral become race-based through law enforcement practices," as Mary Romero puts it.[11]

"Build a wall!" has become the battle cry for right-wing governments around the world. We know Trump's ideal border wall would be surrounded by a moat full of alligators and topped with electrified fencing, flesh-piercing spikes, and armed snipers shooting migrants down.[12] Using billions of dollars of Pentagon military funding, construction on Trump's wall will guzzle an estimated eighty-four thousand gallons of water daily.[13] His administration plans to use migrants blocked by the wall and apprehended at the border as guinea pigs in a massive biometric DNA collection program, to be turned over to FBI databases.[14] Centrists like Bill Clinton, Barack Obama, and Joe Biden have proven they too are "tough on immigration" by securing the border against people, while commodities and capital move freely. Appeals to border walls have emotive political traction and construct the nation-state as "simultaneously vulnerable, victimized, righteous, and powerful."[15] The border merges a range of discursive figures: the illegal, the terrorist, the criminal, the foreigner, the invader, and walls are the most visible and visceral deterrent to these caricatures. Walls and walling performances, as Wendy Brown asserts, "do not simply respond to existing nationalism or racism. Rather, they activate and mobilize them."[16] Walls thus solidify the idea of a homogenous nation-state, emphasizing difference and separation from those deemed undesirable. Since the fall of the Berlin Wall, seventy walls now exist in our barbwired and walled world.[17]

Securitization has also turned the border into a dystopic testing ground, constituting a five-hundred-billion-dollar border security industry[18] that flaunts virtual walling through intrusive electronic surveillance technologies, automated decision-making, predictive data analytics, facial recognition software, and biometric systems tested on migrants and refugees by blood-sucking leeches like Amazon, Palantir, Elbit Systems, and European Dynamics. Migrants and refugees are at the forefront of becoming, as Shoshana Zuboff calls it, "the sources of surveillance capitalism's crucial surplus: the objects of a technologically advanced and increasingly inescapable raw-material-extraction operation."[19] These physical, digital, and symbolic changes to border security are "the most durable and profound consequence of the global war on terror" and are some of the most expensive projects undertaken by states.[20] Cutting through and hurting fragile habitats and armed with surveillance drones hunting humans, border walls are key technologies of state governance. To be a modern state, in fact, presupposes the existence of a secured border.

Aside from walls, detention and deportation are the most visible and violent forms of exclusion. Deportations, entailing the physical removal and expulsion of people by state authorities, have exploded. There were a shocking 287,741 deportations—each one an act of state violence—from the US in 2018.[21] Immigration imprisonment in the US has also risen, growing an astounding twentyfold in the past four decades.[22] Immigration and Customs Enforcement (ICE) is currently incarcerating more than 52,500 people a day in more than two hundred detention centers.[23] Spatialized capture and confinement in detention centers reinforces criminalization across race and gender.

The US detains half a million mostly Latinx and Caribbean immigration prisoners annually who, according to César Cuauhtémoc García Hernández, include those incarcerated by the predatory ICE agency, as well as US Marshals Service, Bureau of Prisons, and state agencies.[24]

Immigrant incarceration is a form of gendered violence enacted and enforced by the state. The number of Honduran, El Salvadoran, and Guatemalan women escaping violence and crossing into the US has nearly tripled.[25] These survivors are seeking safety but find themselves subjected to the gendered violence of incarceration. Solitary confinement, lack of access to reproductive healthcare, strip searches, and sexual violence are commonplace. Between 2012 and 2018, detainees filed 1,448 complaints of sexual violence against ICE and 33,126 complaints of abuse between 2010 and 2016.[26] In immigration detention, as in carceral settings generally, trans women are particularly susceptible to violence and report sexual harassment, strip searches by male guards, denial of access to medical care, and solitary confinement under the guise of protective custody. Immigration detainee Nicoll Hernández-Polanco recounts guards subjecting her to invasive strip searches: "They would touch my genitals, my breasts. They would open my legs and touch my buttocks with a latex glove. The guard pulled my hair, pushed me against the wall, and told me that I should remember that I was in a men's detention center."[27] Trans women are routinely incarcerated in all-male immigration detention facilities and, in 2017, were incarcerated for periods twice as long as the average length of detention.[28]

Paralleling the rise in immigration detention, private detention centers have exploded. One of the sickest symptoms of neoliberal capitalist states is the subcontracting of incarceration to private companies. Seventy-five percent of immigration detainees in the US are now incarcerated in facilities operated by private companies like GEO Group and CoreCivic, and 9.7 percent of federal immigration enforcement budgets fund the private sector.[29] G4S is one of the world's largest security companies and private sector employers. Its violent tentacles extend throughout Australia, Israel, the Netherlands, the UK, and the US, and it operates in these countries' inner-city prisons, immigrant detention centers, youth incarceration facilities, and torture camps holding political prisoners. Private prisons gained a foothold in the industry of incarceration through recession-proof immigration detention contracts in the 1980s. CoreCivic opened the US's first privately owned detention facility in 1984 and spent $9.7 million lobbying the House Appropriations Committee Homeland

Security Subcommittee to pass detention-oriented policies. It paid off handsomely; one-quarter of the company's profits now derive from ICE contracts and its stocks rose 137 percent after Trump's administration expanded detention.[30] Border militarization contractors such as Lockheed Martin, General Dynamics, Northrop Grumman, Raytheon, and Boeing are the largest campaign backers to the House Appropriations Committee, having contributed a combined $27.6 million over twelve years.[31] A judge was even convicted for receiving $2.8 million in kickbacks from private detention centers in exchange for increasing the sentences of migrant children.[32] Nonprofits are also making a killing. Southwest Key Programs receives $955 million in federal contracts to operate immigrant youth custody facilities.[33]

Although private entities are profiting from immigration detention and their lobbying incentivizes incarceration, Jackie Wang cautions that "economic exploitation does not explain the phenomenon of racialized incarceration."[34] Liberal emphasis on privatization as a basis of opposition to immigration detention ignores the fact that detention centers in most countries are *public* institutions structured to maintain state violence. The carceral complex primarily regulates racial capitalism and warehouses its surplus populations, thus maintaining state violence against oppressed communities. Secondarily, the carceral industrial complex serves as a booming market for corporations *and* state governments and agencies. ICE is holding $204 million in immigrants' bond money, and thousands of municipalities extract fines and court fees from predominantly Black residents as a source of local revenue.[35]

Liberal opposition to immigration detention also draws distinctions between civil detention and criminal incarceration. We are told that migrant detainees are not criminals and that immigration detention is incarceration without crime. Such articulations create a distinction between innocent victims and those who presumably "deserve" to be locked up. Despite liberal myths of the presumption of innocence, all carceral institutions are subtended by the presumption of guilt as their central logic. In the US and Canada, a disproportionate number of prisoners in the criminal injustice system are Indigenous and Black people, who are racially profiled, loaded with charges, thrown into custody without bail, convicted of minor offenses (especially drug and poverty-related offenses), impacted by mandatory sentencing laws, beaten and raped in prison, and tortured in solitary confinement. Their lives are also marked by post-incarceration exclusions including the shackles of electronic monitoring and unemployability, creating a revolving door to recidivism.

Prisons are the "new residential schools"[36] and the "late modern 'plantations'"[37] with Indigenous and Black women as some of the fastest-growing incarcerated populations. Black women in the US are incarcerated at twice the rate as white women.[38] Michelle Alexander argues that mass incarceration "functions more like a caste system than a system of crime control," as she details the trajectory between slavery, Jim Crow, and mass incarceration, three primary anti-Black systems of control.[39] Lisa Monchalin similarly argues that the incarceration of Indigenous women in Canada is not merely an issue of "overrepresentation" but a pillar of gendered settler-carceral governance.[40] Settler colonialism is not only a pipeline to prisons but also a gendered carceral system itself, structured through land dispossession, imposition of the Indian Act disenfranchising tens of thousands of Indigenous women and regulating the Indian status and band membership of many more, and state removal of Indigenous children from their families.

In racial-capitalist economies marked by debt and austerity, the consolidation of carceral governance correlates with wealth hoarding, deindustrialization and outsourcing, the dismantling of public services, spatialized segregation between gated mansions and ghettos, and the simultaneous production and policing of precarious employment and unemployment. Innocence is a limiting political stance since criminality, like illegality, is a political construction. Criminality is made through shifting definitions of crime and policed as a race-making and property-protecting regime. Gilmore thus informs us that our political task is not to prove innocence, but "to attack the general system through which criminalization proceeds."[41] Police and prison abolitionists seek the transformation of carceral captivity and criminalization in all state relations and social ecosystems. Abolition, Dylan Rodríguez elucidates, "is constituted by so many acts long overlapping, dispersed across geographies and historical moments, that reveal the underside of the New World and its descendant forms—the police, jail, prison, criminal court, detention center, reservation, plantation, and 'border.'"[42] Drawing on Black-led abolition movements, calls to abolish immigration enforcement replace assimilationist calls for immigration reform. The movement organized around the DREAM Act, for example, emphasized "good" and "deserving" migrants with college degrees, employment history, and clean criminal records and was, therefore, a political campaign mobilizing around appeals to innocence. In contrast, as Mijente organizers underscore, "#Not1More was a call for a moratorium on deportations—an idea at the heart of the notion that ICE should be abolished. It was the radical idea—at the time—that no one should be subject to the harm of immigration enforcement."[43]

Territorial diffusion

The second strategy of border governance is territorial diffusion through the internalization and externalization of border enforcement. Territorial diffusion relies on biometric surveillance and disciplinary practices *within* the state, as well as imperial outsourcing *beyond* the state's borders. Put another way, the border is elastic, and the magical line can exist anywhere. Crossing the border does not end the struggle for undocumented people, because the border is mobile and can be enforced anywhere within the nation-state. Internal bordering differentiates those within the nation-state who are citizens from those who are not. Some of the most progressive welfare states, such as the Nordic countries or Canada, have some of the strictest restrictions on undocumented people accessing welfare, healthcare, education, childcare, or even a driver's license. This mutates the working class—nurses, teachers, social workers—into border guards, and the reproduction of borders becomes a workplace ritual.

The internalization of border enforcement also includes collaboration between agencies through shared databases such as the Secure Communities initiative in the US and devolution of immigration enforcement to local health, school, transit, employment, and policing authorities. Despite important sanctuary city declarations by municipalities to guarantee undocumented residents' access to public services and limit cooperation with immigration agents, police operating in besieged neighborhoods are the main pipeline to deportation. Kesi Foster writes, "Even if local officials don't let ICE walk in the front door of our schools to take our children, local militarized police forces are taking Black and Brown youth out of the back door in handcuffs."[44] About half of all interior deportations in the US are through the Criminal Alien Program, targeting noncitizens for immigration, drug, and traffic charges, and the majority of immigration apprehensions happen through jails, prisons, and the criminal injustice system.[45] Stop-and-frisk policing and immigration raids are thus intertwined systems of criminalization impacting low-income Black, Indigenous, Latinx, Muslim, queer, and trans migrants. Furthermore, US CBP has expansive interior jurisdiction, including legal powers to stop and search vehicles one hundred miles inward from the border—zones where roughly two-thirds of people in the country live.[46] Border internalization, therefore, creates a ubiquitous regime of bordering enacted through racialized surveillance, instilling fear of the everyday and making the lives of undocumented people intolerable in order to encourage self-deportation. Like its internalization, the border is also externalized and operates far beyond its territorial jurisdiction, which I explore in the final section of this chapter.

Commodified inclusion

The third strategy of border governance is the commodified inclusion of migrants and refugees as undocumented or temporary workers with deliberately deflated labor power to guarantee capital accumulation. The looming risk of deportation, even if it does not occur—neither the state nor capital's interests lie in deporting everyone—increases social and labor exploitation. Fifty-two percent of companies in the US threaten to call immigration authorities on workers during union drives.[47] In 2019, one of the largest immigration raids in recent US history took place in Mississippi, with 680 arrests of workers at Peco and Koch processing plants. Run by billionaire Joseph Grendys, Koch Foods was an active site of Latinx worker organizing after a unionization drive in 2005, followed by a seven-year lawsuit for discrimination and sexual harassment. This lawsuit was settled for $3.75 million in favor of the workers, interestingly, just prior to the 2019 ICE raid.[48]

The Koch Foods raid is not a unique moment of state repression against migrant workers. There are echoes of the Bisbee Deportation of 1917, when 1,300 striking miners affiliated with the Industrial Workers of the World (IWW) were deported by deputized vigilantes, and the 1936 deportation of Jesus Pallares, a labor leader of the 8,000-strong Liga Obrera de Habla Espanola. While workers are declared illegal, the surplus value they create is never deemed illegal. The subjugated and commodified inclusion of migrant labor relies on the first two border governance strategies that create exclusion and illegalization. This renders migrants as *deportable* subjects, who are not actually deported if they remain compliant laborers. Capitalism therefore relies on the social and racial exclusions engendered through borders to subordinate migrant labor, the focus of chapter 7.

Discursive control

The fourth strategy of border governance occurs through discursive control, most evident in the maneuvering between "refugee crisis" and "migrant crisis." Refugees are often characterized as fleeing persecution in search of safety, while migrants are depicted as "bogus refugees" moving for economic reasons and hence undeserving of protection. Furthermore, migrants are also differentiated from immigrants, who are typically perceived and selected by the state as upwardly mobile economic actors, while refugees claiming asylum are separated from UN Convention refugees, who are "accepted" or "resettled" with UN or state-designated legal status. The distinction between refugees and migrants, however, is blurry, especially given their unsanctioned, irregular flights of escape and co-constituted networks. The terrorism of extraction and the precarity of war are not easily teased apart. As Teju Cole tells us, "Sometimes the gun aimed at your head is grinding poverty, or endless shabby struggle, or soul crushing tedium."[49] Or as Suketu Mehta asserts, "Whether you're running from something or running toward something, you're on the run."[50] I use "migrants and refugees" together, not to conflate lived experiences or collapse material differences, but to refuse binaries of forced and voluntary, deserving and undeserving, real and bogus, and to depict irregular migration as an autonomous force defying and exceeding state characterizations and controls.

Crucially, Eurocentrism and anticommunism inform the international legal order, and hence, discursive order, governing refugees and migrants. The 1951 United Nations Refugee Convention, which defines a Convention refugee as someone who flees because of "well-founded fear of persecution for reasons of race, religion, nationality, membership of a particular social group or political opinion," was conceived by European states responding to the Nazi-created Holocaust, while ontologically distancing themselves from displacements wrought by their own empires.[51] Aimé Césaire condemned Europeans because they "tolerated Nazism before it was inflicted on them . . . because, until then, it had been applied only to non-European peoples."[52] Furthermore, in a sleight of hand, the Convention codifies the right to seek asylum from persecution but does not require signatory states to actually grant asylum. Throughout the 1950s, the US created a preference for an ideologically charged category of refugees it called "escapees" who, because of persecution on account of race, religion, or political opinion, "fled from the Union of Soviet Socialist Republics or other Communist, Communist-dominated or Communist-occupied area of Europe."[53] The International Organization for Migration (IOM), one of the world's largest intergovernmental organizations, is another pillar of migration management. Also founded in 1951, the IOM was initially propped up by the US to provide services and logistics to contain global migration in line with the Cold War agenda. Today, it is one of the primary facilitators of "assisted voluntary returns," pressuring people to self-deport.[54] In this way, international institutions governing migrants and refugees have created a slew of legally distinct categories and a hierarchy of rights in order to manage, divide, and control people on the move.

Externalization as Border Imperialism

Less visible than the horrific images of immigration raids and overflowing detention centers are the more sophisticated and dangerous front-end technologies resulting in the externalization of borders: interdiction, offshore detention, safe third country agreements, and outsourcing of border control to third countries. Border externalization, part of the second governance strategy of territorial diffusion described above, encompasses all extraterritorial state technologies and actions intended to prevent migrants and refugees from reaching the legal jurisdiction of the state. Signatory states to the Refugee Convention are bound, in principle, to process asylum claims and uphold the principle of non-refoulement. Non-refoulement is the international legal obligation ensuring that no state forcibly returns refugees back to a country where they face persecution. However, a political consensus exists, especially among Western countries, that migrants and refugees should remain in their places of origin or, at most, seek asylum in their neighboring countries. Border externalization governs through prevention and deterrence far beyond the border itself, such that "the definition of the border increasingly refers not to the territorial limit of the state but to the management practices directed at 'where the migrant is.'"[55]

Interdiction is the preemptive apprehension of people by applying carrier sanctions on airlines transporting people without proper visa documentation or patrolling to intercept migrant and refugee boats before they reach territorial waters. Maritime interdictions by European countries in the Mediterranean and by Australia in the Oceania region have been taking place for decades, framed in recent years by governments as an "anti-smuggling" measure, with flimsy boats proactively seized and destroyed. The US also has a Migrant Interdiction Program, the origins of which are discussed in chapter 2, through which the coast guard interdicts boats arriving from the Caribbean, and passengers are detained at Guantánamo Bay before being deported. The coast guard describes its work as enforcing immigration laws at sea, claiming that "intercepting these offenders at sea means they can be safely returned to their country of origin without the costly processes required if they had successfully entered the United States."[56] In Canada, Canada Border Services Agency officers work with commercial airlines overseas to integrate interdiction surveillance. In 2018, a record number of 7,208 people, mostly from Romania, Mexico, India, Hungary, and Iran, were barred from boarding flights to Canada due to "improper documentation."[57] Canada's earliest interdiction efforts date back to the 1900s, when railway staff were informed by authorities not to sell train tickets to Black people coming from the US.[58]

Australia's offshore detention system involves the transfer of refugees to Australian-funded detention centers on Manus Island and Nauru; the system is explored further in the next chapter. Outside Australia is an entire extraterritorial refugee regime, guided by the notorious Pacific Solution, which includes a number of interrelated strategies, such as interception by militarized Australian Defence Force operations, excising islands from Australia's migration zone so refugees arriving at these locations can be denied asylum protection, and offshore detention. Offshoring captivity deflects government responsibilities in two key ways: governments can avoid their legal obligation to offer asylum and also avoid accountability for detention conditions by placing blame on third governments. The EU is also expanding offshore detention through what it calls "transit processing centers" across northern Africa, and the US operates offshore detention on military bases in Guantánamo and Guam, sites already marked by histories of imperial invasion.

Safe third country agreements are bilateral agreements requiring refugees to seek refuge in the first country they reach, prohibiting them from seeking asylum elsewhere. In place since 2004, the US–Canada Safe Third Country Agreement prohibits most refugees from seeking asylum at a regular land port of entry in either country if they first landed in the other one. Given that most refugees transit through the US into Canada and not the other way around, the agreement reduced the number of refugee claims at Canadian land crossings by 49 percent when it was first implemented.[59] After Trump's Muslim ban and suspension of temporary protected status, thousands of refugees arrived at the Canadian border. Many were encouraged by Prime Minister Trudeau's PR stunt; "To those fleeing persecution, terror & war, Canadians will welcome you, regardless of your faith. Diversity is our strength #WelcomeToCanada," he tweeted. In reality, most of the 45,517 Central American, African, and Caribbean migrants and refugees from the US had to contend with the safe third country agreement and were forced to make hazardous journeys.[60] Several lost limbs to frostbite after walking for hours in freezing temperatures.

Mavis Otuteye, a 57-year-old Ghanaian grandmother, was found dead from hypothermia in a ditch near the Canada–US border in 2017. Around 7,787 Haitian refugees arrived in Canada during the first year of Trump's presidency, and many were held captive at the Canadian border in army camps.[61] Based on the US–Canada Safe Third Country Agreement, Trump announced a series of agreements with Mexico, Guatemala, El Salvador, and Honduras, forcing those countries to accept asylum applications from refugees in transit. This makes it virtually impossible for refugees to flee north and claim asylum in the US. In the EU, the Dublin Regulation returns asylum seekers to a previous country of arrival, and the EU–Turkey deal is based on the presumption that Turkey is a safe third country. Such agreements are becoming a popular mechanism of immigration diplomacy to block refugees from claiming asylum in their country of choice and, instead, forcibly returning them to a transit country.

Outsourcing of migration control to third countries is also increasingly deployed as a form of imperial intervention, revealing how the relationship between imperialism and migration is not simply one of cause and effect but, rather, how externalization of migration controls has *itself* become a method for imperialism in this era. Europe's contemporary border externalization regime dates back thirty years. Countries on the African continent are especially pressured to accept outsourcing of EU borders, and most aid agreements now force African countries to implement migration controls. Detailed in chapter 6, EU border externalization employs a sophisticated system of control that includes Mediterranean drone surveillance, EU Border Assistance Missions conducting joint border patrols in dozens of non-EU countries, and European boots on the ground across the Sahel region.

Not to be outdone, US Customs and Border Protection has trained fifteen thousand border agents from one hundred different countries.[62] Todd Miller remarks, "Close your eyes and point to any landmass on a world map, and your finger will probably find a country that is building up its borders in some way with Washington's assistance."[63] In Afghanistan and Iraq, US Border Patrol special forces and tactical units works closely with the US military to further the imperialist occupations of those two countries.[64] In Central America, the US Strategy for Engagement in Central America receives US funding to beef up border security and migration prevention efforts. The US also trains and funds immigration enforcement in El Salvador, Guatemala, Honduras, and Mexico through the Grupo Conjunto de Inteligencia Fronteriza and fuses border intelligence by sharing databases to prevent asylum claims from alleged gang members. The widely reported kidnappings of migrants—almost 9,800 in Mexico within six months—are not random acts of violence by crime syndicates, but rather reflect the deliberate reorganization of social and property relations as the war on drugs conjoins with the war on migrants.[65] As explained in chapter 2, the US-led war on drugs enables neoliberal dispossession, enforces austerity through carceral governance, and sanctions the terror of paramilitary counterinsurgency operations. The imposition of these processes compels migration from Mexico, while also justifying the US outsourcing of border enforcement to Mexico, where the US is currently training both Mexican police and border guards. The discourse of narco-trafficking also serves to control migration through militarization and paramilitarization, through which non-state forces detain, extort, and sometimes massacre and disappear migrants under state supervision. Shortly after the US launched the Mexico-Guatemala-Belize Border Region Program, Homeland Security officials declared "the Guatemalan border with Chiapas is now our southern border."[66] The US has even deployed border agents and investigative forces into Guatemala to restrict migration. In response, three hundred members of the Assembly of Peoples of Huehuetenango took over the Mesilla checkpoint on the Guatemala–Mexico border in 2019 and drew links between resource extraction, land dispossession, forced migration, and border militarization.[67]

US imperial outsourcing is most evident in Trump's recent Migrant Protection Protocols, or "Remain in Mexico" policy as it is commonly known, under which migrants and refugees, including sixteen thousand children and minors, have been forced to remain in Mexico while awaiting a hearing in the US.[68] During its first year of implementation, over fifty-nine thousand people were turned back into Mexico to have their asylum claims processed, and only eleven people were granted asylum in the US.[69] Citing the coronavirus pandemic, US immigration authorities temporarily suspended all asylum hearings in April 2020, leaving thousands of people stranded in the Mexican border town of Matamoros in a teeming migrant camp without electricity or running water.[70] Predating these protocols is the US–Mexico Mérida Initiative, a multibillion-dollar program whose core pillars are fighting narco-trafficking and strengthening immigration enforcement at Mexico's southern border. Initiated by Bush and expanded under Obama, Mérida includes US training and funding of Mexican enforcement agents as well as police and military equipment for training. Mexico's Communications and Transport Ministry also reclaimed ownership of "La Bestia" railroad in 2016, increasing apprehensions of migrants who commonly use this rail line to travel through Mexico.

The militarization and paramilitarization of Mexico led to the apprehension of 520,000 Central American migrants in Mexico between 2015 and 2018.[71] Seventy thousand other migrants disappeared in Mexico between 2006 and 2016—what the Mesoamerican Migrant Movements calls "a migrant holocaust"—and thousands more were assaulted and raped.[72] Eighty percent of Central American migrant women reported sexual extortion and rape.[73] This horror accelerated with the deployment of Mexico's National Guard to the border in 2019 as part of a promise by the Mexican government to take "unprecedented steps" to curb migration, made after Trump threatened punitive tariffs. A battery of migration and police checkpoints now await all travelers arriving in Mexico, beginning in southern Chiapas and ending at the US–Mexico border, and the detention of Central American migrants in Mexico has doubled since these crackdowns began in 2019.[74] In early 2020, Mexican forces blocked and teargassed 4,000 predominantly Honduran migrants and refugees, immediately detaining and deporting more than 1,800.[75] During the 2020 pandemic, hundreds of mostly Honduran and Salvadoran detainees in five Mexican immigration detention centers held protests over their continued detention in overcrowded and unsanitary conditions. In a desperate act, detainees in the Tenosique detention center set fire to the facility and one Guatemalan refugee, Héctor Rolando Barrientos Dardón, tragically died.[76]

Africans are also trapped and detained by the Remain in Mexico policy. The number of African migrants and refugees in Mexico has tripled since 2017.[77] Traveling for months across oceans, rivers, jungles, and mountain ranges through over a dozen countries and forced to leave behind friends who perished along the way, they are now stranded in Chiapas because Mexico has denied them documentation to reach the US. Migrants and refugees in Mexico used to receive documents ordering them to leave the country within twenty-one days, during which time they would travel to the northern border into the US. Now, documents order them to leave through the southern border and prohibit them from journeying north. More than three thousand people from Angola, Burkina Faso, Cameroon, Central African Republic, Democratic Republic of the Congo, Eritrea, Ethiopia, Ghana, Guinea, Liberia, Mali, Mauritania, Republic of Congo, Senegal, Sierra Leone, and Togo have created an Assembly of African Migrants in Tapachula. In a message to the world, they shone light on their collective condition: "Since we left our countries, for us life has been a state of permanent escape. We feel despair, hopelessness, fear, demoralization, loneliness and abandonment."[78] Their protests in the fall of 2019 demanding basic rights for food, hygiene, housing, and mobility were met with armed officers and the National Guard, and they remain immobilized in Mexico.

These forms of border externalization shared across countries, coupled with militarization of the border itself, have allowed imperial states to erect not only walls but entire *fortresses* stretching far beyond the border. The Five Country Conference, for example, is an immigration and border security collaboration between Australia, Canada, New Zealand, the UK, and the US, including shared databases of fingerprints, biometric data of refugees, and the eerie Five Eyes espionage and surveillance network. Further, externalized fortresses are, not coincidentally, often imposed on third countries already subjugated through imperialism. Immigration diplomacy through the soft power of aid agreements or outright threats of trade war compels countries across Africa, Latin America, the Middle East, and Oceania to accept outsourced migration controls, which cements imperial relations and globalizes the racial violence of detention. The next two chapters trace these systems of border externalization and immobilization in and beyond Australia, through the colonial founding of White Australia and its contemporary Pacific Solution, and the EU's Fortress Europe, constructed especially in relation to Africa through an intricate web of imperial control. Just like the entanglements structuring US border formation and immigration policy described in earlier chapters, these fortresses securing Australia and Europe are built on the genealogies of empire, settler colonialism, transatlantic slavery, and indentured labor. As Angela Davis asserts, "The refugee movement is the civil rights movement of our time."[79]

CHAPTER 5

Australia and the Pacific Solution

We are four hundred people
Four hundred lost souls in a tightly confined space
Four hundred prisoners
Anticipating the nights
. . . so we can leave
. . . and enter our nightmares.
—Behrouz Boochani, *No Friend but the Mountains:*
Writing from Manus Prison

Behrouz Boochani, a Kurdish refugee from Iran, won Australia's eminent literary prize in January 2019 for his book *No Friend but the Mountains: Writing from Manus Prison*, which details his ongoing detention since 2013 and the condition of other detainees in Manus Island Regional Processing Centre in Papua New Guinea.[1] Formerly colonized by Germany, Britain, and Australia, Papua New Guinea now houses one of Australia's many externalized, offshore immigration detention centers. Boochani wrote the book one text message at a time while detained, using a smuggled cellphone. He chronicles systemic abuse by guards, a lack of electricity or running water, daily lineups for food, countless incidents of self-harm, and wearing down of prisoners until they self-deport. The torture is daily—dried sweat and human waste producing a smell "so vile that one feels ashamed to be part of the human species"—and deeply psychological, with unbearable isolation and the painfully slow passage of each day bringing an endless loss of time.[2] When

93

Boochani won the prize, he was still captive on Manus Island and forbidden from entering Australia to receive it.

A few weeks later, in February 2019, Abdul Aziz Muhamat, a Zaghawa refugee from Sudan, was named the 2019 Martin Ennals Laureate in Switzerland. Also incarcerated on Manus Island since 2013, Muhamat was a prominent voice against Australian detention. He sent voice messages for broadcast on the outside, organized a mass hunger strike, and advocated for medical care. He was granted special permission to leave Manus Island on a temporary visa to accept the prize. His acceptance speech described being "locked like an animal in a cage." He further explained how incarceration on Manus Island ultimately benefits Australian politicians and their dog-whistle politics, and also announced that he faced detention upon return.[3] After international outrage at the absurdity and cruelty of the situation, Switzerland granted Muhamat asylum in June 2019. Later that same year, Boochani was granted a visa to enter and remain in New Zealand.

Right after the election of conservative Australian prime minister Scott Morrison in 2019, there was a mental health crisis on Manus Island, with fifty incidents of self-harm reported in three weeks.[4] Detainees on Manus Island have no access to healthcare at the prison camp. Health services are contracted to an off-site clinic, which a coroner found provided inadequate care and was responsible for the death of at least one refugee.[5] Instead of ensuring care in response to this mental health crisis, the government discussed repealing a medevac law that had allowed for transfers of sick refugees from offshore sites to Australia for treatment. Equally alarming, Papua New Guinea's paramilitary police squad, which is partially funded by the Australian Immigration Department, was deployed to patrol the prison camp.[6] Provincial police commander David Yapu sadistically told the *Guardian* that refugees would continue to self-harm "unless they see policeman wearing a uniform at the camp. That will change that."[7]

Papua New Guinea's notorious paramilitary police squad has been linked to repression and rapes of Indigenous Papua New Guineans opposing mining, fracking, and logging. In 2009, the squad evicted and burned down more than one hundred homes on the Ipili people's customary lands in the mining lease area of Porgera Gold Mine.[8] Gold mining at Porgera constitutes 12 percent of the country's total exports.[9] The mine is 95 percent owned and operated by Canada-based Barrick Gold Corporation, the world's largest gold mining corporation, which requested and materially supported the squad deployment.[10]

One man refusing to leave his home was locked inside his residence by officers and the house was set on fire.[11] While he survived, worldwide killing of land defenders by private security groups, state forces, and contract killers is highest in the mining sector.[12] Seventy-five percent of the world's mining companies are based in Canada, responsible for a disproportionate amount of the world's mining-related rights violations.[13] Mining corporations also play a sordid role in immigration detention; CI Resources, a phosphate mining company, operates Australia's Christmas Island detention center. As I explore in this chapter, such seemingly disparate violences against Indigenous peoples and refugees across distant geographies entwine resource colonialism and externalized immigration detention through the interconnected structures of colonial dispossession, racial state formation, and carceral control. Australia's oppressive offshore detention system, including on Manus Island in Papua New Guinea, is squarely connected to the genocidal history of colonization and racist regulation of migration by White Australia.

Colonial Production of White Australia

Australia has the most entrenched policies of mandatory and offshore detention in the contemporary world. Australian offshore detention centers are located on Manus Island in Papua New Guinea, the Republic of Nauru, and the Australian overseas territory of Christmas Island. The past haunts, with today's offshore detention centers on Manus Island and Nauru perpetuating prison policy as a key mode of Indigenous dispossession since the first New South Wales penal colony. Some of the first Europeans in Australia in the late 1700s were British and Irish convicts forcibly transported to prison colonies there. Between 1787 and 1868, more than eighty thousand prisoners were forcibly shipped to Australia.[14] With them came British administration and a project of commercial and territorial expansion. British administrators wielded brutal violence and adopted the doctrine of terra nullius to expropriate Aboriginal and Torres Strait Islander lands.[15]

Named after a South Australian politician, the Torrens system of land registration was first enacted in the colony of South Australia.[16] Later exported across the British empire, this system of land registration combined the colonial doctrines of discovery and racist discourses of uninhabited and uncultivated land with capitalist models of private property ownership and land commodification.[17] Renisa Mawani explains that the Torrens system borrowed directly from imperial slave ship manifests and, through it, land was seized from Indigenous social and legal organization and transferred as private property to settlers.[18] Based on colonial dispossession and capitalist private ownership working together to uphold white settler property, this land registration system sanctioned colonizers' claims of ownership to the entire continent. Augmenting the legal and military theft of Indigenous land were the Aboriginal Protection Acts, authorizing the forced removal of children as well as a carceral infrastructure of confinement and impoverishment on various offshore island reserves. Half the Indigenous people forcibly relocated to Flinders Island died.[19] Racial-colonial ordering is always a spatial ordering, and carceral islands in the early colonial period foreshadowed offshore immigration detention.

The transformation of land into a sedentary commodity and policies criminalizing migration are both antithetical to a rich history of land stewardship, trade, voyaging, and kinship networks between islands in Oceania. This way of living was devastated by colonization, slavery, and indentureship. After the formal abolition of chattel slavery in the US, European imperial markets relied on enslavement and forced labor in other colonies to establish plantations. From the 1860s until the early 1900s, South Sea Islanders were kidnapped and either enslaved or forcibly indentured on sugar and cotton plantations in British-controlled northern Australia, supplanting forced unpaid Indigenous labor and supplementing Asian indentured labor.[20] One-third of the South Sea Islanders died, and others were later deported.[21]

Dispossession, enslavement, and indentureship were the motors of accumulation in Australia and fixed it to a "racial destiny" shared by Canada, New Zealand, South Africa, and the US.[22] Amid a chorus of white opposition to Pacific Islander as well as Chinese indentured labor, a series of Australian restrictions were passed. The Victorian Act introduced a poll tax and restrictions on Chinese arrivals, the Pacific Island Labourers Act outlawed imported labor, the Immigration Restriction Act limited non-European migration through the use of language testing, and the Post and Telegraph Act stipulated that only white workers could work on vessels carrying mail. These policies were the first anti-Chinese legislation in the British colonial world and became a template for US and Canadian anti-Chinese exclusion, working to effectively bar non-white migration and secure, as then-attorney general Alfred Deakin put it, a "White Australia." Just as apartheid Israel imagines itself as an "oasis of democracy" in the Middle East, Australia today projects itself as the sole "Western civilization" in an ocean full of Asian and Pacific Islander countries.

Not only was Australia's design of property registration and immigration exclusion exported, but it exerted its own expansionist drive within Oceania. Australia's contemporary externalization of detention can be traced to a colonial relationship between Australia, Nauru, and Papua New Guinea. As Stuart Hall notes, "In the case of the colonial and post-colonial, what we are dealing with is not two successive regimes but the simultaneous presence of a regime and its after-effects. Colonialism persists, despite the cluster of illusory appearances to the contrary."[23] From the turn of the last century until 1975, Papua New Guinea was under Australian colonial rule as well as an Australian trusteeship agreement authorized by the United Nations. The long trajectory of Australian control over Papua New Guinea has been characterized by mass executions, legislated control through the Native Regulations and Ordinances, conscription of forced labor, and imposition of industrial mining such as the Rio Tinto Panguna mine. Today, extracted palm oil is the country's primary export, and "special agricultural and business leases" cover over two million hectares, leading to rapid deforestation in one of the world's largest remaining tropical forests.[24] An explosive investigation in 2020 by Global Witness revealed a planned rubber plantation on Manus Island, propped up by multinational corporations and global financial institutions, is likely a front for illegal logging.[25]

Nauru, the world's smallest island nation, was a colony of Germany in the 1880s, after which an Australia–New Zealand–UK tripartite agreement took over all rights to phosphate mining on the island. In 1947, the United Nations authorized an international trusteeship of Australia, New Zealand, and the UK over the territory of Nauru, with Australia holding effective administrative and trusteeship power. Until formal independence in 1968, Nauru's land was rapaciously devoured and economy underdeveloped, while Australian mining interests and agribusiness flourished. Nauru received just 7.6 percent of revenues from phosphate mining in 1964, and 80 percent of Nauruan lands were strip-mined for export in the global fertilizer industry.[26] In a stunning indictment of its own colonial administration, Australia declared Nauru uninhabitable in the 1960s and offered to resettle people on another island. The people of Nauru refused, and, in a David-and-Goliath battle at the International Court of Justice, Australia was forced to settle a claim for failure to remedy environmental damage. Though an important measure of justice, the settlement could not reverse the extreme impoverishment and decimation of local economies.

Imperialism "lingers where it has always been," as Edward Said reminds us, "in a kind of general cultural sphere as well as in specific political, ideological, economic and social practices."[27] Resource colonialism, ecological devastation, and forced dependency made Papua New Guinea and Nauru into present-day Australian penal colonies, a "residual material haunting through neo-colonial control."[28] Most liberal commentaries depict the people of Nauru or Manus Island as uniformly anti-refugee—and often as more racist than Australians—with little acknowledgment of how Australian offshore detention continues imperialism and land dispossession. Writing about Nauru, Anthea Vogl remarks, "Off shore processing extends and continues Nauru's ongoing relationship with Australia of dependence and aid, which began with Australia's exploitation of Nauru's land."[29] Today, the detention center on Nauru sits next to an active mine site. Liberal opposition to offshore detention often portrays Manus Island and Nauru as "remote jungles" with "savage locals" and "corrupt administrations," relying on anti-Indigenous tropes of modernity. Though employed to force Australia to end offshore detention, the trope of modernity as civilizing actually conceals colonial relations that are the very condition of possibility for border externalization. Ending offshore immigration detention, then, must also eviscerate Australia's colonial relations of dispossession and carceral control.

Mandatory and Offshore Detention

Detention centres should not exist in any capacity.
—RISE: Refugees, Survivors and Ex-detainees,
"Our Position"

Ongoing anxiety about maintaining White Australia continues to animate racial settler formation, producing one of the world's most punitive detention systems. Dating back to 1992 under the Labor government of Paul Keating, Australia mandated that any person without a valid visa be detained, and time limits were removed, thereby permitting indefinite detention. The average length of detention in the Australian onshore detention system is five hundred days, far longer than the US, UK, or Canada.[30] Some people remain in captivity much longer. After being tortured by the Indian army and fleeing the Indian occupation of Kashmir, Peter Qasim was detained for almost seven years.[31] Since 2000, there have been at least 2,026 deaths at sea before reaching Australia's shores, following deportation from Australia, and in Australian onshore and offshore detention centers, including at least 24 deaths by suicide in detention centers since 2010.[32]

On Manus Island and Nauru in 2019, about 75 percent of refugees had a serious physical health condition and 82 percent suffered from depression.[33] The National Ethnic Disability Alliance notes the disproportionate detention of people with disabilities, as well as the institution of detention itself contributing to disabling people.[34] Children as young as seven years old have experienced "repeated incidents of suicide attempts, dousing themselves in petrol, and becoming catatonic."[35] During the coronavirus pandemic, detainees in Australia's onshore and offshore detention centers were identified as one of the populations most susceptible to transmission of the virus, both due to the impossibility of physical distancing and the already-compromised health of many detainees. Further, detention is sexual violence, as captured in the testimony of a woman detained on Nauru: "I went inside. Dogs came in too. Man took off all his clothes and showed me his private parts."[36] When faced with a government-commissioned review cataloging violence including sexual assault of children and guards coercing sexual favors from women, then–Australian prime minister Tony Abbott disgustingly retorted, "Things happen."[37] Perhaps most harrowing, yet emblematic, of Australia's border violence are the struggles of detainees who become pregnant as a result of rape in detention and are nevertheless denied healthcare and reproductive rights in Australia. Amnesty International summarizes these conditions as "a calculated system of neglect and cruelty to increase the hardship suffered by refugees and asylum seekers."[38]

Australian offshore detention centers (or prison camps, as detainees call them) date back nearly two decades, garnering support from both the Australian Labor Party and the conservative Liberal Party. In August 2001, a Norwegian freighter, MV *Tampa*, rescued 433 mostly Afghan refugees and entered near the waters off Christmas Island. After a tense standoff, during which Australia refused to accept the refugees, Australia struck a deal with Nauru and forcibly transported most of the refugees there like cargo. Nauru, whose ecology and economy was devastated through extractive colonialism, received a sizable thirty-million-dollar aid package in exchange.[39] The following month, instrumentalizing the 9/11 attacks to stir up both warmongering and anti-migrant fervor, conservative prime minister John Howard implemented the Pacific Solution. Thus began the interception of boats, with asylum seekers being sent to offshore camps rather than landing on Australian state territory. Under a new Border

Protection Act, the Australian Navy was also deployed to interdict and forcibly return any "suspected illegal entry vessels" near Indonesia. Within just a few weeks, these concerted militarization efforts led to risky sea journeys, and, on October 18, 2001, a boat carrying mainly Iraqi and Afghan passengers sank. Approximately 353 people, including 150 children, died. Yet Immigration Minister Philip Ruddock crudely commented, "This tragedy may have an upside" in terms of deterring future arrivals.[40]

The Pacific Solution also excised external territories such as Christmas Island from Australian migration policy, meaning that refugees arriving at these locations were considered not to have officially entered Australia. They were denied access to Australian asylum protection and were instead detained on Nauru and Manus Island, where their claims were processed. Offshore detention thus serves not only to isolate refugees and as a racist deterrence strategy, but also to create "interstitial legal categories."[41] The first two years after the implementation of the Pacific Solution, Australia interdicted and detained 1,544 refugees on Manus Island and Nauru and also increased aid to Nauru, amounting to one-third of the country's GDP.[42] When Labor Prime Minister Kevin Rudd briefly ended offshore detention in 2007, there was swift backlash from both his own party and the opposition. Under the subsequent Labor leadership of Julia Gillard, detention centers on Manus Island and Nauru were reopened in 2012, in addition to several new detention centers, including "the Gitmo of Australia" on Christmas Island. Gillard also extended the Pacific Solution to include migrants arriving on the Australian mainland by boat, who could then also be sent to offshore detention centers. Shortly after Rudd returned as prime minister, this time blatantly playing to a racist base, he shamelessly announced that any asylum seeker arriving by boat—even if legally determined to be a Convention refugee—could never become a resident of Australia. In this way, excising more territories and expanding offshoring functioned to circumvent Australia's international legal obligation to offer asylum protection. Since these announcements by Gillard and Rudd, more than 4,177 refugees have been forcibly transferred to either Nauru or Papua New Guinea.[43]

In addition, Australia began funding efforts to prevent boats from leaving Indonesia. In yet another example of Australia's "incentivised policy transfer," Indonesia was pulled into the geopolitical orbit of White Australia and colonial carcerality.[44] Like Nauru and Papua New Guinea, Indonesia receives ongoing financial incentives and training to construct detention centers and enhance its border control measures. Australia consistently deflects responsibility for those preemptively detained in Indonesia or for refugees incarcerated on Nauru and Manus Island. However, it is Australian—and not Nauruan or Papua New Guinean or Indonesian—refugee policy that is warehousing refugees. Australia also presents offshore detention as an economic partnership between sovereign countries, when in fact aid to impoverished countries is used as a bargaining chip in the outsourcing of Australia's border policies.

Since 2002, Australia has invested significant resources into combating irregular migration through the criminalization of human smuggling. While criminalizing smuggling is often presented by state actors as a measure to "protect" migrants from "evil" human smugglers, enforcement measures serve to multiply border controls and further constrain the mobility of migrants and refugees. Under Australian domestic law, a number of new criminal offenses, mandatory sentences, and interdiction measures have been introduced to combat "people smuggling." At the international and regional level, the Australian government has linked the smuggling of migrants to national security and pressured Indonesia and other neighboring countries into a regional anti-smuggling and anti-trafficking forum. Through the multilateral "Bali Process on People Smuggling, Trafficking in Persons and Related Transnational Crime," irregular migration networks are now criminalized as "smuggling" and "trafficking" to prevent refugees from migrating with the necessary assistance of others. The recent Operation Sovereign Borders is a "zero-tolerance policy" to prevent, through military-led interdiction and turnbacks, any and all refugees arriving in Australia by boat. Government officials tout the operation as an effort to protect refugees from "crime networks" and prevent drownings at sea. Because migration assistance is criminalized as smuggling, state interdiction perversely becomes rescue.

Finally, the twinning of the migration crisis with the climate crisis has intensified Australia's border security. Global warming is an existential threat for small Pacific Islands, evident through extreme weather changes, tropical cyclones, and sea level rise. Eight small atoll islands have already been submerged, and others like Tuvalu and the Marshall Islands face complete submersion within the next three decades.[45] In 2014, Pacific Climate Warriors from twenty island states blockaded the world's largest coal port in Newcastle, Australia in their outrigger canoes. Declaring "We are not drowning, we are fighting," they demanded the Australian government stop fossil fuel expansion exacerbating climate change and displacement in the region. Australia is planning on doubling its coal exports and has some of the highest per capita carbon emissions in the world. While climate change is itself ignored, climate migration is presented as a border security issue and the latest excuse for wealthy colonial states to fortify their borders. In July 2019, Australian Defence Forces Chief Angus Campbell warned that he was planning to increase military patrols around Australia's waters to intercept climate refugees.[46] As explored in chapter 11, eco-fascist tendencies are on the rise, with racist Malthusian theories of Third World overpopulation now overlaid by settler anxieties about climate refugees.

This manufacturing of the extremely exclusionary Pacific Solution to secure White Australia is the crux of the never-ending and torturous captivity at Manus Island and Nauru today. The United Nations High Commissioner for Refugees says detainees are "languishing in unacceptable circumstances" of "extensive, avoidable suffering."[47] Even though up to 97 percent of detainees have been found to be Convention refugees with well-founded fears of persecution, they can never become residents of Australia simply because, seeking safety, they crossed the expanse of the ocean by boat.[48] In 2016, the Supreme Court in Papua New Guinea ruled the prison camp on Manus Island was illegal and a breach of the country's constitution, and ordered it be shut down. Australia still refuses to accept the refugees or end its externalized detention regime and, aside from one-time resettlement deals for some refugees, the detainees are now in "refugee transit centers" throughout the island. In the Australian-funded Bomana immigration detention center, opened in Port Moresby, Papua New Guinea, after the court ruling shut down the Manus prison camp, an Iranian refugee describes conditions "designed to torture people" including starvation, no telephone access, and solitary confinement.[49] At the end of 2019, as many as 674 refugees still remained in Papua New Guinea and Nauru.[50] Although routinely condemned by the UN and international human rights organizations, Australia's mandatory detention and externalization policies have become a global template. Mandatory detention was briefly adopted in Canada after the arrival of Tamil refugees aboard the MV *Ocean Lady* and MV *Sun Sea* in 2010, and Europe is outsourcing processing of refugees through the $6.6 billion EU–Turkey deal and "transit processing centers" across northern Africa.

While Australian detention is repressive, the resistance by detainees in Australia's offshore and onshore detention centers is relentless, from the Woomera detention center in the early 2000s to the 2017 revolts on Manus Island. Built on a former military site, the Woomera detention center was overcrowded, without phone access, and children comprised one-third of detainees. The detention center was closed in 2003 after widespread hunger strikes and riots by detainees, including the legendary Woomera breakout, where more than one thousand people on the outside helped tear down fencing to allow some detainees to escape. In October 2013, Nauru was ground zero for one of the most disruptive prison riots in Australia with hundreds of detainees pelting guards and burning down most of the center. In 2017, when Manus prison camp was scheduled to close, over six hundred detainees, including Boochani and Muhamat, refused to be transferred and demanded freedom in Australia or another country. They held protests and hunger strikes for more than three weeks, until they were violently removed and forcibly relocated by the Papua New Guinea paramilitary squad.

Detainees in Australian detention also routinely sew their lips shut. Self-mutilation, either as resistance to forced feeding during hunger strikes or as a desperate yet defiant form of protest, is commonplace in detention centers, including in Woomera and Baxter, and on Christmas Island, Manus Island, and Nauru. Children in detention suffer from intense trauma but also engage in their own forms of dissent. In 2014, a group of refugees on Nauru, including children, sewed their lips shut to reject a forcible transfer to Cambodia as part of a forty-five-million-dollar resettlement deal struck by Australia.[51] The next year around Christmas, photographs of dozens of children incarcerated on Nauru were released, in which they held signs with the numbers of days of their incarceration, most marking over three years. During the global pandemic in 2020, detainees in detention centers across Australia held protests to demand their release.

As a result of their constant and courageous confrontations, detainees have won essential reforms, including improved healthcare access, phone use, closure of detention centers like Christmas Island and Manus Island, an end to the detention of children on Nauru through the Kids Off Nauru campaign, and a seventy-million-dollar settlement for detainees at Nauru to be paid by the Australian government and contractors such as G4S and Broadspectrum. Australia's refugee and migrant solidarity movements are some of the most active migrant justice movements worldwide. There are hundreds of local solidarity collectives and national refugee support organizations, regular protests bring thousands of people onto the streets, and large-scale campaigns across the country coordinate to free detainees. Militant direct actions have included disrupting government offices, blockading border security offices and deportation flights, and helping people escape from detention centers. These ongoing forms of resistance and rebellion by detainees and their allies have broken the intended isolation and invisibility of offshoring and thrust the violence of Australian detention onto the world map. Freedom, though, remains elusive, as White Australia remakes itself by externalizing border controls onto countries themselves caught in Australia's matrix of colonial dispossession.

CHAPTER 6

Fortress Europe

you have to understand,
that no one puts their children in a boat
unless the water is safer than the land
no one burns their palms
under trains
beneath carriages
no one spends days and nights in the stomach of a truck
feeding on newspaper unless the miles travelled
means something more than journey.

—Warsan Shire, "Home"

In the last week of July 2015, about 3,500 people in Calais rushed the fifty-kilometer Channel Tunnel in an attempt to enter Great Britain. The UK declared it would deport anyone among the "swarm" who made it through, while France deployed its riot police.[1] Yet, night after night, desperate and rebellious migrants and refugees tried to subvert the juxtaposed controls by stowing away in cargo trucks or trains, sitting on the axles of trucks, or climbing underneath vehicles using the tunnel to the UK. One young Sudanese man, Saleh, was found dead after being crushed by an oncoming truck. That month alone, there were at least nine more deaths of Pakistanis, Sudanese, and Eritreans attempting to cross the border at Calais.[2] Others ended up imprisoned alongside over forty-seven thousand people held in French detention centers.[3] Those who averted detention were considered "lucky"; after all, they had survived death-defying journeys, traversing multiple sea and land borders, to make it this far north. The migrants and refugees all lived in a makeshift camp on a landfill outside Calais, known around the world by its racialized moniker, "the Jungle." At its peak between 2015 and 2016, the camp was home to some seven thousand people in packed tents without adequate sanitation, electricity, heat, or food. The majority were from Afghanistan, Eritrea, Sudan, and Syria, and one-fifth were unaccompanied minors.[4] In 2016, amid local citizens' anti-refugee fervor, French authorities declared the site a "danger" and "blight," and bulldozed the entire camp. Much like the aftermath of gentrification and slum clearances around the world, this community was dispersed, thousands still awaiting their opportunity to cross the Channel.

The year 2015 was a watershed one: the media was inundated with images of toddler Alan Kurdi, seven hundred nameless people capsized in the world's worst migrant drowning disaster, and one million people crossed into Europe. Since then, the constant invocation of "crisis" has not ended the causes of displacement or opened borders but, rather, has expanded state power to immobilize refugees and prevent them from generating the imagined demise of white hegemony in Europe. During the post–World War II era, the EU emerged under various different names to preserve the power of France and Germany, as well as to expand European capitalist interests. As Europe continues to open its borders to commodities—diamonds, oil, uranium, coltan—extracted under capitalism, borders closed to migrants and refugees induce irregular and tragically perilous migrations. In 2018 and 2019, as many as 4,184 migrants died in the Mediterranean, comprising 40 percent of border deaths worldwide.[5] This amounts to almost six lives lost every day. The International Organization for Migration (IOM) calls it "the world's deadliest border," where 33,761 people have died or gone missing between 2000 and 2017.[6] Ninety percent of those attempting the crossing were from Afghanistan, Bangladesh, Eritrea, Iraq, Nigeria, Pakistan, Somalia, Sudan, Syria, and The Gambia.[7]

While recent media reports pronounce a decreasing number of deaths, mounting militarization has decreased the number of crossings, from 1,000,573 in 2015 to 84,345 in 2018, while increasing the death *rate*.[8] Reece Jones underscores that one out of every four people attempting to enter Europe by boat dies en route.[9] The route through the Sahara Desert to get to Libya, one of the primary gateways in Africa to cross the Mediterranean into Europe, is even more deadly. Europe's externalized controls to Algeria have meant that most refugees from west and central Africa are now prohibited from crossing through Algeria into Libya. Instead, Algerian officials force people to walk south through the desert into Niger, where they are abandoned by authorities to continue through Niger, Chad, and Sudan into Libya. For every person dying in the Mediterranean, another two people are dying in the Sahara Desert in their attempts to reach Libya.[10] Christina Sharpe writes that movements of Africans are imagined "as insects, swarms, vectors of diseases; familiar narratives of danger and disaster that attach to our always already weaponized Black bodies" in order to justify vicious anti-Black migration controls and border deaths.[11]

Like rape culture, victim-blaming responses to border deaths put responsibility on people for "choosing" to make unsafe journeys. But restrictive policies compel irregular migration and coercive state powers—not migrants—are responsible for these deaths. Even the passive terminology of "border deaths" to describe what happened to Saleh and tens of thousands of others obscures the violent warscape of premeditated fatalities. The doctrine of deterrence *requires* mass border deaths to instill fear and prevent migration. Suffocation in cargo trucks, dehydration in blistering heat, hypothermia in freezing waters, unmarked graves in deserts, and wet cemeteries are the racialized deathscape of those killed by border imperialism around the world. Kazim Ali fittingly observes, "The law marks the body, documents it, scrutinizes it, it registers it, it permits it, manipulates it, suppresses it, denies it, forbids it, kills it."[12]

In this chapter I emphasize the law and policy bricks of Fortress Europe—including maritime interceptions, joint border patrol missions, readmission agreements, and outsourced migration controls—rather than highlight the endless specter of death at the world's deadliest border. We are bombarded with images of Black and brown people drowning in the Mediterranean or being enslaved in Libya, mirroring the viral videos of anti-Black police shootings on the other side of the Atlantic. Many political projects believe an economy of suffering that graphically publicizes injustices is necessary to hold the state to account and grieve these deaths through empathetic identification, regardless of the traumatic impact on Black and racialized people through the perpetuation of white supremacist sadism. Sara Ahmed maintains that "empathy sustains the very difference that it may seek to overcome" through the creation of spectacle and consumption of the other,[13] which Clare Hemmings describes as "cannibalization of the other masquerading as care."[14] Writing on anti-Blackness as a focal point of the voyeuristic spectacle of violence, Tamara

K. Nopper and Mariame Kaba elucidate, "Spectacle as the route to empathy means the atrocities itemized need to happen more often or get worse, to become more atrocious each round in hopes of being registered."[15] Scenes of border death maintain structures of racial violence and, as statistics of deaths pile up, we cannot evade an interrogation of the *source* of this violence shaped through imperial, racialized, and spatialized control.

Imperial Containment

An intricate system of border security underpins Fortress Europe, on which the EU plans to spend $38.4 billion between 2021 and 2027.[16] The EU has already devoted billions of euros to surveillance, patrols, and over one thousand kilometers of walls—the equivalent of six Berlin Walls.[17] Physical walls, however, are not the EU's primary mode of deterrence. The Dublin Regulation mandates that refugees seek asylum in their first country of arrival, enforced through the Eurodac fingerprint database and a biometric "smart borders" system. The Schengen Agreement is a double project of professedly opening up internal borders while strengthening external borders, and the entry of several southern countries into the Schengen Zone was delayed until they could better securitize their external borders. Harmonized border controls and visa imposition policies across the Schengen Zone create a "vast machine of illegalization" by decreasing legal routes for non–EU nationals.[18] Even for EU nationals like the Roma—constructed as racialized and rootless—the harmonization of policies across the EU's internal borders has had a profound impact. The biggest ethnic minority in Europe and attacked by right-wing leaders such as Viktor Orbán and Matteo Salvini, Roma refugees can no longer seek asylum in Europe, and also face interdiction when seeking safety outside Europe.

Border externalization and upstream securitization have been in place since 1992 through the Spain–Morocco readmission agreement, which compels Morocco to readmit deportees returned from Spain. Since 2015, border externalization has become a cornerstone of EU policy. European border externalization encompasses a bundle of extraterritorial technologies and agreements to prevent and deter migrants and refugees from reaching European borders. Carrier sanctions are regularly implemented on airlines transporting people without proper documentation, the EU border agency Frontex has expanded patrols and interceptions in the Mediterranean, and the European Border Surveillance System (EUROSUR) has introduced drone surveillance.

Countries intending to join the EU, such as Ukraine and Moldova, are part of the Eastern Partnership and EU Border Assistance Missions. The European Commission now requires most development, aid, and trade agreements with Middle Eastern and African countries to include readmission agreements, which obligate non-European countries to preemptively control migration and readmit all expelled deportees.

African countries are especially pressured to accept outsourcing of migration controls. Ampson Hagan lucidly lays out how the "anti-immigration and xenophobic policies of Europe with respect to Black Africans has been able to lean on the assumedly 'non-racial' and 'technocratic' migration projects within Africa."[19] The Khartoum Process was established in 2014 between the African Union Commission and the European Commission to tackle migrations into Europe from eastern African countries, especially Eritrea, Ethiopia, South Sudan, and Sudan. The Khartoum Process was followed by the Valletta Summit in 2015, where African countries were promised financial resources in exchange for reducing migration to Europe. The Migration Partnership Framework explicitly integrates the EU's migration policy into its foreign policy, and the EU Emergency Trust Fund for Africa diverts billions of euros earmarked for aid to twenty-six African countries into surveillance and military equipment to prevent refugees from leaving the continent through the Orwellian-sounding Better Migration Management program.

Through the African Peace Facility program, the EU is training a new counterterrorism and anti-migration force, called the G5 Sahel Cross-Border Joint Force, with Burkina Faso, Chad, Mali, Mauritania, and Niger. In addition, the Transnational Institute reveals UK soldiers are training Tunisian armed forces; Italy has redeployed troops from Iraq and Afghanistan to Niger, Libya, and Tunisia; France has forces in Tunisia and Niger; Germany is training border guards in Libya; and French and German militaries are training agents in Mali.[20] Based on Australia's abhorrent Pacific Solution, the EU is also now offshoring refugees to "transit processing centers" across the Sahel region. Externalization of the EU border necessarily proliferates such internal controls within non-EU countries. Border externalization thus outsources responsibility, and the EU conveniently blames other countries when atrocities, like those unfolding in Libyan detention centers, hit the news. This architecture of externalization has turned African countries into, as Mark Akkerman writes, "Europe's new border guards."[21]

Routes of Securitization and Externalization

We demand papers so that we no longer suffer the humiliation of controls based on our skin, detentions, deportations, the break-up of our families, the constant fear.

—Manifesto of the Sans-Papiers

The EU externalizes border controls based on three primary routes. The western route traverses the border between Morocco and the enclaves of Ceuta and Melilla, which are claimed by Spain and form the only land border between Africa and Europe, as well as across the Strait of Gibraltar to the European mainland or across the Atlantic from Morocco or Mauritania to the Canary Islands. The eastern route crosses the Aegean Sea from Turkey to Greece and encompasses the Balkan routes to Hungary. The central route involves transit through Libya or Tunisia across the Mediterranean to the Italian mainland or its island of Lampedusa. In a cyclical fashion, migrants respond to border militarization by attempting alternative routes, which in turn shifts migration controls, and then other routes are tried. Though the media characterizes them as "new migrant routes"—as though migrants are merrily Columbusing their way around—these paths are actually "EU-organized channels."[22] No route is simple; there are few ladders and many snakes. As Taish, a Kurdish refugee, conveyed to BBC News, "We are between two deaths."[23] All journeys are rife with debt extortion, forced invisibility, starvation, assault, incarceration, injuries, and the constant threat of death. Surviving sexual violence is a ubiquitous experience for all genders and, as such, is on a continuum with wartime rape as a strategy of racial sexual domination.[24] Despite omnipresent violence, migrants overcome bordering practices. With increased militarization of the central route after 2017, the eastern and western routes again became the most active, with 87 percent of landings in 2019 happening in Spain and Greece.[25]

Western route

The western route was the primary route during the 1990s and early 2000s, and some of the earliest European efforts at outsourcing migration controls were in Morocco, Mauritania, Senegal, and Cape Verde. The engineering of Fortress Europe began with the fencing of Melilla and Ceuta in 1993, and, according to scholars, "Europeanisation of the two enclaves remain key long-term goals of Spain's border control policy."[26] As the enclaves were fenced, they remained open to the flow of goods, capital, and low-wage workers from

Morocco to sustain the contraband enclave economy, comprised of 70 percent women.[27] Spain increased monitoring and razor wire fencing in 2005, a year which saw a spike in deaths in Ceuta and Melilla.[28] The Association Malienne des Expulsés in Mali issued an unflinching "Declaration on the Repression of African Immigrants," holding Europe responsible for these deaths and the general climate of exclusion for African migrants.[29]

Spain's history of empire and imbrication with the European civilizational project—constructed upon and against the Muslim world since the Reconquista—makes it an eager participant in physically and conceptually fencing its enclaves on African soil. Spain's marginal status within the EU has also influenced its migration policies. Especially after the Eurozone debt crisis of 2010 and the imposition of EU policies of austerity on Portugal, Ireland, Italy, Greece, and Spain, these peripheral countries have been further subjected to the dictates of the EU. Funded by the EU, a six-meter-high, twelve-kilometer-long, three-tier fence now marks the Morocco–Spain border, and the Spanish Guardia Civil illegally yet routinely forces migrants back behind it. In February 2014, more than five hundred African migrants tried to cross into Ceuta, fifteen of whom were killed after rubber bullets were shot at people in the water.[30] A few months later, dozens of migrants and refugees perched on top of the Melilla fence for ten hours, only to be forcefully returned to Morocco by the Guardia Civil. Immediate, summary returns to Morocco take place without any formal admission process into Spain, which many lawyers argue is in violation of the legal principle of non-refoulement and the international legal obligation to not forcibly return or expel refugees to persecution on account of their race, religion, nationality, membership of a particular social group, or political opinion.

Those violently returned to Morocco often suffer severe injuries at the hands of both the Guardia Civil and Auxiliary Forces of Morocco. In 2014, no fewer than 743 injured migrants were hospitalized.[31] According to an earlier comprehensive survey by Médecins Sans Frontières (MSF) in 2012, close to 63 percent of migrants and refugees in Morocco had experienced violence, with a majority reporting assaults by Moroccan security forces.[32] Twenty-two-year-old Ibrahim told MSF that security forces "hit me with the batons. I wanted to run, but they hit me and I fell down. They started hitting me again. I tried to protect my head and they broke my arms."[33] Of those surveyed, 21 percent also reported racial attacks by civilians and, over a two-year period, MSF treated 697 migrant survivors of sexual violence. Furthermore, Moroccan authorities consistently raid and burn down makeshift camps in the forests. In 2014, there were 261 raids and, in one single day in 2015, over one thousand people were detained.[34] There are tens of thousands of African migrants and refugees immobilized in Morocco, waiting for months and years to attempt the crossing into Europe. In 2018, the EU approved 148 million euros for an updated EU–Morocco Action Plan to ensure that they cannot enter, and in 2019, Morocco forcibly prevented seventy thousand people from crossing into Spain.[35]

Shortly after fencing around Melilla and Ceuta multiplied, more people attempted the Atlantic route to the Canary Islands. The islands were claimed by Spain as an overseas territory after it colonized the Indigenous Guanches in the fifteenth and sixteenth centuries and imposed a plantation economy of sugarcane and cochineal through African enslavement that predated the Middle Passage. In 2006, twelve hundred migrants and refugees from Mauritania reached the Canary Islands within a thirty-six-hour period.[36] That year, over thirty-one thousand migrants and refugees landed on the island and another six thousand perished or went missing attempting the crossing.[37] Spain and Frontex responded with Operation Hera I, aimed at preventing migration from Senegal, The Gambia, and Mali to the Canary Islands. With EU funding, the Guardia Civil also created the Seahorse Atlantic Network for joint maritime operations with Morocco, Mauritania, Senegal, and Cape Verde, allowing EU ships to access territorial waters of African countries and intercept and return boats as quickly as possible. Building on the Australian model, Spain opened a detention center in Mauritania and pioneered the militarized humanitarian model of "rescue and return." As Ruben Andersson remarks, "Migrants are at once rescued and caught," and EU-led enforcement operations become laundered as humanitarian intervention.[38] By 2010, only two hundred migrants and refugees arrived on the Canary Islands.[39]

Taken together, all the routes to Spain were essentially shut down by 2010, and Spain's combination of policing, intelligence gathering, and purportedly humanitarian rescue created the conceptual groundwork for future EU operations.[40] Following the declaration of a "European refugee crisis" in 2015, the EU boosted the surveillance capacity of Mali, Mauritania, and Senegal and launched the West Sahel Project, training Mauritanian border patrol officers to conduct joint anti-migration patrols with the Guardia Civil. The Pan-African Network in Defense of Migrants' Rights condemned these repressive policies, describing them as "hunting policies for migrants that grow everywhere on the African continent with the support of the European institutions under the guise of the fight against 'irregular' migration."[41] Since 2017, when the central route became the focus of EU operations, migrants and refugees are again afoot on the western route. During one weekend in 2019, as many as 250 people attempted the crossing into Ceuta, and 90 people were arrested after getting cut by razor wire on the fence and teargassed by authorities.[42]

Eastern route

With the initial militarization of the western route, the eastern route became busier. During the height of the Syrian displacement crisis in 2015, when 1.3 million Syrian refugees reached Europe, the number of people crossing between Turkey and Greece increased tenfold within a year.[43] Refugees forcibly removed from others parts of Europe to Greece through the Dublin Regulation, as well as the 850,000 who crossed onto Greek islands through Turkey, turned the southern country into a bottleneck.[44] Greece fortified its border against Turkey by building a wall at the Evros River based on the Melilla model and expanded migrant detention centers. In one of the largest Greek detention centers, an investigation revealed that "hit squads" habitually tortured detainees.[45] The fascistic Golden Dawn party also soared in the polls with their belligerent, racist calls for the immediate deportation of all irregular migrants, and their street militias physically attacked hundreds of migrants.[46] In a 2018 report focused on refugee women in Greece, a Syrian mother of four young children depicts her overall experience, with no state or social support: "This is very difficult now, they haven't given us anything, not even blankets to put on the floor. All we have we've collected from the street."[47]

Alongside the imposition of disciplinary austerity measures against Greece by European Commission strongmen, the undemocratic European Central Bank, and the ruthless IMF, jointly referred to as the Troika, the EU designated the Greek Aegean Islands as "hotspots" where people are mandatorily and indefinitely contained to prevent their movement into Europe. The Moria refugee camp on Lesbos island, Europe's largest refugee camp, was supposed to hold 3,000 people, but now immobilizes over 19,000 people, approximately 40 percent of whom are minors.[48] More than 44,000 people are contained in five island hotspots, with up to 10 people per tent, no running water or electricity, and exposure to flowing human sewage and freezing cold temperatures.[49] A teenager from Afghanistan describes, "For two months, we slept in a small tent near the toilet. . . . There was no electricity and it was very cold. And when it rained, the water soak[ed] through the tent."[50]

Women, girls, queer, and trans people suffer violent attacks and avoid using the showers or going to the toilet. The UNHCR received some 174 reports from migrants and refugees who suffered sexual and gender-based violence in the island hotspots.[51] The excruciating confinement and compounding traumas, which many refugees describe as "psychological war," also severely impact mental health.[52] MSF provides emergency care to an average of one person a day for attempted suicide and self-harm at the Lesbos hotspot.[53] The crisis for refugees contained in the Greek island hotspots came to a head during the coronavirus pandemic, with conditions in the overloaded and unsanitary camps creating an ideal breeding ground for transmission of the virus. In the Vial camp on Chios Island, refugees set fire to parts of the camp's administrative buildings to protest the death of an Iraqi woman whom they believed to have died of Covid-19.[54]

Along with the EU-designated hotspots, the EU–Turkey deal is a cornerstone of border policy along the eastern route and turns refugees into tradeable commodities. The 2016 EU–Turkey deal is "one for one," stipulating that refugees irregularly crossing into Greece are deported back to Turkey and, in return, (only) Syrian refugees in Turkey are legally resettled in the EU. As a result, Turkey built a 764-kilometer wall and stepped up security at its border with Syria. The Turkish coast guard committed to working with Greece and the EU to patrol the Aegean Sea, where NATO has also deployed fully militarized warships as part of interdiction efforts. According to the Syrian Observatory for Human Rights, 336 Syrian refugees were killed by Turkey's border forces within the first year of the EU–Turkey deal.[55] To clinch the deal, President Recep Tayyip Erdoğan received six billion euros and promises of visa liberalization for Turkish citizens entering the EU. Erdoğan's partnership with the EU has bolstered his legitimacy despite his government's fascistic repression, including a military offensive against Kurds in Afrin, war crimes in Rojava, declaration of a state of emergency across Turkey, and the arrest of 160,000 dissidents, mostly on false terrorism charges, who have been subjected to electroshock and waterboarding in prison.[56]

The EU–Turkey deal unraveled in early 2020, and refugees were caught in the cross fire of growing political tensions between Turkey and Greece over the war in Syria. Turkey declared it would open its land border with Greece, and consequently, within days, between ten and fifteen thousand refugees rushed to the Evros border region.[57] Greece's conservative New Democracy government responded with a heavy hand, deploying police and military forces to the mainland border, firing tear gas and rubber bullets, stripping and beating people, suspending the right to asylum, and summarily turning refugees back in violation of the international legal principle of non-refoulement.[58] The restrictions on asylum extended to all of Greece's borders, and at least 625 people who arrived on Lesbos were denied the right to seek asylum over an eighteen-day period.[59] MSF characterized these measures as "some of the most restrictive and punitive measures against people seeking protection in the world," yet the Greek response was backed by EU officials, who called Greece the "shield" of Europe.[60] The EU has pledged seven hundred million euros for securing Greece's borders and is also bribing some five thousand refugees in the island hotspots with two thousand euros each to "voluntarily" self-deport.[61]

Alexis Tsipras, socialist leader of Greece's Syriza party, also supported the conservative government's violent repression in Evros and decision to suspend asylum, stating it "was right in closing the borders."[62] Earlier, in 2014, Tsipras had campaigned on migrant rights and the abolition of detention centers but changed his tune shortly after he was elected prime minister in 2015. He oversaw violent evictions of migrants from squatter camps in 2018, and remarked he was proud of the country's migration policy and its detention centers. Tsipras's eventual centrism and Syriza's capitulation to the Troika's imposed conditions of neoliberal austerity wiped them out of the 2019 election. The New Democracy conservative government came to office promising to abolish asylum appeals, increase border patrols, limit the number of refugees in Greece, and replace the camps in the hotspots with detention centers. Irrespective of the duplicity of politicians, dozens of migrant and refugee groups are involved in protests against state violence. Natasha King reports that twenty major hunger strikes by migrants and refugees in Greece have taken place over six years, including a historic and ultimately victorious action in 2011, undertaken by three hundred men for forty days to demand regularization of their immigration status.[63]

From the Greek mainland, migrants and refugees often continue on the Balkan routes through Macedonia and Bulgaria to Serbia, and then Hungary, toward Austria and Germany. In Hungary, Viktor Orbán's right-wing government built a security fence and closed the border with Serbia, now patrolled by Frontex, and passed legislation to imprison all those who cross. Orbán also refused flat out to participate in the Dublin Regulation, which would have returned refugees who crossed through Hungary into other EU countries back to Hungary, their first country of entry into the EU. An investigation in 2011 exposed Hungarian detention center guards using thousands of doses of drugs to sedate 922 detained refugees.[64] Now, upon arrival, people are immediately and often indefinitely detained in "transit zones," a euphemism for open-air pens where food deprivation is a matter of policy.[65] Those who do make it into Hungary have to attempt safe passage yet again. Seventy-one bodies, including a baby's, were found decomposing in a sealed meat truck near the Hungarian border in August 2015. A few days later, one thousand refugees from Syria and Afghanistan defiantly marched along the highway, flouted the border, and walked into Austria.[66] That year, around one million people—mostly from Afghanistan, Iraq, Pakistan, and Syria—attempted the Balkan routes.[67] Austria, Bulgaria, Czech Republic, Germany, Hungary, Poland, Slovakia, and Slovenia responded by implementing internal border controls, building walls, and/or refusing to accept refugees under European refugee redistribution plans.

As internal borders were fortified, a channel emerged further south through Albania, Montenegro, and Bosnia into Croatia. In 2018, the number of migrants crossing through Bosnia to get to Croatia increased thirty-three-fold, and the EU gave Croatia one hundred million euros to increase patrols on the EU's longest external border.[68] Croatia is a member of the EU but not yet part of the Schengen Zone, and it has been eager to prove its disciplinary governance as the newest brick in Fortress Europe. One-third of migrants and refugees in Croatia report systematic police beatings and shootings, theft of their documents, and illegal expulsions into Bosnia.[69] Expelled into Bosnia, thousands from Afghanistan, Iraq, Morocco, Pakistan, and Syria are crowded into the Vucjak camp, built on top of a chemical dump site with high levels of methane, littered with land mines from the war, infested with snakes, and without electricity or sanitation. Border controls along the Balkan routes, as well as EU-funded policies of exclusion and carceral containment in Greece, have deliberately produced torturous conditions on the eastern route, where refugees and migrants are immobilized and blocked from moving further into Europe.

Central route

After the eastern and western routes were sealed, the central Mediterranean became the most active route. It is also the deadliest. In 2008, Italian prime minister Silvio Berlusconi and Libyan colonel Muammar Gaddafi signed a friendship treaty with financial compensation, purportedly for Italy's colonial crimes. Italy's main intention, though, was not reparations but externalization of migration controls. Italy funded detention centers in Libya that became torture camps, increased joint border patrols, and compelled Libya to accept refugees interdicted and deported by Italy.[70] The European Court of Human Rights found Italy guilty of intercepting and forcibly returning African migrants and refugees, especially from Somalia and Eritrea, to Libya. Despite this, the EU continued to work with Libya. Shortly before the NATO invasion of Libya, Gaddafi demanded five billion euros annually to prevent people from departing across the Mediterranean. He blackmailed the EU with the threat of Europe becoming "another Africa."[71]

Shortly after Gaddafi was ousted through Western intervention, Italy and Libya struck another deal for additional detention centers, border surveillance equipment, training of border and coast guards, and continued marine interdiction and return. Devastating drownings started making headlines. In October 2013, a total of 366 people mainly from Eritrea and Somalia drowned, including all of the children on board, and another 200 were reported missing after their boat caught fire.[72] Survivors were detained in Lampedusa and denied permission to attend the state funeral for their friends and loved ones. One week later, 268 migrants and refugees, mostly Syrians and including 30 children, drowned. Media leaks revealed Italian authorities avoided distress calls for hours, and officials Leopoldo Manna and Luca Licciardi now face charges of manslaughter and negligence for delaying the rescue. For the next two years, deaths on the central Mediterranean route increased, with 3,149 deaths in 2015 and 4,581 deaths in 2016.[73]

Italy and the EU responded to the increased crossings and deaths with Operation Mare Nostrum and a militarized mission, Operation Sophia, which deployed naval warships into the Mediterranean. Sophia's mandate was not only to intercept but to destroy migrant boats. Within one year, 358 boats were destroyed.[74] Almost identical to the stance adopted by the Australian government, European politicians are increasingly framing the warscape in the central Mediterranean as "destroying criminal smuggling and trafficking networks." The latest mantra on migrant smuggling and trafficking justifies the proliferation of border controls and punitive criminal sanctions, thus driving migration further underground. Just like narco-trafficking was conscripted in the US war on drugs to expand state enforcement while deflecting responsibility from state actors, smuggling and trafficking narratives enable "a European moral economy of salvation,"[75] locating the crisis as external to Europe and untethered to border imperialist power. European maritime operations are reconstituted as benevolent and humanitarian: saving "trafficked victims" being exploited by "foreign" networks of "organized crime." These crackdowns eclipse state violence as the sole raison d'être for irregular and dangerous migration. Border restrictions create conditions rife for exploitation; the economy for extorting traffickers would collapse if there were no border controls. Bridget Anderson argues that through anti-trafficking legislation and the language of harm, the state emerges as the protector of victims even though state practices are the primary force in constructing vulnerability.[76]

Many European politicians also analogize trafficking to "modern-day slavery" to further restrict migration. The UK's much-lauded Modern Slavery Act criminalizes individuals but fails to address legislated state violence. Migration control is the root cause of manufactured vulnerability within networks of irregular migration and work. Criminalizing migration as a form of slavery leaves migrants and refugees more susceptible to exploitation, and, simultaneously, the logics bolstering white supremacist saviordom and racial modernity are reinforced. Robyn Maynard argues that appropriating Black abolitionist struggles to increase state criminalization is a perverse co-optation of abolition while increasing violence against Black, trans, sex-working, and migrant women.[77] When former Italian prime minister Matteo Renzi equated human traffickers with slave traders, four hundred scholars released an open letter demanding European politicians "stop abusing the history of transatlantic slavery to legitimate military and migrant deterrent actions, and instead recall, and act upon the demands for freedom of movement, or 'a right of locomotion' articulated by African American anti-slavery activists of the nineteenth century."[78]

Not only does the vocabulary of "trafficking and smuggling" shift responsibility from state violence and serve to actually restrict migration, it has also become a potent weapon in the criminalization of solidarity. In the face of deliberate state cruelty, hundreds of activist efforts have cropped up across Europe to provide rescue or humanitarian support, such as food, water, shelter, and transport, to migrants and refugees. Many of these courageous solidarity movements are now facing criminal charges under the guise of "facilitation of irregular entry and stay," a measure intended to combat human smuggling into Europe. An Amnesty International investigation into the criminalization of migrant and refugee solidarity efforts across Croatia, France, Greece, Italy, Malta, Spain, Switzerland, and the UK found that police and prosecutors were manipulating flawed anti-smuggling laws to target solidarity efforts, including laying spurious charges against activists who handed out warm clothes, offered shelter, and saved lives at sea.[79] In Greece, Syrian refugee Sarah Mardini and

Vietnamese refugee Seán Binder spent one hundred days in pretrial detention and now face twenty-five years in prison on serious charges, including espionage and facilitating human smuggling, for rescuing people in dinghies trying to reach Lesbos and providing them with food, blankets, and medical assistance.[80] The Institute of Race Relations documents prosecutions of eighty-nine people under trafficking and smuggling laws across Europe in 2018, with a majority of charges actually laid against NGO search and rescue missions.[81]

Under the particularly hard line of the fascist Italian leader Salvini, migrant crossings across the Mediterranean into Italy were explicitly criminalized. Salvini referred to immigration as "ethnic replacement" and "a Muslim problem," and his tenure consisted of a series of decrees to radically restrict migration. Minimally rescue-oriented operations were suspended and a security decree was passed to confiscate and fine private vessels carrying migrants and refugees into Italian territorial waters up to one million euros. Criminalizing solidarity efforts became a front line in Salvini's war on migrants, with NGO rescue boats being fined and seized, and captains Carola Rackete and Pia Klemp dragged through Italian court proceedings on trumped-up charges, facing years in prison simply for rescuing migrants in the Mediterranean. To avoid the maritime obligation of aiding a vessel in distress, Salvini also suggested replacing surveillance ships with aerial drones. Charles Heller and Lorenzo Pezzani observe: "The Mediterranean has been made to kill through contemporary forms of militarized governmentality of mobility which inflict deaths by first creating dangerous conditions of crossing, and then abstaining from assisting those in peril."[82] Salvini is now facing criminal kidnapping charges for blocking over one hundred migrants from disembarking from an Italian coast guard ship in 2019.[83] Furthermore, Salvini evicted more than five hundred people from one of Italy's largest refugee centers and eliminated humanitarian protection permits for refugees. As a result of these cumulative crackdowns, crossings into Italy dropped a dramatic 55 percent between 2016 and 2018.[84]

While militarizing the Mediterranean, Salvini also extended the Libyan coast guard's international jurisdiction to prevent Africans from leaving Libya toward Italy, a policy that has remained largely intact under the subsequent Italian leadership of Luciana Lamorgese. In the first two weeks of 2020, approximately 953 migrants and refugees were intercepted by the Libyan coast guard and detained.[85] As former Italian interior minister Marco Minniti told reporters, "Securing Libya's southern border means securing Europe's southern border."[86] Indeed, the EU is providing 237 million euros to train the Libyan coast guard.[87] They are also propping up efforts geared toward self-deportation and funding detention centers operated by the bluntly named Directorate for Combating Illegal Migration. Denying safe passage across the Mediterranean has led to murderous captivity in Libya, where outsourced migration controls embolden Libyan authorities and militias. There are 641,398 migrants and refugees, 94 percent of whom are from twenty-eight different African countries, detained or immobilized in Libya.[88] They face abuse, overcrowding, lack of sanitation, starvation, electrocution, torture, rape, extortion, executions, forced labor, and enslavement.[89] Armed militias operating in detention centers or extralegal torture camps kidnap migrants and refugees in order to extort money and then sell them to another armed militia group. As one detainee anonymously told the *Guardian*, "Libya is a market of human beings."[90] Migrants and refugees are forcibly recruited into militias or become human shields during combat between the Government of National Accord and General Khalifa Haftar. Detainees also risk being hit by air strikes with no escape. Fifty-three people were killed when the Tajoura detention center was bombed, and many reported being shot at by guards when attempting to flee.[91] The Libyan coast guard is notorious for involving armed militia members, who have attacked, tortured, or shot at migrants and refugees, and opened fire on NGO boats. Europe has undeniably contributed to this terror.

After international outcry over conditions in Libya, the EU began funding the evacuation of thousands of migrants and refugees from Libya—not to Europe but to centers in Niger, where border securitization is also being imposed and "transit processing centers" are being piloted.[92] Under pressure from Europe, Niger officially criminalized human smuggling in 2015. Since then, the EU has supplied border control equipment, trained Niger's National Guard, deployed Frontex officers, set up organizations to raise awareness about the "risks of migration" with the intended goal of deterrence, and funded campaigns compelling migrants transiting through Niger to agree to "voluntary returns." During the coronavirus pandemic, 2,371 migrants were immobilized and stranded without food or sanitary supplies in the transit processing centers in Niger, many of whom were pressured to return to their home countries through the International Organization for Migration's Assisted Voluntary Return and Reintegration program.[93] Combined with the networks of surveillance intensifying in Mali, Mauritania, Morocco, The Gambia, and Senegal in the western region, such efforts in the east work to wall the entire Sahel and make migration more treacherous.

The EU has also had a partnership with the dictator Omar Hassan Ahmad al-Bashir in Sudan. Through the Khartoum Process, Valletta Summit, and the EU Emergency Trust Fund for Africa, the EU exchanged 155 million euros in trade, aid, and development funding for al-Bashir's policing of migration through Sudan, which is considered both a transit country to Libya and a country of origin for migrants and refugees.[94] Policing of Sudanese borders is controlled by the Rapid Support Forces (RSF) and Janjaweed militias, a paramilitary force that engaged in war crimes and ethnic cleansing in Darfur, fueling the displacement of approximately three million people in the region. Fatin Abbas argues the Darfur genocide and Sudan must be understood within the context of slavery, state-mediated social relations, and the Khartoum government's failure to equally distribute wealth, rather than through "myths of cultural and ethnic purity."[95] IMF-imposed structural adjustment policies, including fuel subsidy cuts and land grabs, have further driven the displacement of farmers and producers.[96] To block migration, the EU and Italy have provided Sudan and the RSF with millions of euros for border security and a readmission agreement. Sudan has also been financially bolstered by Saudi Arabia in exchange for deploying RSF mercenaries to Yemen.

The terror imposed by the RSF is inseparable from these geopolitics. In 2017, the RSF bragged about intercepting 1,500 people at the border and, like Gaddafi, RSF leader General Mohamed Hamdan Dagalo (Hemedti) has extorted Europe, claiming, "We are hard at work on behalf of Europe in containing the migrants, and if our valuable efforts are not well appreciated, we will (re)open the desert to migrants."[97] Migrants and refugees report being sold to Libyan militias by RSF members; EU's partnership with Sudan, therefore, bolsters the fascistic RSF and Janjaweed militias, as well as Libyan militias. An open letter by Eritrean and Sudanese organizations condemns the European Council and its migration prevention processes, which they say have "emboldened the criminal exploitation and extortion of refugees and migrants, increased the capacities of unaccountable militia to act with impunity, and give[n] increased legitimacy to governments who repress their people and drive them out of their countries."[98]

Disrupting Liberal "Welcome"

In the face of growing far-right calls from Viktor Orbán, Matteo Salvini, and Marine Le Pen to completely prevent migration on all migration routes, liberal elite responses—as exemplified by Angela Merkel—tend to mobilize around the empathy-oriented project of "refugees welcome." Albeit with different intentions, both center refugees as abject subjects and European whiteness as the arbiter of migration. Liberal elite responses center humanitarian benevolence and Europeans materialize as saviors, while refugees are burdened with the expectation of performing gratitude and assimilating into the racial social order and capitalist markets. Further, the rhetoric of "refugees welcome" masks the inhospitable reality for nearly nine hundred thousand refugees still in limbo across Europe in 2019—most languish in hotspots or camps, sleep on the streets or in overcrowded housing, are underpaid and exploited in the informal economy, and anxiously wait for their claims to be approved. Refugee claim rejection rates have actually doubled between 2016 and 2019.[99]

Germany's much-lauded *Willkommenskultur* (welcome culture) evaporated once refugees were accused of not integrating, characterized as a drain on resources, and blamed for gendered violence. The brief charitable moment also eclipsed the longer, politicized struggle of refugees, including the two-year-long Oranienplatz campaign of civil disobedience. This campaign demanded real systemic change, including the abolition of *lagers* (refugee housing camps), removal of the *Residenzpflicht* mandatory residence law confining refugees to certain districts, open work and study permits, and an end to all deportations from Germany. Napuli Langa describes: "We organised many actions: we occupied a vacant school, we occupied Brandenburg Gate, we went on demonstrations and hunger strikes, we occupied the tree at Oranienplatz, we occupied the roof of the school at Ohlauerstrasse, we occupied the parliament in the district of Kreuzberg, we occupied the federal office of the Green party, we occupied the church, we occupied the UN office, we occupied embassies."[100]

Most troubling about liberal welcome culture is the erasure of European complicity in creating displacement through colonial conquest, land theft, slavery, capitalist extraction, labor exploitation, and war profiteering. Refugees and migrants defying Fortress Europe do not require the variable empathy of Europeans; their movement is ultimately a form of decolonial reparations. Glossing over structural responsibility and restitution, the social grammar of benevolence maintains, as Ida Danewid argues, "A colonial and patronising fantasy of the white man's burden—based on the desire to protect and offer political resistance *for* endangered others—which ultimately does little to challenge established interpretations that see Europe as the bastion of democracy, liberty, and universal rights."[101] Or as Ali, an Iranian refugee in Calais, crystallizes the liberal savior industrial complex: "Sundays in the Jungle: pity. Outside the Jungle: hatred."[102]

Disrupting white European innocence requires refusing selective amnesia and shifting the gaze away from migrants and refugees, and toward the enduring project of Europe. Migration is treated as a recent phenomenon, even though the genocide, displacement, and movement of millions of people was unequally structured by European colonialism for three centuries, with European emigrant settlers in the Americas and Oceania, the transatlantic slave trade from Africa, and imported indentured laborers from Asia. As Paul Gilroy writes on the intimacies of these histories, "The reflexive cultures and consciousness of the European settlers and those of the Africans they enslaved, the 'Indians' they slaughtered, and the Asians they indentured were not, even in situations of the most extreme brutality, sealed off hermetically from each other."[103] But these ongoing colonial encounters are conveniently erased in the constitution of Europe's migration crisis. Instead, the EU's liberal political establishment claims to welcome refugees while firmly embedding anti-migration controls to fortify the physical and conceptual idea of Europe, purports to serve the working class while maintaining capitalist austerity, speaks of democracy while ensconcing the EU in technocratic policy and unaccountable bureaucracies, and espouses postcolonialism while expanding imperial networks built on an anti-Black racial order.

Black Mediterranean

Water is another country.
—Dionne Brand, *A Map to the Door of No Return: Notes to Belonging*

It is impossible to discuss the intensifying control of sea routes between Africa and Europe outside the history of transatlantic slavery, which strengthened imperial networks through juridification of maritime space and consolidated white supremacy. Renisa Mawani details how maritime laws were mobilized to entrench racial hierarchies and govern movement on the seas: "Whereas British and US admiralty law granted ships a legal personality, the laws of slavery and the laws of the seas denied African captives their humanity."[104] Discussions about the European migrant crisis must acknowledge the history of plunder and racial subordination underwriting deaths in the Mediterranean.

The term "Black Mediterranean," coined by Alessandra Di Maio as an extension of Gilroy's Black Atlantic, has emerged to locate murderous European border policies in the material relations and routes of anti-Blackness. In *The Black Atlantic*, Gilroy conceptualizes African diaspora political engagement as "first, in active pursuit of self-emancipation from slavery and its attendant horrors; second, toward the acquisition of substantive citizenship denied by slavery; and finally, in pursuit of an autonomous space in the system of formal political relationships that distinguishes occidental modernity."[105] SA Smythe calls the Black Mediterranean a "radical, anarchic, collective, Black and queer" political project built on "an abolitionist vision that sees a world without border regimes and the Mediterranean as a site of cultural syncretism and radical possibility rather than a watery grave and site of dispossession."[106] The Gilets Noirs (Black Vests), the largest collective of undocumented migrants in France, assert their presence as an accounting for the ongoing colonization and exploitation that is a precondition for the existence of Europe. They boldly pronounce: "We are the freedom to move, to settle down to act. We will take it as our right. In the name of all those who did not make it here, and to save ourselves, and for all those who want to make it out here."[107]

Pan-Africanist revolutionaries tirelessly detailed how imperialism, slavery, and capitalism enriched Europe at the expense of Africa. Thomas Sankara depicted imperialism operating through a matrix of military interventions and corporate plunder, prophetically describing the relationship between the Burkinabé revolution and the battle against desertification: "This struggle to defend the trees and forests is above all a struggle against imperialism. Because imperialism is the arsonist setting fire to our forests and our savannas."[108] Mabel Ellen Dove penned a scorching indictment of colonialism: "The supposed Christians of Western civilization have to throw away their cant, humbug, hypocrisy and sheer malevolent brutality in Africa."[109] Julius Nyerere's vision of *ujamaa* rebuked capitalist development. "Capitalism means that the masses will work, and a few people—who may not labor at all—will benefit from that work. The few will sit down to a banquet, and the masses will eat whatever is left over," he wrote.[110] Walter Rodney theorized development as a relational process, where underdevelopment expresses "a particular relationship of exploitation." Rodney elucidated: "Capitalists of Western Europe were the ones who actively extended their exploitation from inside Europe to cover the whole of Africa," including ongoing investment in "land, mines, factories, banks, insurances companies, means of transportation, newspapers, power stations."[111]

The same European colonizers—Belgium, France, Germany, Italy, Portugal, Spain, and the UK—maintain their hold over Africa with circuits of financialized power and land grabs. As land is expropriated through an economy of dispossession that reconfigures both property and social relations (described in chapter 3), highly subsidized European agribusinesses are dumping food into African markets and further displacing farmers. Tomatoes, grains, dairy products, and coffee are flooding African markets. Meanwhile, oil, copper, cobalt, diamonds, uranium, zinc, iron, bauxite, coal, coltan, and gold are dug up and exported for corporate profit. The Democratic Republic of the Congo is home to one of the world's largest displacement crises, with over four million internally displaced people. Major drivers of Congolese displacement are mining-related invasions and conflicts over diamonds, cobalt, copper, coltan, and gold, placing the country at the epicenter of violence and forced child labor related to "blood diamonds" and "blood batteries," which implicates corporate criminals like Apple, De Beers, Google, Microsoft, and Tesla. To top it off, EU arms giants like Finmecannica and Airbus sell billions of euros worth of weapons fueling conflicts, while raking in billions of euros worth of contracts in the business of militarizing Fortress Europe.[112]

Europe is also pushing free trade agreements across the continent, promoting policies of capitalist investment and neoliberal liberalization at the expense of local producers. Jean Nanga writes, "The growth of free trade increases the (re)production and aggravation of inequalities and pauperization."[113] The Euro-Mediterranean Free Trade Area has been established, and a series of export processing zones (EPZs) with minimal tax and labor laws are being proposed. One of the most offensive, yet constitutive, juxtapositions of border imperialism is the activity of European anti-migration operations alongside European fishing trawlers off the coast of Mauritania. Europe's fishing agreement with Mauritania gives over a hundred EU vessels access to Mauritania's fishing waters, resulting in the devastation of local livelihoods.[114] Yet, if impoverished fishers attempt to migrate, they get apprehended by an EU surveillance vessel. Despite European complicities in creating displacement, barely 3 percent of African refugees make it to Europe.[115]

Pundits frequently pronounce on "failed African states" by mobilizing capitalist ideals of development, relying on racist tropes of delinquency and inferiority, and deliberately disregarding present legacies of conquest and intervention. An uninterrupted trajectory of imperialism and capitalism is undeniable, from the formal colonial period to Cold War–era destabilizations, such as the assassination of Patrice Lumumba and the overthrow of Kwame Nkrumah, to forced structural adjustment policies and neoliberal privatization in the

1980s and 1990s, the establishment of the US Africa Command (AFRICOM), land grabs and free trade plunder, and current policies of border externalization. Tryon P. Woods and P. Khalil Saucier assert that "antiblack violence in the Euro-Mediterranean Basin has its roots in the earliest fifteenth century African slave trade and the subsequent 'voyages of discovery' that further established European dominance of the Mediterranean and Atlantic coasts."[116] Exclusions of heterogeneously racialized people traversing the Mediterranean are built on the policing of migration as the capture of Blackness—punishment for "people out of place." Even among progressives, Woods and Saucier argue, the emphasis on deracialized politics of border securitization or refugee exclusion dodges a necessary excavation of our "social organisation premised on antiblack sexual violence."[117] Anti-Muslim racism in Europe, discussed in chapter 10, is woven into anti-Blackness to buttress Fortress Europe, beginning with the enslavement of African Muslims and subsequent imperial policies targeting Muslim-majority countries during the Cold War and war on terror. Sohail Daulatzai and Junaid Rana maintain the racialization of Muslims is central to race making and European empire, with Islam "made distinct as a racial object of white supremacy," dating back to the Reconquista and the expulsions of Muslims from Spain.[118] The rise of the far right, white nationalism, and fascism are thus not singular moments or isolated events; they are an extension of the societies and economies upon which the glory of Europe is unceasingly built.

It is not enough to demand the reformation or even elimination of border policies; rather, we must abolish the racial social organization subtending the criminalization of migration. Despite the disproportionate exclusions of Africans, Nesima Aberra points out, "the heart-wrenching pictures and stories that are circulated in the media about refugees are mostly light-skinned, conventionally attractive, and Arab."[119] Ruben Andersson, in conversation with officials at an EU command center, uncovers how EU maritime operations routinely racialize boats and their passengers into "Sub-Saharan Africans," who are more likely to be forced into the dangerous hold, and "North African Maghreb."[120] Even projects of humanitarian assistance, such as refugee camps on the African continent, coalesce into a bordered regime of spatialization and containment. Vilna Bashi argues a transnationalization of this anti-Black sentiment has resulted in imperial racial hierarchies of immigrants and a "global blockade to Black migration."[121]

News headlines frequently decry the end of the EU. We are told the Schengen Agreement is breaking down with internal walls going up; core and peripheral countries are squabbling about the Dublin Regulation; technocrats are debating how to best manage migration flows; and far-right and liberal-centrist parties are divided on refugee quotas. In reality, the entire EU is unified in expanding maritime interdiction, preventing migration, and externalizing the border, especially into Africa. Writing about the formal colonial period, Peo Hansen and Stefan Jonsson note "the unification of Europe and a unified European effort to colonize Africa were two processes that presupposed one another."[122] We see this continuing today with a European consensus on the imposition of externalized migration controls throughout the Sahel region. The primary disagreement between EU states about "sharing the burden of refugee distribution" is, fundamentally, a quarrel over racial imperial management. It harkens back to the colonial distribution of territory during the Partition of Africa and the Berlin Conference of 1884–85, resulting in colonial borders throughout the continent and violations of self-determination. No EU member state is actually discussing an end to forced displacement; after all, they are invested in maintaining the extractions and exploitations of racial capitalism, while preventing migration to a Europe they sanctimoniously declare their own. However, as Achille Mbembe poignantly puts it, "African and diasporic struggles for freedom and self-determination have always been intertwined with the aspiration to move unchained."[123]

PART 3

Capitalist Globalization
and Insourcing of Migrant Labor

CHAPTER 7

Temporary Labor Migration
and the New Braceros

On June 2, 2018, a scorching summer day in Italy's southern Calabria region, Soumayla Sacko and his coworkers gathered aluminum sheets for their San Ferdinando tent city. Suddenly, a car drove up and the men inside pointed a rifle at Sacko, shooting him in the head. The killing is widely believed to be a targeted assassination given Sacko's organizing as a migrant farmworker from Mali and labor leader with the Unione Sindacale di Base.[1] His brutal murder occurred in the context of both a wave of anti-migrant and anti-Black violence after the election of far-right leader Matteo Salvini as well as agribusiness backlash against migrant farmworker organizing.

One-third of farmworkers in Italy are migrant workers, earning an average of twenty to thirty euros a day for up to fourteen hours of work.[2] Many workers are recruited through the *caporalato* (gangmaster system), under which their wages are often withheld, they are coerced to take performance-enhancing drugs, and they experience routine violence by employers and labor brokers. Workers are segregated outside towns and forced to live in shacks they build from scrap metal and cardboard. These makeshift tent cities have no running water, electricity, healthcare, or sanitation. When an encampment gets too large, officials raze it to the ground. One of the cruelest ironies of capitalist globalization is the proletarianization of displaced peasants into migrant farmworkers. In Ghana, for example, trade liberalization policies have caused

131

an influx of cheap imported Italian tomato puree and the decline of local tomato production.[3] Consequently, Ghana has become one of the world's largest importers of tomato paste, 90 percent of which comes from the EU, mainly from Italy, which is one of the world's largest tomato producers.[4] Farmers from Ghana now have to pick and process tomatoes for the same Italian agribusinesses that decimated their livelihoods.

The extreme abuse of migrant farmworkers in Italy is linked both to Italian trade policies and to repressive refugee policies. Border controls, governing through illegalization and deportability, serve a critical function in the political economy by producing pliable labor. Border controls manufacture spatialized difference not to completely exclude all people but to capitalize on them, what Nicholas De Genova calls an "active process of inclusion through 'illegalization.'"[5] Here we see the third border governance strategy referenced in chapter 4: the disciplining of labor through immigration controls and transfiguring irregular migration into what is known in international policy circles as "managed labor migration." In the US, neoliberal, pro–Democratic Party commentator Thomas Friedman says candidly, "We have a real immigration crisis and . . . the solution is a *high wall with a big gate—but a smart gate*" (emphasis in original).[6]

While many migrant farmworkers in Italy are undocumented, others are brought in through the "smart gate" of temporary authorizations. Under Italian law, an annual flows decree sets a quota for contractual and seasonal migrant workers to live and work for up to nine months a year.[7] The residence permit is contingent upon a formal employment contract tied to an employer, creating a systemic tool of exploitation. As Sacko's comrade Aboubakar Soumaoro writes, "Soumayla did have a temporary permit to stay in Italy. But even such a status does not guarantee stable living conditions, for it is linked to a specific work contract. The employer can also use this as a form of blackmail against the worker who decides to speak out against exploitation or form a union, for he can threaten not only their sacking but also to put an end to their permission to remain in the country."[8]

The experience of migrant farmworkers in the fields of Italy is neither an anomaly nor a recent phenomenon. Before World War I, an estimated half a million seasonal farmworkers crossed the border annually into Germany.[9] After World War II, migrant worker programs were formalized during the reconstruction period. Over a twenty-year period, millions of migrant workers, or *Gastarbeiter*, mostly from Algeria, Greece, Italy, Morocco, Portugal,

Spain, Tunisia, Turkey, and Yugoslavia, worked in Germany, France, the UK, the Netherlands, Belgium, Sweden, and Switzerland.[10] Workers endured severe geographic segregation, were sequestered into low-wage industries, could not bring their family members, and had no rights to permanent residency. In the People's Republic of China in the 1950s, the introduction of the *hukou* system of governmental household registration served as an internal bordering regime to bifurcate the national labor market by dividing the population into urban and rural residents, each with distinctly different entitlements. The temporary migration of rural surplus labor to the urban centers was controlled through this administrative system, channeling migrant peasants into certain low-wage sectors and without the accompanying benefits of urban hukou. C. Cindy Fan describes this as a de facto migrant labor regime, enabling "labor-intensive industrialization and urban development at low cost" to consolidate China's socialist market economy.[11]

The International Labour Organization (ILO) estimates there are 164 million migrant workers around the world today.[12] I use "migrant workers" here not to refer to all people who move for work but specifically those migrants conscripted under transnational labor migration programs. Liberal elites present labor migration as a triple win because high-income receiving countries fill labor shortage needs, low-income sending countries decrease unemployment and generate revenue through remittances, and migrants support their families with higher wages due to exchange rates between sending and receiving countries. The Global Compact for Migration is the first UN agreement on a global approach to all forms of migration. One of its central principles is to facilitate labor mobility through "temporary, seasonal, circular, and fast-track programmes in areas of labour shortages."[13] The compact was finalized in 2018 amid right-wing opposition in Australia, Austria, Canada, Hungary, Israel, Poland, and the US. Liberal capitalists present temporary and circular labor migration as the more "humane" (i.e., market supply–oriented) alternative to right-wing calls for complete migrant exclusion. The *Economist* argues that denying migrant workers' voting rights, charging them extra taxes, and restricting their access to public services is "horribly discriminatory" but still "better for the migrants than the status quo, in which they are excluded from rich-world labor markets."[14]

Migrant workers provide liberal capitalist interests with cheapened labor without altering the racial social order through permanent immigration. Of the tens of thousands of farmworkers coming annually to Canada, for instance,

98 percent return to their place of origin upon completion of the seasonal contract, hoping to legally return the following season; they do not remain and become undocumented in Canada.[15] Kerry Preibisch argues this forced rotation is the reason for Canada's agricultural migrant worker program's international reputation: "This high degree of 'circularity' in policy-speak—or cyclical labor migration that does not result in permanent settlement—is a fundamental benchmark for which the 'success' of guest-worker programs is measured."[16] Liberal discussions about reforming Canada's migrant worker programs tend to be limited to piecemeal protections for migrant workers without analyzing how capitalism, imperialism, exclusion, and criminalization all shape temporary migration to simultaneously manage labor pools and control migration flows. Canadian migrant worker programs, detailed in chapter 9, are structured around market demands for cheapened labor, and workers' economic and social mobility is constrained by the very design of the program. While migrant workers are temporary, temporary migration is itself permanent.

In the US, the most well-known migrant worker program is the bracero program, which operated between 1942 and 1964. Initiated due to a labor shortage during World War II, the program allowed millions of Mexican workers to enter the country legally but under conditions of precarity. A key feature of the program was the tying of a bracero's temporary residency to an individual employment contract. Braceros did not have the right to permanent residency, and family members were not allowed to accompany them. The deportation of undocumented Mexicans, as exemplified through Operation Wetback, funneled Mexican workers through the bracero program, thus revealing the linkages between immigration exclusion and commodified inclusion. Even while more than 1 million Mexicans were being deported from the US during the 1950s,[17] as many as 4.8 million Mexican workers were contemporaneously brought in as temporary braceros.[18] The bracero program was beneficial to the Mexican government, which managed surplus populations through labor exportation, and lucrative for US agribusinesses, which used it as a tool of labor discipline by controlling braceros' wages, governing braceros' living conditions, and using braceros as strikebreakers against local farmworkers.

After the program ended, the recruitment and exploitation of workers continued through the H-2 program, the country's oldest and the world's second-oldest migrant worker program, first initiated to recruit workers from the Bahamas, Barbados, and Jamaica during World War II.[19] As more mostly

Jamaican workers were brought in under the H-2 program after the end of the bracero program, strike waves and deportations involving thousands of H-2 migrant workers became commonplace, especially in Florida's sugar industry, itself an outgrowth of US imperial interests and capitalist investments in Cuban sugar. As Cindy Hahamovitch explains about Florida's sugar industry, "Expropriated Cuban sugar moguls adopted the labor practices pioneered by the US Sugar Company, importing mostly Jamaican peasant farmers as temporary workers and deporting those who refused to accept their terms."[20] On the Florida plantation of the Fanjul brothers, the notorious Cuban sugar barons, Caribbean cane cutters engaged in a work stoppage in November 1986 to protest their wages being lower than their contracts stipulated.[21] A few days later, 385 workers on the property were rounded up at gunpoint and deported, some barefoot and with injuries sustained from police dog bites.[22]

Today, there are 257,666 mostly Mexican and Central American workers in the US under the H-2A temporary foreign agricultural worker program.[23] The Departments of State, Agriculture, Labor, and Homeland Security have all announced they will be "streamlining" the program to ease regulations for grower associations and ensure labor flexibility, a euphemism for labor super-exploitation and expendability. Honesto Silva Ibarra, a 28-year-old farmworker on an H-2A visa, collapsed on the Sarbanand Farms in Sumas, Washington, and died in August 2017. Prior to his death, Ibarra and six hundred other workers had been given the order: "Al menos que se estén muriendo, no falten" (Unless you are dying, don't miss work).[24] Days later, seventy of his fellow workers held a strike to protest his death and their mistreatment, including lack of health and safety protections, meals contaminated with insects, and picking quotas. They were promptly fired, evicted, deported to Mexico, and blacklisted by recruiters from returning. A number of workers are now filing class action lawsuits for unlawful termination and use of deportation as an intimidation tactic against organizing.

The concurrent expansion and privatization of the US military has led to an increase in migrant workers in the military industrial complex. In addition to the well-documented, privatized killing machine of foreign mercenary armies like Blackwater operating with "immunity and impunity,"[25] thousands of invisible, low-wage workers labor under outsourced contracts. Sarah Stillman reports that a seventy-thousand-strong logistical army of cooks, cleaners, construction workers, and beauticians served the US military's deadly occupations in Iraq and Afghanistan. Stillman reports that these workers were "robbed of wages, injured without compensation, subjected to sexual assault, and held in conditions resembling indentured servitude by their subcontractor bosses."[26]

One of the first companies to bring migrant workers to Iraq was Halliburton, also the first major private partner in the occupation of Iraq and one of the occupation's largest corporate beneficiaries. Former US vice president Dick Cheney was a former chairman and CEO of Halliburton and still retained stock options in the company when it was awarded a seven-billion-dollar government contract. In the mid-2000s, when one thousand Iraqis were killed weekly, Iraqi forces began targeting migrant worker convoys to pressure third governments into refusing work for the US military.[27] In one gruesome incident, thirteen Nepalese workers were contracted by a Halliburton subsidiary, under false pretenses, to cook and clean for US forces. Nepal had already banned migrant workers from going to Iraq and these workers thought they were being recruited to Jordan, but their passports were confiscated upon arrival in Jordan and a Halliburton recruiter forcibly transported them to Al Asad Air Base in Iraq. There, twelve of the workers were kidnapped, shot, and beheaded by the Ansar al-Sunna Army. The families of the slain workers were barred from pursuing liability claims against the military contractors after a US federal judge found the deaths occurred extraterritorially, beyond US legal jurisdiction.[28]

Even though migrant workers—precarious and deportable—are some of the most vulnerable during times of economic crisis, they are the most likely to be scapegoated for "stealing" jobs and resources. Migrant workers are discursively and physically attacked for "causing unemployment" and become the targets of rising xenophobia. The real culprits—bosses receiving bonuses or corporate giants getting bailed out—get off scot free. In Malaysia, for example, migrant workers mostly from Bangladesh, Indonesia, India, Nepal, Vietnam, and Myanmar constitute one-fifth of the country's workforce. In addition to enduring dangerous working conditions, they survive vigilante abuse at the hands of Ikatan Relawan Rakyat Malaysia (RELA), a 500,000-strong paramilitary group hunting down migrants.[29] This volunteer militia was created in the 1970s to track communists and in 2005 was given legal authority to stop people to check identification, raid homes, make arrests without warrants, use firearms, and even take over management of detention centers.[30] After scores of testimonies of assault and extortion, a new law was passed in 2012 that limits RELA's enforcement powers but maintains the militia's role in surveilling migrant workers. As such, RELA serves a key function in the Malaysian political economy: maintaining social and economic control over a large section of the workforce, discouraging migrant workers from leaving the employer to whom they are bound, ensuring fast deportability in moments of economic downturn, and entrenching the "foreignness" of all migrant workers, regardless of their length of residency and legal status.

Five Features of Migrant Worker Programs

Migrant workers have a myriad of unique experiences and individual subjectivities. Here I examine the forms of *structural* power regulating the lives of millions of temporary migrant workers and, hence, exacerbating their vulnerability. In analyzing labor migration programs worldwide, Daniel Costa and Philip Martin find notable similarities across jurisdictions.[31] Low-wage migrant workers are tied to one employer by contracts and visas and cannot bring their children or other family members. They are subjected to dangerous working conditions, forced labor, long work hours without overtime pay, and wage theft. Most workers are indebted to recruiters. Workers face legal or de facto barriers to unionization, are denied access to labor protections and social services, and have no real path to permanent immigration status. Speaking out against abuse almost always results in retaliation, termination, deportation, and blacklisting.

Abuses under temporary labor migration programs are not a coincidence. The manufactured vulnerability of migrant workers is both generated by and constitutive of racial capitalism; the architecture of labor migration is *intended* to guarantee capital accumulation and uphold racialized gendered citizenship. The next two chapters focus on the kafala system in the Arab Gulf region and the Temporary Foreign Worker Program in Canada. While routinely and singularly condemned in the media, the kafala is not exceptional. Like other migrant worker programs, the kafala is a feature of racial-capitalist statecraft with a pronounced reliance on unfree migrant workers. In comparison, the Canadian program is upheld as the five-star model for labor migration even though its origins and current configuration are rooted in the organization of labor extraction within a settler-colonial economy. I delve into both programs in the following chapters and demonstrate that they are structurally informed by similar global dynamics of capital flows, labor segmentation, and regimes of exclusionary citizenship, as described below.

Though every jurisdiction has distinct regulations governing migrant workers, five overlapping features characterize most migrant worker programs around the world.

First and foremost, migrant worker programs are state-sanctioned programs of *indentured work*. These programs can be traced back to the indentureship of more than 1.3 million people from the South Asian subcontinent, facilitated by the interests of empire and emerging colonial states.[32] The British East India Company and then the British raj regulated the emigration of indentured workers to sugar, cotton, rubber, and tea plantations and for railroad construction across the British empire, including to Guyana, Fiji, Jamaica, Kenya, Malaysia, Mauritius, South Africa, Tanzania, Trinidad, and Uganda, for nearly one century. Approximately a quarter million of those indentured were women, many of whom were sex workers, widowed, or escaping domestic violence.[33] Even though indentureship was deemed voluntary contract labor, the movement of mostly class- and caste-oppressed South Asian indentured labor throughout the British colonies, and later other European colonies, created some of the first state interventions in migration and facilitated the conditions of unfree labor migration. As part of an imperial labor strategy in the aftermath of the formal abolition of chattel slavery, indentured labor maintained a disciplined racialized labor force subordinated to colonial-capitalist production.

Today's migrant workers are similarly bound to a designated employer or sector, and employment is a requirement of migration. Employers can discard migrant workers through termination and deportation when their labor is no longer needed, actions having mutual benefit to capital and state interests in providing a valve to control unemployment and demographics. Migrant workers are therefore either legally or de facto unable to leave their employer without losing their immigration status, making their labor indentured. David McNally writes: "It's not that global business does not want immigrant labour to the West. It simply wants this labour on its own terms: frightened, oppressed, vulnerable."[34] This indentureship is underwritten by ableism since capitalism is always undergirded by ableist ideas of productivity. The ILO recognizes migrant workers face endemic conditions of coerced productivity: "forced labour, low wages, poor working conditions, virtual absence of social protection, denial of freedom association and union rights, discrimination and xenophobia, as well as social exclusion."[35] The Migrants' Trade Union in South Korea, one of the world's most active migrant worker organizations, launched with sustained actions against labor crackdowns and worker deportations.[36] Comprised mostly of South Asian and Southeast Asian workers, the union advocated for an end to indentureship through an open work visa system and full immigration status for migrant workers, and, in a historic victory, won the right to union certification in 2015.

Second, migrant worker programs are a form of *legalized segregation*. Indentureship facilitated by the state legally sanctions the stratification of labor cast as racialized outsiders. Despite working alongside citizen workers, migrant workers are differentially included in the nation-state. Migrant workers can return to the same community and workplace for several generations, but being legally classified as "temporary" or "foreign" conceptually places them outside the nation-state and outside the bounds of belonging. Workers are often spatially and socially segregated: they are housed in separate labor camps, they are unprotected by national labor laws or unionization, they are unable to fully access public services such as healthcare, and their family members cannot accompany them. The entire cost of social reproduction is borne by migrant workers themselves and, as Susan Ferguson and David McNally put forward, "the social reproduction of the global working class crucially entails processes of migration and racialization that are inseparable from its class and gender dimensions."[37] Migrant worker programs therefore represent an extreme neoliberalization of both immigration and labor policies, where the deliberate design of national and racial difference results in "internal segregation in host countries."[38]

Third, as such, migrant worker programs are a form of *neoliberal insourcing*, the flipside of neoliberal outsourcing. The denial of permanent residency is precisely what creates an extranational segmentation of labor. Even though migrant workers are laboring alongside citizens, their labor power and social relations are organized to oxymoronically position them as "foreign." This maintains a global division of labor pools, reinforces a border within the international working class, and segments migrant workers as "Third World" workers. Like the outsourced workforce in export processing zones and maquiladoras, migrant workers are subject to suppressed wages and intense labor discipline. Hence, insourced and outsourced labor are two sides of the same capitalist coin: deliberately deflated labor power imbricated with hierarchies of race, caste, gender, sexuality, and citizenship. Critically, migrant worker programs make it clear that borders do not collapse under neoliberal globalization; rather, border imperialism segments labor and acts as a spatial fix for capital accumulation.[39] Migrant workers therefore represent the ideal, insourced workforce; they are commodified and exploitable, flexible and expendable.

Fourth, migrant worker programs constitute a *distinct mode of racialization*, both the result of and reproducing racism. Class relations cannot be reduced to relations of production, and, as Brenna Bhandar notes, "[r]ace and racism, gender, and sexuality shape the nature and form that class relations take and, significantly, how they are experienced."[40] The devaluation of migrant workers is animated by the specific devaluation of the racialized bodies performing the work. Migrant worker programs are not only racially discriminatory; they are themselves a race-making regime. Migrant workers are racially constructed and ordered through the very design of these programs as a distinct and segregated labor regime. Capitalism relies both on the division of labor *and* the division of laborers. Racialized, as well as gendered, divisions are supplemented by divisions between citizen workers and migrant workers, what Sandro Mezzadra and Brett Neilson term the "multiplication of labor," emphasizing the heterogeneity of labor bifurcated by a border.[41] The denial of permanent immigration status to migrant workers and their racialization as "foreigners" normalizes racism. Race is a contingent structure, and this distinct ordering of legal-but-deportable labor generates structural hierarchies between racialized migrant workers and citizen workers, and further affixes race to citizenship.

Fifth, migrant worker programs are a *carceral regime* with intense control, discipline, and surveillance of not only labor conditions or immigration status but the totality of life. Carceral spaces are "sites and relations of power that enable and incentivize the systematic capture, control, and confinement of human beings through the structures of immobility and dispossession."[42] Migrant workers routinely report the confiscation of identification documents and passports, long work hours, wage theft, forced labor, violence, imposition of curfews, denial of visitors and phone access, food deprivation, and being locked in and prevented from leaving employer-provided accommodations— all of which leave them immobilized. This is particularly heightened for migrant domestic workers; a recent report on the abuse of migrant domestic workers in Lebanon is fittingly titled "Their Home Is My Prison."[43] Like prisons, migrant worker programs manage surplus populations and discipline labor through racial social ordering, citizenship regulation, and restructuring of capital–labor relations in national labor markets. We see the logic of plantation relations operating here: to capture labor while also exceeding the logic of labor alone, or, as Fred Moten argues, "more than just the constitutive outside of bourgeois capitalism."[44]

Domestic Work and Global Care Chains

I would get about three to four hours sleep. I would be constantly washing or ironing clothes and if the clothes were not clean enough I would have to wash and iron them again. My hands split and bled because of the work.
—Migrant worker in Qatar, quoted in
Amnesty International, *"My Sleep Is My Break": Exploitation of Migrant Domestic Workers in Qatar*

The five features of migrant worker programs are exemplified in domestic work, where a growing proportion of workers are migrants in gendered, sexualized, and racialized positions of precarity. The unevenly gendered work of the social reproduction of labor within the domestic sphere, an essential condition for the reproduction of capitalism, means the private domain of the home has long been a site of struggle to make this feminization of labor visible. The International Wages for Housework campaign in the 1970s, led by Marxist feminists, demanded that class struggle include women's unpaid domestic labor as a pillar of patriarchal cisheteronuclear organization and capitalist accumulation. While the slogan focused on wages, the campaigners made clear it was a rhetorical device to make housework visible and highlight patriarchal social structuring under capitalism. Raj Patel estimates that the value of women's unpaid work constitutes more than half the world's entire labor output.[45] In 2020, the *New York Times* pegged the value of women's unpaid labor around the world at an overwhelming $10.9 trillion.[46] This naturalization of reproductive work as unpaid, gendered work lays the foundation for underpaid domestic work in the wage economy. Maria Mies writes, "Women are the optimal labour force because they are now being universally defined as 'housewives,' not as workers; this means their work, whether in commodity production or use value, is obscured."[47]

The *racialized*, feminized nature of domestic and reproductive work further destabilizes the moorings of domestic work as women's "natural work." Patricia Hill Collins argues, "The assumed split between the 'public' sphere of paid employment and the 'private' sphere of unpaid family responsibilities has never worked for US Black women."[48] The International Black Women for Wages for Housework campaign specifically linked unwaged housework to reparations for slavery and imperialism, drawing links between the subsidization of capitalism by factory wages and unwaged labor in the home and on plantations, strengthened through immigration controls and laws criminalizing sex work. "Black/Third World women internationally, the majority of the majority of the world's people, carry the major burden of the world's work and get the least wealth in return," they described.[49] Black women in the US were kidnapped from their children and violently enslaved in homes, where they were forced to cook, clean, and care for and act as wet nurses for white children. Even after the formal abolition of chattel slavery, Marvel Cooke and Ella Baker wrote about the hundreds of street corners in New York, which they referred to as "slave markets," where Black women were hired as domestic day laborers by white employers.[50]

Before she was deported, Claudia Jones spent much of the 1940s and 1950s raising the issues of Black domestic workers. She chastised unions for their failure to center domestic workers: "It is merely lip service for progressive unionists to speak of organizing the unorganized without turning their eyes to the plight of the domestic worker, who, unprotected by union standards, is also the victim of exclusion from all social and labor legislation."[51] She argued that Black working women are "the most oppressed stratum of the whole population" and "far out of proportion to other women workers, are the main breadwinners in their families."[52] Jones focused on the Black domestic worker, whose super-exploitation was justified through the "white chauvinist stereotype as to where her place should be."[53]

Domestic worker struggles have largely been marginalized in mainstream feminist and labor movements because of this history of domestic work as a Black, feminized sector in the hypersurveilled and privatized domain of the home—characterized by a master–servant, not employer–employee, relation and exemplified by terminology like "the help." Due to legal and de facto segregation, 90 percent of Black working women in the southern US were domestic workers who endured long hours, earned low wages, and experienced intense discipline and violence.[54] Linking slavery of the past to servitude of the present, thousands of workers organized from the 1950s onward, redefining domestic work and winning important victories such as the inclusion of domestic labor in wage and hour laws.[55] Premilla Nadasen writes, "Domestic work, so representative of white racial oppression for the African American community, became an important platform for the politics of black liberation."[56]

The current international division of labor has also created an international division of domestic labor. According to the ILO, an estimated sixty-seven million adult domestic workers are employed worldwide, of whom 80 percent are women.[57] Sixty-six percent of domestic workers in high-income countries are migrant workers.[58] The expansion of capitalist relations and introduction of women's waged work have transformed global conditions of social reproduction and labor relations. The concept of "global chains of care" refers to the transnational networks of paid and unpaid care work, formed to reproduce and maintain life in a range of settings, from the private home to the senior home.[59] The global care chain links low-income women oppressed by race, caste, class, sexuality, and nationality to their employers, privileged by those same hierarchies in the advanced capitalist countries of the Global North and, increasingly, also the Global South. In turn, migrant workers' own families—often forbidden from accompaniment—are cared for by other family members or another chain of domestic workers. Care chains are multiplied as a result of neoliberal and structural adjustment policies. In high-income, imperialist countries, austerity measures have privatized senior care, healthcare, and childcare, thus shifting feminized care work away from public institutions into the private and privatized domain of the home.

In many countries in the Global South, colonial legacies of impoverishment, coupled with intensified capitalist expropriation, have compelled circuits of labor migration. For instance, labor migration policy was first introduced in the Philippines under the US-backed dictatorship of Ferdinand Marcos, and the country is now one of the largest labor-exporting countries in the world. Ten percent of the population work overseas, and migrant domestic workers constitute a whopping 70 percent of all migrant workers leaving the country.[60] US imperialism has influenced this exodus. Soon after Frederick Jackson Turner declared the archipelago an American frontier, the Philippines became a US colony, which it remained from 1898 until 1946. Approximately 1.4 million people were killed during the Philippine-American war, where waterboarding and scorched-earth tactics were first battle-tested by the US.[61] Under colonial rule, workers from the Philippines were recruited by the Hawaiian Sugar Planters' Association to work the plantations and serve US imperial interests there.

Even after the Philippines won independence, conditions like a fixed exchange rate between the peso and dollar were imposed to protect US companies. Within two decades, the Philippines was forced to follow the dictates of IMF and World Bank structural adjustment programs. World Bank lending increased a staggering eightfold during the period of martial law, and Marcos subsequently mandated budget appropriation for debt service, making the Philippines the only country in the world with an automatic debt appropriation law.[62] Caught in a debt spiral, the impact was severe: public services were privatized, currency was devalued, user fees were raised, food production was industrialized and geared for export, and wages were depressed. The country also served as a pilot project for the World Bank's global urban development strategy, slating slums for redevelopment and displacing poor people, while generating profits for developers.[63] Against this backdrop, the institutionalization of labor migration became a means of quelling dissent, shrinking local unemployment and poverty rates, using remittances to service debt, and positioning the Philippines in the global economic order as a supplier of racialized and gendered labor, constantly produced and disciplined. Migrante International calls the government's labor export policy "state-sponsored human trafficking."[64]

The feminization of poverty, the feminization of labor, and the feminization of migration, therefore, intersect and are sustained by a matrix of racial, imperial, and class power. Silvia Federici argues that the labor of migrant domestic workers contributes to the accumulation of wealth for middle-class and rich women in advanced, capitalist countries, who become "liberated" from housework in order to climb corporate ladders. For Federici, migrant domestic workers are "a colonial solution to the 'housework problem.'"[65] This exploitative division of labor cements the hierarchies between middle- and upper-class white women in the so-called productive economy and low-income racialized migrant women in the undervalued and underpaid economy of domestic labor. Bridget Anderson maintains that employing domestic workers in the home consolidates social status and class, and that the highly exploitative conditions associated with domestic work exist because it is "the worker's 'personhood,' rather than her labour power, which the employer is attempting to buy."[66]

In response to these exploitative labor relations and carceral social formations, the International Domestic Workers Federation brings together domestic workers' unions and associations from Africa, Asia, the Caribbean, Central America, South and North America, and Europe. The first global union organization run by women, it won a historic Decent Work for Domestic Workers Convention, adopted by the ILO in 2011. Geraldine Pratt and Migrante BC powerfully argue, "Although domestic work is feminized, the strength of domestic worker organizing disrupts the conventional images of femininity and must be understood in terms of the spatiality and materialities of domestic workers' lives."[67] Around the world, migrant workers are spearheading vital labor, feminist, antiracist, and migrant justice campaigns calling for an end to policies of temporary labor migration that facilitate racialized, gendered indentureship based on citizenship status. Migrant worker networks such as Alianza Americas, International Trade Union Confederation, La Via Campesina, Migrant Forum in Asia, Pan-African Network in Defense of Migrants' Rights, and Women in Migration Network are mobilizing across borders and demanding the right to permanent residency upon arrival, full access to social services, protection of collective bargaining rights, and living wages for all.

CHAPTER 8

The Kafala System in the Gulf States

*I worked and worked. My boss would slap me and beat me. He said: "If you
do not remove your clothes I will cut your neck."*
—Adia, quoted in Anna Dubuis, "We Spoke to Domestic Workers
Who Were Trapped in the Middle East's 'Formal Slave Trade'"

The Gulf Cooperation Council (GCC) is the main destination for labor
migration in the Global South, making it a key region for an analysis
of the dynamics of capital accumulation, labor control, and citizenship regulation in relation to migration.[1] Migrant workers in the oil-rich GCC states of
Bahrain, Kuwait, Oman, Qatar, Saudi Arabia, and the United Arab Emirates
(UAE) constitute anywhere from 40 to 90 percent of each country's population. Regionally, non-nationals represent 51 percent of the total population
and 67 percent of the total labor force.[2] Eighty percent of the private sector
labor force in Qatar is made up of migrant workers, and migrant workers make
up almost the entire private sector labor force in the UAE and Saudi Arabia.[3]

Particularly in Saudi Arabia, authoritarian rule repressing political dissidents, illustrated by the assassination of journalist Jamal Khashoggi in 2018,
is inextricable from control of the migrant workforce. Saudi Arabia is one of
the top five destination countries worldwide for migrant workers, with a population of 2.3 million migrant domestic workers.[4] Most work fifteen to twenty
hours a day, and many experience labor super-exploitation, intense regulation,
confinement, assault, and rape.[5] In 2014, Filipina domestic worker Marilyn
Porras Restor was kidnapped by a royal family.[6] Restor had been working for

another family under the kafala system for a decade before she was abducted. Even though a formal complaint was filed with Saudi officials regarding Restor and a number of other missing and kidnapped migrant women, Restor's family got no information for over a year, until they received the distressing news that she was dead. The reported cause of death was unknown but believed to be fatal injuries sustained from being pushed off a roof.

The kafala system is the dominant form of governance of migrant workers in the six GCC states, as well as in Jordan and Lebanon. In the GCC countries, nearly thirty million people worked under the kafala system in 2017.[7] Kafala's main feature is sponsorship by a citizen or corporate employer, which contractually binds the worker to the *kafeel* (sponsor) to maintain immigration status. Migrant workers generally require the kafeel's permission to enter or exit the country, transfer to a different sponsor or place of employment, or change the conditions or period of employment. The kafeel, on the other hand, can unilaterally change contract terms, including wages and working conditions. An entire industry is wrapped around the system. Even before migrants set foot in their place of employment, they accumulate an immense debt from fees owed to recruiting agencies and labor brokers that acts as an additional form of discipline. Andrew Gardner argues the system is structurally violent against migrant workers because of "the transnational character of the contracts and debt incurred in their sojourn to the Gulf, the control of the foreign workers' passports by the kafeel, the linguistic and cultural barriers that limit their strategic responses to the dilemmas they face, and the spatial aspects of this system of dominance."[8]

The carceral immobility and proprietorial dimension of this bonded labor manifests in one vicious word: runaway. In a stark parallel to the enforcement of slavery, "runaways" who leave the kafeel are often charged with "absconding" and subsequently detained and deported. In Saudi Arabia, twenty thousand domestic workers mostly from Ethiopia, Indonesia, the Philippines, and Sri Lanka abscond every year.[9] As soon as a charge of absconding is registered by a kafeel, the worker's visa is canceled. Migrant workers, especially domestic workers, become unemployed, criminalized, and undocumented all at once, compounding their manufactured vulnerability and leaving them susceptible to deportation.

State Development and Gulf Capitalism

Moral misgivings about the kafala system pervasive in liberal media tend to implicate culture instead of structure. Such critiques rely on Orientalist tropes portraying the system as somehow peculiarly Arab, with limiting explanations of "premodern" hospitality traditions, rather than an indictment of the *modern* global structuring of capitalism through borders. While the role of the kafeel as a guarantor to the state certainly has roots in Sharia law, the kafala system is not uniquely Arab or Islamic in its control of migrant labor in the present day. These representations mirror the problematic yet durable utilization of culture or religion to analyze political authoritarianism in the region, when, in fact, capitalism, and specifically oil as a global commodity enmeshed in imperial relations, is intimately connected to the maintenance of authoritarian regimes. Egregious abuses under the kafala system are not a matter of uniquely unscrupulous Arab employers, but a result of immigration status being tied to a sponsor-employer to collapse labor and political power. We must, therefore, refrain from explaining the kafala through the lens of essentialist cultural difference since the system cannot be cleaved from the continuum of migrant worker programs exploding worldwide. Instead, I explore regional dynamics within an international ordering of racial capitalism, dispossessive forces in the formation of political economies, and the balance of power between the ruling and the working class.

The key bureaucratic tenets of the kafala system originated during British colonial rule in the Gulf, especially strong in Bahrain. The British first introduced passports in Bahrain in 1929 for "foreign subjects" falling under British jurisdiction. According to Omar AlShehabi, the movement of pearl divers from other regions into Bahrain—comprising nearly half the island's labor force—was regulated by the British through a sponsorship system to control movement and maintain surveillance.[10] Ship captains were required to have valid permits and visas to work in Bahrain, and they were also responsible for all foreign divers on their ships. This sponsorship system in the pearl diving industry, and subsequently for workers from colonial India in the oil industry in Bahrain in the 1930s, was a form of indirect colonial rule by the British to ensure labor discipline and population control. As AlShehabi asserts, the roots of the kafala lie in "a legal-bureaucratic complex regulating migrant labour, not as an age-old practice in the Arabian Peninsula from time immemorial, but as a very modern product of British colonial practices to control labour and police empire across the Gulf and the Indian Ocean."[11]

The evolution of the kafala system throughout the region follows a similar trajectory into the 1950s, heightened with the spread of Gulf capitalism and Western interests. Adam Hanieh argues the wealth accumulated from extracting crude oil for global markets and the insertion of the Gulf region as a key zone in the international economy has been completely contingent on Western-backed state formation of the Gulf monarchies, which at once both excludes citizens from productive labor and exploits migrant workers as a permanently temporary workforce to quell dissent.[12] In the 1950s, competing British and American oil interests were resisted by anticolonial nationalist forces, as exemplified by Iranian prime minister Mohammad Mossadegh nationalizing oil and Egyptian president Gamal Abd al-Nasser nationalizing the Suez Canal. This pan-Arab nationalism inspired dissident groups and strikes in the GCC countries to oppose imperial interests and ruling monarchies. During this period, three interconnected processes unfolded to contain pan-Arab nationalism. First, there was massive repression. Second, the ruling monarchies oversaw distribution of oil revenues to citizens through programs such as cheap housing, education stipends, and zero income tax, purchasing their loyalty—with loyalty to the state *as* loyalty to its rulers. Gilbert Achcar describes the rentier state as one with patrimonial political structures, where oil is the primary source of rent for GCC states and the state is considered the property of the ruling family.[13] The third process to take hold was the transformation of the working class into a migrant worker labor force with diminished labor power and no citizenship. The outcome of these processes was that, as Abdulhadi Khalaf argues, "the majority of the economically active population is excluded from politics, while citizens, who are a minority, would continue to rely on the ruling families to allocate the resources required to sustain citizenship privileges in highly competitive markets."[14]

These key processes of state formation and political governance required a highly controlled and segregated regime of labor. As Hanieh explains, "Class congealed spatially around temporary migrant labor flows and was demarcated through the institution of citizenship."[15] At first, migrant workers from neighboring Yemen, Egypt, and Palestine formed the majority of the migrant labor force in GCC countries through sizable movements of people. Palestinians were the single-largest non-Kuwaiti demographic in Kuwait in the 1980s.[16] Arab migrant workers became increasingly involved in left, socialist, and Palestinian movements, while also making demands on GCC countries for permanent settlement. GCC rulers responded by shifting their labor migration programs first to South Asia and then also to Southeast Asia, and between 1975 and 2002, the Arab proportion of migrant workers dropped by 40 percent.[17] It is this history of state formation through rapid capital accumulation, labor suppression, and restrictive citizenship that forms the basis of the extreme exploitation of migrant workers in the region today. Hanieh concludes: "A vital element to challenging capital and state in the Gulf must be a defense of the region's migrant workers. The exploitation of these workers is an integral part of how working classes have formed in the Middle East and is essential to the ways that Gulf capitalism continues to project its power."[18]

The dynamics of labor migration are also overlaid by the supra-structure of the GCC. The GCC is a regional economic zone with unified external tariffs, tax-free mobility of goods and services produced in member countries, and integration of capital markets. This political power structure is currently solidified around the devastating Saudi- and Emirati-led war on Yemen, experiencing one of the world's worst famines, and the UAE domination of military and commercial logistics in a maritime space stretching from the Red Sea to the Indian Ocean.[19] Even as circuits of finance and logistics have become internationalized, nationalist redistributive programs are maintained as much as possible. Jane Kinninmont writes: "The legal, political and economic construction of citizenship by Gulf regimes has been designed partly to provide incentives for Gulf nationals to support the existing nations rather than being swayed by stronger pulls toward transnational Arab or Islamic identities."[20] Though the integrated economic zone is predicated upon transnational relations guaranteeing flow of commodities and capital across borders, it is still anchored to the hierarchies of *national* citizenship that configure class and political formations. The kafala system, where both the precarious condition of migrant workers and their alienation from citizens is embedded, further manages class relations through national citizenship.

As elite rulers intend, the construction of an exclusionary regime of national citizenship and legalized segregation of migrant workers from citizens acts as an effective firewall against solidarity. When major labor strikes do occur, they are often along nationalist lines with anti-immigrant demands as an affirmation of workers' rights. Jill Crystal details how one of the first major labor strikes in Qatar was centered around the demand to deport Dhofari workers. Two hundred fifty Dhofaris were deported before the striking Qatari workers agreed to return to work.[21] This deflection of class consciousness into nationalist consciousness was formalized in the country's first labor law in 1962, institutionalizing a hiring preference for Qataris. This nationalist dynamic is currently amplified, as a decade of economic downturn and rising citizen unemployment has resulted in the scapegoating of migrant workers.

Saudi Arabia's Crown Prince Mohammed bin Salman announced the Vision 2030 national framework to combat bubbling dissent due to declining oil prices, rising unemployment, shrinking state programs, and imposition of taxes on citizens for the first time. A key element of the framework is the Nitaqat campaign, launched in 2011, for the Saudization of the workforce, especially in the private sector.[22] In 2013, as part of Nitaqat, an enforcement initiative was undertaken to deport irregular migrant workers, resulting in raids, fatal xenophobic attacks by state forces alongside citizens armed with machetes, and mass detention.[23] In the first two days after the campaign was announced, 20,000 people were detained, and within six months around 427,000 were deported, mostly to Yemen and Ethiopia.[24] In 2017, Saudi Arabia launched another expulsion campaign, resulting in a staggering 2.1 million arrests in one year.[25] This scapegoating and mass repression not only quashes the possibility of joint struggle between Saudi dissidents and migrant workers, but also reinforces the authoritarian rule of the ruling monarchies.

Kafala as Capture and Control

Three features of the kafala system distinguish it from most other migrant worker programs. First, the centrality of migrant labor to the GCC economy cannot be overstated, with migrant workers representing a majority of the total labor force and half of the entire population.[26] Relatedly, most of the private labor market, such as domestic, service, and retail work, is dependent on migrant labor and results in the devolution of immigration obligations from governments to dispersed citizen sponsors or companies. The differentiation between citizen and noncitizen becomes further entrenched with kafeels positioned in the active surveillance, control, and discipline of migrant workers. Finally, transfer of the responsibility of migrant workers from one kafeel to another is a customary practice, for instance, as an "inheritance" to another citizen sponsor in the event of the kafeel's death.

The contractual dependence of migrant workers on the kafeel for income, residency, and immigration status leads to egregious abuses, and the litany of violations endured by migrant workers is long. While there are some middle-class, white-collar workers sponsored under the kafala system (and, in unusual circumstances, non-nationals can sponsor themselves), the vast majority of migrant workers in the GCC are low-income laborers from Bangladesh, Ethiopia, India, Indonesia, Nepal, Pakistan, the Philippines, Thailand, and Sri Lanka.

These workers are imperiled by illegal confiscation of passports and travel documents, excessive recruitment fees by agents, nonpayment or withholding of wages, long work hours, dangerous conditions including confinement to the home, physical and sexual violence, false accusations of theft as punishment and discipline, and constant threat of deportation. Trade unions are banned and consequences for mobilizing include arrest, deportation, and bans on return. Each country's ministry of the interior, an enforcement arm equivalent to the US Department of Homeland Security, administers and oversees the kafala system. Citizenship laws are generally based on the principle of jus sanguinis, requiring paternal lineage, leaving migrant workers with few avenues to become citizens. Despite years of residency, contributions to the political economy, and strong kinship networks, workers are in a liminal and contingent position inside the nation-state; they are hierarchically categorized as permanent outsiders. It is no surprise, then, that desperation is a stifling reality. One migrant worker attempted or committed suicide every two and a half days in Kuwait in 2010, and an average of three suicides were committed every week by construction workers in the UAE over a similar period.[27]

Migrant workers make up over 95 percent of construction workers and domestic workers in the region.[28] The political economy of oil extraction has led to a building frenzy with the construction of massive industrial infrastructure and retail ventures such as luxury apartments and malls. Beneath the glittering skylines of Gulf metropolises like Dubai are millions of construction workers experiencing deadly conditions. In one year alone, India, Pakistan, and Bangladesh repatriated the bodies of 880 construction workers from the UAE.[29] The ironically named Saadiyat Island (island of happiness)—hosting branches of the Louvre, the Guggenheim Museum, and New York University, as well as golf courses, private residences, and hotels—is an island of misery for the workers tasked with building it in extreme heat for twelve hours a day. The average annual salary for migrant workers on Saadiyat is $2,575.[30] Employers habitually withhold wages and passports, and workers are housed in cramped and unsanitary accommodations. When workers went on strike in 2014, the swift response of authorities was to interrogate, detain, and deport hundreds. One worker told Human Rights Watch that five hundred men were either deported or had their work visas canceled after the action.[31]

In Qatar, the International Trade Union Confederation estimates that at least 5,200 workers will die—almost a dozen workers a week—in the frenzy to build stadiums, hotels, and infrastructure for the World Cup in 2022.[32] A

Guardian investigation revealed that workers toil in 50°C temperature (122°F) for ten hours a day, a dozen men sleep in one room, and many workers are not paid. Ram Kumar Mahara describes: "We were working on an empty stomach for 24 hours; 12 hours' work and then no food all night. When I complained, my manager assaulted me, kicked me out of the labour camp I lived in and refused to pay me anything. I had to beg for food from other workers."[33] The *Guardian* further reported that seven hundred Indian workers died in Qatar between 2010 and 2012, and, in a separate investigation, that Nepalese workers died at a rate of almost one worker per day during 2013.[34]

In response to international pressure, Qatar introduced regulations replacing the term "sponsor" with "recruiter" and proclaimed an end to the kafala. However, the kafala structure remains in place. New regulations, such as one allowing many workers to leave the country without employer permission, are smoke screens, because employers can still withhold passports, and workers are still unable to change jobs, and will be charged with absconding if they do.[35] The ongoing vulnerability of migrant workers in Qatar was unambiguously evident in March 2020, when hundreds of workers were arbitrarily rounded up, detained in crowded cells with one piece of bread each, and summarily deported without the wages owed to them. Most troubling was the authorities' use of the pandemic as a cover; the workers were falsely informed they were being transported to health centers to get tested for the coronavirus.[36] Other migrant workers still in the country were forcibly locked down in a migrant labor camp housing thousands of men, with 8 to 10 crammed in a room without adequate access to healthcare or sanitary supplies, after 351 workers tested positive for the virus.[37]

While the majority of migrant workers in the region are men, the most vulnerable workers are women laboring and living in the home, excluded from labor laws in all GCC countries.[38] The feminization of labor in private households is characterized by the entwined devaluation of domestic work and subjugation of migrant women workers. Migrant domestic workers in the GCC "provide a substitute for the unwaged labor of women within households, allowing the latter to take up more remunerative employment outside of the household, focus on quality time with her family, and/or enjoy a life of leisure."[39] According to a 2014 Human Rights Watch report, most migrant domestic workers interviewed in the UAE said employers confiscated passports, physically and sexually abused them, forced them to work long hours without breaks, denied them adequate food and medical treatment, and confined them to the home.[40] Half of the domestic workers interviewed by another researcher in the UAE said they had not left the employer's home alone in over two years.[41] An Amnesty investigation of Qatar revealed that the majority of workers reported similar carceral immobility and exploitation: working a hundred hours per week, experiencing severe restrictions on being able to leave the house or make phone calls, verbal harassment, and violence. Workers fleeing violence are punished with charges of absconding, and 90 percent of migrant women detained in Qatar in 2013 were domestic workers.[42] A gruesome illustration of pervasive gendered violence these women workers face is the case of Indonesian migrant worker Tuti Tursilawati in Saudi Arabia. She was executed in 2018 after being convicted for murdering her employer in an act of self-defense after an attempted rape. Tursilawati was the third Indonesian domestic worker executed in Saudi Arabia in a single year.[43]

Despite horrific working and living conditions, as well as the constant cudgels of termination and deportation, migrant workers have waged intrepid resistance against the kafala system. Filipina worker Jennifer Dalquez defended herself against her predatory employer, who attempted to rape her at knifepoint. Sentenced to death, she was later acquitted with the support of a global campaign demanding her freedom. In the UAE, there have been at least three large labor strikes against Arabtec, a major construction company contracted to build the Louvre Abu Dhabi on Saadiyat and the world's tallest building, Burj Khalifa, in Dubai. Thirty thousand migrant construction workers went on a ten-day strike against the company in 2007, three thousand migrant workers took strike action in 2011, and hundreds of workers refused to leave their accommodations and announced a strike in 2013.[44] Beneath these protests and strikes is a web of transnational relations among migrant workers that destabilize citizenship, sabotage omnipresent state-capital power, and defy notions of belonging intended to constrain their lives and labor mobility in the region. As Aimee Bahng highlights, such migrant networks of existence and resistance "extend networks of care beyond national narratives of 'risky subjects' and the calculations of global financialization."[45]

CHAPTER 9

Permanently Temporary:

Managed Migration in Canada

Under the temporary foreign worker program, the boss has all the power—over your money, house, status, everything. They have you tied to their will.
—OPT, quoted in UNIFOR, "Landmark Human Rights Ruling Highlights Systematic Abuse of Temporary Foreign Workers"

In 2015, the Human Rights Tribunal of Ontario awarded two hundred thousand dollars to two Mexican migrant workers—known publicly by their initials OPT and MPT—who had experienced sexual harassment and discrimination at the Presteve Foods fish processing plant. They were part of a group of thirty-nine migrant farmworkers from Mexico and Thailand who brought forward complaints of violence. The two workers recounted appalling details of assault and rape by Jose Pratas, the owner of Presteve Foods. OPT testified Pratas repeatedly "touched her legs and her vagina through her clothes" and "penetrated her with his penis."[1] MPT was similarly sexually assaulted and was subsequently terminated and deported for leaving the employer-provided accommodation. In his decision in favor of OPT and MPT, adjudicator Mark Hart emphasized their particular vulnerability as migrant workers. "As a temporary foreign worker in Canada, OPT was put in the position of being totally reliant upon her employer," he wrote.[2] The #MeToo movement has largely ignored this kind of gendered violence against migrant workers, even though violence is systemic and embedded in migrant worker programs.

Canada's current Temporary Foreign Worker Program (TFWP) was creat-ed in 2002, though Canadian history of indentured migrant labor is longer. Two of the most significant programs within the TFWP are the Seasonal Agricul-tural Worker Program (SAWP) and the Caregiver Program, tying farmworkers and domestic workers, respectively, to an employer. Since 2002, the number of migrant workers entering Canada has almost quadrupled. In 2019, as many as 98,335 migrant workers, approximately 18 percent of whom were women, en-tered under the TFWP.[3] Although TFWP streams exist for higher-paid work-ers, the majority of TFWP arrivals are migrant workers in low-wage sectors. Successive governments have justified the TFWP as a response to short-term labor shortages, but, in reality, there are, as Nandita Sharma puts it, "shortages of cheapened and politically subjugated labour power."[4]

Migrant workers in Canada do some of the most dangerous jobs that form the backbone of the economy. From the agricultural sector to resource extraction to construction work, migrant workers are forced to handle toxic pesticides, dig open-pit mines, and dangle from skyscrapers to maintain accu-mulation in a settler-colonial economy. While no official statistics are kept on migrant workers' deaths, a number of fatalities have been recorded, including the deaths of three Mexican migrant farmworkers in the province of Ontario during the first few months of the Covid-19 pandemic.[5] Justice for Migrant Workers estimates that thirty-three migrant farmworkers have died over one decade in that province alone.[6] On Ontario's farms, the unrelenting deaths of Jamaican farmworkers have propelled the demand for mandatory inquests. In 2002, Ned Peart was crushed to death on a tobacco farm, Paul Roach and Ralston White collapsed in a giant tank filled with toxic fumes on an apple farm in 2010, and Omar Graham was fatally injured when the pickup truck and trailer pack he was driving flipped off the road in 2011. In the province of Alberta, the toxic tar sands, the world's largest energy project and Canada's largest source of industrial greenhouse gas emissions, is poisoning Indigenous people and their lands as well as killing migrant workers. In 2007, four mi-grant workers were critically injured and two migrant workers from China, Genbao Ge and Hongliang Lui, died when a storage tank roof collapsed on them at a tar sands industrial site. Fifty-three workplace charges were laid but the companies got away with pleading guilty to only three charges. In a single year in Alberta, more than eight hundred complaints were made by migrant workers regarding working conditions and safety concerns.[7]

Despite its name and Canada's justification for it, there is nothing temporary about the TFWP. The naming of workers as "temporary foreign workers" ideologically removes them from the nation-state. Migrant workers are also spatially isolated from other workers, materially denied the same fundamental rights and social benefits afforded to citizens, and considered interlopers even though migrant workers labor and live for years alongside citizens. While pathways to citizenship exist in some sectors, scores of farmworkers have been toiling on Canadian farms for decades. Even after their tenth year in Canada, only 2 percent of SAWP workers can become permanent residents.[8] Forced rotation is, as Sharma argues, "less about restricting access to the territory of the national state than about differentiating those within it while obfuscating the source of the discrimination faced by workers named as foreigners."[9]

Like in the kafala system, the TFWP work permit is tied to an employer or a sector. While the degrees of abuse may differ between the kafala and the TFWP, their structures and racial logics are similar. Chris Ramsaroop describes Canada's migrant worker program as "an apartheid system," where Black and brown migrant workers whose ancestors endured enslavement and indentureship are now similarly forced to endure a different set of legal and social rights than Canadian workers.[10] Ramsaroop co-organizes Harvesting Freedom, an annual 1,500-kilometer caravan through the fields and farms of southern Ontario raising awareness about the plight of migrant farmworkers and demanding full labor rights and permanent immigration status. Migrant workers under the TWFP are forced to work long hours with no overtime pay, excluded from basic rights such as minimum wage regulations, controlled through curfews and prohibitions on leisure activities, subjected to physical violence, and crammed and surveilled in employer-provided housing. Between 2009 and 2019, Mexican migrant farmworkers in Canada filed 3,100 complaints with the Mexican Secretariat of Labor, with 1,245 of those complaints being about unsafe and inadequate housing, including accommodations filled with rats, snakes, bedbugs, broken amenities, and overflowing fecal matter.[11] These conditions are not limited to a few bad employers, as is often portrayed by the mainstream media. The program is designed to keep workers in abject living and working conditions, and their compliance is coerced by dangling the threats of termination, deportation, and blacklisting. Syed Hussan estimates each migrant farmworker and each domestic worker is robbed of twenty thousand and ten thousand dollars, respectively, in unpaid wages at the end of their two-year contract, illustrative of an enhanced system of accumulation built on extreme labor discipline and bordered exclusion.[12]

Myth of Multicultural Canada

A fantasy of inclusion is a technique of exclusion.
—Sara Ahmed, *Living a Feminist Life*

Canadian liberalism, peacekeeping, and multiculturalism are praised around the world. Contrary to this popular perception, the country exports violence, not generosity. Perfected Canadian technologies of racial settler state formation, imperial expansion, and labor precarity serve as international blueprints. Canada's model of spatial confinement of Indigenous people through the reserve and pass system was adopted by apartheid South Africa and later imported by Israel. Canada also spearheaded the imperialist UN "Responsibility to Protect" doctrine, which legalizes diplomatic, financial, and military state intervention of UN member states into sovereign countries. The doctrine, an updated version of the old concept of humanitarian imperialism and the white man's burden, was mobilized to justify the coup against President Jean-Bertrand Aristide in Haiti in 2004 and NATO attacks on Libya in 2011.[13] Critical to our discussion about migrant workers, the TFWP has emerged as the global prototype for labor migration. The antecedents for this program can be traced back to the late 1800s, when fifteen thousand Chinese men were brought to Canada to construct the country's first transcontinental railroad. The workers endured low wages and deadly conditions, including landslides and explosions, that killed one worker for every mile of track laid through the Rocky Mountains.[14] Today, as states contend with irregular migration, Canada's TFWP—built upon this legacy of exploiting disposable migrant labor—is considered a model of "managed migration." Western states consider the Canadian SAWP a best practice for agricultural workers, and the Caregiver Program has been declared the world's "Rolls Royce" of migrant labor programs.[15] Declarations of Canadian multiculturalism work to effectively mask the reality of this commodified inclusion within sustained racial-capitalist governance.

The foundation of current Canadian migrant worker programs lies in the Caribbean Domestic Scheme of the 1950s and the Commonwealth Caribbean SAWP of the 1960s. Based on racist assumptions about Black women's proclivity for domestic work, the Caribbean Domestic Scheme was established between Canada, Barbados, and Jamaica in 1955. Single women with no children could become domestic workers and apply for landed immigrant status after one year of live-in work but were subjected to gendered anti-Black controls, including invasive medical examinations and deportation if they became pregnant in

Canada, demonstrating, as Christina Sharpe points out, how "slavery's violences emerge within the contemporary conditions of spatial, legal, psychic, material and other dimensions of Black non/being."[16] The Commonwealth Caribbean SAWP established Canada's first official migrant agricultural worker program. Thousands of farmworkers came primarily from Jamaica, Trinidad and Tobago, and Barbados. Operational guidelines included a stipulation that Canada would provide Caribbean countries with a priority list of specifically named workers and their arrival dates as required by the employer.[17] Like the kafala, immigration enforcement was downloaded onto individual employers, who selected and surveilled workers. This continues today; farmworkers are disciplined through the prospect of employer selection for return.

Through the Caribbean SAWP, employers also controlled the totality of workers' lives through a carceral regime, including curfews, bans on telephones and television, and limiting mobility off the farm.[18] Robyn Maynard stresses that "the very inception of these worker programs was informed by the devaluation of Black life and labour under slavery," which she argues are "an extension and consolidation of Jim Crow-style labour practices in Canada."[19] Even after slavery was abolished, the persistence of anti-Black racism meant that at least 80 percent of Black women in Canadian cities were domestic workers.[20] Similarly, attempts in the US to control predominantly Black workers in agricultural and domestic work, and the exclusion of those sectors from federal labor protections during the New Deal era, reflected an extension of the plantation economy and, drawing on Katherine McKittrick, geographies of "black displacement, black placelessness, black labor, and a black population that submissively stays 'in place.'"[21]

Canadian multiculturalism glosses over such histories of racial capitalism and continuities of violence. Rinaldo Walcott argues that the emphasis in multicultural discourse on culture, ethnicity, and heritage "strategically denies a longer Black presence in this country," with Black people in Canada "an absented presence always under erasure" despite the continuous profiling and punishment of Black life since slavery in the early 1600s.[22] Official multiculturalism positions diverse racialized communities as "distinct cultures" yet problematically homogenizes them as "immigrants." The flattening and depoliticization of racism into culture and diversity discussions evades an interrogation of the specific dynamics of empire, class, caste, cisheteropatriarchy, anti-Blackness, and Islamophobia within heterogenous immigrant communities.

State discourses of multiculturalism also collapse diverse Indigenous nations into grammars of culture and ethnicity, reproducing what Jodi Byrd calls a "historical aphasia of the conquest."[23] In the early 1900s, immigration was an unconcealed expression of conquest; the Canadian immigration department was called the Department of Immigration and Colonization. Today, despite state claims of reconciliation, as Glen Coulthard argues, Indigenous land dispossession is still the dominant structure enabling Canadian state formation.[24] There are almost 2,300 reserves in Canada, but they are small, fragmented, chronically underfunded, and account for only 0.28 percent of the land base.[25] This settler occupation, like settler-colonial states elsewhere, is built through genocide, dispossession from land, deliberate impoverishment, forced dependency, and quotidian oppression,[26] and it forms the backdrop for white settlers today to position themselves as hosts—literally and metaphorically on top of Indigenous nations—to "welcome" racialized immigrants into Canadian multiculturalism.

Canada was the first country in the world to adopt multiculturalism as government policy. Declared in 1971, it was presented as turning the page on explicitly race-based immigration exclusions, such as the Chinese Exclusion Act, Japanese Canadian internment, regulations barring Black migration, the Continuous Journey law prohibiting migration from South Asia, and the turning back of Jewish refugees fleeing Nazi Germany. These were not singular incidents; explicit references to "preferred nationalities and races" in immigration policy until 1967 meant that in 1961, as much as 95 percent of immigrants were from Europe or the US, and as late as 1981, at least 86 percent of the Canadian population was of European origin.[27] Canada's policy of multiculturalism, however, has not altered these relations of white settler racial power. Sunera Thobani writes that state multiculturalism facilitates "a material inclusion of increased numbers of immigrants within the population and their simultaneous exclusion from the nation, primarily through their reification as cultural outsiders."[28] Culture—sometimes celebrated through festivals but mostly scrutinized—becomes the "primary modality for mediating relations among nationals, immigrants, and the state."[29]

White anxieties about "cultural difference" and "excessive diversity" are especially heightened since 9/11 with anti-Muslim violence, adjoined to anti-migrant xenophobia, on the rise. During the past two decades in Canada, Muslim refugees and permanent residents have been detained on spurious security certificates, a killer shot people after evening prayers in a Quebec City mosque, and refugee housing buildings were targeted in arson attacks. A law was implemented in Quebec in 2019 banning public workers from wearing religious symbols and requiring women to uncover their faces to receive certain public services. In the same year, a nationwide poll found that 40 percent of Canadians believe not only that immigration is too high, but that specifically *non-white* immigration is too high.[30] Between 2015 and 2019, the number of far-right groups roughly doubled.[31]

Notably, multiculturalism was proclaimed two years before migrant worker programs were implemented through the Non-immigrant Employment Authorization Program of 1973, giving workers temporary residency contingent on their employment. Multiculturalism worked in tandem with migrant worker programs to reinforce the ideological "foreignness" of all racialized people, which justified the heightened exclusions of migrant workers. This also solidified the association between immigration and labor and, more specifically, between racialized temporary migrants and low-wage work. Sedef Arat-Koç argues that "just when Canada started to define itself as 'multicultural,' it developed policies which defined some groups of immigrants as 'workers only,' disposable non-members who, despite their contributions, are given no acknowledged part in the 'nation' or 'nation-building' project."[32] Despite the enduring yet false myth of Canada as a "country of immigrants," Canada has admitted more temporary migrant workers than permanent residents since 2006.[33] Multiculturalism therefore cements white settler coloniality and racial-capitalist political economies by managing racialized communities and capturing migrant labor.

Seasonal Agricultural Worker Program

> *We come here with closed work permits that tie us to a farmer. What happens when we speak out? We get deported. It's a recipe for exploitation, it's 18th century conditions.*
>
> —Gabriel Allahdua, quoted in Harvesting Freedom, "Migrant Farmworkers Travel 1500km to Demand Permanent Residency in Canada on 50th Anniversary of Farmworker Program"

Farmworkers entering Canada through the SAWP make up the largest proportion of workers in the TFWP. Every year, more than thirty thousand migrant farmworkers from the Caribbean, Central America, and Mexico come to Canada annually for a maximum of eight months per year, but they can be selected by employers to return without limit. Two private sector farm owner organizations work directly with the federal immigration department and provincial labor ministries to process worker requests from employers and administer operations for the SAWP. Agribusiness interests wield enormous influence over immigration policy to meet their needs of "flexible labour with reductions in regular farm employment, an extension of growing/harvesting seasons, a move away from on-farm employment, deepening gender and racial segmentation, and the intensification of work."[34] Because of the power of this lobby, farmworkers are excluded from many labor protections, including health and safety regulations. Working in concert with the state, agribusiness corporate interests have also secured successive reservoirs of racialized low-wage workers, including Chinese Canadian workers, interned Japanese Canadians, and Indigenous people, who all toiled on Canadian farms and fields prior to the heavy reliance on labor migration programs. Kerry Preibisch maintains that "state policy has played a key role in enhancing flexibility within the labour market for farm and food industry workers by increasing the availability of migrants, by granting access to the global labour market to a wider range of agribusinesses, and by broadening the global pool of labor reserves."[35]

The most striking example of the commodification and expendability of migrant farmworkers is medical deportation. Racist and ableist, the medical deportation of workers unable to continue working due to health conditions is ubiquitous and casts Canada's renowned reputation as a provider of universal healthcare in a different light. Take the situation of Sheldon McKenzie, a Jamaican man who had been going to Canadian farms for twelve years. He was working on a farm in Leamington—Canada's tomato capital—when he sustained a severe injury in January 2015, leaving him in a coma. While on life support, he was stripped of his work visa and healthcare coverage as officials attempted to deport him. Only after McKenzie's cousin, Marcia Barrett, launched an advocacy campaign was his deportation temporarily delayed. He passed away shortly after, in September 2015, leaving behind his wife and daughters. In a study of farmworkers in just one province, researchers documented 787 medical repatriations between 2001 and 2011.[36] The most frequent grounds for repatriation were external injuries, including poisoning, and surgical reasons. Since all farmworkers already undergo extensive medical examinations before arrival—another capitalist and ableist feature of the program—most of the health conditions resulting in medical deportation are not preexisting, as employers often try to argue, but rather develop over the course of working and living in Canada. As Barrett candidly told media, "It's worse than slavery—they dispose of them."[37]

Further illustrating the connection between capitalist wealth hoarding and migrant worker exploitation is the case of Golden Eagle Farms, a SAWP employer owned by the Aquilini family in the province of British Columbia. With an estimated net worth of $3.6 billion, the Aquilinis are one of the country's wealthiest families; one of their many assets is the Canucks hockey team. Canada is not a redistributive utopia; the Aquilinis and nine other billionaire families in the province have a combined net worth of $24.9 billion, equal to the total worth of a whopping 1.3 million poor and low-income people in the province.[38] The obscene wealth of the Aquilinis exists alongside the exploitation and impoverishment of workers on their farms. In fact, all of Canada's richest CEOs make more in one day than an average worker earns in one full year.[39] This is not a coincidence; rather, it is the consequence of capitalism, a trickle-up system extracting and exploiting the labor of the many to enrich the few. Samir Amin elucidates, "The specific logic of the fundamental laws that govern the expansion of capitalism leads to a growing inequality and asymmetry on a global level."[40]

For more than fifteen years, Golden Eagle Farms has been a site of migrant worker strikes and lawsuits. In 2006, a group of thirty-two Mexican farmworkers organized a wildcat strike and issued an open letter detailing grave injustices:

> There is only one bathroom which is full of excrement, in other words when we have to do our physiological necessities (i.e., go to the bathroom) we have to go in the open. This is an embarrassing situation and risky for us. For this reason some of the workers are sick with diarrhea, nevertheless the worst part is that they do not give us medicine and they don't take us to the doctor because the supervisors say that we do not have the right to medical service.[41]

In 2011, the Aquilinis were fined $125,402 for failing to maintain basic safety standards for migrant workers on one of their farms, including failing to provide accessible first aid for workers, failing to take necessary precautions to prevent injuries, and failing to keep farm vehicles in safe operating condition.[42]

In 2019, a group of 174 farmworkers from Guatemala at Golden Eagle Farms won $133,632.56 in back wages, vacation pay, and overtime. Heartened by the decision in their favor, some of the women in the group spoke publicly about the appalling work and living conditions they endured. They described ninety-eight women crammed into two houses with inadequate appliances or showers, working in the freezer area for fifteen hours a day without warm clothing, workplace injuries with no first aid or medical attention, being denied water breaks during the long summer months, managers and supervisors entering the accommodations at night, and being threatened with termination and deportation.[43] The senior vice president of the Aquilini Investment Group, Jim Chu, who is—in an Orwellian turn—also Vancouver's former police chief, launched a media smear campaign suggesting the complaints were an attempt to extort the company. Even though they face public hostility, legislated restrictions on unionization, and the threat of deportation, migrant workers like those toiling on Golden Eagle Farms remain on the front line of labor organizing.

Caregiver Program

> [M]y employer, sometimes when he gets drunk, is like he wanted to use me sexually. And then the wife is treating me like garbage. I wasn't safe at all in this house.
> —Phyllis, quoted in Care Givers' Action Centre and Migrant Workers Alliance for Change, *Care Worker Voices for Landed Status and Fairness*

In *Care Worker Voices for Landed Status and Fairness*, an unprecedented 2018 report convening care workers across Canada, workers like Phyllis describe working an average of ten hours a day, fifty-four hours a week, without overtime or vacation pay.[44] They also endure substandard housing, sexual violence, dangerous work, forced family separation, and being tied to employers. According to the report, this pervasive exploitation is "rooted in the vulnerability that is created by the terms of Canada's temporary labour migration programs."[45]

Racial state formation and racial capitalism has played a vital role in influencing the design of domestic worker programs. Genocidal residential schools trained Indigenous girls in domestic work, forcibly sending them to white settler homes as child laborers. The majority of enslaved Black women were also forced to labor in the homes of white settlers.[46] Migrant domestic workers were first recruited from the UK in the early 1900s. Single, working-class British women worked for six months as live-in caregivers in the homes of upper-class, white Canadian women. Regarded as "daughters of the empire" and "mothers of the race," white British domestic workers were readily granted immigration status.[47] This stood in contrast to the way Black migrant domestic workers, who arrived from the British-ruled Caribbean between the 1910s and 1930s, and then under the Caribbean Domestic Scheme after World War II, were treated. Women from the Caribbean were subjected to invasive gynecological examinations and pregnancy tests, could only apply for immigration status after a year of live-in work, and were paid substantially less than British and other European domestic workers.[48]

The 1950s and 1960s marked a shift toward a distinctly racialized workforce of domestic workers, coinciding with a global shift in the chains of care work. The Canadian government then became overwhelmed by the prospect of Caribbean domestic workers sponsoring their family members—"a West Indian sponsorship explosion" as one immigration officer put it—and drastically shifted the program.[49] The Temporary Employment Authorization Program was launched in 1973, providing temporary visas to caregivers, who could remain in Canada only as long as they were employed as domestic workers. The temporary visas could be renewed, but workers were not allowed to remain as permanent immigrants.[50] This program also entrenched care work as a so-called low-skill category in immigration policy, solidifying the treatment of migrant domestic workers as "cheap, exploitable and expendable."[51] This happened, not accidentally, shortly after explicitly racist categories of "preferred" races and nationalities were removed from policy and, instead, a point system established for "high-skilled" professionals in a nod to neoliberal multiculturalism. Immigration restrictions and conditions of unfree labor were shifted onto low-wage migrant workers, exploitable through temporary labor programs. A key restriction was the bar on permanent immigration for domestic workers with spouses and children. In 1977, Canada wanted to deport a group of domestic workers who had allegedly misrepresented their family status. The struggle of the seven Jamaican mothers brought together domestic workers and community groups to counter this racialized gendered discrimination with the slogan of "Good enough to work, good enough to stay."[52]

In response to this wave of organizing, led nationally by the organization Intercede, the Foreign Domestic Movement program was established in 1981, and all domestic workers became eligible for permanent residency after two years of domestic work—but only after being evaluated on their "suitability" to live in Canada.[53] The live-in requirement, indenturing workers not only to an employer but also to their home, was another key condition, and it was maintained under the subsequent Live-In Caregiver Program until the new Caregiver Program in 2014, under which mostly Filipina and Indonesian migrant caregivers arrive to Canada.[54] The live-in aspect is intensely abusive. Workers participating in a community report by the Filipino Women's Organization in Quebec described how they could not use fans or the internet, lock their rooms, entertain visitors, or leave the home when not working. Almost all workers reported privacy invasions by employers, who would enter their rooms without notice. The live-in requirement also blurs the boundaries of work duties, and all workers reported performing additional responsibilities and working sixteen hours a day at an average of six dollars an hour. As one caregiver put it, "I became a dog with a leash to my employer."[55] Now, as a result of grassroots advocacy and changes to the Caregiver Program, caregivers can live in the employer's home only if the employer and worker both agree. Consent, though, is constrained by a huge imbalance of power. As Audrey Macklin summarizes, "The domestic worker is admitted into Canada but barred from political membership, employed in a workplace but often excluded from worker-protection laws, resident in a household but not a part of the family."[56]

Even though they are some of the most precarious workers and marginalized immigrants in Canada, migrant caregivers have been leading struggles ever since the movement of the seven Jamaican mothers. The Juana Tejada Law was named in honor of Filipina caregiver Juana Tejada, who developed cancer in Canada and was deemed inadmissible as a permanent resident. She then led a valiant, and ultimately victorious, fight to scrap medical admissibility regulations until her dying breath in 2009. In 2014, migrant domestic workers won the elimination of the abusive live-in requirement. In 2019, they successfully forced the government to allow caregivers to bring their families to Canada, have open work permits not tied to an employer, and pursue a pathway to permanent residency. Kara Manso lays out the uncompromising vision of migrant caregivers who refuse to express gratitude for the pittances of multiculturalism and temporary migration and, instead, assert their right to permanently live and labor with dignity. As Manso says, "It's a tremendous victory and testament to our organizing and it's not enough. Migrant care workers take care of families, and have been for centuries, this is a permanent program with a permanent solution and that means permanent resident status upon arrival for future workers, and full immigration status for all migrant workers."[57]

PART 4

Making Race,
Mobilizing Racist Nationalisms

CHAPTER 10

Mapping the Global Far Right
and the Crisis of Statelessness

*Oh true, crises like this one don't come alone. They are accompanied by all
the acrobats of history: prophets, leaders, supreme saviors, new religions,
the "change begins with oneself." The "help yourself and I will help you."
The "think positively." The "Smile we're gonna win." The "We will be your
worst nightmare."*

—Subcomandante Galeano, "The Method, the Bibliography, and a
Drone Deep in the Mountains of the Mexican Southeast"

Networks among the nationalist far right are, perhaps paradoxically, increasingly transnational. Brexit cheerleader Nigel Farage appeared at
a Trump rally in 2016, former executive chairperson of Breitbart News Steve
Bannon became the cochair of the Republican Hindu Coalition in 2019, President Jair Bolsonaro in Brazil was the guest of honor at India's Republic Day
celebration hosted by Prime Minister Narendra Modi in 2020, and the Christchurch shooter as well as Norwegian killer Anders Breivik both glorified the
Bosnian Serb army's ethnic cleansing of Bosnian Muslims and the creation
of the ethnostate Republika Srpska. Contrary to the myth of the lone wolf,
one-third of white supremacist killers around the world were inspired by and
connected to one of the other 350 white supremacist attacks in recent years.[1]
The Ukrainian Azov movement, for example, has furtively turned Kiev into
a capital for the far right, actively training neo-Nazis from all corners of the

world. Azov has recruited tens of thousands of people into a parallel fascist state with its own political party, social infrastructure, paramilitary street force, and military wing. Created in 2014 to fight in a US proxy war against pro-Russian forces, the Azov Battalion is a Ukrainian National Guard regiment and the world's only overt neo-Nazi militia integrated into a military. On an electoral level, Lega Nord in Italy, the Rassemblement National (formerly known as the Front National) in France, Alternative für Deutschland in Germany, and the Party for Freedom in the Netherlands are leading an effort toward a unified far-right bloc in the European Parliament. Former Canadian prime minister Stephen Harper heads the International Democratic Union, the largest global alliance of its kind with eighty right-wing parties.

In the US, white supremacists account for 71 percent of civilian terror attacks, and all mass shooters are men, most with a known history of misogynist violence.[2] While their misogyny is often noted in circulating commentary, the dominant narrative of intimate violence as a "gateway" to mass violence problematically relegates gendered violence to the individual sphere. Confronting racism and patriarchy must go beyond an analysis of personal traits; rather, gendered violence and racial violence, and their interconnections, are always mass structural violences. Such oppressions, and the ideologies that justify them, are the basis for the rise of the far right. The far right is an intersectional oppressor, driven by a rapacious hate of many. And while far-right forces are not fully united, with their own conflicts and contradictions, their ideological synergies point toward escalating social warfare. One unifying narrative is the anti-Semitic conspiracy theory of "cultural Marxism," upon which the Christchurch killer, Chabad of Poway synagogue shooter John Earnest, and Breivik all hinged their hatred. A ubiquitous reference in online spaces and legitimized in intellectual circles by the likes of Jordan Peterson, it is alt-right code for the destruction of civilization by feminists, atheists, Jews, multiculturalists, communists, and queers.

Preoccupied by a restrictionist agenda of family values and gender roles, the far right also loathes access to abortion, legalization of same-sex marriage, and trans and queer liberation. An alliance exists between many trans-exclusionary feminists (TERFs) and the far right, with both sharing biologically determinist ideologies of gender. Just as white supremacists hide behind "race science," TERFs disguise their oppression using the myth of "gender ideology." Upholding the gender binary synergizes with ethnonationalist discourses positioning the nation-state as a "family," simultaneously reproducing racism, heteropatriarchy, and transmisogyny. Free speech is another coalescing mantra, even though the "crisis of free speech" is a self-victimizing strawman, as left-wing academics are purged from campuses, Zionists routinely censor Boycott, Divestment, and Sanctions (BDS) activities, corporate conglomerates control mainstream media, millions are disenfranchised from the political system, and private property rights trump the right to dissent. Further, intolerant speech without consequence is not an inalienable legal right. Aleksandar Hemon surmises, "The practice of fascism supersedes its ideas, which is why people affected and diminished by it are not all that interested in a marketplace of ideas in which fascists have prime purchasing power."[3]

Of particular interest to us here is the dogma of racial citizenship, yet another unifying issue among the far right. This chapter investigates some of the world's most threatening far-right governments who are working to entrench the ideology of racial citizenship, including its escalation to the legal stripping of citizenship. Far-right demagogues have arisen out of the failures of neoliberalism and overcome the legitimacy crisis of the ruling classes by offering authoritarian visions and xenophobic solutions. Even though far-right populism engages the working class by decrying the lack of democracy under liberal elitism, far-right demagogues present themselves as authoritarian saviors, providing stability and reestablishing social hierarchies. As I explore here, leaders in the US, India, Israel, the Philippines, Brazil, and across Europe draw on a range of interlocking ideologies such as ethnonationalism, penal populism, welfare nationalism, and imperial gendered racism to maintain a hierarchical social order. For the sake of focus, I have briefly mapped these tendencies separately, but they are overlapping phenomena. We typically understand these far-right ideologies to converge around "nativism," which is xenophobia targeting immigrants. However, as the examples below reveal, the real dividing line is *the social organization of difference* and the political, economic, and spatial processes by which race and class are reproduced. Legal but subjugated citizens from Muslim, Dalit, Indigenous, Black, Roma, and urban poor communities are characterized as "undesirables" and "aliens," just as migrants are, and all of them suffer attacks from the far right.

In some cases, an escalation to the legal disenfranchisement of citizens has occurred, turning people into stateless migrants in their own places of birth. State-defined racial citizenship is the fulcrum of racist nationalism, and the last section offers sketches of the systematic exclusion and deliberately manufactured statelessness of millions of Muslim Indians of Bengali origin, Rohingya in Myanmar, people of Haitian descent in the Dominican Republic, and Bidoon in the Arab Gulf region. Race and the nation, Paul Gilroy argues, are "now primary sources of groupness and absolute ethnicity."[4] The frightening process of turning legal citizens into either othered subjects or stateless noncitizens is as essential to producing racist nationalism as the expulsion of migrants. To end anti-migrant xenophobia, criminalization of migrants through detention and deportation, and migrant worker exploitation, we must dismantle the wider structure of racial social violence upholding exclusionary citizenship.

White Nationalism, Zionism, Hindutva: Ethnonationalist Bedfellows

The most dangerous alliance in the world today exists between US president Donald Trump, Israeli prime minister Benjamin Netanyahu, and Indian prime minister Narendra Modi, each of whom controls some of the world's largest and most powerful militaries. The US is one of India's main arms suppliers and the two countries conduct joint military exercises; Israel is the largest recipient of US military aid; and India is the largest importer of Israeli arms, with the two countries collaborating in developing military technologies.[5] Israeli and Indian lobby groups in the US are solidifying their geopolitical interests through alliances between the American Israel Public Affairs Committee and the United States India Political Action Committee. Especially since 9/11, the US, Israel, and India have framed their geopolitical expansions as part of the global war on terror, secured their borders with more than 5,700 kilometers of walls, and implemented antiterror legislation with broad powers of surveillance and detention to maintain racial repression.[6]

The ideologies of these three figureheads are celebrated throughout far-right networks as well as cemented in state policy. The manifesto of the El Paso shooter took up Trump's xenophobic description of a "Hispanic invasion," and Breivik praised India's Bharatiya Janata Party (BJP) in his rambling manifesto. Meanwhile Trump's Muslim ban has barred at least 42,650 people from entering the US, Netanyahu has approved thousands of new Jewish-only settlements in the occupied West Bank, and Modi has annexed Indian-occupied Kashmir.[7] Trump, Netanyahu, and Modi all peddle their poison—white nationalism, Zionism, and Hindutva—congealed in anti-Muslim racism. Trump has routinely tweeted about "a Muslim problem"; Netanyahu formed an electoral alliance with Otzma Yehudit, a brazenly anti-Arab party linked to Meir

Kahane's terrorist organization that calls for ethnic cleansing; and Modi has openly declared war on Muslims.

White nationalism in the US is vehemently anti-Semitic and racist, so the far-right embrace of Zionist Israel and Hindutva India may seem contradictory. Synagogues and temples are frequent sites of racist attacks, and anti-Semitic conspiracies are a theoretical linchpin of white nationalism.[8] Ethnonationalism and demographic racism explain this paradox. Days after Nazis marched on Charlottesville in August 2017, white supremacist leader Richard Spencer appeared on Israeli TV and called himself "a white Zionist" securing a white homeland.[9] Ethnonationalist states such as Israel, founded on violent dispossession and separation, serve as models for white power organizations. Further, the Zionist idealization of an exclusive Jewish state is not contradictory to and is, in fact, buoyed by the anti-Semitic ideology of white Christian fanaticism calling for the expulsion and containment of Jews elsewhere.

Many Zionist organizations in the US are often willing to portray Palestinian resistance and BDS campaigns—and not actual white supremacists—as anti-Semitic. Wendy Elisheva Somerson writes, "While spreading anti-Semitic myths and allying with actual anti-Semites, the Israeli government keeps insisting that anti-Zionists are the ones forwarding anti-Semitism."[10] To manage opposition to Israeli apartheid, the International Holocaust Remembrance Alliance has proposed a definition of anti-Semitism conflating legitimate criticisms of Israel with anti-Semitism. This flawed definition has been adopted by the US, Canada, and EU countries at the urging of Netanyahu. At the same time, in order to secure economic deals to militarize Hungary's border, Netanyahu has dismissed the real anti-Semitism of Viktor Orbán's praise for Hitler's ally Miklós Horthy. In the US, the Republican Jewish Coalition and the Israeli ambassador both defended the appointment of Bannon as Trump's chief strategist. Regarding Trump's own comments about Jews' "disloyalty," echoing anti-Semitic charges of Jewish dual loyalty, Israel lobby groups were largely quiet.[11]

Just as white nationalists can malign Jews but exalt a powerful ethnonationalist Zionist state, Hindutva forces can harm Muslims but align with the authoritative states of the Gulf Cooperation Council (GCC). The GCC is India's largest regional bloc trading partner and primary source of imported oil. Despite Modi's unambiguous Islamophobia, he has been conferred both the United Arab Emirates (UAE) and Saudi Arabia's highest civilian honors for deepening economic ties with the GCC. Modi is, after all, one of the world's most business-friendly politicians, with a ruthless agenda of deregulation, private investment in the manufacturing and agricultural sectors, corporate subsidies, and regressive taxation. Hindutva forces also find common cause with Nazism. Early Hindutva fascist leaders, like M. S. Golwalkar, justified Nazi genocide and lionized Hitler for maintaining "racial purity," an obsession for *savarna* (caste) Hindus, and there are now a growing number of Hindu Nazis. Textbooks used in the state of Gujarat, under the rule of then–chief minister Modi, have also glorified Hitler. For their part, many white supremacists propagate the theory of ancient "Aryans" conquering and settling in what is now northern India to form a Hindu Rashtra. Given strict caste and religious endogamy, these Nazis declare Brahmins to be descendants of the Aryan race, claiming that white nationalism and Hindutva share the same lineage.[12]

While the current reign of Trump, Netanyahu, and Modi brings venomous violence to the fore, all three states were founded on ethnonationalist violence. Having discussed US and Israeli state formation in earlier chapters, I focus here on Hindutva fascism, dating back to the founding of the Rashtriya Swayamsevak Sangh (RSS) in 1925. Openly advocating for a Hindu Rashtra, the RSS is the world's largest voluntary paramilitary organization, comprised of six million members.[13] Like Zionism, Hindutva is a political ethnonationalist ideology, propagating Hindu brahminical domination and expansion to justify violence against Muslims, Sikhs, Christians, Adivasis, and Dalits. With Hindutva now enshrined as state policy under Modi, at least 1,092 violent incidents, including lynchings and horrifying assaults by vigilantes and cow-protection mobs, have unleashed terror since 2014, especially upon Muslims and Dalits.[14] Modi has openly provoked violence against Muslims and stoked a growing far-right Hindutva base, culminating in both legislated state violence and state-sanctioned vigilante violence.[15] In one of the worst outbreaks of violent carnage in the country's capital in decades, fifty-three mostly Muslim people were killed, mosques were burned, and Muslim neighborhoods were ransacked and vandalized by armed Hindu supremacist goons, many carrying saffron flags, as police watched on and BJP politicians incited hatred with anti-Muslim provocations, such as "Desh ke gaddaron ko, goli maaro saalon ko" (traitors of the nation, shoot them).[16] This targeted violence in early 2020 came on the heels of Muslim women mobilizing against new BJP laws implementing mass population registration, the political disenfranchisement of Muslims, and the exclusion of Muslim migrants and refugees from citizenship, described in this chapter's last section. A few months later, the coronavirus pandemic became a pretext to further anti-

Muslim racism, with Islamophobic propaganda about "Coronajihad" spurring boycotts of Muslim businesses and prohibitions on Muslims entering villages.[17]

Casteism is another foundational system of power upholding Hindutva violence, and India, renowned as the world's largest democracy, was a site of immense repression well before Modi or even the British raj. The hereditary and hierarchical caste system is centuries old and a quotidian marker of apartheid in Indian life. British colonialism strengthened brahminical oppression, which endured in the post-1947 Indian state. Dalit leader and scholar Dr. B. R. Ambedkar critiqued the preservation of caste in the Indian independence struggle, challenging what freedom would truly mean in a society so completely structured by caste violence.[18] His words ring true in India today, with the country's richest 10 percent of brahmin households holding 60 percent of all wealth.[19] A violence encompassing the totality of life, caste-oppressed people are compelled to wear caste-specific attire; forced to perform jobs as manual scavengers and clean human filth with their bare hands; abandoned by local administrators in the provision of basic services, such as electricity and sanitation; denied access to cultivate land or draw water; refused entry into upper-caste homes and temples; required to eat and live in separate and segregated areas; and are subjected to daily beatings, humiliation, rape, butchery, and barbaric murder by upper-caste savarnas.

Also present among non-Hindus, casteism is most pronounced as a staple of Hinduism through its rituals of purity and pollution, and it is exported into the diaspora through migration. In a watershed report on caste in the US, a majority of Dalit people said they were subjected to casteist discrimination and violence.[20] Like Zionism, casteist and Islamophobic Hindutva is ideologically propped up beyond India. One of the main propagandists of Hindutva abroad is a far-right Flemish publisher, Koenraad Elst.[21] Vishwa Hindu Parishad, a militant Hindutva organization, is another international front; it has been operating in the US since the 1970s and has branches in Canada, Australia, and Germany. These fundamentalist fronts funnel millions of saffron dollars into Hinduization projects and Hindutva election campaigns in India.[22] International phenomena such as "Overseas Friends of BJP" or "Hindus for Trump" are best explained through the prism of Hindutva's brahminical supremacy and adjoining Islamophobia, rather than typical explanations of whitewashed, model minorities or upward class mobility; savarna caste supremacy and Islamophobia tether but are not synonymous with these symptoms.

The ruling class ideology of India has consistently combined the deadly potion of casteism, religious chauvinism, and colonialism. Since Indian state formation in 1947, minoritized communities have been repressed all over the country, and not a year has passed without the deployment of armed forces. Arundhati Roy captures this consummate state violence: "Almost from the moment India became a sovereign nation, it turned into a colonial power, annexing territory, waging war."[23] Most noticeable is the six-decade-long Indian imposition of the Armed Forces Special Powers Act (AFSPA) in the northeastern region, where secessionist movements have opposed forced integration into India and domination by the central government. Based on a pre-independence British ordinance, the AFSPA grants de facto and de jure immunity to state forces engaging in torture and extrajudicial killings in militarized regions, such as the northeast. After the Malom Massacre in Manipur in 2000, during which ten civilians were ruthlessly shot and killed at a bus stop by the Indian paramilitary force Assam Rifles, Irom Sharmila went on the world's longest hunger strike.[24] She refused to eat for sixteen arduous years, demanding AFSPA's repeal while being force-fed through a nasal tube in police custody, but the act remained in force. In Panjab, the AFSPA was enacted in the 1980s and 1990s as part of a counterinsurgency campaign resulting in the detention, torture, rape, execution, mass cremations, and enforced disappearances of tens of thousands of Sikhs.[25]

The war on terror augmented the rise of religious chauvinist forces and provided cover for mass state violence. In Gujarat in 2002, Modi was chief minister when two thousand Muslims were horrifically massacred, women and children raped, homes burnt down, and two hundred thousand people displaced by organized Hindu majoritarian violence and ethnic cleansing.[26] In 2009, the Indian government launched Operation Green Hunt under the guise of fighting Maoist Naxalites. In reality, the so-called Maoist heartland is also a mining heartland, with more than three hundred extractive special economic zones planned without consent on Adivasi lands. Over one-quarter of the world's Indigenous population are Adivasis living within the borders of India.[27] During Green Hunt, close to 250,000 police, armed forces, and counterinsurgency teams were deployed against Adivasi communities, vigilante groups like Salwa Judum received state support, and the US provided military intelligence.[28] An average of forty civilians were killed weekly to destabilize and dispossess Adivasi communities and push through forcible land acquisitions.[29]

India's Hindu brahmanical foundation is further solidified under Modi's vision of a Hindu Rashtra and Hindutva's imperial ambitions, similar to the hardening of existing ethnonationalist settler-colonial ambitions under Trump in the US and Netanyahu in Israel. One of Modi's most egregious moves was the illegal annexation of Kashmir, the world's most militarized zone and the largest region occupied by state security forces. In 2019, Modi unilaterally abrogated Article 370, a constitutional provision recognizing some semblance of Kashmir's semi-autonomous status. Modi also bifurcated the state of Jammu and Kashmir and placed the region's entire population in an open-air prison camp through a military siege with curfews, a communications blockade, mass arrests, and killings. Furthermore, Article 35A, empowering Kashmir's state legislature to define employment and property rights afforded only to Kashmiri permanent residents, was revoked, thereby opening Kashmir to Indians to impose economic projects and buy property—a clear project of neoliberal development and demographic settlement. For Azad Essa, the annexation paves the way for "a full settler-colonial project in Kashmir with the next stage likely to involve Hindu-only enclaves, much like Jewish settlements in the West Bank."[30] A statement from the BDS National Committee echoes these parallels: "As Palestinians, we deeply feel the suffering of the people in Kashmir under military repression that in so many cases is similar to Israeli forms of subjugation and control."[31]

The colonial annexation of Kashmir laid bare a decades-long, de facto occupation, with successive Indian governments diminishing Kashmir's autonomy and failing to honor UN resolutions calling for a plebiscite by using rhetoric referring to an "internal" Indian dispute or a "territorial" dispute with Pakistan. A specifically gendered imperial racism pervades the occupation, which Nitasha Kaul describes as "the exoticisation of Kashmir as a territory, which results in a feminisation of the Kashmiri landscape and Kashmiri bodies."[32] In the immediate aftermath of Kashmir's annexation, Indian websites were overtaken by Indians obsessed with marrying "fair" Kashmiri women and owning a slice of Kashmiri "paradise," underscoring possessive, masculinist discourses inherent to this violent conquest. Reports document at least 95,238 killings, eight thousand enforced disappearances, and one in six Kashmiris having endured torture over the past three decades as part of India's continuous efforts to quash Kashmiri resistance and independence.[33] The ruthless totality of genocidal occupation—militarization, electoral interference, extrajudicial killings, torture, unmarked graves, rapes, maiming through mass blinding, enforced disappearances, confinement, and collective punishment—is defined by Mohamad Junaid as "a triad of spatial dominance over public space, military control of everyday life, and routinized administration of violence."[34]

Alongside the colonization of Kashmir and systemic violence against minoritized communities, border fortification through walling against Pakistan
and Bangladesh has also worked to secure India's status as an imperial power.
Today, the India–Bangladesh border has the shameful honor of being the border with the highest number of deaths at the hands of an enforcement agency.[35] The culprit, the Indian Border Security Force (BSF), is also the world's
largest border security force.[36] Between 2000 and 2018, as many as 1,144 Bangladeshis were killed, 1,078 injured, 1,367 abducted, and fifteen raped by the
BSF.[37] In the first two weeks of 2020 alone, three Bangladeshis were killed by
the BSF.[38] Justifications for these lethal violations feed on vicious anti-Muslim
racism, with Muslims from Bangladesh called invaders or infiltrators, while
Hindus from Bangladesh and Nepal are referred to as refugees. The BJP has
long fixated on migration from Bangladesh, specifically asserting that *Muslim*
migration from the neighboring country is a demographic threat. The party's
national executive passed a resolution in 1992 claiming fifteen million Bangladeshis were "illegals" and constituted a security threat. Deputy Prime Minister
L. K. Advani of the ruling BJP issued a national directive in 2003 to identify
and "throw out" undocumented Bangladeshi migrants; 18,801 Bangladeshis
were deported that year.[39] Thus, like in the US and Israel, anti-migrant xenophobia in India is an extension of ethnonationalism and the dogma of imperial racial citizenship.

Penal Populism under Duterte and Bolsonaro

Penal populism is another far-right ideology solidifying the social organization of difference and reproducing racial class warfare. The far right frequently
exploits and exaggerates issues of petty crime by removing such acts from wider socioeconomic contexts and, instead, assigning blame to particular social
groups and pressuring for stricter law-and-order policies. President Rodrigo
Duterte in the Philippines and President Jair Bolsonaro in Brazil are two of
the world's most openly fascistic leaders, both coming to power after running
strict law-and-order campaigns, using brazen rhetoric of outright violence
against the urban poor, land defenders, and political dissidents. This rhetoric
is gravely real. As mayor of Davao City, a position he held for twenty-two
years, Duterte founded a police death squad that killed at least fourteen hundred petty drug dealers, journalists, and political opponents.[40] When Duterte
won the 2016 presidential election, he promised a drug war to kill every drug

dealer and user, vowing to dump their bodies in Manila Bay to "fatten the fish." Duterte's war on drugs has resulted in twenty-seven thousand deaths of mostly the urban poor, who are victims of extrajudicial killings by paid vigilantes and national police.[41] Arbitrary neighborhood drug-watch lists with up to one million names have been turned over to police to become kill lists, with police recruiting paid killers or executing people themselves.[42] One of those killed under Duterte's reign was Jerwin Rivera, a 36-year-old who organized basketball games in his neighborhood, worked part-time in construction, and was a former small-time dealer recently out of rehab. He was shot to death by over two dozen officers while playing cards at his neighbor's house.[43] For Duterte, these killings are not enough. "Hitler massacred 3 million Jews . . . there's 3 million drug addicts. There are. I'd be happy to slaughter them," he has outrageously (and erroneously) stated.[44]

David Johnson and Jon Fernquest describe Duterte's regime as one of penal populism, where overt policies of criminalization and extrajudicial executions of the urban poor, stereotyped as drug dealers, have popular support from the other classes.[45] Penal populism escalates the state's law-and-order agenda by justifying and popularizing harsh punishment and carceral institutions within society. Duterte boasts about how he would ride his motorcycle and look for people to kill, demonstrating to police forces, "If I can do it, why can't you."[46] Like the broken windows model of policing in the US but even further intensified, penal populism under Duterte targets the urban poor for criminalization to deflect from neoliberal policies that create widespread poverty and stimulate the drug trade. In 2017, Trump called Duterte to congratulate him on the "unbelievable job on the drug problem."[47] Rather than dealing with the underlying political economy of landlessness and unemployment, Duterte's regime has employed the drug war as a pretext for controlling urban poor people. The global health pandemic in 2020 provided Duterte the cover he needed to further the drug war, and he implemented a militarized curfew with orders to police and military forces to arrest and shoot any violators.[48]

Kadamay, a national alliance of the urban poor, links Duterte's drug war to attacks on landless and Indigenous communities in a cyclical process of creating and then criminalizing impoverishment. Almost half a million people were forcibly evicted from rural communities between July 2016 and December 2018, and martial law was declared in mineral-rich Mindanao in 2017, lasting more than two years.[49] On Negros Island in 2019, the armed forces and national police launched counterinsurgency operations of mass killings and arrests, aimed at landless farmer groups and impoverished sugar workers advocating for land reform of colonial-era sugar plantations. That same year, Duterte became an overnight international environmental hero after threatening to declare war on Canada for dumping one hundred containers of nonrecyclable waste on the Philippines. The president, though, is no environmentalist. The Lumad people continue to face threats to their lands and livelihoods from extractivism, and have long been fighting to uphold their customary laws and cultures against a "systemic war of extinction."[50] Threats to their communal lands have increased under the forces of transnational capitalist plunder. Copper, nickel, gold, chromite, coal, and gas are mined and extracted, and communal lands are declared uncultivated and turned over by the state to agribusinesses to export oil, bananas, rubber, and pineapples. Under Duterte's reign, more than thirty Lumad schools have been forcibly closed, and 225 military attacks have been carried out on other schools vilified as training centers for terrorists.[51] In one month alone in 2019, two Lumad farmers and organizers, Alex Lacay and Jeffrey Bayot, were murdered by state forces.

In addition to posturing about environmentalism, Duterte also espouses anti-imperialist rhetoric. He says he will oust foreign troops; however, he has benefited from an expanding US presence in the region. Under the guise of fighting "Jihadi extremism," the US launched Operation Pacific Eagle—Philippines in 2017 and maintains a Marine Corps mission in the country, continuing the long legacy of imperial presence on the archipelago. The Philippines remains the largest regional recipient of US military aid, totaling $193.5 million for weapons and aerial surveillance in 2018, and Duterte also received more than $58.5 million for policing the drug war and counterinsurgency operations.[52] In 2020, Duterte signed a draconian anti-terrorism law authorizing warrantless arrests to further target government dissidents. Political dissidents, including land defenders, labor leaders, journalists, human rights activists, and communists affiliated with the New People's Army and Communist Party of the Philippines, have been consistently policed and targeted by Duterte's regime, with 222 victims of political killings, 2,171 political arrests, and 85,236 incidents of political intimidation between July 2016 and December 2018.[53] In 2018, approximately 18 percent of worldwide killings linked to environmental protection took place in the Philippines, making it the world's deadliest country for land defenders.[54]

Under Bolsonaro, Indigenous communities in Brazil are also facing state and paramilitary violence, illegal incursions on their land, and policies of land grabbing and resource theft. One of the biggest threats posed by Bolsonaro is to the Amazon, the world's largest rainforest, home to 305 Indigenous communities and 10 percent of our planet's biodiversity.[55] Within a few months of taking office in October 2018, Bolsonaro slashed the budgets of the environmental and Indigenous agencies, while agricultural and mining ministries were expanded to fast-track approvals for agribusiness and extractive projects. As a strategy to force open Indigenous lands to commercial agriculture and mining, he also froze Indigenous land titling (a legal process recognizing Indigenous peoples' rights of use and management over their lands and resources). The post-junta Brazilian constitution had provided some safeguards for lands demarcated as Indigenous territories, making them off-limits to industrial projects and cattle ranching. Following the commodity boom of the 2000s, the powerful agro-industrial sector (*ruralistas*) and landed oligarchy pushed back, playing a key role in former president Dilma Rousseff's impeachment and former president Lula's persecution. Now, Bolsonaro's cabinet and advisory staff is stacked with prominent ruralistas, including Luiz Antônio Nabhan Garcia, who is the president of Ruralista Democratic Unity, a landowner organization staunchly opposed to Indigenous land demarcations and agrarian redistribution reform championed by the Landless Workers' Movement (MST).

Under Bolsonaro, deforestation has spiked 67 percent, at a rate of three football fields per minute, and fires have swelled 84 percent.[56] Bolstered by Bolsonaro, who has said the Brazilian cavalry should have been more efficient in exterminating Indigenous people, miners and loggers are also illegally invading lands in the Amazon at a rate 150 percent higher than before his presidency.[57] These invasions are lethal. In one incident, 68-year-old Chief Emyra Waiãpi was assassinated by *garimpeiros* (illegal miners), who were armed and accompanied by a pit bull. Alongside the Philippines, Brazil is now one of the world's deadliest countries for land defenders, with the Pastoral Land Commission recording a 20 percent increase in land-related murders in 2018.[58] The same year, three thousand Indigenous women organized a nationwide Indigenous women's march to protest attacks on Indigenous people and rollbacks of environmental legislation. Sônia Guajajara told the media: "Ever since Bolsonaro said that there will not be one more centimeter of land demarcated for Indigenous peoples we have marched because, with this affirmation, he declared war not only on Indigenous peoples but also on Indigenous women. This totally authoritarian, conservative government seeks to erase and exploit our territories, negating our right to exist."[59]

Bolsonaro's prescription for one of the country's worst recessions is geno-cidal colonialism and voracious capitalism. Hundreds of multinational corpora-tions, commodity traders, banks, and investors (including a top Trump financier, the investment firm Blackstone) are currently staking a claim on Indigenous lands for forest-based exports of soy, beef, and paper products. Bolsonaro is also actively courting an updated US–Brazil free trade agreement, alongside im-plementing market-friendly pension reform, eliminating a swath of labor reg-ulations, and cutting education budgets for public universities he deems dens of "cultural Marxism." Bolsonaro wants a cleansing of the left, which he holds responsible for unemployment and crime. A former military officer, Bolsonaro is also a fervent admirer of the CIA-backed military dictatorship that ruled Brazil for two decades and has openly remarked, "The situation of the country would be better today if the dictatorship had killed more people."[60]

Vincent Bevins contends that Bolsonarismo is best understood as "a vio-lent obsession with destroying the left combined with contempt for democratic institutions."[61] Indeed, Bolsonaro espouses authoritarianism and an extirpation of socialism to ensconce a Christian, settler, racial-capitalist order disguised as majoritarianism. In a revanchist move, Bolsonaro has declared, "Not a centi-meter will be demarcated either as an Indigenous reserve or as a *quilombola*" (free Black communities founded by many of the five million Africans who escaped enslavement in the region), subsequently vitalizing the right-wing, Christian-settler coup against President Evo Morales in Bolivia.[62] Bolsonar-ismo also emboldens patriarchal homophobia and transmisogyny. At a press conference with Trump, Bolsonaro proclaimed, "Brazil and the United States stand side-by-side in their efforts to share liberties and respect to traditional and family lifestyles, respect to God, our creator, against the gender ideology of the politically correct attitudes, and fake news."[63] Bolsonaro once pronounced that he would rather his son be dead than gay. Bolsonaro's rise as a fascist has wedded all these strands: the *antipetismo* (anti–Workers' Party) mobilization of the white landowning oligarchy against moderate redistributive reforms, evangelical conservatism, the power of the military establishment, and popular anti-incumbent concerns for security in cities experiencing some of the world's highest homicide rates, of which 53 percent of victims are Black.[64]

Like Duterte, Bolsonaro's strongman image is rooted in penal populism; his signature move is gesturing with both hands, two fingers pointing two guns. Black and brown residents of favelas are already subject to police, military, and paramilitary forces, yet Bolsonaro approves American-style gun ownership and wants *bandidos* to "die in the streets like cockroaches." He is pushing legislation to shield state forces and civilians from prosecution if they shoot alleged criminal offenders. In the first year of Bolsonaro's presidency, police killed an average of five people per day in Rio de Janeiro alone.[65] The 2018 assassination of Marielle Franco, a Black, queer, favela-born city councilor from the Socialism and Liberty Party, is widely believed to have been carried out by *milícias* linked to Bolsonaro.[66] The notorious paramilitary milícias in Rio often consist of active and retired police and military members, who control swaths of urban territory and engage in extortion, arms and drug trafficking, land expropriation, and contract killing under the guise of fighting drug crime. Franco, whose staunchly left career was built on exposing this parallel state network, was advocating for favela residents against real estate extortion and militarization at the time of her assassination.[67] Luciane Rocha writes:

> The Black population's lives are heavily shaped by violence, systemic racism, and the militarisation of public space, whether by the army or militias. They ruin and often claim the lives of poor young Black men working at the retail end of the drug trade. Those men's lives are dismissed as irrelevant, even as a blind eye is turned to white elites who profit from arms and drugs trafficking on a grand scale. Meanwhile, two out of three women murdered in Rio are Black.[68]

Thus, in Brazil, like the Philippines, penal populism is a fascist strategy to intensify the militarization of social control under neoliberal capitalism.

European Welfare Nationalism and Imperial Gendered Racism

The ideological intersection of racial capitalism and racial citizenship is evident in European far-right critiques of immigration. Though such critiques are long-standing in Europe, the recent concerted rise of the far right is alarming, including Norbert Hofer and the Freedom Party (FPÖ) in Austria, Vlaams Belang in Belgium, United Patriots in Bulgaria, Danish People's Party (DPP) in Denmark, Front National in France, Alternative für Deutschland (AfD) and Patriotic Europeans against the Islamization of the Occident (Pegida) in Germany, British National Party and UK Independence Party in Great Britain, Golden Dawn in Greece, Fidesz and Jobbik in Hungary, Lega Nord in Italy, Partij voor de Vrijheid (Party for Freedom) in the Netherlands, Prawo i Sprawiedliwość (Law and Justice) in Poland, Vox in Spain, Janez Janša and the Slovenian Democratic Party (SDS) in Slovenia, and Sverigedemokraterna (Sweden Democrats) in Sweden.

Although the parliamentary success of these parties has waxed and waned, they repeatedly reemerge even after electoral defeat. For example, Golden Dawn, one of the oldest European ultranationalist parties, lost all its seats in the 2019 Greek elections, with sixty-eight Golden Dawn members facing charges, including for hate crimes and murder, in one of the country's largest criminal trials ever.[69] However, this does not necessarily mark the party's demise. In 2005, under similar circumstances of electoral defeat, Golden Dawn retreated, only to resurface a few years later with a slight rebranding. And while the European liberal media condemns the Golden Dawn as extremist, its far-right views are being popularized in Greek society and state policy. Refugee aid buildings have been torched in acts of hate, armed vigilante groups are patrolling the border, and the New Democracy government is adopting a hardline approach to immigration with plans to construct a 2.7-kilometer-long floating barrier in the Aegean Sea.[70]

Across Europe, neoliberal centrist and conservative governments are normalizing far-right platforms. French Front National policies, for instance, were adopted by then-president Nicolas Sarkozy, who imposed a public ban on the burqa, sought to prevent Muslim and Jewish students from accessing non-pork meals in schools, and promised to end "mass immigration." Similarly, although the number of DPP's seats sunk in recent elections, Mette Frederiksen's Social Democrats captured some of the far-right vote with an anti-immigration platform, advocating a cap on "non-Western" immigrants and claiming uncontrolled immigration is allegedly eroding the social welfare state.[71] The collapse of the far-right FPÖ in the 2019 Austrian elections led to a Conservative–Green coalition government, whose female-majority cabinet promises a ban on niqabs and expansion of detention centers.[72]

Anti-immigration sentiments are the primary reason voters support far-right electoral parties across Europe.[73] The invocation of a migration crisis by the European far right dangerously links immigration to myths about crime, terrorism, scarcity of jobs and resources, cultural invasion, lack of integration, contagious disease, and social backwardness—a right-wing revanchism converging around racism. This European-wide surge in xenophobic nationalism is based on racist fears of mass immigration but not its actuality, since most migrants are immobilized outside Europe. Despite significant differences between far-right forces across Europe, race and immigration operate as omnibus issues through which other concerns, such as social relations, public services, and EU integration, are funneled.[74] In western Europe, Front National President Marine Le Pen has argued that "immigration is an organised replacement of our population," and UK Home Secretary Priti Patel has vowed to "end the free movement of people once and for all."[75] To the south, far-right Italian leader Matteo Salvini linked the large-scale outbreak of the coronavirus in his country to African migrants, and in Greece, Golden Dawn's manifesto articulates an opposition to "demographic alteration, through the influx of millions of illegal immigrants."[76]

In central Europe, the FPÖ in Austria centered its election propaganda on "migrant invasions" and "Islamization," with Viennese Citizen's Initiatives launched against the construction of mosques.[77] At a provincial level, the FPÖ imposed a ban on the construction of mosques and minarets, sloganeering about the "sound of church bells instead of muezzin song."[78] In Hungary, Victor Orbán refuses to accept refugees allocated by the EU and has declared zero tolerance for immigration, purportedly to defend Christianity from the creation of "mixed-race nations." New textbooks in the country ask students to "spot the European." In eastern Europe, the post–Cold War transition managed by the US has resulted in revanchism across religious and ethnic lines, with a pronounced casting out of Muslims and Roma.[79] In Serbia, far-right vigilante groups have begun patrols to surveil, harass, and intercept migrants and refugees in Belgrade.[80] Despite constituting less than 0.1 percent of the population, Muslims in Poland have become the target of the Law and Justice party, the largest party in parliament.[81] One of the world's largest far-right gatherings took place in Warsaw in 2018, where sixty thousand ethnonationalist neo-Nazis chanted, "Europe will be white or depopulated."[82]

Poland and Hungary are home to some of the smallest migrant populations in Europe yet have some of the most xenophobic governments on the continent. There, Roma are also a primary target for persecution and cast similarly to migrants: racialized, mobile, and poor. One of the founders of Orbán's Fidesz party has called Roma "animals . . . unfit to live among people."[83] The Magyar Gárda, a paramilitary wing of Hungary's Jobbik party, conducted extremist rallies in Roma villages before being banned by Hungarian courts for threatening and violating human rights.[84] Roma oppression is a foundational violence upon which nascent forms of xenophobia—amid nationalist articulations of Hungary's debt crisis and the migrant crisis—are registered.

Nordic countries, often glorified for low levels of inequality and their redistributive welfare, are similarly marked by an enduring racism. Social democrats worldwide often look to Nordic social democracy as a model. Nordic exceptionalism, however, elides a colonial present. When Trump tweeted about buying Greenland, Danes were outraged at the absurdity of his suggestion, but few acknowledged the majority Inuit population's long history of Danish colonization, beginning in 1721. Indigenous Sámi people across Norway, Sweden, Finland, and the Kola Peninsula are also fighting for their land, culture, and self-determination. For more than two centuries, landowners and logging companies seized Sámi lands, economies of herding and hunting were decimated, people were forcibly relocated and Christianized, languages were outlawed, and women were mass sterilized. Nordic countries built their economic security with revenues from extractive industries and industrial power projects, turning much of Sámi lands into resource colonies and sacrifice zones. Sámi resistance against land grabbing today manifests as opposition to state hydropower and green-power projects. State-led industrial development, upon which redistribution programs in many Nordic countries rely, cannot vindicate colonization. For Indigenous peoples around the world, especially those occupied by nation-states with resource-driven economies, multinational corporations *and* state-run projects are equally complicit in colonial land theft. The utmost expression of racist nationalism, after all, is expansionist frontier colonialism, where genocidal violence, dispossession, infrastructure development, and resource extraction—from railroads to pipelines—are justified in the name of "national interest."

Vanessa Barker argues that Nordic nationalism also gives rise to punitive policies against migrants. Writing about Sweden, she maintains that "the backbone of the welfare state, Folkhemmet, the People's Home, is at once demos, democratic and egalitarian and ethnos, a people by blood, exclusionary and essentialist."[85] For Barker, the key component of Nordic exceptionalism in Sweden hinges on the relationship of welfare to work and the nation. While welfare policies are redistributive, they are also disciplinary against those who don't or can't work, along with immigrants characterized as not belonging to the nation. The far-right Sweden Democrats made major electoral breakthroughs at the federal and municipal levels by campaigning with chauvinistic slogans like "Keep Sweden Swedish" and linking immigration to a rise in crime, pressure on the welfare system, and a drain on healthcare.

While less pronounced than in advanced neoliberal regimes, the Swedish welfare state model has been deteriorating with the influx of transnational capital since the 1990s. Like in other countries, far-right forces, such as the Sweden Democrats, then fault immigration for the impacts of neoliberal globalization by relying on tropes of cultural incompatibility and decay. The Sweden Democrats point to "foreign ethnic minorities" and "remote cultures" as causes of the decline of a golden age, defaulting to racial exclusion to express their longing for an era of egalitarianism. Other Nordic far-right parties are similarly fixated on immigration. While the DPP in Denmark has roots in neoliberal protest *against* the welfare state, its rise was possible precisely because it eventually incorporated tenets of the welfare state into its program while simultaneously shifting its focus toward an anti-migrant agenda. Birte Siim and Susi Meret note that welfare nationalism in Denmark, like Sweden, is already marked by "clear exclusionary drives,"[86] further weaponized in advocating anti-migrant ethnonationalism as a means of bordering welfare. Denmark now has some of the most restrictive immigration laws in Europe.[87] In Iceland, the Icelandic National Front rejects multiculturalism and says it will fight mosque construction and ban burqas.

Anti-Muslim racism in Europe is not new; it draws on the inheritance of imperialism at the nexus of religion, race, and colonization. Edward W. Said laid the groundwork for interrogating homogenizing racial panics about Islam. "How really useful is 'Islam' as a concept for understanding Morocco *and* Saudi Arabia *and* Syria *and* Indonesia?" he probes.[88] Orientalism, Said pens, is "a kind of Western projection onto and will to govern over the Orient," a constituted entity based on structures from the past, "secularized, redisposed and re-formed."[89] In the Netherlands, for instance, anti-Muslim racism as the willed positional superiority of imperial racism can be traced from the country's three-hundred-year colonization of Indonesia, which has the largest Muslim population in the world, to Dutch politician and Party for Freedom leader Geert Wilders's current fanatic fixation on Islam. Wilders claims that Islam is an existential problem for women's issues, crime, and the country's public services. Wilders wants the closure of every mosque, a ban on the niqab in government buildings, and prohibition of the Koran—which he equates with *Mein Kampf*. Saba Mahmood notes, "The events of September 11, 2001 have only served to strengthen the sense that it is a secular-liberal inquisition before which Islam must be made to confess."[90] Wilders is notable in his co-optation of progressive values, particularly queer liberation, feminism, and opposition to anti-Semitism, in denouncing Islam as "premodern." This mimics a pernicious racism, as Sohail Daulatzai and Junaid Rana argue, vocalized through seemingly progressive platforms "grounded in deep civilizational discourses about the 'Muslim problem' and threats that mosque building, migrants, refugees, the veil, and other signs of 'Islam' will pose to a white Christian Europe."[91]

Under the guise of liberalism and feminism, laws banning the niqab or burqa in Austria, Bulgaria, Belgium, Denmark, France, and the Netherlands mark Black and brown Muslim women for surveillance and white feminist savior missions through a seductive representation of Muslim women's victimhood. Sherene Razack maintains, "For Muslim societies, the veil's significance and functions have varied historically whereas for the West, the veil has remained a static colonial image that symbolizes Western superiority over Eastern backwardness."[92] Compulsory unveiling is posed as liberating, a racialized discourse in which Muslim women are simultaneously projected as victims of patriarchy *and* as gendered subjects unwilling to integrate into secular (Christian) society. The patronizing proposition that women can be rescued through professed humanitarian intervention is antithetical to feminist principles of autonomy over one's body, clothing, gender identity, and labor. Writing about gender and sexuality as a generated political structure, Judith Butler observes that "the body gains meaning within discourse only in the context of power relations."[93]

The appropriation of gender and sexuality in the service of power has a capacious trajectory: imperial feminism justifies military interventions to save women from patriarchy, homonationalism claims to liberate queers from sexually repressive cultures, carceral feminism vindicates prison expansion under the guise of victims' rights, trans-exclusionary feminism reduces gender to biological determinism, and secular femonationalism[94] unveils migrant women from their allegedly primitive religions. In Germany, the AfD weaponized incidents of sexual assault in late 2015 to formulate a campaign framed as "Der Islam gehoert nicht zu Deutschland" (Islam doesn't belong in Germany), gaining 15 percent of labor union member votes.[95] In January 2016, the racists at French magazine *Charlie Hebdo* drew a cartoon of lascivious, pig-like men with outstretched groping hands next to drowned toddler Alan Kurdi, questioning, "What would little Aylan [*sic*] have grown up to be?" Daulatzai and Rana conclude that "to be a Muslim as a faith category and a racial figure entails a dangerous existence amid a vocal and public turn that vilifies Islam as antimodern and antihuman."[96]

Liberal responses to vitriolic racism are best encapsulated by Hillary Clinton's remarks about the rise of far-right leaders in Europe. Instead of offering a fight-back challenging white entitlement and European colonialism, she enabled reactionary far-right rhetoric on immigration. Clinton claimed: "Europe needs to get a handle on migration because that is what lit the flame. . . . Europe has done its part, and must send a very clear message—'we are not going to be able to continue provide refuge and support'—because if we don't deal with the migration issue it will continue to roil the body politic."[97] Former British prime minister Tony Blair, in typical, Third Way centrist fashion, similarly victim-blamed migrants, stating their failure to integrate produced far-right bigotry and proposing "civic integration contracts" as a condition of immigration.[98]

Clinton, Blair, and other politicians justify their restrictionist views on immigration through the failed strategy of centrist compromise. They posit that some negotiation with the far right is necessary to dampen the fires of xenophobia. However, the very opposite is true. The preservation of state, capitalist, and racial violence by liberal centrists actually normalizes and *fuels* the far-right forces of ethnonationalism, penal populism, welfare nationalism, and imperial gendered racism across Europe, as well as in the US, India, Israel, the Philippines, and Brazil. This politics of fear, discussed further in the next chapter, provides both a necessary scapegoat for capitalist inequality and a material basis for further alienation of racialized communities. Therefore, the political ideology of liberalism, the economic dogma of neoliberalism, and right-wing nationalism inflected by race, gender, and citizenship are all connected and must be dismantled together.

Statelessness in a State-Centric World

> *The contemporary world's work has become policing, halting, forming policy regarding, and trying to administer the movement of people. Nationhood—the very definition of citizenship—is constantly being demarcated and redemarcated in response to exiles, refugees, Gastarbeiter, immigrants, migrations, the displaced, the fleeing, and the besieged.*
>
> —Toni Morrison, "Home"

Immigration and citizenship are race-making regimes, and exclusionary race making is most explicit in the threatening process of turning legal citizens into stateless noncitizens, unfolding in all corners of the world. In India, the BJP and RSS agenda to animate India as a Hindu Rashtra relies on the dual dog whistle of Muslim migrants as infiltrators and Muslim Indians as threats, as described above. This is pronounced in the casting out and produced statelessness of Muslim Indians in the northeast region of Assam using the National Register of Citizens (NRC), a tool of racist disenfranchisement mainly of Muslim Indians of Bengali origin, now deemed noncitizens despite generations of birth and residency in the region. The politics surrounding Assam's NRC date back to the Assam Agitation of the 1970s and 1980s. Refugees fled into Assam during the struggle for Bangladeshi independence in the 1970s, and border fortification along Assam's border with Bangladesh began in the 1980s. This sparked an "anti-foreigner" movement in Assam, subjecting especially Muslim Indians of Bengali origin to legal discrimination and political exclusion. While some sections of the Assamese movement positioned themselves as an autochthonous movement in what has been an undeniably resource-rich but deliberately underdeveloped and colonized region since the British-imposed tea plantation economy, the Assam Agitation (or Axom Andalon) was primarily an ethnonationalist movement propagated through the All Assam Students' Union. In one of the world's bloodiest massacres, two thousand Bengali Muslims were slaughtered in a single day in the 1983 Nellie Massacre.

Modi's BJP reignited this tinderbox during a court-ordered updating of the NRC that, in 2019, rendered 1.9 million people "foreigners" in their own homes. If someone is unable to prove their Indian citizenship, regardless of their actual residency or birth certificate, the Foreigners Tribunal then orders their detention and eventual deportation, in most cases to an undetermined destination. In a media interview, Saleha Begum expressed worries about her future: "My parents were born here. We have all the documents. Still, my family's names are not on the list. I'm scared. I don't know if the police will put us into a detention center or deport us to Bangladesh."[99] As of November 2018, more than 1,037 people had already been declared foreigners and been detained.[100] Ten massive new detention camps are being built. Saying it would help rid India of "termites," the BJP has been vociferously championing this ethnic cleansing and wants to extend population registration to a national level. In an amendment to the citizenship laws designed for Hindus impacted by the NRC, Modi has allowed citizenship to be fast-tracked for Hindus, Sikhs, Buddhists, Jains, Parsis, and Christians—but not Muslims—from Afghanistan, Bangladesh, and Pakistan. Together, the Citizenship Amendment Act and the NRC are legal routes to mass disenfranchisement for Muslim citizens, sparking massive Muslim women- and student-led protests and civil disobedience across the country in 2019. Hindutva ethnonationalism, therefore, maps onto anti-migrant xenophobia in three ways: Bangladeshis in the borderlands face the guns and goons of India's Border Security Force, Muslim migrants (as opposed to "Hindu refugees") in India are dehumanized as infiltrators and expelled, and mainly Muslim Indians face disenfranchisement and deportation despite being citizens.

This ethnonationalist casting out mirrors the condition of Rohingya in Myanmar. Under the watch of state counsellor and Nobel laureate Aung San Suu Kyi—the decades-long darling of Western governments—the Myanmar military has committed appalling atrocities against the Rohingya. Enabled by Israeli and Indian arms sales, it has engaged in rape, mass killings, torture, infanticide, and torching of entire villages in the western Myanmar state of Rakhine. Legalized social control includes unpaid military labor, segregated schools, a two-child limit, and regulations on which villages or townships Rohingyas may live in. Aung San Suu Kyi denies UN contentions that this is ethnic cleansing and genocide.[101]

The racist othering of Rohingyas is part of the project of Buddhist majoritarian domination and Buddhist Rakhine nationalism. Dating back to the British strategy of importing labor to extract rice profits from the region and colonial policies of divide and rule that exacerbated tensions between communities, Buddhist fundamentalism has now escalated with virulent Islamophobia. As a result, Rohingyas are regarded as Muslim "illegals" or "invaders" from Bangladesh and stripped of citizenship rights under the 1982 Citizenship Law, which grants citizenship to "national races" based on residency prior to 1823. Preceding the First Anglo-Burmese War and subsequent British administration of the territory as an Indian province, the designation of this particular year, 1823, intentionally excludes descendants of imported laborers. This treacherous nationalism essentializes ethnicity, evades the historical heterogeneity of the borderlands, excludes the descendants of laborers settled since the colonial period, and scapegoats Muslims who have actually lived in the region since the fifteenth century—rendering Rohingyas one of the world's largest stateless populations.

With more than seven hundred thousand Rohingyas forced to flee heightened violence since 2017, dozens of scorched and bulldozed villages are now being claimed as government-managed lands. Rohingyas who remain are forced into internment camps, while new settlements pop up rapidly, facilitated by the military junta and sponsored by Buddhist nationalist organizations. A 2018 independent fact-finding mission report describes the unfolding process of dispossession: "Appropriation of vacated land and terrain clearance, erasing every trace of the Rohingya communities, and the construction on this land of houses for other ethnic groups."[102] The insertion of Myanmar into the global supply chain has also opened lands to capital investment for agribusiness, industrial manufacturing, timber extraction, geothermal projects, and mining. India and China, with their respective Look East policy and Belt and Road Initiative, have invested in multimillion-dollar infrastructure projects, including pipelines and ports in the Rakhine region, dubbed "Asia's final frontier." The social engineering, ethnic cleansing, and expropriation of land eerily mirrors Palestine. Indeed, India, Israel, and Myanmar are regional allies in perpetuating abominable ethnonationalism. Israel and Myanmar have signed a bilateral education agreement allowing each country the authority to engage in mutual revisionism of textbooks, censoring histories of Palestinian and Rohingya persecution. Aung San Suu Kyi has also stated that Myanmar is "facing the same problem as India is facing in Kashmir," while Modi expressed his support for her as India and Myanmar held joint military exercises in 2017, the very year of heightened genocidal violence against Rohingyas.[103]

A crisis of statelessness is similarly unfolding in the Dominican Republic. In 2013, the country's Constitutional Tribunal stripped citizenship from Dominicans born to those deemed "in transit" or "illegal foreigners," retroactive to 1929. Overnight, the ruling left more than two hundred thousand residents of Haitian descent, including Dominican children, as unauthorized migrants and, hence, deportable. Targeting of Dominicans of Haitian descent accelerated as a result of nationalist welfare policies, with increased reports of public service denial, alongside an intensification of vigilante ethnonationalist attacks. Claude Jean Harry, a Haitian shoeshine worker, was lynched in the center of Santiago in February 2015. In response to international outrage about escalating social violence and the arbitrary expulsion of Dominicans of Haitian descent, President Danilo Medina passed a naturalization law allowing people to reclaim citizenship with proof of a birth certificate. As the government had already systemically denied birth certificates to Dominican-born children of Haitian descent, based on their parent's immigration status, the new law was a mere smoke screen and few were able to get their citizenship back. People were also told to register in the "book of foreigners" in order to remain. Those who did register now endure the indignity of being legal foreigners in their country of birth, facing an omnipresent fear of deportation. At least 214,962 people have been deported, pushed out by police or social terror, or felt compelled to self-deport.[104]

Since the Spanish and French colonial period on Hispaniola, the original crime scene of the so-called New World, *antihaitianismo* has been a particular feature of Dominican nationalism. According to Silvio Torres-Saillant, after the revolution unified the entire island, the Dominican Republic became a nation-state to juridically distance itself from an independent Black Haiti.[105] As part of efforts to encourage permanent white immigration to the Dominican Republic, a 1911 regulation stipulated, "Agricultural companies are forbidden from importing for their labor needs immigrants who do not belong to the white race."[106] US military occupation of the country between 1915 and 1934 further influenced US-backed authoritarian rulers, including Rafael Trujillo, to promote a contrived nationalism emphasizing European ancestry, mestizo identity, and racial stratifications.[107] Trujillo entrenched the border in the permeable borderlands, while signing bilateral agreements with Haiti to ensure a supply of Haitian laborers, living in isolated *bateyes* (shanty towns) and working under conditions of indentureship in the US-controlled sugar economy. In 1937, Trujillo ordered the ruthless massacre of thirty thousand Haitians at the border, echoing the current crisis for people of Haitian descent in the Dominican Republic. Since 2006, the US has helped the Dominican Republic set up a special forces border security unit, Cuerpo Especializado en Seguridad Fronteriza Terrestre (CESFRONT), to patrol the border with Haiti.[108] The contemporary statelessness of Dominicans of Haitian descent is thus produced through enduring racial social hierarchies policed by the interests of empire and elites.[109] J. Michael Dash reminds us, "The Caribbean needs to be understood not in terms of the romantic fantasy of the other Island but rather in terms of that larger, relational context of the other America."[110]

In the Arab Gulf countries, highly restrictive citizenship conjoined with welfare nationalism places migrant labor outside the bounds of political rights, as detailed in chapter 8, and creates *bidoon jinsiyya* (stateless residents).[111] In Kuwait, 106,000 Bidoon have no citizenship, are forced to use distinct identity cards, cannot purchase property, and face discrimination in accessing government services and employment.[112] After Kuwaiti independence, many migratory communities were unwilling or unable to obtain territorially defined citizenship and became forcibly stateless. Also, since citizenship is paternal, the children of Kuwaiti women who marry Bidoon men are considered Bidoon. This "foreignness" was legalized in 1986, when Bidoon were subjected to the Alien Residence Law. Then, during the Iraqi invasion of Kuwait, Bidoon were deemed Iraqi enemy aliens and tens of thousands were deported. Since 2012, the government has forbidden Bidoon marches, citing the Public Gatherings Law barring *noncitizens* from participating in public gatherings.

In 2014, Kuwait arranged for Bidoon to receive "economic citizenship" from Comoros, though the plan has yet to go into effect. Comoros permits sale of its citizenship, an example of the lucrative business of economic citizenship. Under French colonial rule until 1975, Comoros now receives money from certain GCC countries in the form of development aid and, in turn, registers Bidoon people under Comorian passports. The UAE was the first champion of this scheme and has paid two hundred million euros to register approximately forty thousand Bidoon—without their consent—as citizens of Comoros.[113] No Bidoon person has yet relocated to Comoros; all remain in the UAE under provisions allowing them residency as foreign nationals, but face the constant threat of deportation to a soil they have never set foot on. In one widely reported case, prominent Bidoon activist Ahmed Abdelkhaleq was jailed for his activism and then deported from the UAE on a Comorian passport, but Comoros refused to accept him. "We never had citizenship, but we belonged to the UAE. Now we belong to a country that is not ours in any sense of the word," Abdelkhaleq stated in an interview.[114] He was then deported to Thailand and eventually claimed asylum in Canada.[115] Citizenship has long been a commodity—with investors able to fast-track citizenship in their country of choice—but these citizenship schemes to displace disenfranchisement through mass population transfer are particularly terrifying in an era of exclusionary racist nationalism.

These sketches of statelessness illustrate the glaring convergence of racist nationalism and border imperialism. Ethnonationalism, penal populism, welfare nationalism, and imperial gendered racism around the world are providing fuel for the fires of exclusionary racial state citizenship, with manufactured statelessness emerging as an alarming consequence. The refrain of "minority groups" in human rights discourse takes the category of citizenship for granted. But the construct of citizenship itself, as an institution of governance reifying *how* one is minoritized, must be interrogated. State citizenship is less about collective participation in governance of life and more about an authoritarian system of governance *over* life. State citizenship thus becomes the legal basis of asserting state sovereignty through "define and rule" to hierarchize and manage difference.[116] The 1952 Nationality Law in Israel, for example, mobilized citizenship as a key pillar of colonization to produce Palestinian statelessness by granting citizenship to any Jewish immigrant but depriving many Palestinians the right to acquire citizenship in Israel. Around the world, state-defined citizenship is already and always tenuous and troubled: assigned by colonizers drawing arbitrary lines, an imposition on Indigenous communities annexed by settler states, or a shell game for those already cast out by race, caste, religion, gender, sexuality, ability, or class. William Anderson and Zoé Samudzi write, "The anarchistic and *noncitizen* nature of blackness positions us as foreign invaders and threats to white order" (emphasis added).[117] Now, the disenfranchisement of already-subjugated citizens is also legally rendering millions of people noncitizen migrants in their places of birth, stateless in a state-centric world. In bold contrast, thinking beyond the constraints of the state and defying citizenship as a technology of control, Erica Violet Lee lyrically depicts Indigenous liberation: "When I am old, I will tell you I remember learning about freedom beyond anthems and passports. And how we never went back once we knew the kind of love bound only by shorelines, prairie skies, and forest floors."[118]

CHAPTER 11

Refusing Reactionary Nationalisms

What keeps a poor child in Appalachia poor is not what keeps a poor child in Chicago poor—even if from a distance, the outcomes look the same.
—Ijeoma Oluo, *So You Want to Talk about Race*

D onald Trump infamously tweeted at four Democratic congresswom-
en—Alexandria Ocasio-Cortez, Rashida Tlaib, Ayanna Pressley, and
Ilhan Omar—asking why they didn't "go back and help fix the totally broken and crime-infested places from which they came." His tweet was clearly
personally racist, but the taunt of "go back home" also upholds the structural
violence the Americas are built on. It casts racialized people as perpetual outsiders, erases Indigenous nations, normalizes European colonization, reproduces an anti-Black racial order, and is the ideological basis for all deportation
policies. From this century's global war on terror to the coronavirus pandemic,
racialized people are scapegoated during times of crisis and subjected to the
constant white supremacist violence of being labeled a "dangerous terrorist"
or "vector of disease." Over eight hundred documented hate crimes involving
assault in the US between 2015 and 2019 included variations of the taunt "go
back to your country."[1]

Some of the most common xenophobic tropes target immigration.
Economic arguments characterize migrants as lazy welfare scammers and,
somewhat contradictorily, also as stealing jobs. Völkisch blood-and-soil arguments depict migrants as invaders altering demographically fragile societies, and gibberish race science rationalizes racial homogeneity as evident

in "white genocide" and "great replacement" conspiracy theories. Cultural arguments portray migrants as the cause for social breakdown, crime, and disintegration of alleged secular liberal values. Political arguments represent migrants as trespassing queue-jumpers threatening territorial sovereignty. In a vicious cycle, nationalism escalates racism, racism strengthens the border, and borders produce nationalism. This places anti-migrant xenophobia at the center of the reproduction of race, caste, cisheteropatriarchy, ableism, capitalism, and imperialism, bringing attention to the production of power through space. Anti-migrant xenophobia is, thus, inseparable from exclusionary and hierarchal ideas of belonging and entitlement buttressing the nation-state. In this chapter, I analyze the nationalist dimensions of racial violence and eco-fascism and locate the practices of making and mobilizing anti-migrant racism as constitutive of far-right nationalism.

It is no coincidence that the rise of the far right is happening in the aftermath of the Great Recession and has emerged as a reactionary alternative to neoliberalism and liberalism, both suffering a profound legitimacy crisis. Though they are distinct ideologies, the far right is the Frankenstein of liberalism. The prevailing liberal ideologies of individualism, freedom of opportunity, tolerance, respectability, and techno-solutionism have cultivated the far-right mobilizations now calling for the very destruction of liberalism. One of the far right's main targets is the liberal articulation of multiculturalism, discussed in the Canadian context in chapter 9. For liberals, multiculturalism is synonymous with essentialized ethnic identity formation and shallow representational politics. Keeanga-Yamahtta Taylor observes, "Cold War liberalism was a political framework that viewed American racial problems as existing outside of or unrelated to its political economy and, more importantly, as problems that could be fixed within the system itself."[2] The prevailing creed of the culture of poverty, culture of terrorism, and culture of evil are all birthed by liberal multiculturalism functioning as state racism. Himani Bannerji contends multiculturalism is "a mode of the workings of the state, an expression of an interaction of social relations in dynamic tension with each other."[3] Liberal multiculturalism produces and essentializes ethnicity and race as markers of "cultural difference," which has become a foundation for the demographic racism of the far right. Mahmood Mamdani, for example, argues the liberal placing of Muslims within "culture talk"—removed from politicized discussions of Cold War imperial expansionism into Muslim-majority states—animates Islamophobia.[4]

Liberal multiculturalism also assumes a false solidarity between the racialized working class and racialized elite, who are directly implicated in oppression as bosses, landlords, and agents of the state, and contains radical demands in favor of promoting tokenistic diversity within the status quo. Elizabeth Povinelli argues that liberal multiculturalism is an adaptation of late capitalism to naturalize capitalist accumulation through categories of social difference and imaginaries of national cohesion. She maintains that multiculturalism calls on people to "perform an authentic difference in exchange for the good feelings of the nation."[5] Liberalism and far-right populism are, therefore, not completely contrasting ideologies when it comes to antiracism. Ghassan Hage notes, "White racists and white multiculturalists share in a conception of themselves as nationalists and of the nation structured around a White culture, where Aboriginal people and non-white 'ethnics' are merely national objects to be moved or removed according to a White national will."[6] Discourses emphasizing immigrants as hard-working, tax-paying, contributors-not-criminals, and model minorities mask an underlying ableism and white supremacy by demanding immigrant gratitude and assimilation within a racial-capitalist order while reinforcing a category of undeserving immigrants. Superficial tolerance talk, like Canadian prime minister Justin Trudeau's or German chancellor Angela Merkel's much-acclaimed statements welcoming refugees, is not a force opposing the far right because it does not alter the relations of racial nationalist power centering white citizens as the ultimate authority *over* multiculturalism. Our opposition, then, must strike at the heart of the assumptive racialized national space and challenge the racist assumptions about national identity shared by both liberal multiculturalism and the far right.

Class through the Prism of Race

Race is thus, also, the modality in which class is "lived," the medium through which class relations are experienced, the form in which it is appropriated and "fought through."

—Stuart Hall, "Race, Articulation and
Societies Structured in Dominance"

On countering the rise of Christian white power in the US, debates have emerged around whether to emphasize the racial hostility or the material insecurity of the white working class. We know the highest proportion of white voters for Trump in the 2016 election were actually middle-class or rich, their votes directed at maintaining the status quo of racial capitalism. That said, there is an undeniable upswing of overt white supremacy in all classes across the US and Western world. Those who believe white nationalism is primarily an impact of capitalist forces squeezing the white working class proselytize that economic redistribution will automatically alleviate racial hostility. Contrary to such deracialized rationalizations, however, growing white supremacy is not solely a product of neoliberal austerity. Though economic recessions do lead to amplified racial scapegoating, the far-right Freedom Party (FPÖ) in Austria, Lega Nord in Italy, and Danish People's Party (DPP) in Denmark, for instance, recorded significant electoral success during a period of low unemployment.[7] And while there are countless examples of whiteness being conscripted to break multiracial class solidarity, strikingly evident in Nixon's southern strategy, Bill Fletcher Jr. argues that it is important not to reduce white working-class support for leaders like Trump to class fears alone: "This segment of the white population was looking in terror at the erosion of the American Dream, but they were looking at it through the prism of race."[8]

The crisis of neoliberalism for working people—debt, wage stagnation, rising costs of living, and downward mobility—is weaponized by far-right forces who position themselves as anti-establishment. But far-right leaders prescribe a messianic rescue, not actual redistribution, from the upheavals of neoliberalism. Anticommunist demagogues may agitate the masses, but their rescue route involves uprooting class from material relations and, instead, overlaying it with projections of who rightfully constitutes the nation-state. The far right constructs threats to the working class across ethnic or racial lines, leading to the intensification of vicious ethnonationalism while maintaining an elitist status quo. Charleston shooter Dylann Roof was infatuated with white racial purity and Black enslavement as the means of class uplift and social belonging.[9] For Roof and others, the indictment is not of poverty in general but of poverty as unfittingly experienced by white men. Their perceived loss of status does not necessarily correlate with a loss of economic security but, rather, with a loss of social privilege, an anxiety of so-called racial inferiors being treated as equals, and their revanchist belief that globalization results in the waning power of white males. Listen Chen and Ivan Drury write, "Working class white men who have been made homeless may, rather than rage against the economic and political system that has tossed them out, instead pine for their lost race and gender power."[10] David Roediger, drawing on W. E. B. Du Bois's formulation of a public and psychological wage, argues that working-class racism cannot be explained only through the lens of economic disadvantage but must also be understood as racial conservatism inherent to a class identity forged *through* whiteness as anti-Blackness.[11] "White working class" works alongside constructs such as "white power," coined by white nationalist George Lincoln Rockwell to oppose Black Power movements.[12] Thus, the identity formation of the "white working class," in explicit antagonism to a multiracial class identity, is a modality of race making at the expense of *all* working people.

Of course, not all white workers identify with the category of the white working class, white workers are not necessarily more racist than white elites, and low-income whites are not the main beneficiaries of racial violence. Nevertheless, racism is simultaneously a manipulative tactic of divide-and-conquer and the basis of material social relations. Whiteness is more than just a privilege; it is a public identity politic including class convergence around white supremacy. In 1928, US labor leader William Green charged that there were "too many Mexicans" and demanded immigration restrictions to protect American workers. Ranging from the Knights of Labor seeking the expulsion of Chinese workers to the AFL-CIO's opposition to undocumented workers, the centrality of race to the organization of labor cannot be ignored. Cheryl Harris argues racial identity and property are interrelated and that whiteness is a form of property contingent on the right to exclude.[13] She traces enslavement and colonization—anti-Black and anti-Indigenous racial social formations solidifying whiteness in the US—as also establishing racially contingent property rights codified through law, thus guaranteeing racialized supremacy and economic hegemony. In a similar vein, Lou Cornum puts forward, "The transformation of land into property, which could then be seized, is inseparable from the transformation of people into property, who could then be banned from considerations of humanity."[14]

Whiteness is a possessive force and a system of patronage affording white people the full status and protection of citizenship, as well as income-bearing value and asset inheritance for white workers, while racialized workers are enmeshed in the property relations of racial capitalism. The nostalgia for a union-wage-based, Fordist industrial economy ignores how such an economy has always been subsidized by both colonial extraction and the racialized, gendered, low-wage, service economy. Ultimately, an obsession with analyzing the exaggerated trauma of the white working man ends up reinforcing patriarchal whiteness, invisibilizes the disproportionate impoverishment of racialized women workers, and undermines antiracist, feminist leadership in class struggles. Half of the fastest-growing jobs in the US are in the feminized care sector of social reproduction, like nurse practitioners and home care aids, and during the Covid-19 pandemic, one in three jobs held by women was designated as essential.[15] These care sector jobs are overwhelmingly held by racialized women workers who are leading working-class movements such as Fight for \$15 and the Green New Deal for secure and healthy jobs, legislative drives to protect domestic workers socially reproducing the world, and nationwide strikes against corporate criminals such as Amazon and Whole Foods. Robin D. G. Kelley points out, "The idea that race, gender, and sexuality are particular whereas class is universal not only presumes that class struggle is some sort of race and gender-neutral terrain but takes for granted that movements focused on race, gender, or sexuality necessarily undermine class unity and, by definition, cannot be emancipatory for the whole."[16]

Making of "Foreigner" through Nationalist Identities

The manufacturing of a national working class, as opposed to the international working class, is fraught with the same problematic. An extreme example is the establishment of labor Zionism. A workers' utopia, with joint ownership of production through kibbutzim, was a means of ensuring the primacy of Jewish workers. Labor Zionism enforced ethnic separatism in the labor force and militarized Zionist control over Palestine under the colonial slogan "Make the desert bloom." Seraj Assi pens, "Socialist Zionism thus entailed the total racialization of the class struggle and the reconfiguration of labor along strictly demarcated ethnic lines."[17] Today, the construction of the national working class is also used to pit citizens against noncitizens. In Greece, for example, the migrant crisis is seen as exacerbating Troika-imposed austerity. In early 2020, Greek residents of Lesbos protested and rioted against the construction of a new detention center. Their opposition was not an act of solidarity with migrants, but rather against the very presence of migrants whom they characterized as an economic encumbrance.[18] In this interpretation, hostility toward migrants is portrayed as an unfortunate but logical outcome of a squeezed citizenry. But positioning the primary victims of austerity as Greek citizens, and not *also* migrants suffering more acutely under the same regime, creates a bordered logic and formulates both the austerity and migrant crises as ultimately a burden upon (white) citizens. Frantz Fanon offers us poignant insight in distinguishing national liberation from nationalist exclusion: "National consciousness, which is not nationalism, is the only thing that will give us an international dimension."[19]

One of the most pernicious forms of white supremacy on the left today is the animation of the working class along nationalist lines. Like appeals to whiteness, the conditioning of class *through* citizenship is not simply a social identity; it is imbued with economic value as a form of property. Calls on citizens to "protect our jobs" puts working-class movements on a path away from collective ownership of the means of production and, instead, toward an ambiguous sense of ownership of the nation-state. Uplift for the people becomes synonymous with uplift of the state, thus aligning labor interests with the state. Welfare nationalism then emerges to control public services, not as egalitarian institutions based on social solidarity, but as a form of bordered exclusion to allegedly defend the nation's workers. Even in vaguely social democratic countries such as Canada, Sweden, and Denmark, ideological shoring up of the nation-state targets migrants and refugees for "welfare tourism," restricting them from full access to social services. These restrictions operate as a de facto wealth test, as well as a nationalist form of exclusion against "undesirable" immigrants.

Welfare nationalism is not unique to welfare states; it is a spacious orientation linking social security to nationalist ideas. Welfare nationalism merges seamlessly with austerity regimes to argue that scare resources cannot be provided to migrants and, additionally, that migrants are actually responsible for the scarcity. Migrants are portrayed as stealing *our* jobs and taking *our* services, with racial entitlement reproducing racial citizenship. Trump has deceptively proclaimed, "Working-class Americans are left to pay the price for mass illegal immigration: reduced jobs, lower wages, overburdened schools, hospitals that are so crowded you can't get in, increased crime, and a depleted social safety net."[20] Such rhetoric generates support for anti-immigration measures, escalates hate crimes, and pits neighbors and workers against one another. For migrants to be successfully pitted against workers presupposes that migrants are not *also* workers participating in and leading class struggles.

Furthermore, racialized xenophobia blunts class consciousness and allows elites like Trump, who has full or partial ownership of five hundred companies, to effortlessly impose austerity measures and expand capital accumulation. In 1993 in Austria, brewing class antagonisms were shifted onto migrants by far-right forces who began calling for "Austria First," a referendum on immigration issues. More recently, a billboard campaign in Canada against "mass immigration" and in support of the far-right People's Party of Canada was paid for by an organization headed by a mining company CEO. The Brexit "Vote Leave" campaign, funded by five of the UK's richest businessmen, unveiled posters featuring refugees alongside the slogan "Breaking Point."[21] Right-wing nationalism is a bourgeois nationalism, and in our struggles against capitalist austerity we must emphasize that our enemy arrives in a limousine and not on a boat.

The identification of global capitalist institutions as "foreign"—rather than the home to both domestic and transnational capitalist interests—also bolsters the nation-state. Far-right opposition to the EU during the Brexit referendum in 2016 was framed as a challenge to foreign imposition, rather than collaboration between global and national elites. This was crucial, since the Leave leadership of the far-right UK Independence Party was aligned with Thatcherite neoliberal conservatives in the Conservative Party. The identification of elite powers as foreign, instead of capitalist, dovetailed perfectly into their anti-immigration campaign and the subsequent election of Boris Johnson, a surge in reactionary Blue Labour, and the defeat of the Remain vote. Alongside a working-class rejection of the EU's catastrophic status quo agenda, one of the principal drivers of the vote for Brexit was white racial anxiety about immigration rates should the UK remain in the EU.[22]

Brexit also added fuel to the fire of other far-right movements, whose opposition to globalization and the EU directly correlates with imperial nostalgia and anti-immigration sentiments. The primary issue of right-wing Eurosceptics with the EU liberal elite is migration policy, articulated as a negative influence on their imagined national societies, and they target the EU as a boon to "Islamization" and "the immigration agenda." The dogma of racial citizenship is the universal motivating factor for far-right voters across the EU.[23] For their part, liberal elites counter the far right with affective claims to generosity and hypocritical gestures of multicultural welcome for migrants, refugees, and migrant workers into a status quo system of racial oppression and labor exploitation that does nothing to challenge white supremacy, imperial subjugation, or capitalist dispossession. These liberal public relations stunts simply heighten the forces of xenophobia, with nationalist accusations of "taking care of others before our own," pretending to care about domestic impoverishment, even as right-wing cuts to public services actually produce it. Nearly every far-right party has a variation of Trump's "America First" slogan. In Bulgaria, for instance, Ataka aims to end *foreign* control of companies through renationalization. At the same time, Ataka's contempt for *foreign* "Islamization" prompted an attack by Ataka militias on one of Bulgaria's biggest mosques, and its vigilantes patrol the border.[24]

This pattern is global and ranges from accusing "foreign" money of flooding housing markets—rather than an indictment of commodification of housing facilitated by domestic elites—to scapegoating "foreign" workers for state and capital's labor suppression. The problem isn't *foreign* capital, it's capital; the problem isn't *foreign* workers, it's labor segmentation. Writing on the Caribbean, Peter Hudson documents how anti-finance capitalism expressed through national sovereignty resulted in attacks on Haitian workers, including Cuba's deportation of twenty-five thousand Haitian workers from US-controlled sugar plantations in 1937. These workers became positioned as anti-nationalist symbols of foreign control; as Hudson remarks, "The critique of foreign domination by finance occurred through an attack on the presence of the black labor brought in by foreign capital.[25]

In the Pacific regions of the US, Australia, and Canada, nationalist protectionism can be traced back to white racial and settler-colonial unity among labor organizations actively lobbying for the expulsion of Chinese workers and prohibition against "Asian coolie labor." Kornel Chang writes, "The racialization of Asian migrants as degraded foreign labor mobilized a diverse array of Euro-American and Canadian workers into a transnational white working class."[26] Denis Kearney, an Irish populist who led the Workingmen's Party of California, unified white, working-class men by blaming Chinese workers for unemployment. He led a ten-thousand-strong march in San Francisco on Thanksgiving Day in 1877, demanding that the country get rid of Chinese laborers, characterized by Kearney as "tools of the capitalists."[27] Kearney's efforts eventually helped secure the Chinese Exclusion Act, the first US law restricting immigration based on race.

In the mid-1970s, shortly after the historic and victorious Delano grape strike in California, farmworker leader César Chávez led a campaign against "wetbacks" and reported undocumented workers to federal authorities. His cousin Manuel Chávez led union members in setting up a "wet line" of tents along a stretch of the border to detect, prevent, and even assault undocumented migrants crossing from Mexico. For Chávez, undocumented laborers were strikebreakers who undermined the power of local farmworker organizing. The far right is now co-opting the otherwise-heroic legacy of Chávez with proposed legislation to declare his birthday National Border Control Day. This is disturbing but unsurprising, as anti-migrant calls by Kearney and Chávez were mistaken and failed to understand that the border cannot work against globalized capital because the border is itself a "method for capital."[28] Free capital *requires* bordered and immobilized labor.

Today, growing demands by labor unions to keep jobs out of the hands of "foreign"workers as a purported defense against neoliberal globalization should concern us. The demand for increased enforcement against migrant workers reproduces the logic of scarcity upon which austerity depends, maintains the international division of labor upon which capitalism relies, and aligns with far-right racism. The perceived loss of national and economic sovereignty, as argued by *both* the far right and many labor organizations, is blamed on migrant workers, thus rendering their protection of the working class as racially and nationally inscribed. As Lauren Berlant notes, the "implicit whiteness and maleness of the original American citizen is thus itself protected by national identity."[29] Instead, we should assert that migrant workers don't suppress wages; bosses and borders do. Labor movements must align with migrant worker organizations demanding an end to a system of indentureship that establishes highly racialized, gendered, and nationalist labor pools and regimes of citizenship. We need full immigration status and labor protections for all workers. This is similar to the call to decriminalize sex work and recognize it as work, instead of a punitive enforcement agenda that increases the manufactured vulnerability of sex workers. Ensuring labor protections and citizenship status is the most ethical and effective counter to the far right's anti-migrant racism. Otherwise, attacks on migrant workers—buttressed by ubiquitous anti-Indigenous, anti-Black, anti-Muslim, anti-Roma, and anti-Latinx racism—will continue to work as intended for capitalist interests: channeling irregular migration into precarious labor migration, lowering the wage floor for all workers, and expanding carceral governance. Justin Akers Chacón prophesizes that "at the center of the conflicts to come will be whether labor can internationalize its understanding of the class struggle, build unity between workers within and across borders, and not fall victim to the barrage of xenophobia, reactionary nationalism, and scapegoating."[30]

Far-right forces are not alone in mobilizing a problematic nationalism as an opposing force to the failures of neoliberalism. While the far right mobilizes racist nationalism as a cover for escalating capitalist austerity, many leftists also call for nationalist state protections in the face of transnational capital. Given deterritorialized capital, nationalism is positioned as a positive territorializing force. These banal left critiques of neoliberalism point to a contracted state under globalization, most evident in state cuts to feminized care economies and public services. Budget cuts, however, never include cuts to corporate subsidies or expenditures for the police, prison, military, security, or border industrial complexes. Current Black-led calls to defund carceral state institutions expose this hypocrisy of neoliberal austerity. The expanding neoliberal penal state provides the ideological and material foundation for the overt penal populism of the far right. After all, Clinton's 1996 laws and Obama as "deporter-in-chief" laid the ground for Trump's cruelty at the border. Capitalist globalization is not contingent on a small state; a muscular state is actually required to discipline and criminalize populations under austerity regimes. Therefore, those who believe the state can protect us against capitalism misrecognize the state as having "withered" under globalization.

Among the Keynesian left, a lack of historical clarity exists about the genealogy of the nation-state, forged through racial capitalism and colonial empires. Here, the propositions of the mainstream left and the far right insidiously converge. Neoliberal globalization as a *new* phenomenon infringing national sovereignty only holds if the globalized cataclysms of enslavement, conquest, and indentureship—central to Western national economies—are erased and the violences of the past are sanitized. The formation of the state has been the condition of possibility for the simultaneous grounding and expansion of capital; class relations and state formation are generated through one another. The state creates the conditions for capital investment; protects private property; implements tax rates; subsidizes banks and corporations; regulates the flow and flexibility of surplus populations, including through borders and prisons; and authorizes an entire legal regime sanctioning the violence of dispossession, extraction, and commodification of land and labor. The state, therefore, enshrines capitalist relations and, as Romain Felli summarizes, "It is a form through which the accumulation and expansion of capital are secured and the insecurity produced by this very expansion is managed or displaced."[31]

It is precisely because state intervention is positioned as an opposing force to neoliberalism that Trump's protectionist trade wars are viewed by some leftists as a radical turn from transnational neoliberalism. Though Trump's opposition to trade agreements such as NAFTA and the Trans-Pacific Partnership (TPP) is a break from the elite consensus on globalization, it has nothing to do with actually opposing the system of neoliberalism. Trump advocates bilateral trade agreements, capitalist deregulation, and some protectionist policies to advance the interests of US capital in the face of declining imperial fortunes. When Trump talks about restoring manufacturing jobs lost to free trade (83 percent of manufacturing jobs are now in the Global South[32]), he is talking about restoring the heyday of US unipolar economic power, increasing profits for US corporations, and continuing the exploitation of workers domestically and internationally. Indeed, the new NAFTA gives *more* power to US corporations and investors, and import tariffs further empower US capitalists within imperialist free trade regimes.

Given that globalized capital relies on the organization of the state, nationalisms bound to the state cannot be a real opposition to neoliberalism. Subsidies for the corporate sector and national markets, particularly through imperialist state protection, have long formed a disciplining pillar of international markets. Ninety-six percent of the world's largest corporations are incorporated in just eight countries.[33] Lisa Lowe notes, "Capital has maximized its profits not through rendering labor 'abstract' but precisely through the social productions of 'difference,' of restrictive particularity and illegitimacy marked by race, nation, geographical origins, and gender."[34] Instead of racist nationalism defining who constitutes the nation-state or the working class, we need a robust and internationalist struggle committed to dismantling the conjoined forces of capitalism, the state, racism, and all hierarchized relations, while nurturing a kinship of relationality and place-based stewardship.

Flames of Eco-fascism

> *Mother Nature—militarized, fenced-in, poisoned—demands that we take action.*
>
> —Berta Cáceres, quoted in Moira Birss,
> "Criminalizing Environmental Activism"

Eco-fascism is another alarming weapon in the arsenal of white nationalism. Eco-fascism pioneer Madison Grant was a renowned conservationist who served as an executive officer of both the American Eugenics Society and the Immigration Restriction League. More recently, the Christchurch killer railed that "continued immigration into Europe is environmental warfare," and, across the ocean, the El Paso killer announced, "If we can get rid of enough people, then our way of life can become more sustainable."[35] Malthusian theories blame high birth rates and immigration for environmental degradation and food scarcity, while green nationalism weaponizes the threat of climate devastation and the myth of human (not corporate) carrying capacity to argue that racial exclusion is necessary for survival. Eugenics and immigration controls become the bedrock of Darwinian lifeboat theories, fueled by apocalyptic nihilism and race war fantasies. These are also masculinist savior ideologies, which merge saving the "pure" race with "guarding" a fragile earth. Even as far-right politicians are considered climate change deniers, they dive into the burgeoning field of "climate security," prioritizing militarized borders and eco-apartheid in a warming world. The migration crisis is increasingly linked to the climate crisis, and shutting down climate migration has become their pressing concern. Marine Le Pen, for example, campaigns on an exclusionary ecological localism, where immigrants are compared to foreign invasive species, and her party puts forward screeds such as "Borders are the environment's greatest ally; it is through them that we will save the planet."[36]

Global warming accelerates existing inequalities created through colonialism and capitalism. Writing on Haiti, Keston Perry observes, "Hurricanes destroyed housing, food production, livelihoods and infrastructure and a severe drought dried up the island's water resources."[37] These inequities are solidified in colonial responses to climate refugees. After the devastating earthquake in 2010 displaced one million Haitians, the US responded by ramping up interdiction, opening up a detention center, and broadcasting an aerial message across Haiti: "If you leave, you will be arrested and returned."[38] The US has also launched Operation Vigilant Sentry off the Florida coast and created Homeland Security Task Force Southeast, a standing task force of marine interdiction and deportation of Caribbean passengers in the aftermath of disasters. When Hurricane Dorian hit the Bahamas in 2019, hundreds of survivors were blocked from boarding evacuation ferries to Florida. A US Pentagon–commissioned report encapsulates this hostility to climate refugees: "Borders will be strengthened around the country to hold back unwanted starving immigrants from the Caribbean islands (an especially severe problem), Mexico, and South America."[39]

Liberal elites barely offer any moral opposition to this eco-apartheid. They avoid the core issues of mitigating climate change, ending forced displacement, and ensuring the rights of climate refugees. Instead, they turn displaced people into a humanitarian cause or a funnel of temporary labor migration. We know that if the environment were a bank, the elite would have saved it. Instead, ecosystems and displaced people are considered superfluous, while the elite—including those who publicly present as climate deniers—save themselves by weatherproofing their mansions, hoarding water, investing in climate-disaster technologies, and fortifying their green oases with gated communities and militarized borders.

While eco-fascist views are an extremist tendency, they are an outgrowth of the limitations of liberal movements struggling for the environment as a "white sanctuary."[40] The Sierra Club was embroiled in vicious debates about immigration and population control throughout the 1990s and 2000s. Like those on the left who inaccurately believe we can fight austerity through border controls, Sierra members advocated immigration restriction as a method of environmental protection. Environmental liberalism is steeped in such false solutions, evident in the rise of Elon Musk–style techno-solutionism. We are also presented with attempts to greenwash industrial extraction and corporate profiteering with propaganda for carbon markets, natural gas, and clean coal by corporations interested in sustaining their windfall profits, not the earth. The CEOs of these toxic corporations are boosted by G7 governments providing one hundred billion dollars in oil, gas, and coal subsidies.[41] We are all assigned individual responsibility to recycle and change consumer habits, even though just one hundred corporations are responsible for 71 percent of global emissions and the poorest half of the world are responsible for only 10 percent.[42] Many environmentalists applaud green militarism, such as the Zionist Jewish National Fund greening the occupation of Palestine through tree planting, or the US military, as the world's largest institutional consumer of hydrocarbons,[43] announcing it will green its killing machine. But militarism is fueled by endless resource extraction, and war devastates the landscape; it simply cannot be greened.

This litany of false solutions stems from environmental liberals' blind spots to militarism, capitalism, and environmental racism—from ignoring the disproportionate impact of climate catastrophe on racialized communities around the world to land-grabbing conservation efforts erasing Indigenous jurisdiction and perpetuating colonial terra nullius. Instead of individualist, incrementalist, and imperialist liberalism, we must tackle climate catastrophe and the impending extinction of one million species as emerging *from* extractivist colonialism and capitalism.[44] Decarbonizing would necessarily require demilitarization, decarceration, and decolonization because the climate crisis is a symptom and not the cause of our existential crisis. Importantly, the escalation of eco-fascism and the far right cannot be overcome by or through the settler-colonial nation-state, because eco-fascism is not a racist aberration of an otherwise-humane system. Instead, decolonization and Indigenous liberation are the strongest and longest front lines resisting commodification and degradation of land and water. Indigenous people comprise less than 5 percent of the world's population but steward 80 percent of the planet's biodiversity and, as a result, most acutely experience the impacts of ecological genocide.[45] Eriel Deranger emphasizes, "The complex interrelations between energy poverty, the price of food, access to clean water and climate change disproportionately impact Indigenous peoples."[46]

Yet, just as white workers express resentment toward migrant workers for stealing *their* jobs, workers in extractive industries are often hostile toward Indigenous land defenders for ruining *their* (settler) economy. Working-class identity *as* settler-worker identity and the characterization of Indigenous lands as "public" lands in an expression of terra nullius elide the colonial theft of Indigenous territories as an indispensable subsidy to the settler polity and the industries workers are laboring in. The positioning of workers against Indigenous environmentalists also invisiblizes land defenders and water protectors who labor in highly skilled, noncapitalist Indigenous economies of hunting, gathering, fishing, cultivation, and harvesting. Indigenous land defenders are, in fact, *working* to protect a way of life and reciprocal relations with the land and all its creations.

Two essential anticolonial reorientations for settlers laboring on Indigenous lands are, first, the recognition of Indigenous land defense as generative labor and, second, solidarity with Indigenous blockades as picket lines preventing state and capital's expropriation of land by asserting legitimate Indigenous jurisdiction. This is urgent because in this time of frontier extractivism, the price for Indigenous caretaking labor and land stewardship is high. Across Turtle Island, warriors in the Idle No More, Protect Mauna Kea, Standing Rock, Stop Keystone XL, Tiny House Warriors, and Wet'suwet'en movements have faced the intensity of armed state repression. Worldwide, the horrific murders of environmental land defenders, overwhelmingly Indigenous resisters, has doubled over the past fifteen years, with four people killed every week, and land defenders making up 40 percent of targeted killings of all human rights defenders in 2019.[47]

Far-right revanchism is, in conclusion, inseparable from the making of class identity through race, the scapegoating of foreigners solidifying anti-migrant xenophobia, and the reproduction of settler entitlement. Therefore, we must unequivocally discard class struggles structured through racist nationalism and environmental justice movements animated through eco-fascism.

Exclusionary projections of who belongs and has the right to life uphold ruling-class and right-wing nationalism, thus breaking internationalist solidarity and solidifying global apartheid. A political and economic system that treats land as a commodity, Indigenous people as overburden, race as a principle of social organization, women's caretaking as worthless, workers as exploitable, climate refugees as expendable, and the entire planet as a sacrifice zone must be dismantled.

Conclusion

The world was born yearning to be a home for everyone.
　　　　　　　　—Eduardo Galeano, "Through the Looking Glass:
　　　　　　　　　　　　　Q & A with Eduardo Galeano"

Calls for nationalist protectionism against neoliberal globalization have only emboldened the far right and heightened anti-migrant xenophobia. Far-right organizations are even weaponizing resistance to fascism as a nationalist cause. In France, anti-immigration and Islamophobic forces present themselves as a new Resistance, a direct reference to forces fighting Nazi occupation. Similarly, Italian resistance to Nazi occupation is being memorialized and shaped by far-right forces in that country as a white patriotic movement—nationalist at its core—fighting *foreign* occupation. This conveniently erases the more than fifty nationalities, including thousands of migrants in Italy, represented in the internationalist Resistance against the Nazis and Mussolini's fascism.[1] The anticolonial dimension of the Resistance is also omitted, as are those who fought Italian fascism in the colonies.

In the US, white nationalists deploy the trope of the "vanishing Indian" and appropriate Indigenous struggles to position themselves as victims of and defenders against an imagined migrant invasion. That white supremacists spuriously claim an affinity with Indigenous nations is a disgusting conflation of the nation-state with Indigeneity, particularly abhorrent in contexts where Indigenous people are resisting the weight of centuries of genocidal settler colonialism. Racist nationalism in the US and other colonial states is built upon Indigenous nations and tethered to coercive power, not relationships to place or land. Trump's fascination with Andrew Jackson illustrates how settler colonialism is the most violent form of far-right nationalism and stands in sharp contrast to Indigenous articulations of place, nationhood, kinship, and economies of reciprocity. Leanne Betasamosake Simpson imagines Indigenous futures as ones that "reject dispossession and settler colonialism and the violence of capitalism, heteropatriarchy, white supremacy, and anti-Blackness that maintains them." To her, "Indigenous nationhood is a radical and complete overturning of the nation-state's political formations."[2] In assessing anticolonial movements, Adom Getachew asserts that African, African American, and Caribbean nationalists were not primarily concerned with the building of nation-states. "Against the standard view of decolonization as a moment of nation-building," Getachew writes that Black anticolonial nationalism of this period was actually a global anticolonial "worldmaking" rooted in the principles of internationalism, nondomination, and redistribution.[3] Simpson and Getachew point to a vision of the future beyond state formations, which uphold social control.

Anti-migrant xenophobia, immigration enforcement, detention centers, migration controls, and border securitization are ultimately the tentacles of a much-larger ideological monster: the rule of racist, nationalist borders. I align with a leftist politics of no borders, since the borders of today are completely bound up in the violences of dispossession, accumulation, exploitation, and their imbrications with race, caste, gender, sexuality, and ability. A no borders politics is not abstract; it is grounded in the material and lived impacts of our world, scarred by warfare and warming. Like the regime of private property, borders are not simply lines marking territory; they are the product of, and produce, social relations from which we must emancipate ourselves. The borders of advanced capitalist and imperialist states, including Australia, Canada, the EU, Israel, Japan, New Zealand, and the US, demarcate a fortress hoarding 73 percent of global wealth and only 14 percent of the world's population, and passports from these regions guarantee the most mobility worldwide.[4]

A no borders politics is more expansive than an open borders one; it calls on us to transform the underlying social, political, and economic conditions giving rise to what we know as "the migration crisis." A meaningful no borders politics requires an end to forced displacement caused by the brutalities of conquest, the voraciousness of capital, and the wreckages of climate change. We must wage resistance to displacement and immobility in all its forms: drone warfare, military occupations, policing agencies, mass incarceration, reservations, ghettos, gentrification, capitalist trade agreements, special economic zones, sweatshops, land grabs, resource extraction, and temporary labor programs. Dismantling borders requires that we abandon capitalism, which has only given us the merciless expropriation of land and exploitation of labor. We need to urgently jettison regimes of private property, reject dispossessive forces of colonialism, forsake extractive labor markets, and abolish carceral regimes. To fully undo the rule of borders, we must also undo the apartheid racial-social organization subtending the criminalization of migration and upholding ethnonationalism as citizenship. A no borders politics, then, is a politics of refusal, a politics of revolution, and a politics of repair.

Revolutions stretch our imaginations and manifest our desires. Political struggle is a purpose and a practice. In between utopic romanticism and demobilizing fatalism—both of which foreclose the future as a process *we* generate—is our collective commitment to revolutionary struggles blossoming around us and ushering in a different world. Our profound planetary crisis has propelled groundswells of resistance to racial-capitalist, border imperialist, and far-right nationalist rule. Following a surge of xenophobic violence in South Africa in 2019, hundreds of refugees and migrants, mainly from the Democratic Republic of the Congo, Ethiopia, Somalia, and Zimbabwe, occupied the streets and buildings of Cape Town for six continuous months. Many migrant domestic workers, most from Indonesia and the Philippines, joined the 2019 democracy movement in Hong Kong and organized migrant union affiliates within the Hong Kong Confederation of Trade Unions. In the US in 2019, thousands of "Close the Camps" mobilizations, demanding closure of detention facilities incarcerating migrant children and families, swept across the country. On May Day of the following year, mostly immigrant and racialized retail, warehouse, and food service workers at Amazon, Target, Whole Foods, and Instacart led protests and strikes for higher pay and better safety protections during the Covid-19 pandemic, while also refusing a return to pre-pandemic "normalcy." Around the same time, tens of thousands of jobless and desperate mostly caste-oppressed migrant workers and day laborers in India's major cities defied a national lockdown, thousands of them battling with police as they attempted to make their way home to their villages.

In Bosnia in early 2020, seven hundred refugees broke through the fence surrounding the Miral camp and proceeded to blockade the road leading to the Croatian border. In February 2020, on the Greek hotspot of Lesbos, over two thousand refugees revolted against their confinement on the island and the horrific conditions of malnutrition, lack of sanitation, and exposure to the cold in the camp. Though they faced riot police who fired tear gas, they chanted "Freedom! Freedom!" and marched on foot toward the capital of Lesbos. In a brilliant stroke of metaphor, the undocumented migrants' organization Black Vests (Gilets Noirs) in France and the refugee group Black Sardines in Italy are loudly asserting their presence within the working-class Yellow Vests and anti-Salvini Sardines social movements. Through visible protests, defiant occupations, and viral manifestos, the Black Vests and Black Sardines are revealing the real underbelly of austerity, racial capitalism, and far-right populism in Europe, just as incendiary Black-led rebellion is pushing forward abolitionist struggle in the US.

While power is omnipresent, shaping every aspect of our lives, these and other movements remind us that injustice is not ordained to determine our future. Empires crumble, capitalism is not inevitable, gender is not biology, whiteness is not immutable, prisons are not inescapable, and borders are not natural law. We *can* abolish the organization of difference, through citizenship, race, caste, gender, sexuality, ability, and neoliberal atomization, which underwrites relentless state and social violence despite hollow proclamations of tolerance. We *can* narrow the schisms between the international working class and reimagine the working class as the capacious global proletariat, and labor—beyond the confines of accumulation and extraction—as feminist economies of care and Indigenous land stewardship. We *can* weave solidarities through the lens of abundance, rather than scarcity, and celebrate the interdependence of the particularities of our humanities. We *can* reconstruct egalitarian social ecosystems, where we cultivate depropertied, decommodified, decarceral, decolonial, and democratic relations. Considering that millions of people are differentiated and managed under border imperialism, we *can* and *must* embrace a basic yet expansive vision: no human being is illegal.

Even as bordering practices fragment internationalist solidarities and exert seemingly totalizing power over who migrates and under which conditions, the mere existence of autonomous "illegal" migration—an expression of revolt, redistribution, and reparation—defies attempts to control it. This is our starkest reminder that man-made borders shall never fully thwart human movements compelled by the upheavals of our era. This book against borders is ultimately a book about "worldmaking" as a process of homemaking, and I close with the prophetic words of Toni Morrison: "In this new space one can imagine safety without walls, can iterate difference that is prized but unprivileged, and can conceive of a third, if you will pardon the expression, world 'already made for me, both snug and wide open, with a doorway never needing to be closed.' Home."[5] The freedom to stay and the freedom to move are revolutionary corollaries refusing imperial bordered sovereignties, with home as our shared horizon.

Afterword

Aplanet torn asunder from centuries of pillaging and theft is on the brink of collapse. Rising temperatures and sea levels correlate with growing inequality and violence. The unnatural divisions within humanity sharpen. Wealth accumulates into the hands of eight white men, who own half the world's social wealth as of 2017. The world's golf courses, a symbol of affluence, consume enough water to keep 4.7 billion people on the planet hydrated, yet large portions of humanity live without access to clean drinking water. The enforced scarcity of precious resources necessary for life is not a deviation; it is the desired outcome of global capitalism. The lethal inefficiency of neoliberalism to fulfill the needs of the vast majority of people, however, has created a political vacuum, and some find answers in neofascism and authoritarianism. The imagination of a world otherwise appears to be in short supply.

Those who live in zones of suffering and war are separated from those who live with a dangerous illusion of peace, while actively denying that their countries not only produce misery but stand in the way of humanity's freedom. Wealth is allowed to flow to the centers of global capital but never outward. The mobility of capital never applies to the wretched of the earth, who are forced to traverse deadly water and land passages across borders, not of their making, and are unwelcome in countries that may have destroyed theirs. Only punishment awaits them. Their mobility is made criminal, their existence made illegal. While it is framed as a migrant or refugee crisis, it is really a crisis of humanity, the failure of the current system to offer any real alternatives other than the demonization of the other.

Like global ecological collapse benignly called climate change, a term that suggests "natural" origins versus system-induced fallout, the protracted violence of the Covid-19 pandemic has gripped humanity. The neoliberal order that eviscerated social welfare, public healthcare systems, and international cooperation created the disaster. There is nothing natural about a body count that overwhelming includes the colonized people of the so-called First World, who are already deemed expandable. From where I write in Tiwa Territory, Native relatives fall ill and die, leaving holes in the tight-knit kinship systems and networks of care. Elders have taken with them the knowledge of a history that was and a future that could have been—the stories that will not be told. We have holes in our hearts that are quickly filling with a prophetic fire.

The colonizers have fallen deeper into their deadly hallucinations of blaming the Chinese, migrants, Indigenous people—everything but the system itself. As we contact-trace the spread of the virus, we can also contact-trace the purveyors of violence all the way up the chain of command. Vijay Prashad has given us the term "Coronashock" to understand the intensifying international class struggle underway: on one side human solidarity, best represented by mutual aid and healthcare workers, and on the other pure barbarism.

This is a bleak vision.

But the humble of the earth are not passive or easily defeated. The second decade of the twenty-first century was one of rebellion. The year 2019 witnessed the resurgence of a Latin American left, defying the new Plan Condor that brings a return of the dirty wars and death squads of the 1970s and 1980s. The US-backed fascist coup in Bolivia may have temporarily knocked Indigenous movements from state power, but in the mountains, the Indigenous plot their return to history's stage, chanting the mantra of the assassinated Quechua leader Túpac Katari: "I will return, and I will be millions." In Ecuador, Chile, Peru, Honduras, Argentina, Colombia, and Brazil—everywhere there has been crushing structural adjustment and austerity—Indigenous people came from the mountains, altiplanos, llanos, and forests encircling capital cities, demanding an end to crushing neoliberal policies and an overthrow of a comprador class of neocolonialists who bow to multinational corporations. In Haiti, the descendants of Touissant L'Ouverture, the leader of the first free republic in the Western Hemisphere, besieged a puppet government of the US in a near overthrow of the brutal regime. These are not yet torrential hurricanes, but breezes that have the potential to evolve and grow, if properly nurtured and allowed to breathe.

Some commentators on the recent uprisings point to weakening US hegemony regionally and worldwide. The inability of the US and its allies to successfully mount a full-scale invasion or intervention in countries attempting to de-link from the imperialist supply chain, however, does not mean we should underestimate threats to peace. The rise of right-wing strongmen such as Bolsonaro in Brazil, Modi in India, and Trump in the US points to deepening catastrophe. This is where Harsha Walia's cogent and unfolding analysis of border imperialism is most effective: borders are ordering technologies of the world, the material and political divisions of humanity, and the crushing obstacles for futures otherwise. Fortress America, Fortress Europe, and the deepening national security projects of states such as India, Brazil, Saudi Arabia, and Israel show that neoliberalism, and capitalism more generally, not only exist comfortably side by side with authoritarianism; the relationship is also highly lucrative. Neofascism is simply the unmasked character of capitalism. Concentration camps, endless border walls and concertina wire, and armed groups of fascists are not contradictions to a First World consumer culture of electric cars, Starbucks, and online shopping. As Walia shows, these elements of the global commodity supply chain are co-constitutive and necessary elements of the for-profit system.

"Those who are against fascism without being against capitalism are like people who wish to eat their veal without slaughtering the calf," Bertolt Brecht wrote in 1935. This is the illusion of peace we are sold as an alternative to the current crisis—a return to normalcy, to the more enlightened times insulating the few from the immiseration of the many. Those who invoke the halcyon days of Roosevelt, Obama, or Trudeau ignore how these liberals, respectively, facilitated mass displacement of Indigenous peoples and theft of Indigenous lands to save settler economies during the Great Depression; expanded the Bush Doctrine, war on terror, and the mass imprisonment of migrant families; and violently plundered Global South countries through Canadian mining corporations. More recently, both liberals and conservatives agreed to drill their way out of the Great Recession at the expense of Indigenous lands and lives. The meek pay for the crimes of the powerful. The invocation of a settler past—always based on exclusion, theft, and genocide—deviates little from the cynical slogan of "Make America great again." The foundations of settler states are the problem, not the solution. A settler identity is a cruel fiction, the falsehood of a hegemonic white working class. Walia reminds us in these pages and on the front lines that teachers, domestic workers, nurses, service workers, single mothers, and land defenders are leading political struggle and, in many ways, are the most militant arms of the class struggle. This hinges on a critical dialectic between foreign and domestic policy to truly understand settler colonialism—or, more accurately, settler imperialism.

Walia writes from the Global North, while not being entirely of it. We cannot be entirely of a system that we oppose, but we also cannot fully extricate ourselves from it at this moment. That is the paradox of a revolutionary: the politics we espouse come from the future supplanted in a nightmarish present held hostage by an equally horrific past. Likewise, there cannot be a protest where everyone is welcome. (Who is Trudeau protesting when he marches at a climate march? He is, after all, the man in charge.) We have to draw lines. There are class enemies, the enemies of Mother Earth, who need to always be identified and defined. Walia implores us to be clear on this. But, more importantly, she reminds us who our friends are: the humble people of the earth, those caught in the maws of this death system. These pages are written in wind and fire. The wind is your friend, pushing at your back, propelling you headlong into a future without prisons, borders, and bosses. And the fire burns those in the path of freedom, clearing the ground for the freedom-making business called revolution. Correct relations with humanity and the nonhuman world begin by nurturing and caretaking those relations and knowing your comrades and potential friends. The future of the planet requires us to get it right.

Nick Estes

Notes

Introduction

1. Vivek Shraya, *I'm Afraid of Men* (Toronto: Penguin Canada, 2018), 61.
2. Harsha Walia, *Undoing Border Imperialism* (Oakland: AK Press, 2013), 5–6.
3. Sasha Abramsky, "Trump Wants to Treat Undocumented Migrants like Enemy Combatants," *The Nation*, November 19, 2019, www.thenation.com/article/archive /trump-immigration-military-terrorism/.
4. Erik Prince, "A Public-Private Partnership Will Solve Europe's Migration Crisis," *Financial Times*, January 3, 2017, www.ft.com/content/d95057a2-c907-11e6 -9043-7e34c07b46ef.
5. Catherine Dauvergne, *The New Politics of Immigration and the End of Settler Societies* (Cambridge: Cambridge University Press, 2016), 135.
6. Peter Nyers, "Abject Cosmopolitanism: The Politics of Protection in the Anti-Deportation Movement," *Third World Quarterly* 24, no. 6 (December 2003): 1069–93.
7. Marcus Rediker, "A Motley Crew for Our Times?," interview by Radical Philosophy, *Radical Philosophy* 2.07 (Spring 2020), www.radicalphilosophy.com/interview /a-motley-crew-for-our-times#fnref13.
8. Matina Stevis-Gridneff, "'Protecting Our European Way of Life'? Outrage Follows New E.U. Role," *New York Times*, September 12, 2019, www.nytimes.com/2019 /09/12/world/europe/eu-ursula-von-der-leyen-migration.html.
9. Nicholas De Genova, "Introduction: The Borders of 'Europe' and the European Question," in *The Borders of "Europe": Autonomy of Migration, Tactics of Bordering*, Nicholas De Genova, ed. (Durham: Duke University Press, 2017), 6.
10. Radhika Mongia, *Indian Migration and Empire: A Colonial Genealogy of the Modern State* (Durham: Duke University Press, 2018), 139.
11. Michael Liedtke, "Jeff Bezos Now Richest in World, as David Thomson Tops Canadian Billionaires," Associated Press, March 7, 2018, www.bnnbloomberg.ca /jeff-bezos-now-richest-in-world-as-david-thomson-tops-canadian-billionaires -1.1019997; Casey Quackenbush, "The World's Top 26 Billionaires Now Own as Much as the Poorest 3.8 Billion, Says Oxfam," *Time*, January 21, 2019, https://time

.com/5508393/global-wealth-inequality-widens-oxfam/.

12. Sandro Mezzadra and Brett Neilson, *Border as Method, or, the Multiplication of Labor* (Durham: Duke University Press, 2013), 5.

13. Joseph Sterphone, "'Mut Zu Deutschland!' On the Populist Nationalism of the Alternative für Deutschland," in *Populist Nationalism in Europe and the Americas*, Fernando Lopez-Alvest and Diane E. Johnson, eds. (New York: Routledge, 2019), 101.

14. Whitney N. Laster Pirtle, "Racial Capitalism: A Fundamental Cause of Novel Coronavirus (COVID-19) Pandemic Inequities in the United States," *Health Education and Behavior*, April 26, 2020, https://doi.org/10.1177/1090198120922942.

15. Ruth Wilson Gilmore, "Making Abolition Geography in California's Central Valley with Ruth Wilson Gilmore," interview by Leopold Lambert, The Funambulist, February 2019, https://thefunambulist.net/making-abolition-geography-in-californias -central-valley-with-ruth-wilson-gilmore.

16. UN High Commissioner for Refugees, "Beware Long-Term Damage to Human Rights and Refugee Rights From the Coronavirus Pandemic: UNHCR," April 22, 2020, www.unhcr.org/news/press/2020/4/5ea035ba4.html.

17. Chris Scicluna, "Malta Refuses to Let Ship Carrying 57 Rescued Migrants Dock," *Independent*, May 1, 2020, www.independent.co.uk/news/world/europe/malta -migrant-rescue-ship-dock-eu-mediterranean-a9494536.html; Patrick Kingsley and Haley Willis, "Latest Tactic to Push Migrants from Europe? A Private, Clandestine Fleet," *New York Times*, April 30, 2020, www.nytimes.com/2020/04/30/world/europe /migrants-malta.html.

18. "Italy Closes Ports to Refugee Ships Because of Coronavirus," Al Jazeera, April 8, 2020, www.aljazeera.com/news/2020/04/italy-closes -ports-refugee-ships-coronavirus-200408091754757.html; Faisal Mahmud, "Rohingya Stranded at Sea, Bangladesh Says Not Its Responsibility," Al Jazeera, April 23, 2020, www.aljazeera.com/news/2020/04/rohingya-stranded-sea-bangladesh -responsibility-200425082607464.html; Lydia Gall, "Hungary Weaponizes Coronavirus to Stoke Xenophobia," Human Rights Watch, March 19, 2020, www.hrw.org /news/2020/03/19/hungary-weaponizes-coronavirus-stoke-xenophobia.

19. Human Rights Watch, "Lebanon: Refugees at Risk in COVID-19 Response," April 2, 2020, www.hrw.org/news/2020/04/02/lebanon-refugees-risk-covid-19-response.

20. Hsiao-Hung Pai, "The Coronavirus Crisis Has Exposed China's Long History of Racism," *Guardian*, April 25, 2020, www.theguardian.com/commentisfree/2020/apr /25/coronavirus-exposed-china-history-racism-africans-guangzhou; Geoffrey York, "African Diplomats Protest Alleged Racism and Inhumane Treatment of Migrants in China," *Globe and Mail*, April 12, 2020, www.theglobeandmail.com/world/article -african-diplomats-protest-alleged-racism-and-inhumane-treatment-of/.

21. Rozanna Latiff, "Malaysia Rounds Up Migrants to Contain Coronavirus, U.N. Warns of Detention Risks," *Chronicle Herald*, May 2, 2020, www.thechronicleherald.ca /news/world/malaysia-rounding-up-migrants-to-contain-coronavirus-spread -police-say-444914/.

22. Camille Baker, "Conditions for Migrants Are So Dire That Covid-19 Isn't Even Their Deadliest Threat," Quartz, April 9, 2020, https://qz.com/1834508/what

-dealing-with-covid-19-is-like-for-homeless-migrants/.

23. Camilo Montoya-Galvez, "'Exporting the Virus': Migrants Deported by US Make Up 20% of Guatemala's Coronavirus Cases," CBS News, April 27, 2020, www.cbsnews.com/news/deported-migrants-guatemala-coronavirus-cases/.

24. Franco Ordoñez, "White House Seeks to Lower Farmworker Pay to Help Agriculture Industry," NPR, April 10, 2020, www.npr.org/2020/04/10/832076074 /white-house-seeks-to-lower-farmworker-pay-to-help-agriculture-industry.

25. Monique O. Madan, "Millions of Immigrant Families Won't Get Coronavirus Stimulus Checks, Experts Say," *Miami Herald*, March 26, 2020, www.miamiherald.com /news/local/immigration/article241531211.html#storylink=cpy.

26. Americans for Tax Fairness and Institute for Policy Studies, "Tale of Two Crises: Billionaires Gain as Workers Feel Pandemic Pain," May 21, 2020, https:// americansfortaxfairness.org/wp-content/uploads/2020-5-21-Billionaires-Press -Release-at-Two-month-Covid-Pandemic-FINAL.pdf.

27. Eren Orbey, "Trump's "Chinese Virus" and What's at Stake in the Coronavirus's Name," *New Yorker*, March 25, 2020, www.newyorker.com/culture/cultural-comment /whats-at-stake-in-a-viruss-name; Salvador Rizzo, "Trump's Wobbly Claim That His Wall Could Stop the Coronavirus," *Washington Post*, March 12, 2020, www .washingtonpost.com/politics/2020/03/12/trumps-wobbly-claim-that-his-wall -could-stop-coronavirus/.

28. Arelis R. Hernández and Nick Miroff, "Facing Coronavirus Pandemic, Trump Suspends Immigration Laws and Showcases Vision for Locked-Down Border," *Washington Post*, April 3, 2020, www.washingtonpost.com/national/coronavirus-trump-immigration -border/2020/04/03/23cb025a-74f9-11ea-ae50-7148009252e3_story.html.

29. Geoffrey York, "African Countries Move to Restrict European Visitors amid Coronavirus Pandemic," *Globe and Mail*, March 11, 2020, www.theglobeandmail.com/world /article-african-countries-move-to-restrict-european-visitors-amid-coronavirus/.

30. S. Lamble, "Transforming Carceral Logics: 10 reasons to dismantle the Prison Industrial Complex through Queer/Trans Analysis and Action," in *Captive Genders: Trans Embodiment and the Prison Industrial Complex*, Eric A. Stanley and Nat Smith, eds. (Oakland: AK Press, 2011), 237.

31. Sunera Thobani, *Exalted Subjects* (Toronto: University of Toronto Press, 2007), 147.

32. Sara Ahmed, *Living a Feminist Life* (Durham: Duke University Press, 2017), 32.

33. Ghassan Hage, "Fears of 'White Decline' Show How a Minor Dent to Domination Can Be Catastrophic for Some," *Guardian*, April 15, 2019, www.theguardian.com /commentisfree/2019/apr/15/fears-of-white-decline-show-how-a-minor-dent-to -domination-can-be-catastrophic-for-some.

34. Jason Buzi quoted in Oliver McAteer, "A Millionaire Wants to Move the World's 60 Million Refugees to an Island," Metro, July 28, 2015, https://metro.co.uk/2015/07/28 /a-millionaire-wants-to-move-the-worlds-60-million-refugees-to-an-island-5315744/.

35. Harry Minas quoted in Frank Chung, "Real Estate Mogul's 'Radical Solution' to the Global Refugee Crisis," News Corp Australia, July 27, 2015, www.news.com.au /finance/economy/real-estate-moguls-radical-solution-to-the-global-refugee-crisis /news-story/c78f094595d65e394b90c997901822de.

36. Global Witness, *Enemies of the State? How Governments and Business Silence Land and Environmental Defenders*, July 2019, www.globalwitness.org/documents /19766/Enemies_of_the_State.pdf.

37. Missing Migrants Project, "Missing Migrants: Tracking Deaths Along Migratory Routes," International Organization for Migration, https://missingmigrants.iom.int/.

Chapter 1

1. RAICES Texas, "Children Should Not be 'Apprehended' at the Border," May 16, 2019, www.raicestexas.org/2019/05/16/children-should-not-be-apprehended-at -the-border/.

2. Cynthia Pompa, "Immigrant Kids Keep Dying in CBP Detention Centers, and DHS Won't Take Accountability," American Civil Liberties Union, June 24, 2019, www.aclu.org/blog/immigrants-rights/immigrants-rights-and-detention/immigrant -kids-keep-dying-cbp-detention; American Immigration Lawyers Association, "Deaths at Adult Detention Centers," December 2, 2019, www.aila.org/infonet /deaths-at-adult-detention-centers.

3. "US Held Record 69,550 Migrant Children in Custody in 2019: Report," Al Jazeera, November 12, 2019, www.aljazeera.com/news/2019/11/held-record-69550-migrant -children-custody-2019-report-191112132803440.html.

4. Eliot Spagat, "5,400 Children Separated at U.S.-Mexico Border Since July 2017: ACLU," Associated Press, October 25, 2019, https://globalnews.ca/news/6081217 /migrant-children-separated-tally-aclu/; American Civil Liberties Union, "Family Separation: By the Numbers," www.aclu.org/issues/immigrants-rights/immigrants -rights-and-detention/family-separation; Associated Press, "Tally of Children Split at US Border Tops 5,400 in New Count," Al Jazeera, October 24, 2019, www.aljazeera.com/ news/2019/10/tally-children-split-border-tops-5400-count-191025020652717.html.

5. Sara Boboltz, "18 Migrant Infants and Toddlers Separated for Weeks or Months, House Report Finds," Huffington Post, July 12, 2019, www.huffingtonpost.ca/entry /migrant-infants-toddlers-separated_n_5d288c60e4b0060b11eb0ec7; Associated Press, "'I Can't Feel My Heart': Children Separated Under Trump Show Signs of PTSD, Watchdog Finds," *Guardian*, September 5, 2019, www.theguardian.com /us-news/2019/sep/04/child-separation-ptsd-trump-zero-tolerance.

6. Gaby Del Valle, "The Most Horrifying Allegations in the ACLU's Newest Family Separation Lawsuit," Vice, October 4, 2019, www.vice.com/en_ca/article/8xwvy5 /the-most-horrifying-allegations-in-the-aclus-newest-family-separation-lawsuit.

7. Ted Hesson and Mica Rosenberg, "U.S. Deports 400 Migrant Children under New Coronavirus Rules," Reuters, April 7, 2020, www.reuters.com/article/us-health -coronavirus-usa-deportations/u-s-deports-400-migrant-children-under-new -coronavirus-rules-idUSKBN21P354; Nick Miroff, "Under Coronavirus Immigra-tion Measures, U.S. is Expelling Border-Crossers to Mexico in an Average of 96 Minutes," *Washington Post*, March 30, 2020, www.washingtonpost.com/immigration /coronavirus-immigration-border-96-minutes/2020/03/30/13af805c-72c5-11ea -ae50-7148009252e3_story.html; Nina Lakhani, "US Using Coronavirus Pandemic

to Unlawfully Expel Asylum Seekers, Says UN," *Guardian*, April 17, 2020, www .theguardian.com/world/2020/apr/17/us-asylum-seekers-coronavirus-law-un.

8. Nick Miroff, "Under Trump Border Rules, U.S. Has Granted Refuge to Just Two People since Late March, Records Show," *Washington Post*, May 13, 2020, www .washingtonpost.com/immigration/border-refuge-trump-records/2020/05/13/93e-a9ed6-951c-11ea-8107-acde2f7a8d6e_story.html.

9. Griffin Connolly, "House to Probe Rise in Hate Crimes since Trump Was Elected," Roll Call, April 4, 2019, www.rollcall.com/news/congress/lawmakers-to-probe-rise -of-hate-crimes-and-white-nationalism-in-u-s; Southern Poverty Law Center, "SPLC Answers Questions about Antigovernment Extremists Who Detain Mi-grants along the U.S.-Mexico Border," April 23, 2019, www.splcenter.org/news /2019/04/23/splc-answers-questions-about-antigovernment-extremists-who-detain -migrants-along-us-mexico.

10. Simon Romero, "Militia in New Mexico Detains Asylum Seekers at Gunpoint," *New York Times*, April 18, 2019, www.nytimes.com/2019/04/18/us/new-mexico-militia.html.

11. Todd Miller, *More Than a Wall: Corporate Profiteering and the Militarization of US Borders*, Transnational Institute, September 2019, www.tni.org/files/publication -downloads/more-than-a-wall-report.pdf.

12. Caitlin Dickerson, "ICE Faces Migrant Detention Crunch as Border Chaos Spills into Interior of the Country," *New York Times*, April 22, 2019, www.nytimes.com/2019 /04/22/us/immigration-detention.html.

13. Lisa Lowe, *The Intimacies of Four Continents* (Durham: Duke University Press, 2015), 7.

14. Greg Grandin, *The End of the Myth: From the Frontier to the Border Wall in the Mind of America* (New York: Metropolitan Books, 2019).

15. California African American Museum, "#blackhistory: On February 2, 1848, Mexico and the United States Sign the Treaty of Guadalupe Hidalgo, Transferring California to the US," February 2, 2020, https://caamuseum.org/learn/600state/february -2-1848-mexico-and-the-united-states-sign-the-treaty-of-guadalupe-hidalgo-ending -the-mexican-american-war-and-transferring-california-arizona-new-mexico -nevada-and-utah-from-mexico-to-the-united-states.

16. Richard R. Valencia, *Chicano Students and the Courts: The Mexican American Legal Struggle for Educational Equality* (New York: New York University Press, 2008), 155.

17. Laura E. Gómez, *Manifest Destinies: The Making of the Mexican American Race* (New York: New York University Press, 2007); Mae M. Ngai, *Impossible Subjects: Illegal Aliens and the Making of Modern America* (Princeton: Princeton University Press, 2014).

18. Roxanne Dunbar-Ortiz, "Stop Saying This Is a Nation of Immigrants!," *Monthly Review*, May 29, 2006, https://mronline.org/2006/05/29/stop-saying-this-is-a-nation -of-immigrants/.

19. Chief Justice John Marshall quoted in "The Doctrine of Discovery, 1493," Gilder Lehrman Institute of American History, 2012, www.gilderlehrman.org/sites/default/ files/inline-pdfs/04093_FPS.pdf.

20. Jodi A. Byrd et al., "Predatory Value: Economies of Dispossession and Disturbed Relationalities," *Social Text* 36, no. 2 (June 2018): 2.

21. Leanne Betasamosake Simpson, *As We Have Always Done: Indigenous Freedom*

through Radical Resistance (Minneapolis: University of Minnesota Press, 2017), 13.

22. Shannon Speed, *Incarcerated Stories: Indigenous Women Migrants and Violence in the Settler-Capitalist State* (Chapel Hill: University of North Carolina Press, 2019).

23. Patrick Wolfe, *Settler Colonialism and the Transformation of Anthropology: The Politics and Poetics of an Ethnographic Event* (London: Cassell, 2011), 209.

24. Jenna M. Loyd, "Prison Abolitionist Perspectives on No Borders," in *Open Borders: In Defense of Free Movement*, Reece Jones, ed. (Athens: University of Georgia Press, 2019).

25. Ngai, *Impossible Subjects*.

26. Brenden W. Rensink, *Native but Foreign: Indigenous Immigrants and Refugees in the North American Borderlands* (College Station: Texas A&M University Press, 2018).

27. Roxanne Dunbar-Ortiz, *An Indigenous Peoples' History of the United States* (Boston: Beacon Press, 2015), 231.

28. Audra Simpson, *Mohawk Interruptus: Political Life across the Borders of Settler States* (Durham: Duke University Press, 2014), 18, 99.

29. Laleh Khalili, *Time in the Shadows: Confinement in Counterinsurgencies* (Stanford: Stanford University Press, 2013), 18.

30. Maggie Blackhawk, "The Indian Law That Helps Build Walls," *New York Times*, May 26, 2019, www.nytimes.com/2019/05/26/opinion/american-indian-law-trump.html.

31. George Manuel and Michael Posluns, *The Fourth World: An Indian Reality* (Minneapolis: University of Minnesota Press, 2019).

32. Nick Estes, *Our History Is the Future* (New York: Verso, 2019), 148.

33. Jodi A. Byrd, *The Transit of Empire: Indigenous Critiques of Colonialism* (Minneapolis: University of Minnesota Press, 2011).

34. Esmeralda Lopez and Melissa Hastings, "Overlooked and Unprotected: Central American Indigenous Migrant Women in Mexico," *New York University Journal of International Law and Politics* 48, no. 4 (Summer 2016): 1105–24.

35. Emil Keme and Adam Coon, "For Abiayala to Live, the Americas Must Die: Toward a Transhemispheric Indigeneity," *Native American and Indigenous Studies* 5, no. 1 (Spring 2018): 42–68.

36. Silvia Raquec Cum quoted in Network in Solidarity with the People of Guatemala, "Guatemala Resists U.S. Border Imperialism," September 2019, https://nisgua.org/wp-content/uploads/R101-fourth-draft.pdf.

37. Speed, *Incarcerated Stories*.

38. Nina Lakhani and Tom Dart, "'Claudia Was a Good Girl. Why Did They Kill Her?' From a Guatemalan Village to Death in Texas," *Guardian*, June 2, 2018, www.theguardian.com/world/2018/jun/02/guatemala-texas-rio-bravo-border-claudia-gomez.

39. Gilberto Gómez quoted in Nina Lakhani, "'I Want Justice': A Year On, Family of Guatemalan Woman Shot Dead in Texas Wait for Answers," *Guardian*, May 22, 2019, www.theguardian.com/us-news/2019/may/22/guatemala-woman-claudia-gomez-texas-border-agents.

40. Iyko Day, *Alien Capital: Asian Racialization and the Logic of Settler Colonial Capitalism* (Durham: Duke University Press, 2016), 33.

41. Martha S. Jones, *Birthright Citizens: A History of Race and Rights in Antebellum America* (Cambridge: Cambridge University Press, 2018).

42. Rinaldo Walcott and Idil Abdillahi, *BlackLife: Post-BLM and the Struggle for Freedom* (Winnipeg: ARP Books, 2019), 22.

43. Robyn Maynard, "Black Life and Death across the US-Canada Border: Border Violence, Black Fugitive Belonging, and a Turtle Island View of Black Liberation," *Critical Ethnic Studies* 5, nos. 1–2 (April 2019): 124–51; Simone Browne, *Dark Matters: On the Surveillance of Blackness* (Durham: Duke University Press: 2015).

44. Maynard, "Black Life and Death across the US-Canada Border," 127.

45. Roberto Lavato, "Juan Crow in Georgia," *The Nation*, May 26, 2008, www.thenation .com/article/juan-crow-georgia/.

46. Philip Kretsedemas, *The Immigration Crucible: Transforming Race, Nation, and the Limits of the Law* (New York: Columbia University Press, 2012).

47. K-Sue Park, "Self-Deportation Nation," *Harvard Law Review* 132, no. 1878 (May 2019): 1879–941.

48. Saidiya Hartman, *Wayward Lives, Beautiful Experiments: Intimate Histories of Social Upheaval* (New York: W. W. Norton, 2018), 243.

49. Frank Wilderson III, "Gramsci's Black Marx: Whither the Slave in Civil Society?" *Social Identities* 9, no. 2 (2003): 238.

50. Angela Y. Davis, *Women, Race and Class* (New York: Vintage Books, 1983), 190.

51. Zoé Samudzi, "White Witness and the Contemporary Lynching," *The New Republic*, May 16, 2020, https://newrepublic.com/article/157734/white-witness-contemporary -lynching.

52. Abby Phillip, "White People in New Orleans Say They're Better Off after Katrina. Black People Don't," *Washington Post*, August 24, 2015, www.washingtonpost.com /news/post-nation/wp/2015/08/24/white-people-in-new-orleans-say-theyre-better -off-after-katrina-black-people-dont/; Richard Florida, "How Natural Disasters Can Spur Gentrification," CityLab, February 12, 2019, www.citylab.com/environment/2019 /02/gentrification-causes-new-orleans-natural-disasters-hurricane-katrina/582499/.

53. Fred Moten, *Stolen Life* (Durham: Duke University Press, 2018), 135.

54. Black Alliance for Just Immigration, *The State of Black Immigrants: Black Immigrants in the Mass Criminalization System*, State of Black Immigrants, http://stateofblackimmigrants.com, 15.

55. Alex Anfruns, "1996–2016: 20 Years after the Harshest Immigration Laws Ever Approved in the US," Investig'Action, June 22, 2016, www.investigaction.net/en/1996 -2016-20-years-after-the-harshest-immigration-laws-ever-approved-in-the-us/.

56. Juliana Morgan-Trostle, Kexin Zheng, and Carl Lipscombe, *The State of Black Immigrants*, NYU Law School and Black Alliance for Just Immigration, January 22, 2016, www.stateofblackimmigrants.com/assets/sobi-fullreport-jan22.pdf.

57. Jamila Osman, "Do Black Lives Matter in the Immigrant Rights Movement?" Al Jazeera, December 10, 2017, www.aljazeera.com/indepth/opinion/black-lives-matter -immigrant-rights-movement-171210095207677.html.

58. Saidiya Hartman, *Lose Your Mother: A Journey along the Atlantic Slave Route* (New York: Farrar, Strauss, & Giroux, 2007), 6.

59. Ju-Hyun Park, "The Alien and the Sovereign: Yellow Peril in Pandemic Times," *Evergreen Review*, Spring 2020, https://evergreenreview.com/read/the-alien-and-the

-sovereign-yellow-peril-in-pandemic-times/.

60. Nikhil Pal Singh, "The Pervasive Power of the Settler Mindset," *Boston Review*, November 26, 2019, http://bostonreview.net/war-security-race/nikhil-pal-singh-pervasive-power-settler-mindset.

61. Gary Clayton Anderson, *The Conquest of Texas: Ethnic Cleansing in the Promised Land* (Norman: University of Oklahoma Press, 2019).

62. Kelly Lytle Hernández, *Migra! A History of the U.S. Border Patrol* (Berkeley: University of California Press, 2010), 20.

63. Rebecca Onion, "America's Lost History of Border Violence," Slate, May 5, 2016, https://slate.com/news-and-politics/2016/05/texas-finally-begins-to-grapple-with-its-ugly-history-of-border-violence-against-mexican-americans.html.

64. David E. Magill, "'Border Panic' and the Bounds of Racial Identity" in *Racism and Borders: Representation, Repression, and Resistance*, Jeff Shantz, ed. (New York: Algora, 2010), 121; Kendrick A. Clements, *The Presidency of Woodrow Wilson* (Lawrence: University Press of Kansas, 1992), 100.

65. Benjamin Madley, "It's Time to Acknowledge the Genocide of California's Indians," *Los Angeles Times*, May 22, 2016, www.latimes.com/opinion/op-ed/la-oe-madley-california-genocide-20160522-snap-story.html.

66. Justin Akers Chacón and Mike Davis, *No One Is Illegal: Fighting Violence and State Repression on the U.S.-Mexico Border* (Chicago: Haymarket Books, 2006).

67. Erin Blakemore, "California's Little-Known Genocide," History, July 1, 2019, www.history.com/news/californias-little-known-genocide; Benjamin Madley, *An American Genocide: The United States and the California Indian Catastrophe, 1848–1928* (New Haven: Yale University Press, 2017).

68. William D. Carrigan and Clive Webb, *Forgotten Dead: Mob Violence against Mexicans in the United States, 1848–1928* (New York: Oxford University Press, 2017).

69. Kelly Wallace, "Forgotten Los Angeles History: The Chinese Massacre of 1871," Los Angeles Public Library Blog, May 19, 2017, www.lapl.org/collections-resources/blogs/lapl/chinese-massacre-1871.

70. Erika Lee, *At America's Gates: Chinese Immigration during the Exclusion Era, 1882–1943* (Chapel Hill: University of North Carolina Press, 2003).

71. Grandin, *The End of the Myth*, 163.

72. Alexis Goldstein, "Mass Movements Can Beat Back Racist Vigilantes like the El Paso Shooter," Truthout, August 7, 2019, https://truthout.org/articles/mass-movements-can-beat-back-racist-vigilantes-like-the-el-paso-shooter/.

73. Nicole L. Novak and Natalie Lira, "Forced Sterilization Programs in California Once Harmed Thousands—Particularly Latinas," The Conversation, March 22, 2018, https://theconversation.com/forced-sterilization-programs-in-california-once-harmed-thousands-particularly-latinas-92324.

74. Chacón and Davis, *No One Is Illegal*, 52.

75. Kathryn S. Olmsted, *Right out of California: The 1930s and the Big Business Roots of Modern Conservatism* (New York: New Press, 2017).

76. Chacón and Davis, *No One Is Illegal*.

77. Francisco E. Balderrama and Raymond Rodríguez, *Decade of Betrayal: Mexican Re-*

patriation in the 1930s (Albuquerque: University of New Mexico Press, 2006); Diane Bernard, "The Time a President Deported 1 Million Mexican Americans for Supposedly Stealing U.S. Jobs," *Washington Post*, April 13, 2018, www.washingtonpost.com/news/retropolis/wp/2018/08/13/the-time-a-president-deported-1-million-mexican-americans-for-stealing-u-s-jobs/.

78. Ngai, *Impossible Subjects*, 75.
79. Cedric J. Robinson, *Black Marxism: The Making of the Black Radical Tradition* (London: Zed Books, 1983).
80. Reece Jones, *Violent Borders: Refugees and the Right to Move* (London and New York: Verso, 2017), 35.
81. Nikhil Pal Singh, *Race and America's Long War* (Oakland: University of California Press, 2019), ix.
82. National Indian Child Welfare Association, "Disproportionality in Child Welfare," September 2017, www.nicwa.org/wp-content/uploads/2017/09/Disproportionality-Table.pdf; Nylah Burton, "Research Shows Incarceration Devastates U.S. Black Families Fifty Percent More than Other Families," *Essence*, October 30, 2019, www.essence.com/news/fwd-us-bail-reform-essence-reports/.
83. Kelly Lytle Hernández, "Amnesty or Abolition?" *Boom: A Journal of California* 1, no. 4 (2011): 65.
84. Radhika Mongia, *Indian Migration and Empire: A Colonial Genealogy of the Modern State* (Durham: Duke University Press, 2018), 113.

Chapter 2

1. Meredith Clark, "Immigrants at ICE Facility Face Retaliation during Hunger Strike," MSNBC, March 11, 2014, www.msnbc.com/msnbc/immigrants-face-threats-during-hunger-strike.
2. UN High Commissioner for Refugees, *Women on the Run: First-Hand Accounts of Refugees Fleeing El Salvador, Guatemala, Honduras, and Mexico*, October 26, 2015, www.unhcr.org/5630f24c6.html; Peter J. Meyer and Maureen Taft-Morales, "Central American Migration: Root Causes and U.S. Policy," Congressional Research Service, June 13, 2019, https://fas.org/sgp/crs/row/IF11151.pdf.
3. Victoria Macchi, "At US-Mexico Border, Africans Join Diversifying Migrant Community," VOA News, August 31, 2019, www.voanews.com/usa/us-mexico-border-africans-join-diversifying-migrant-community; Daniel Gonzalez, "The 2019 Migrant Surge Is Unlike Any We've Seen Before. This Is Why," *USA Today*, September 25, 2019, www.usatoday.com/in-depth/news/nation/2019/09/23/immigration-issues-migrants-mexico-central-america-caravans-smuggling/2026215001/.
4. Don Winslow, "MS-13 Was Born in the USA," Daily Beast, February 28, 2019, www.thedailybeast.com/ms-13-was-born-in-the-usa.
5. Naomi Murakawa, "The Origins of the Carceral Crisis: Racial Order as 'Law and Order' in Postwar American Politics," in *Race and American Political Development*, Joseph Lowndes, Julie Novkov, and Dorian T. Warren, eds. (New York: Routledge, 2008), 236.
6. Angela Davis and Gina Dent, "Prison as a Border: A Conversation on Gender,

Globalization, and Punishment," *Globalization and Gender* 25, no. 4 (Summer 2001): 1236–37.

7. Edward M. Brecher and the Editors of *Consumer Reports Magazine*, "The 1969 Marijuana Shortage and 'Operation Intercept,'" in *Licit and Illicit Drugs* (New York: Little, Brown & Company, 1972).

8. Greg Grandin, *The End of the Myth: From the Frontier to the Border Wall in the Mind of America* (New York: Metropolitan Books, 2019).

9. Ana Raquel Minian, *Undocumented Lives: The Untold Story of Mexican Migration* (Cambridge: Harvard University Press, 2018).

10. Dawn Paley, *Drug War Capitalism* (Oakland: AK Press, 2015).

11. David Harvey, "Neoliberalism Is a Political Project," interview by Bjarke Skærlund Risager, *Jacobin Magazine*, July 2016, www.jacobinmag.com/2016/07/david-harvey -neoliberalism-capitalism-labor-crisis-resistance/.

12. Jordan T. Camp and Christina Heatherton, *Policing the Planet: Why the Policing Crisis Led to Black Lives Matter* (London and New York: Verso, 2016).

13. Michelle Alexander, *The New Jim Crow: Mass Incarceration in the Age of Colorblindness* (New York: New Press, 2010), 101.

14. National Association for the Advancement of Colored People, "Criminal Justice Fact Sheet," www.naacp.org/criminal-justice-fact-sheet/.

15. Victoria Law, *Resistance behind Bars: The Struggles of Incarcerated Women* (Oakland: PM Press, 2012), 165.

16. Jenna M. Loyd and Alison Mountz, *Boats, Borders, and Bases: Race, the Cold War, and the Rise of Immigration Detention in the United States* (Oakland: University of California Press, 2018), 176.

17. Don Tiburcio's testimony quoted in Roddy Brett, *The Origins and Dynamics of Genocide: Political Violence in Guatemala* (London: Palgrave Macmillan, 2016), 6.

18. Noam Chomsky, *What Uncle Sam Really Wants* (Berkeley: Odonian Press, 1992), 42.

19. Gary Cohn and Ginger Thompson, "Unearthed: Fatal Secrets," *Baltimore Sun*, June 11, 1995, www.baltimoresun.com/news/bal-honduras1-story.html.

20. Adán Quan, "Through the Looking Glass: U.S. Aid to El Salvador and the Politics of National Identity," *American Ethnologist* 32, no. 2 (May 2005): 276–93.

21. Suzan Gzesh, "Central Americans and Asylum Policy in the Reagan Era," Migration Policy Institute, April 1, 2006, www.migrationpolicy.org/article/central-americans -and-asylum-policy-reagan-era.

22. Grandin, *The End of the Myth*, 228.

23. "The Candidates Debate; Transcript of the Reagan–Mondale Debate on Foreign Policy," *New York Times*, October 22, 1984, www.nytimes.com/1984/10/22/us/the -candidates-debate-transcript-of-the-reagan-mondale-debate-on-foreign-policy. html; Matthew Longo, *The Politics of Borders: Sovereignty, Security, and the Citizen After 9/11* (Cambridge: Cambridge University Press, 2018), 51; Justin Akers Chacón and Mike Davis, *No One Is Illegal: Fighting Racism and State Violence on the U.S.– Mexico Border* (Chicago: Haymarket Books, 2006).

24. Jennifer G. Correa and James M. Thomas, "From the Border to the Core: A Thickening Military-Police Assemblage," *Critical Sociology* (September 2018): 1–15.

25. Stuart Schrader, *Badges without Borders: How Global Counterinsurgency Transformed American Policing* (Oakland: University of California Press, 2019).

26. Peter J. Meyer and Clare Ribando Seelke, "Central America Regional Security Initiative: Background and Policy Issues for Congress," Congressional Research Service, December 17, 2015, https://fas.org/sgp/crs/row/R41731.pdf.

27. Paley, *Drug War Capitalism*, 16.

28. Nina Lakhani, "Berta Cáceres Court Papers Show Murder Suspects' Links to US-Trained Elite Troops," *Guardian*, February 28, 2017, www.theguardian.com/world/2017/feb/28/berta-caceres-honduras-military-intelligence-us-trained-special-forces; Billy Kyte, "Honduras: The Deadliest Country in the World for Environmental Activism," Global Witness, January 2017, www.globalwitness.org/es/campaigns/environmental-activists/honduras-deadliest-country-world-environmental-activism/.

29. Denise Ferreira da Silva, *Toward a Global Idea of Race* (Minneapolis: University of Minnesota Press, 2007), 3.

30. C. L. R. James, *The Black Jacobins: Toussaint L'Ouverture and the San Domingo Revolution* (New York: Vintage Books, 1963).

31. Jean Saint-Vil, "France Should Return the $40 Billion (U.S) It Ransomed at Gun Point from Haiti between 1825 and 1947," Global Research: Centre for Research on Globalization, January 19, 2010, www.globalresearch.ca/france-should-return-the-40-billion-u-s-it-ransomed-at-gun-point-from-haiti-between-1825-and-1947/17077.

32. Peter James Hudson, *Bankers and Empire: How Wall Street Colonized the Caribbean* (Chicago: University of Chicago Press, 2017), 6.

33. Steve Coupeau, *The History of Haiti* (London: Greenwood Press, 2008).

34. Jean Saint-Vil, "The Real Problem with Haiti," The Canada-Haiti Information Project, https://canada-haiti.ca/content/real-problem-haiti-jean-saint-vil.

35. Keston K. Perry, "What Is Really behind the Crisis in Haiti?" Al Jazeera, September 30, 2019, www.aljazeera.com/indepth/opinion/crisis-haiti-190927092336787.html.

36. Charlotte Hammond, "Coronavirus Deepens Haiti's Unequal Role in Global Garment Supply Chain," Haiti Support Group, April 17, 2020, https://haitisupportgroup.org/garment-factories-reopen-haiti-covid19/.

37. Loyd and Mountz, *Boats, Borders, and Bases*, 42; Nick Davies, "Vietnam 40 Years On: How a Communist Victory Gave Way to Capitalist Corruption," *Guardian*, April 22, 2015, www.theguardian.com/news/2015/apr/22/vietnam-40-years-on-how-communist-victory-gave-way-to-capitalist-corruption.

38. Loyd and Mountz, *Boats, Borders, and Bases*, 72.

39. Todd Miller, *More Than a Wall: Corporate Profiteering and the Militarization of US Borders*, Transnational Institute, September 2019, www.tni.org/files/publication-downloads/more-than-a-wall-report.pdf; William French Smith quoted in Mark Dow, *American Gulag: Inside U.S. Immigration Prisons* (Berkeley: University of California Press, 2005), 7.

40. A. Naomi Paik, "US Turned Away Thousands of Haitian Asylum-Seekers and Detained Hundreds More in the 90s," The Conversation, https://theconversation.com/us-turned-away-thousands-of-haitian-asylum-seekers-and-detained-hundreds-more-in-the-90s-98611; Loyd and Mountz, *Boats, Borders, and Bases*, 162.

41. Loyd and Mountz, *Boats, Borders, and Bases.*
42. Law, *Resistance behind Bars*, 154.
43. Loyd and Mountz, *Boats, Borders, and Bases*, 4.
44. William I. Robinson, "What Is behind the Renegotiation of NAFTA? Trumpism and the New Global Economy," Truthout, July 24, 2017, https://truthout.org/articles/what-is-behind-the-renegotiation-of-nafta-trumpism-and-the-new-global-economy/.
45. Aura Lolita Chávez Ixcaquic quoted in Moira Birss, "Criminalizing Environmental Activism," NACLA, October 4, 2017, https://nacla.org/news/2017/10/04/criminalizing-environmental-activism.
46. Cecilia Olivet, Bettina Müller, and Luciana Ghiotto, "ISDS in Numbers: Impacts of Investment Arbitration against Latin America and the Caribbean," Transnational Institute, December 2017, www.tni.org/files/publication-downloads/isds_en_numerosen2017.pdf.
47. Chacón and Davis, *No One Is Illegal*, 111.
48. Chacón and Davis, *No One Is Illegal*, 121.
49. Gavin O'Toole, "A Constitution Corrupted," NACLA, March 8, 2017, https://nacla.org/news/2017/03/08/constitution-corrupted.
50. O'Toole, "A Constitution Corrupted"; Global Trade Watch, "NAFTA's Legacy for Mexico: Economic Displacement, Lower Wages for Most, Increased Migration," March 2018, www.citizen.org/wp-content/uploads/migration/nafta_factsheet_mexico_legacy_march_2018_final.pdf.
51. Ana de Ita, "Fourteen Years of NAFTA and the Tortilla Crisis," Bilaterals, August 2007, www.bilaterals.org/?fourteen-years-of-nafta-and-the.
52. Laura Dowley, "How an Indigenous Woman Left Her Mark on a Tumultuous Presidential Campaign in Mexico," OpenDemocracy, March 20, 2018, www.opendemocracy.net/en/5050/indigenous-women-presidential-campaign-mexico/.
53. Aldo Gonzalez quoted in Christina Santini, "The People of the Corn," Cultural Survival, December 2006, www.culturalsurvival.org/publications/cultural-survival-quarterly/people-corn.
54. de Ita, "Fourteen Years of NAFTA."
55. Manuel Perez-Rocha, "5 Reasons Mexican Workers Would Cheer the Demise of NAFTA," Foreign Policy in Focus, February 28, 2018, https://fpif.org/5-reasons-mexican-workers-cheer-demise-nafta/; Paley, *Drug War Capitalism*, 101.
56. Reyna Cruz López quoted in Dowley, "How an Indigenous Woman Left Her Mark."
57. Tracy Jan, "With NAFTA in Trump's Crosshairs, Mexico's Border Factories Brace for the Unknown," *Washington Post*, February 21, 2017, www.washingtonpost.com/business/economy/with-nafta-in-trumps-crosshairs-mexicos-border-factories-brace-for-the-unknown/2017/02/21/f91a3960-ee49-11e6-b4ff-ac2cf509efe5_story.html; Patricia Fernandez Kelly, "The 'Maquila' Women," NACLA, September 25, 2007, https://nacla.org/article/%27maquila%27-women.
58. Chacón and Davis, *No One Is Illegal*, 117.
59. John Geddes, "How Many Jobs Has NAFTA Really Cost the U.S.?" *Maclean's*, August 16, 2017, www.macleans.ca/politics/ottawa/how-many-jobs-has-nafta-really-cost-the-u-s/.

60. Kate Bronfenbrenner, "We'll Close! Plant Closings, Plant-Closing Threats, Union Organizing and NAFTA," *Multinational Monitor* 18, no. 3 (1997): 8–14.

61. Robinson, "What Is behind the Renegotiation of NAFTA?"

62. Jonathan Fox and Gaspar Rivera-Salgado, *Indigenous Mexican Migrants in the United States* (La Jolla: Center for U.S.–Mexican Studies / Center for Comparative Immigration Studies, UCSD, 2004).

63. David Bacon, "Globalization and NAFTA Caused Migration from Mexico," Political Research Associates, October 11, 2014, www.politicalresearch.org/2014/10/11/globalization-and-nafta-caused-migration-from-mexico.

64. Bacon, "Globalization and NAFTA."

65. Bill Clinton quoted in Gabriela Flora and Gabriel Camacho, "NAFTA's Not Delivered, Except for Corporations," American Friends Service Committee, www.afsc.org/resource/naftas-not-delivered-except-corporations.

66. Grandin, *The End of the Myth*, 247.

67. Cynthia Bejarano, Maria Cristina Morales, and Said Saddiki, "Understanding Conquest through a Border Lens," in *Beyond Walls and Cages: Prisons, Borders, and Global Crisis*, Jenna M. Loyd, Matt Mitchelson, and Andrew Burridge, eds. (Athens: University of Georgia Press, 2012), 30.

68. Coalición de Derechos Humanos and No More Deaths, *Disappeared: How the US Border Enforcement Agencies Are Fueling a Missing Persons Crisis*, www.thedisappearedreport.org/uploads/8/3/5/1/83515082/disappeared--introduction.pdf.

69. Alexandra Délano Alonso and Benjamin Nienass, "Deaths, Visibility, and Responsibility: The Politics of Mourning at the US–Mexico Border," *Social Research* 83, no. 2 (2016): 421–52.

70. Tanya Maria Golash-Boza, *Deported: Immigrant Policing, Disposable Labor, and Global Capitalism* (New York: New York University Press, 2016).

71. Dow, *American Gulag*, 9; Law, *Resistance behind Bars*, 146.

72. Susan Bibler Coutin, "Exiled by Law: Deportation and the Inviability of Life," in *The Deportation Regime: Sovereignty, Space, and the Freedom of Movement*, Nicholas De Genova and Nathalie Peutz, eds. (Durham: Duke University Press), 357; Miller, *More Than a Wall*.

73. Golash-Boza, *Deported*, 167.

74. Lisa Schaefer, "The 1996 Personal Responsibility and Work Opportunity Reconciliation Act in the US," Centre for Public Impact, October 30, 2017, www.centreforpublicimpact.org/case-study/personal-responsibility-and-work-opportunity-reconciliation-act-the-clinton-welfare-reform/.

75. Premilla Nadasen, "Welfare Reform and the Politics of Race," AHA Today, August 22, 2016, www.historians.org/publications-and-directories/perspectives-on-history/summer-2016/welfare-reform-and-the-politics-of-race-20-years-later.

76. Law, *Resistance Behind Bars*, 165.

77. Alexander, *The New Jim Crow*, 57.

78. Juan Cole, "Top Ten Differences between White Terrorists and Others," Informed Comment, November 28, 2015, www.juancole.com/2015/11/differences-between-terrorists.html.

79. Sunaina Maira, "Radical Deportation: Alien Tales from Lodi and San Francisco," in De Genova and Peutz, *The Deportation Regime*, 304.

80. Maira, "Radical Deportation," 303.

81. ACLU, "New ACLU Report Documents Devastating Effects of Post-9/11 Deportations on Immigrant Communities and Families," December 8, 2004, www.aclu.org/press-releases/new-aclu-report-documents-devastating-effects-post-911-deportations-immigrant.

82. Center for Constitutional Rights, "CMUs: The Federal Prison System's Experiment in Social Isolation," March 31, 2010, https://ccrjustice.org/home/get-involved/tools-resources/fact-sheets-and-faqs/cmus-federal-prison-system-s-experiment.

83. Quoted in Dow, *American Gulag*, 10.

84. Craig Whitlock and Craig Timberg, "Border-Patrol Drones Being Borrowed by Other Agencies More Often Than Previously Known," *Washington Post*, January 14, 2014, www.washingtonpost.com/world/national-security/border-patrol-drones-being-borrowed-by-other-agencies-more-often-than-previously-known/2014/01/14/5f987af0-7d49-11e3-9556-4a4bf7bcbd84_story.html.

85. Nadine Naber and Junaid Rana, "The 21st Century Problem of Anti-Muslim Racism," Jadaliyya, July 25, 2019, www.jadaliyya.com/Details/39830.

86. George W. Bush, "Text: Bush on State of War," *Washington Post*, October 11, 2001, www.washingtonpost.com/wp-srv/nation/specials/attacked/transcripts/bush_text101101.html.

87. Carla Conetta, "Operation Enduring Freedom: Why a Higher Rate of Civilian Bombing Casualties," Project on Defense Alternatives, January 24, 2002, www.comw.org/pda/0201oef.html; Dara Lind, "Trump's Immigration Order Was a 9/11-Style Crisis Reaction—without a 9/11," Vox, January 31, 2017, www.vox.com/policy-and-politics/2017/1/31/14427024/trump-muslim-ban-911.

88. Revolutionary Association of the Women of Afghanistan, "Interview: Afghan Women's Struggles against Patriarchy, Imperialism and Capitalism," September 20, 2019, www.rawa.org/rawa/2019/09/20/interview-afghan-women-s-struggles-against-patriarchy-imperialism-and-capitalism.html.

89. Phyllis Bennis, "The Alarming Rise of Civilian Deaths in the War on Terror," Foreign Policy in Focus, May 10, 2019, https://fpif.org/the-alarming-rise-of-civilian-deaths-in-the-war-on-terror/.

90. Nick Turse, "More U.S. Commandos Are Fighting Wars in the Middle East," The Intercept, September 25, 2019, https://theintercept.com/2019/09/25/special-operations-command-military-middle-east/.

91. Medea Benjamin and Nicolas J. S. Davies, "The Staggering Death Toll in Iraq," Salon, March 19, 2018, www.salon.com/2018/03/19/the-staggering-death-toll-in-iraq_partner/; Martin Chulov, "Research Links Rise in Falluja Birth Defects and Cancers to US Assault," *Guardian*, December 30, 2010, www.theguardian.com/world/2010/dec/30/faulluja-birth-defects-iraq.

92. Jeremy H. Keenan, "Africa Unsecured? The Role of the Global War on Terror (GWOT) in Securing US Imperial Interests in Africa," *Critical Studies on Terrorism* 3, no. 1 (2010): 27–47.

93. Annika Lichtenbaum, "U.S. Military Operational Activity in the Sahel," Lawfare

Institute, January 25, 2019, www.lawfareblog.com/us-military-operational-activity-sahel; Lion Summerbell, "Drones over Djibouti," Africa Is a Country, August 2019, https://africasacountry.com/2019/07/drones-over-djibouti.

94. Stephanie Savell, "Mapping the American War on Terror," Common Dreams, February 19, 2019, www.commondreams.org/views/2019/02/19/mapping-american-war-terror; Watson Institute for International and Public Affairs, "Costs of War," https://watson.brown.edu/costsofwar/papers/summary.

95. Audra Simpson, *Mohawk Interruptus: Political Life across the Borders of Settler States* (Durham: Duke University Press, 2014).

96. International Civil Liberties Monitoring Group, *Civil Liberties, National Security and International Solidarity*, March 27, 2017, https://iclmg.ca/wp-content/uploads/2017/03/CCIC-ICLMG-Exec-Summary-Website-version-FINAL.pdf.

97. United States Conference of Catholic Bishops, "Immigrant Detention Bed Mandate," 2016, https://justiceforimmigrants.org/wp-content/uploads/2017/01/Detention-Bed-Mandate-1-18-17.pdf.

98. No More Deaths, "Factsheet: Operation Streamline," March 2012, https://nomoredeaths.org/wp-content/uploads/2014/10/nmd_fact_sheet_operation_streamline.pdf.

99. Todd Miller, *Border Patrol Nation: Dispatches from the Front Lines of Homeland Security* (San Francisco: City Lights Books, 2014), 259.

100. Michael Dear, *Why Walls Won't Work: Repairing the US-Mexico Divide* (New York: Oxford University Press, 2013), 113; Muzaffar Chisti, Sarah Pierce, and Jessica Bolter, "The Obama Record on Deportations: Deporter in Chief or Not?" Migration Policy Institute, January 26, 2017, www.migrationpolicy.org/article/obama-record-deportations-deporter-chief-or-not.

101. Grandin, *The End of the Myth*, 258.

102. Meredith Hoffman, "What Happened to Arizona's Minutemen?" Vice, March 22, 2016, www.vice.com/en_us/article/xd7jmn/what-happened-to-arizonas-minutemen; Greg Grandin, "How Violent American Vigilantes at the Border Led to Trump's Wall," *Guardian*, February 28, 2019, www.theguardian.com/us-news/2019/feb/28/how-violent-american-vigilantes-at-the-border-led-to-trumps-wall.

103. Longo, *The Politics of Borders*, 53; Associated Press, "Obama Administration Spent $18B on Immigration Enforcement," *USA Today*, January 7, 2013, www.usatoday.com/story/news/nation/2013/01/07/obama-immigration-enforcement/1815667/.

104. Miller, *More Than a Wall*.

105. Dara Lind, "The 2014 Central American Migrant Crisis," Vox, October 10, 2014, www.vox.com/2014/10/10/18088638/child-migrant-crisis-unaccompanied-alien-children-rio-grande-valley-obama-immigration; Dara Lind, "Why Is the Obama Administration Still Fighting to Keep Immigrant Families behind Bars?," Vox, July 29, 2015, www.vox.com/2015/7/29/9067877/family-detention-immigration-flores.

106. John Gramlich and Kristen Bialik, "Immigration Offenses Make Up a Growing Share of Federal Arrests," Pew Research Center, April 10, 2017, www.pewresearch.org/fact-tank/2017/04/10/immigration-offenses-make-up-a-growing-share-of-federal-arrests/.

107. Carlos Rojas, "Why We Confronted Joe Biden on Deportations," interview by Eric Blanc, *Jacobin Magazine*, November 22, 2019, https://jacobinmag.com/2019/11/joe

-biden-deportations-immigration-barack-obama.

108. Natalie Martinez, "Facebook Let Trump's Campaign Run Over 2,000 Ads Referring to Immigration as 'Invasion,'" Media Matters, August 5, 2019, www.mediamatters.org /facebook/facebook-let-trumps-campaign-run-over-2000-ads-referring-immigration -invasion.

109. Medea Benjamin, "America Dropped 26,171 Bombs in 2016. What a Bloody End to Obama's Reign," Guardian, January 9, 2017, www.theguardian.com/commentisfree /2017/jan/09/america-dropped-26171-bombs-2016-obama-legacy.

Chapter 3

1. Sini Saaritsa, Janne Hulkkonen, and Carry Sommers, "Rana Plaza—The Survivors' Stories," Fashion Revolution, October 2018, www.fashionrevolution.org/rana-plaza -the-survivors-stories/.

2. Amirul Haque Amin, "Workers of the World Unite," National Garment Workers Federation, May 29, 2017, www.ilo.org/wcmsp5/groups/public/---asia/---ro-bangkok /---ilo-jakarta/documents/presentation/wcms_555941.pdf.

3. War on Want, Stitched Up: Women Workers in the Bangladeshi Garment Sector, 2011, https://waronwant.org/sites/default/files/Stitched%20Up.pdf.

4. Dana Thomas, "Why Won't We Learn from the Survivors of the Rana Plaza Disaster?," New York Times, April 24, 2018, www.nytimes.com/2018/04/24/style/survivors -of-rana-plaza-disaster.html.

5. World Bank, "Export Processing Zones," Policy and Research Series 20 (Washington, DC: World Bank, Industry Development Division of Industry and Energy Department, Trade Policy Division of Country Economics Department, 1992).

6. Mike Davis, Planet of Slums (London and New York: Verso, 2006), 158.

7. Lisa Duggan, Twilight of Equality: Neoliberalism, Cultural Politics, and the Attack on Democracy (Boston: Beacon Press, 2003), 3.

8. John Chalmers, "Special Report: How Textile Kings Weave a Hold on Bangladesh," Reuters, May 2, 2013, www.reuters.com/article/us-bangladesh-garments-special -report/special-report-how-textile-kings-weave-a-hold-on-bangladesh -idUSBRE9411CX20130502.

9. Debabrata Mondal, "Bangladesh, Global Capitalism, and the Garment Industry," Sanhati, November 24, 2009, http://sanhati.com/excerpted/6726/.

10. Naomi Klein, The Shock Doctrine: The Rise of Disaster Capitalism (Toronto: Alfred A. Knopf, 2007), 97.

11. Walden Bello and Shea Cunningham, "The World Bank and the IMF," Transnational Institute, July 1994, www.tni.org/my/node/5690.

12. Justin Akers Chacón and Mike Davis, No One Is Illegal: Fighting Racism and State Violence on the U.S.–Mexico Border (Chicago: Haymarket Books, 2006), 112; Larry Elliott, "World's 26 Richest People Own as Much as Poorest 50%, Says Oxfam," Guardian, January 21, 2019, www.theguardian.com/business/2019/jan/21/world -26-richest-people-own-as-much-as-poorest-50-per-cent-oxfam-report.

13. "iPhone Workers Today Are 25 Times More Exploited than Textile Workers in 19th

Century England: The Thirty-Ninth Newsletter (2019)," Tricontinental, September 26, 2019, www.thetricontinental.org/newsletterissue/iphone-workers-today-are-25 -times-more-exploited-than-textile-workers-in-19th-century-england-the-thirty -ninth-newsletter-2019/.

14. Anu Muhammad, "Wealth and Deprivation: Ready-Made Garments Industry in Bangladesh," *Economic and Political Weekly* 46, no. 34 (August 2011): 23–27.

15. Tayyab Mahmud, "Debt and Discipline," *American Quarterly* 64, no. 3 (September 2012): 469–94.

16. David Harvey, *Marx, Capital and the Madness of Economic Reason* (New York: Oxford University Press, 2018), 20.

17. Eric Toussaint, "Breaking the Vicious Cycle of Illegitimate Private Debt in the Global South," Committee for the Abolition of Illegitimate Debt, April 26, 2017, www.cadtm.org/Breaking-the-Vicious-Cycle-of,14782.

18. BBC News, "The Bangladesh Poor Selling Organs to Pay Debts," October 28, 2013, www.bbc.com/news/world-asia-24128096.

19. Robert Glennon, "The Unfolding Tragedy of Climate Change in Bangladesh," *Scientific American*, April 21, 2017, https://blogs.scientificamerican.com/guest-blog /the-unfolding-tragedy-of-climate-change-in-bangladesh/.

20. Simon Ingram, "A Gathering Storm: Climate Change Clouds the Future of Children in Bangladesh," UNICEF, April 2019, www.unicef.org/rosa/reports/gathering -storm; Environmental Justice Foundation, "Climate Displacement in Bangladesh," https://ejfoundation.org/reports/climate-displacement-in-bangladesh.

21. Saskia Sassen, *Expulsions: Brutality and Complexity in the Global Economy* (Cambridge: Belknap Press, 2014), 63.

22. Shites Das quoted in AZM Anas, "How Dire Climate Displacement Warnings Are Becoming a Reality in Bangladesh," The New Humanitarian, March 5, 2019, www .thenewhumanitarian.org/news/2019/03/05/how-dire-climate-displacement -warnings-are-becoming-reality-bangladesh.

23. Kristine Kolstad, "Cox's Bazar: The World's Largest Refugee Settlement," Norwegian Refugee Council, August 24, 2018, www.nrc.no/news/2018/august/coxs-bazar -the-worlds-largest-refugee-settlement/.

24. Poppy McPherson, "Dhaka: The City Where Climate Refugees Are Already a Reality," *Guardian*, December 1, 2015, www.theguardian.com/cities/2015/dec/01/dhaka -city-climate-refugees-reality.

25. Saleemul Huq quoted in Tim McDonnell, "Climate Change Creates a New Migration Crisis for Bangladesh," *National Geographic*, January 24, 2019, www .nationalgeographic.com/environment/2019/01/climate-change-drives-migration -crisis-in-bangladesh-from-dhaka-sundabans/#close.

26. Anna Plowman, "Bangladesh's Disaster Capitalism," *Jacobin Magazine*, January 22, 2016, www.jacobinmag.com/2016/01/bangladesh-rana-plaza-rmg-garment-industry -climate-change-environment.

27. Naila Kabeer and Simeen Mahmud, "Rags, Riches and Women Workers: Export-Oriented Garment Manufacturing in Bangladesh," in *Chains of Fortune: Linking Women Producers and Workers with Global Markets*, Marilyn Carr, ed. (London:

Commonwealth Secretariat, 2004), 133–62.

28. Julhas Alam, "Bangladesh Garment Workers Seek Unpaid Wages as Orders Stop," AP News, April 16, 2020, https://apnews.com /181650f23661c91c8757d85c5491c883.

29. Conrad Duncan, "Bangladesh Fire Leaves '50,000 People Homeless' after Slum Destroyed in Capital of Dhaka," *Independent*, August 17, 2019, www.independent .co.uk/news/world/asia/bangladesh-fire-slum-destroyed-homeless-blaze-dhaka -capital-a9063871.html.

30. United Nations, Department of Economic and Social Affairs, "Sustainable Development Goals Statistics," 2019, https://unstats.un.org/sdgs/report/2019/goal-11/.

31. Tanner Howard, "Are Planners Partly to Blame for Gentrification?" Citylab, March 29, 2019, www.citylab.com/equity/2019/03/urban-planning-gentrification-capital -city-samuel-stein/585262/.

32. Gita Dewan Verma, *Slumming India: A Chronicle of Slums and Their Saviours* (New Delhi: Penguin Books India, 2002), xix.

33. Neil Smith, "Gentrification in Berlin and the Revanchist State," Policing Crowds, October 20, 2007, http://policing-crowds.org/urbanization/homelessness/homeless /neil-smith-gentrification-in-berlin-and-the-revanchist-state/.

34. UN, Department of Economic and Social Affairs, *International Migration Report 2017: Highlights* (ST/ESA/SER.A/404), www.un.org /en/development/desa/population/migration/publications/migrationreport/docs /MigrationReport2017_Highlights.pdf.

35. Adam Hanieh, "The Contradictions of Global Migration," in *Socialist Register 2019: A World Turned Upside Down?*, Leo Panitch and Gregory Albo, eds. (London: Merlin Press, 2018): 52–53.

36. US Customs and Border Protection, "U. S. Border Patrol Nationwide Apprehensions by Citizenship and Sector in FY2007," www.cbp.gov/sites/default/files/assets /documents/2018-Jul/usbp-nationwide-apps-sector-citizenship-fy07-fy17.pdf.

37. Hunter Stuart, "The Bangladeshis Are on the Rise in New York City," Huffington Post, April 14, 2011, www.huffingtonpost.ca/2011/03/14/bangladeshi -new-york_n_833641.html.

38. New York Taxi Workers Alliance, "NYTWA Statement on Muslim Ban," www.nytwa.org/solidarity.

39. Manfred Ricciardelli, "Taxi Drivers Face Unique Challenges in Filing Workers' Compensation Claims When Injured While Working," MFR Law Office, www.mfrlawoffice .com/library/challenges-faced-by-taxi-drivers-in-filing-for-workers-comp.cfm.

40. Thompson Reuters Foundation, "Why Are So Many Overseas Bangladeshi Workers Dying?" *South China Morning Post*, January 22, 2019, www.scmp.com/news/asia /south-asia/article/2183220/why-are-so-many-overseas-bangladeshi-workers-dying.

41. Industrial Global Union, "Over 11,600 Bangladesh Garment Workers Lose Jobs and Face Repression," February 11, 2019, www.industriall-union.org/over-11600-bangladesh -garment-workers-lose-jobs-and-face-repression.

42. "Number of Migrants Now Growing Faster Than World Population, New UN Figures Show," UN News, September 17, 2019, https://news.un.org/en/story/2019

/09/1046562; UN High Commissioner for Refugees, "Figures at a Glance," June 19, 2019, www.unhcr.org/figures-at-a-glance.html.

43. Here I am following Elizabeth Povinelli, *Economies of Abandonment: Social Belonging and Endurance in Late Liberalism* (Durham: Duke University Press, 2011), and Ruth Wilson Gilmore, *Golden Gulag: Prisons, Surplus, Crisis, and Opposition in Globalizing California* (Berkeley: University of California Press, 2007).

44. Jennifer Hyndman and Wenona Giles, *Refugees in Extended Exile* (London: Routledge, 2016), xiv, 2.

45. Noura Erakat, *Justice for Some: Law and the Question of Palestine* (Stanford: Stanford University Press, 2019), 52, 55.

46. Noura Erakat, "On Recent Events in Palestine," Jadaliyya, June 19, 2017, www.jadaliyya.com/Details/34382/On-Recent-Events-in-Palestine.

47. Peter Baker and Julie Hirschfeld Davis, "U.S. Finalizes Deal to Give Israel $38 Billion in Military Aid, *New York Times*, September 13, 2016, www.nytimes.com /2016/09/14/world/middleeast/israel-benjamin-netanyahu-military-aid.html.

48. Sasha Chavkin and Michael Hudson, "New Investigation Reveals 3.4m Displaced by World Bank," International Consortium of Investigative Journalists, April 13, 2015, www.icij.org/blog/2015/04/new-investigation-reveals-34m-displaced-world-bank/.

49. "The Sardar Sarovar Dam: A Brief Introduction," Narmada, May 10, 2006, www.narmada.org/sardarsarovar.html.

50. Ratan quoted in Eric Randolph, "Indian Protest over Narmada Dam Builds Awareness of Rights," *National* (UAE), October 31, 2010, www.thenational.ae/world/asia /indian-protest-over-narmada-dam-builds-awareness-of-rights-1.562690.

51. Thomas R. Berger, "The World Bank's Independent Review of India's Sardar Sarovar Projects," *American University International Law Review* 9, no. 1 (1993): 33–48.

52. "Human Impacts of Dams," International Rivers, www.internationalrivers.org/human -impacts-of-dams.

53. Inclusive Development International, "Unjust Enrichment: How the IFC Profits from Land Grabbing in Africa," Oakland Institute, April 2017, www.oaklandinstitute .org/sites/oaklandinstitute.org/files/outsourcing-development-africa.pdf.

54. Kyle F. Davis, Paolo D'Odorico, and Maria Cristina Rulli, "Land Grabbing: A Preliminary Quantification of Economic Impacts on Rural Livelihoods," *Population and Environment* 36, no. 2 (December 2014): 180–92.

55. Timothy A. Wise, "Land Grab Update: Mozambique, Africa Still in the Crosshairs," Food Tank, October 2016, https://foodtank.com/news/2016/10/land-grab-update -mozambique-africa-still-in-the-crosshairs/; Sassen, *Expulsions*, 152.

56. Damian Carrington, "$1m a Minute: The Farming Subsidies Destroying the World– Report," *Guardian*, September 16, 2019, www.theguardian.com/environment/2019 /sep/16/1m-a-minute-the-farming-subsidies-destroying-the-world.

57. "Land Grabbing," Global Agriculture, www.globalagriculture.org/report-topics /land-grabbing.html.

58. Oakland Institute, "World Bank Fuels Land Grabs in Africa through Shadowy Financial Sector Investments," May 1, 2017, www.oaklandinstitute.org/world-bank -fuels-land-grabs-africa-through-shadowy-financial-sector-investments.

59. Sassen, *Expulsions*, 94.

60. James Fairhead, Melissa Leach, and Ian Scoones, "Green Grabbing: A New Appropriation of Nature?" *Journal of Peasant Studies* 39, no. 2 (April 2012): 237–61.

61. "The African People's Land Grab Declaration," Stop Africa Land Grab, 2019, www.stopafricalandgrab.com/declaration.php.

62. Sassen, *Expulsions*, 83.

63. Amina Mama, "Sheroes and Villains: Conceptualizing Colonial and Contemporary Violence against Women in Africa," in *Feminist Genealogies, Colonial Legacies, Democratic Futures*, M. Jacqui Alexander and Chandra Talpade Mohanty, eds. (New York: Routledge, 1997), 61.

64. Lyn Ossome, "Can the Law Secure Women's Rights to Land in Africa? Revisiting Tensions between Culture and Land Commercialization," *Feminist Economics* 20, no. 1 (2014): 170.

65. Silvia Federici, *Witches, Witch-Hunting, and Women* (Oakland: PM Press, 2018).

66. Ana Paula Tuacale quoted in "Peasant Union Concerned at Land Expropriation in Mozambique," Club of Mozambique, October 17, 2017, https://clubofmozambique .com/news/peasant-union-concerned-at-land-expropriation-in-mozambique/.

67. Kate Lyons, "Climate Refugees Can't Be Returned Home, Says Landmark UN Human Rights Ruling," *Guardian*, January 20, 2020, www.theguardian.com/world/2020/jan/20 /climate-refugees-cant-be-returned-home-says-landmark-un-human-rights-ruling.

68. Internal Displacement Monitoring Centre and Norwegian Refugee Council, *2017 Global Report on Internal Displacement*, May 2017, www.internal-displacement.org /global-report/grid2017/pdfs/2017-GRID.pdf/.

69. "Disasters and Climate Change," Internal Displacement Monitoring Centre, www.internal-displacement.org/disasters-and-climate-change.

70. Kanta Kumari Rigaud et al., "Groundswell: Preparing for Internal Climate Migration" (Washington, DC: World Bank, 2018), http://hdl.handle.net/10986/29461; Baher Kamal, "Climate Migrants Might Reach One Billion by 2050," Relief Web, August 21, 2017, https://reliefweb.int/report/world/climate-migrants-might-reach-one -billion-2050.

71. Joshua Axelrod, "Canada's Boreal Clearcutting Is a Climate Threat," NRDC, November 1, 2017, www.nrdc.org/experts/josh-axelrod/canadas-boreal-clearcutting-climate -threat; Deng Tingting, "In China, the Water You Drink Is as Dangerous as the Air You Breathe," *Guardian*, June 2, 2017, www.theguardian.com/global-development -professionals-network/2017/jun/02/china-water-dangerous-pollution-greenpeace.

72. Hans-Joachim Heintze et al., *World Risk Report 2018*, Bündnis Entwicklung Hilft and Ruhr University Bochum–Institute for International Law of Peace and Armed Conflict (IFHV), 2018, https://reliefweb.int/sites/reliefweb.int/files/resources /WorldRiskReport-2018.pdf.

73. Rhett Butler, "Rich Countries Grow at Ecological Expense of Poor Countries," Mongabay, January 21, 2008, https://news.mongabay.com/2008/01/rich-countries-grow -at-ecological-expense-of-poor-countries/; Todd Miller, "Save the Climate, Dismantle the Border Apparatus," *Jacobin Magazine*, June 23, 2019, https://jacobinmag.com /2019/07/green-new-deal-freedom-movement-borders.

74. Climate Reality Project, "How the Climate Crisis Is Driving Central American Migration," May 31, 2019, www.climaterealityproject.org/blog/how-climate -crisis-driving-central-american-migration.

75. Climate Reality Project, "How the Climate Crisis Is Driving Central American Migration."

76. Climate Centre, "UN: Sahel Region One of the Most Vulnerable to Climate Change," November 14, 2018, www.climatecentre.org/news/1066/un-sahel-region-one-of-the -most-vulnerable-to-climate-change.

77. Ibrahim Thiaw quoted in "Building Climate Resilience and Peace Go Hand in Hand for Africa's Sahel-UN Forum," Africa Renewal Information Program, www.un.org/africarenewal/news/building-climate-resilience-and-peace-go -hand-hand-africa%E2%80%99s-sahel-%E2%80%93-un-forum.

78. Stefano M. Torelli, "Climate-Driven Migration in Africa," European Council on Foreign Relations, December 20, 2017, www.ecfr.eu/article/commentary_climate _driven_migration_in_africa; Food and Agriculture Organization of the United Nations, "The Magnitude of the Problem," www.fao.org/3/X5318E/x5318e02.htm; Robert Muggah and José Luengo Cabrera, "The Sahel Is Engulfed by Violence," World Economic Forum, January 23, 2019, www.weforum.org/agenda/2019/01/all -the-warning-signs-are-showing-in-the-sahel-we-must-act-now/.

79. Tim McDonnell, "The Refugees the World Barely Pays Attention To," NPR, June 20, 2018, www.npr.org/sections/goatsandsoda/2018/06/20/621782275/the-refugees -that-the-world-barely-pays-attention-to.

80. Ioane Teitiota quoted in Tim McDonald, "The Man Who Would Be the First Climate Change Refugee," BBC News, November 5, 2015, www.bbc.com/news/world -asia-34674374.

Chapter 4

1. Perla Trevizo, "Tribes Seek to Join Immigration Reform Debate," *Arizona Daily Star*, June 14, 2013, https://tucson.com/news/local/border/tribes-seek-to-join-immigration -reform-debate/article_d4fe1980-46d4-5e90-b690-ce78c5453bf1.html.

2. Michael Dear, *Why Walls Won't Work: Repairing the US–Mexico Divide* (New York: Oxford University Press, 2013), 158.

3. Will Parish, "The U.S. Border Patrol and an Israeli Military Contractor Are Putting a Native American Reservation Under 'Persistent Surveillance,'" The Intercept, August 25, 2019, https://theintercept.com/2019/08/25/border-patrol-israel-elbit -surveillance/; Todd Miller, "How Border Patrol Occupied the Tohono O'odham Nation," In These Times, June 12, 2019, https://inthesetimes.com/article/21903/us -mexico-border-surveillance-tohono-oodham-nation-border-patrol.

4. "Tohono O'odham National Tribal Chairman Says Nation Won't Allow Border Wall to Be Built," ABC 15 Arizona News, November 15, 2016, www.abc15.com/news /region-central-southern-az/other/tohono-oodham-national-tribal-chairman -says-nation-wont-allow-border-wall-to-be-built.

5. Ofelia Rivas quoted in "Silent and Sacred," *USA Today*, www.usatoday.com/border-wall

/story/tohono-oodham-nation-arizona-tribe/582487001/.

6. Ruth Wilson Gilmore, *Golden Gulag: Prisons, Surplus, Crisis, and Opposition to Globalizing California* (Berkeley: University of California Press, 2007), 247.

7. Jasbir Puar, *The Right to Maim: Debility, Capacity, Disability* (Durham: Duke University Press, 2017), 64.

8. Puar, *The Right to Maim*, 81.

9. Alan Gomez, "Homeland Security: More Than 600,000 Foreigners Overstayed U.S. Visas in 2017," *USA Today*, August 7, 2018, www.usatoday.com/story/news/world /2018/08/07/dhs-foreigners-overstayed-visas-2017/924316002/.

10. US Department of Homeland Security, "Entry/Exit Overstay Report: Fiscal Year 2015," January 19, 2016, www.dhs.gov/sites/default/files/publications/FY%2015%20 DHS%20Entry%20and%20Exit%20Overstay%20Report.pdf. Data calculated from Suspected In-Country Over-Stay Total columns; total for all countries is 482,781 suspected in-country overstays.

11. Mary Romero, "Keeping Citizenship Rights White: Arizona's Racial Profiling Practices in Immigration Law Enforcement," *Law Journal for Social Justice* 1, no. 1 (2011): 97–113.

12. Michael D. Shear and Julie Hirschfeld Davis, "Shoot Migrants' Legs, Build Alligator Moat: Behind Trump's Ideas for Border," *New York Times*, October 1, 2019, www.nytimes.com/2019/10/01/us/politics/trump-border-wars.html.

13. Ryan Devereaux, "Mining the Future," The Intercept, October 3, 2019, https:// theintercept.com/2019/10/03/climate-change-migration-militarization-arizona/.

14. Associated Press, "Trump Administration to Expand DNA Collection at Border and Give Data to FBI," *Guardian*, October 3, 2019, www.theguardian.com/us-news /2019/oct/02/us-immigration-border-dna-trump-administration.

15. Wendy Brown, *Walled States, Waning Sovereignty* (New York and Cambridge: Zone Books, 2017), 132.

16. Brown, *Walled States*, 105.

17. Reece Jones, "Introduction," in *Open Borders: In Defense of Free Movement*, Reece Jones, ed. (Athens: University of Georgia Press, 2019), 3.

18. Todd Miller, *Border Patrol Nation: Dispatches from the Front Lines of Homeland Security* (San Francisco: City Lights Books, 2014), 42.

19. Shoshana Zuboff, *The Age of Surveillance Capitalism: The Fight for a Human Future at the New Frontier of Power* (New York: PublicAffairs, 2019), 10.

20. Reece Jones, *Border Walls: Security and the War on Terror in the United States, India, and Israel* (London: Zed Books, 2012), 2.

21. Kate Smith, "Immigrant Deportation Filings Hit Record High in 2018, New Report Shows," CBS News, November 8, 2018, www.cbsnews.com/news/ice-deportations-in -2018-hit-record-high/.

22. Emily Kassie, "Detained: How the US Built the World's Largest Immigrant Detention System," *Guardian*, September 24, 2019, www.theguardian.com/us-news/2019 /sep/24/detained-us-largest-immigrant-detention-trump.

23. National Catholic Reporter Editorial Staff, "Editorial: Don't Look Away from Concentration Camps at the Border," National Catholic Reporter, June 19, 2019, www

.ncronline.org/news/opinion/editorial-dont-look-away-concentration-camps-border.

24. César Cuauhtémoc Garcia Hernández, "Abolishing Immigration Prisons," *Boston University Law Review* 97, no. 1 (2017): 245–300.

25. UN High Commissioner for Refugees, *Women on the Run: First-Hand Accounts of Refugees Fleeing El Salvador, Guatemala, Honduras, and Mexico*, October 26, 2015, www.unhcr.org/5630f24c6.html.

26. Alice Speri, "Detained, Then Violated," The Intercept, April 11, 2018, https://theintercept.com/2018/04/11/immigration-detention-sexual-abuse-ice-dhs/.

27. Nicoll Hernández-Polanco quoted in Adam Frankel, "Do You See How Much I'm Suffering Here? Abuse against Transgender Women in US Immigration Detention," Human Rights Watch, March 23, 2016, www.hrw.org/report/2016/03/23/do-you -see-how-much-im-suffering-here/abuse-against-transgender-women-us.

28. Katalina Hadfield, "The Precarious Position of Transgender Immigrants and Asylum Seekers," Human Rights Campaign, January 4, 2019, www.hrc.org/blog/the -precarious-position-of-transgender-immigrants-and-asylum-seekers.

29. Livia Luan, "Profiting from Enforcement: The Role of Private Prisons in U.S. Immigration Detention," Migration Policy Institute, May 2, 2018, www.migrationpolicy.org /article/profiting-enforcement-role-private-prisons-us-immigration-detention; John Washington, "The Amount of Money Being Made Ripping Migrant Families Apart Is Staggering," *The Nation*, October 28, 2019, www.thenation.com/article/immigration -ice-family-separation/.

30. Luan, "Profiting from Enforcement."

31. Todd Miller, *More Than a Wall: Corporate Profiteering and the Militarization of US Borders*, Transnational Institute, September 2019, www.tni.org/files/publication -downloads/more-than-a-wall-report.pdf.

32. Nancy MacLean, *Democracy in Chains: The Deep History of the Radical Right's Stealth Plan for America* (New York: Viking, 2017), 219.

33. Manny Fernandez and Katie Benner, "The Billion-Dollar Business of Operating Shelters for Migrant Children," *New York Times*, June 21, 2018, www.nytimes.com /2018/06/21/us/migrant-shelters-border-crossing.html.

34. Jackie Wang, *Carceral Capitalism* (New York: Semiotext(e), 2017), 281.

35. Meagan Flynn, "ICE Is Holding $204 Million in Bond Money, and Some Immigrants Might Never Get It Back," *Washington Post*, April 26, 2019, www.washingtonpost.com/ immigration/ice-is-holding-204-million-in-bond-money-and-some-immigrants-might -never-get-it-back/2019/04/26/dcaa69a0-5709-11e9-9136-f8e636f1f6df_story.html; Michael W. Sances and Hye Young You, "Who Pays for Government? Descriptive Representation and Exploitative Revenue Sources," *Journal of Politics* 79, no. 3 (2017): 1090–94.

36. Pam Palmater quoted in Amanda Coletta, "Canada's Indigenous Population Is Over-represented in Federal Prisons—and It's Only Getting Worse," *Washington Post*, July 1, 2018, www.washingtonpost.com/news/worldviews/wp/2018/07/01/canadas-indigenous -population-is-over-represented-in-federal-prisons-and-its-only-getting-worse/.

37. Rinaldo Walcott and Idil Abdillahi, *BlackLife: Post-BLM and the Struggle for Freedom* (Winnipeg: ARP Books, 2019), 44.

38. Equal Justice Initiative, "Incarceration of Women Is Growing Twice as Fast as that of Men," November 5, 2018, https://eji.org/news/female-incarceration-growing -twice-as-fast-as-male-incarceration/.

39. Michelle Alexander, *The New Jim Crow: Mass Incarceration in the Age of Colorblindness* (New York: New Press, 2012), 13.

40. Lisa Monchalin, *The Colonial Problem: An Indigenous Perspective on Crime and Injustice in Canada* (Toronto: University of Toronto Press, 2016).

41. Ruth Wilson Gilmore, "Race, Capitalist Crisis, and Abolitionist Organizing: An Interview with Ruth Wilson Gilmore," interview by Jenna Loyd in *Beyond Walls and Cages: Prisons, Borders, and Global Crisis*, Jenna M. Loyd, Matt Mitchelson, and Andrew Burridge, eds. (Athens: University of Georgia Press, 2012), 43.

42. Dylan Rodríguez, "Abolition as Praxis of Human Being: A Foreword," *Harvard Law Review* 132, no. 1575 (2019): 1577.

43. Tania Unzueta, "We Fell in Love in a Hopeless Place: A Grassroots History from #Not1More to Abolish ICE," Medium, June 29, 2018, https://medium.com/@LaTania /we-fell-in-love-in-a-hopeless-place-a-grassroots-history-from-not1more-to-abolish -ice-23089cf21711.

44. Kesi Foster, "There Are No Sanctuaries," Black Organizing Project, December 16, 2016, http://blackorganizingproject.org/5888-2/.

45. Tanya Maria Golash-Boza, *Deported: Immigrant Policing, Disposable Labor and Global Capitalism* (New York: New York University Press, 2015), 177, 185; Marybeth Onyeukwu, "Black Immigrants' Lives Matter: Disrupting the Dialogue on Immigrant Detention," Truthout, July 22, 2015, https://truthout.org/articles/black-immigrants -lives-matter-disrupting-the-dialogue-on-immigrant-detention/.

46. ACLU, "The Constitution in the 100-Mile Border Zone," June 2018, www.aclu.org /other/constitution-100-mile-border-zone.

47. Joseph Nevins, "Policing Mobility: Maintaining Global Apartheid from South Africa to the United States," in Loyd, Mitchelson, and Burridge, *Beyond Walls and Cages*, 21.

48. Zack Ford, "ICE Raids Followed a Massive Sexual Harassment Settlement at Mississippi Plants," Think Progress, August 8, 2019, https://thinkprogress.org/ice-raids-follow -massive-sexual-harassment-settlement-mississippi-plant-koch-foods-d95eb2720f67/.

49. Teju Cole, "Migrants Are Welcome," Verso Blog, September 7, 2015, www.versobooks.com/blogs/2226-teju-cole-migrants-are-welcome.

50. Suketu Mehta, "This Land Is Their Land," *Foreign Policy*, September 12, 2017, https:// foreignpolicy.com/2017/09/12/this-land-is-their-land-america-europe-fear-of-migrants -trump/.

51. UN General Assembly, *Convention Relating to the Status of Refugees*, July 28, 1951, United Nations, Treaty Series, vol. 189, 137.

52. Aimé Césaire, *Discourse on Colonialism* (New York: Monthly Review Press, 1972), 14.

53. Sarah Lazare, "How the Red Scare Shaped the Artificial Distinction between Migrants and Refugees," In These Times, February 5, 2018, https://inthesetimes.com/article /20888/cold-war-anti-communism-political-refugee-economic-migrant-war-poverty.

54. Fabian Georgi and Susanne Schatral, "Toward a Critical Theory of Migration Control: The Case of the International Organization for Migration" in *The New Politics of*

International Mobility: Migration Management and Its Discontents, Martin Geiger and Antoine Pécoud, eds. (Osnabrück: Institute for Migration Research and Intercultural Studies, 2012), 193–221.

55. Maribel Casas-Cortes, Sebastian Cobarrubias, and John Pickles, "'Good Neighbours Make Good Fences': Seahorse Operations, Border Externalization and Extra-Territoriality," *European Urban and Regional Studies* 23, no. 3 (2016): 231–51.

56. US Coast Guard, "Enforcing Immigration Laws," Go Coast Guard, www.gocoastguard .com/about-the-coast-guard/discover-our-roles-missions/migrant-interdiction.

57. Nicholas Keung, "Record Number of Canada-Bound Visitors Barred from Flights on Advice of Canada Border Agents," *The Star*, July 17, 2019, www.thestar.com/news /canada/2019/07/17/record-number-of-canada-bound-visitors-barred-from-flights -on-advice-of-canada-border-agents.html.

58. Vilna Bashi, "Globalized Anti-Blackness: Transnationalizing Western Immigration Law, Policy, and Practice," *Ethnic and Racial Studies* 27, no. 4 (2004): 584–606.

59. Canadian Council for Refugees, *Closing the Front Door on Refugees: Report on the First Year of the Safe Third Country Agreement*, 2005, https://ccrweb.ca/files /closingdoordec05.pdf.

60. Immigration and Refugee Board of Canada, "Irregular Border Crosser Statistics," https://irb-cisr.gc.ca/en/statistics/Pages/Irregular-border-crosser-statistics.aspx.

61. Statistics Canada, "Just the Facts: Asylum Claimants," May 17, 2019, https:// www150.statcan.gc.ca/n1/pub/89-28-0001/2018001/article/00013-eng.htm.

62. Miller, *Border Patrol Nation*, 199; Todd Miller, *Empire of Borders: The Expansion of the US Border around the World* (New York: Verso, 2019).

63. Miller, *Empire of Borders*, 6.

64. Miller, *Empire of Borders*, 4.

65. Dawn Paley, *Drug War Capitalism* (Oakland: AK Press, 2014), 147.

66. Adam Isacson, Maureen Meyer, and Gabriela Morales, *Mexico's Other Border: Security, Migration, and the Humanitarian Crisis at the Line with Central America*, Washington Office on Latin America, June 2014, www.wola.org/files/mxgt/report/.

67. NISGUA, "Guatemala Resists U.S. Border Imperialism," August 2019, https://nisgua .org/portfolio-items/border-imperialism/?portfolioCats=351%2C362.

68. Kristina Cooke, Mica Rosenberg, and Reade Levinson, "U.S. Migrant Policy Sends Thousands of Children, including Babies, Back to Mexico," Reuters, October 11, 2019, www.reuters.com/article/us-usa-immigration-babies-exclusive/exclusive-u-s-migrant -policy-sends-thousands-of-babies-and-toddlers-back-to-mexico-idUSKBN1WQ1H1.

69. Sandra Cuffe, "One Year into 'Remain in Mexico,' the U.S. Is Enlisting Central America In Its Crackdown on Asylum," The Intercept, January 29, 2020, https://theintercept .com/2020/01/29/remain-in-mexico-year-anniversary-central-america/; Gustavo Solis, "Remain in Mexico Has a 0.1 Percent Asylum Grant Rate," *San Diego Union Tribune*, December 15, 2019, www.sandiegouniontribune.com/news/border-baja-california /story/2019-12-15/remain-in-mexico-has-a-0-01-percent-asylum-grant-rate.

70. Cat Cardenas, "Still Fearing Violence, Migrants Subject to Trump's Remain in Mexico Policy Are Now Bracing for a Pandemic," *Texas Monthly*, April 10, 2020, www .texasmonthly.com/news/matamoros-migrant-camps-coronavirus-remain-mexico/.

71. Clare Ribando Seelke, "Mexico: Evolution of the Mérida Initiative, 2007–2020," Congressional Research Service, June 28, 2019, https://fas.org/sgp/crs/row/IF10578.pdf.

72. Miller, *Empire of Borders*, 22.

73. Deborah Bonello and Erin Siegal McIntyre, "Is Rape the Price to Pay for Migrant Women Chasing the American Dream?" Splinter News, August 10, 2014, https://splinternews.com/is-rape-the-price-to-pay-for-migrant-women-chasing-the-1793842446.

74. Kirk Semple, "Overflowing Toilets, Bedbugs and High Heat: Inside Mexico's Migrant Detention Centers," *New York Times*, August 3, 2019, www.nytimes.com/2019/08/03/world/americas/mexico-migration-conditions.html.

75. Kirk Semple and Brent McDonald, "Mexico Breaks Up a Migrant Caravan, Pleasing White House," *New York Times*, January 24, 2020, www.nytimes.com/2020/01/24/world/americas/migrant-caravan-mexico.html.

76. Human Rights Watch, "Mexico: Free Detained Migrants amid Pandemic," April 14, 2020, www.hrw.org/news/2020/04/14/mexico-free-detained-migrants-amid-pandemic.

77. "Record Number of African Migrants Coming to Mexican Border," PBS News, June 16, 2019, www.pbs.org/newshour/world/record-number-of-african-migrants-coming-to-mexican-border; Simone Schlindwein, "Halfway round the World by Plane: Africa's New Migration Route," Deutsche Welle, August 2, 2019, www.dw.com/en/halfway-round-the-world-by-plane-africas-new-migration-route/a-49868809.

78. "African Migrants Assembly Created in Chiapas," El Enemigo Común, September 2, 2019, https://elenemigocomun.net/2019/09/african-migrants-assembly-created-in-chiapas/.

79. Angela Davis quoted in Lalitha Chelliah and Chris Peterson, "Angela Davis: 'The Refugee Movement Is the Civil Rights Movement of Our Time,'" *Green Left Weekly*, October 29, 2016, www.greenleft.org.au/content/angela-davis-%E2%80%98-refugee-movement-civil-rights-movement-our-time%E2%80%99.

Chapter 5

1. Behrouz Boochani, *No Friend but the Mountains: Writing from Manus Prison,* Omid Tofighian, trans. (Toronto: House of Anasi Press, 2019).

2. Boochani, *No Friend but the Mountains*, 179.

3. Abdul Aziz Adam, "'The Cage Made Me Strong': Manus Island Detainee Abdul Aziz Muhamat Wins Human Rights Award-Video," *Guardian*, February 15, 2019, www.theguardian.com/global/video/2019/feb/15/the-cage-made-me-strong-manus-island-detainee-abdul-aziz-muhamat-wins-human-rights-award-video.

4. Rachel Eddie, "Refugee Sets Self on Fire at Manus Island amid 'Mental Health Crisis'," *Sydney Morning Herald,* June 12, 2019, www.smh.com.au/national/refugee-sets-self-on-fire-at-manus-island-amid-mental-health-crisis-20190612-p51wuk.html.

5. Christopher Knaus and Helen Davidson, "Company Given $21.5m for Manus Healthcare without a Contract," *Guardian,* February 21, 2019, www.theguardian.com/australia-news/2019/feb/22/company-given-215m-for-manus-healthcare-despite-poor-track-record.

6. Rory Callinan, "Australian Funds Lethal Brute Squad," *The Age*, August 4, 2013, www.theage.com.au/national/victoria/australia-funds-lethal-brute -squad-20130803-2r6g1.html.

7. Michael McGowan, "Notorious PNG Police Unit Deployed at Manus Refugee Camp as Tensions Rise," *Guardian*, June 3, 2019, www.theguardian.com/australia-news/2019 /jun/04/notorious-png-police-unit-deployed-at-manus-refugee-camp-as-tensions-rise.

8. Amnesty International, *Undermining Rights: Forced Evictions and Police Brutality Around the Porgera Gold Mine, Papua New Guinea*, January 2010, www.amnesty.org /download/Documents/36000/asa340012010eng.pdf.

9. Chris Albin-Lackey, *Gold's Costly Dividend: Human Rights Impacts of Papua New Guinea's Porgera Gold Mine*, Human Rights Watch, February 1, 2011, www.hrw.org/report/2011/02/01/golds-costly-dividend/human-rights-impacts -papua-new-guineas-porgera-gold-mine.

10. Albin-Lackey, *Gold's Costly Dividend*; Amnesty International, *Undermining Rights*.

11. Valerie Croft, "Forced Evictions around Papua New Guinea Mine Have Canadian Link," *The Straight*, February 4, 2010, www.straight.com/article-286263/vancouver /valerie-croft-forced-evictions-around-papua-new-guinea-mine-have-canadian-link.

12. "Enemies of the State? How Governments and Business Silence Land and Environmental Defenders," Global Witness, July 30, 2019, www.globalwitness.org/en /campaigns/environmental-activists/enemies-state/.

13. Andrew Findlay, "Canadian Mining Companies Will Now Face Human Rights Charges in Canadian Courts," *The Narwhal*, June 7, 2019, https://thenarwhal.ca/canadian -mining-companies-will-now-face-human-rights-charges-in-canadian-courts/.

14. William Walters, "Deportation, Expulsion, and International Police of Aliens," in *The Deportation Regime: Sovereignty, Space, and the Freedom of Movement*, Nicholas De Genova and Nathalie Peutz, eds. (Durham: Duke University Press, 2010), 78.

15. Stuart Banner, *Possessing the Pacific: Land, Settlers, and Indigenous People from Australia to Alaska* (Cambridge: Harvard University Press, 2007).

16. Renisa Mawani, *Across Oceans of Law: The Komagata Maru and Jurisdiction in the Time of Empire* (Durham: Duke University Press, 2018), 223.

17. Brenna Bhandar, *Colonial Lives of Property: Law, Land, and Racial Regimes of Ownership* (Durham: Duke University Press, 2018), 102.

18. Mawani, *Across Oceans of Law*.

19. Katherine Roscoe, "A Natural Hulk: Australia's Carceral Islands in the Colonial Period, 1788–1901," *International Review of Social History* 63, no. 26 (2018): 45–63.

20. Gerald Horne, *The White Pacific: U.S. Imperialism and Black Slavery in the South Seas after the Civil War* (Honolulu: University of Hawaii Press, 2007).

21. Elliose Farrow-Smith, "Australia Still Slow to Remember Its South Sea Islander Heritage and Industry It Helped Create," ABC North Coast, December 20, 2018, www .abc.net.au/news/2018-12-21/south-sea-islander-people-remembered-in-history /10628250.

22. Iyko Day, *Alien Capital: Asian Racialization and the Logic of Settler Colonial Capitalism* (Durham: Duke University Press, 2016), 17.

23. Stuart Hall, *Familiar Stranger: A Life between Two Islands* (Durham: Duke Universi-

ty Press, 2017), 22.

24. Paul N. Nelson et al., "Oil Palm and Deforestation in Papua New Guinea," *Conservation Letters* 7, no. 3 (2014): 188–95.

25. Global Witness, *Bending the Truth*, May 7, 2020, www.globalwitness.org /documents/19894/Bending_the_Truth.pdf.

26. Anthea Vogl, "Sovereign Relations? Australia's 'Off-Shoring' of Asylum Seekers on Nauru in Historical Perspective," in *Against International Norms: Postcolonial Perspectives*, Charlotte Epstein, ed. (London: Routledge, 2017), 158–74; Ben Doherty, "A Short History of Nauru, Australia's Dumping Ground for Refugees," *Guardian*, August 9, 2016, www.theguardian.com/world/2016/aug/10/a-short-history-of-nauru -australias-dumping-ground-for-refugees.

27. Edward Said, *Culture and Imperialism*, (New York: Vintage Books, 1994), 9.

28. Alison Mountz, "The Enforcement Archipelago: Detention, Haunting, and Asylum on Islands," *Political Geography* 30 (2011): 118–28.

29. Vogl, "Sovereign Relations?," 159.

30. Australian Human Rights Commission, "Risk Management in Immigration Detention," June 18, 2019, www.humanrights.gov.au/our-work/asylum-seekers-and-refugees /publications/risk-management-immigration-detention-2019.

31. Amnesty International, *The Impact of Indefinite Detention: The Case to Change Australia's Mandatory Detention Regime* 2005, www.refworld.org/pdfid/ 45b3a41e2.pdf.

32. Border Crossing Observatory, "Australian Border Deaths Database," Monash University, https://arts.monash.edu/border-crossing-observatory/research-agenda /australian-border-deaths-database; "Asylum Insight: Facts and Analysis," Asylum Insight, 2019, www.asyluminsight.com/statistics#.XXsXYZNKhBx.

33. Dana McCauley, "Three Quarters of Refugees on Manus and Nauru Seriously Ill, Doctors Claim," *Sydney Morning Herald*, August 22, 2019, www.smh.com.au/politics /federal/three-quarters-of-refugees-on-manus-and-nauru-seriously-ill-doctors-claim -20190821-p52j8z.html.

34. Jane Flanagan, "The Plight of People Living with Disabilities within Australian Immigration Detention: Demonised, Detained and Disowned," National Ethnic Disability Alliance, 2015, www.neda.org.au/sites/default/files/2017-06/People%20 living%20with%20Disability%20in%20Immigration%20Detention-%20FINAL.pdf.

35. Refugee Council of Australia, "Australia's Man-Made Crisis on Nauru: Six Years On," September 8, 2018, www.refugeecouncil.org.au/nauru-report/2/.

36. Anonymous woman refugee on Nauru quoted in Wendy Bacon et al., "Protection Denied, Abuse Condoned: Women on Nauru at Risk," *Australian Women in Support of Women on Nauru*, June 2016.

37. Daniel Hurst, "'Things Happen': Tony Abbott on Sexual Assault Allegations in Offshore Detention," *Guardian*, May 20, 2015, www.theguardian.com/australia-news/2015 /mar/20/things-happen-tony-abbott-on-sexual-assault-allegations-in-offshore-detention.

38. Amnesty International, *Punishment Not Protection: Australia's Treatment of Refugees and Asylum Seekers in Papua New Guinea*, 2018, www.amnesty.org.au /wp-content/uploads/2018/02/Manus-briefing-FINAL4.pdf.

39. Richard Wazana, "Fear and Loathing Down Under: Australian Refugee Policy and the National Imagination," *Refugee* 22, no. 1 (2004): 83–95.

40. Philip Ruddock quoted in Suvendrini Perera, "'They Give Evidence': Bodies, Borders and the Disappeared," *Social Identities* 12, no. 6 (2006): 637–56.

41. Mountz, "The Enforcement Archipelago," 121.

42. J. Weston Phippen, "Australia's Controversial Migration Policy," *The Atlantic*, April 29, 2016, www.theatlantic.com/international/archive/2016/04/australia-immigration /480189/.

43. Refugee Council of Australia, "Offshore Processing Statistics," October 27, 2019, www .refugeecouncil.org.au/operation-sovereign-borders-offshore-detention-statistics/2/.

44. Amy Nethery and Carly Gordyn, "Australia-Indonesia Cooperation on Asylum-Seekers: A Case of 'Incentivised Policy Transfer'," *Australian Journal of International Affairs* 68, no. 2 (2014): 177–93.

45. John Podesta, "The Climate Crisis, Migration, and Refugees," Brookings, July 25, 2019, www.brookings.edu/research/the-climate-crisis-migration-and-refugees/.

46. "Defence Chief Sounds Warning on Surge of Climate Change Refugees," SBS News, July 15, 2019, www.sbs.com.au/news/defence-chief-sounds-warning-on-surge-of -climate-change-refugees.

47. UN High Commissioner for Refugees, "UNHCR Chief Filippo Grandi Calls On Australia to End Harmful Practice of Offshore Processing," July 24, 2017, www .unhcr.org/en-au/news/press/2017/7/597217484/unhcr-chief-filippo-grandi-calls -australia-end-harmful-practice-offshore.html.

48. Wazana, "Fear and Loathing," 83–95.

49. Jo Chandler, "'Designed to Torture': Asylum Seeker Chooses Iranian Prison over PNG Detention Centre, *Guardian*, November 10, 2019, www.theguardian.com/world /2019/nov/10/designed-to-torture-asylum-seeker-chooses-iranian-prison-over-png -detention-centre.

50. Refugee Council of Australia, "Offshore Processing Statistics."

51. Mark Isaacs, "There's No Escape from Australia's Refugee Gulag," *Foreign Policy*, April 30, 2018, https://foreignpolicy.com/2018/04/30/theres-no-escape-from-australias -refugee-gulag/.

Chapter 6

1. "British PM Under Fire for Calling Calais Migrants a 'Swarm'," France 24, July 30, 2015, www.france24.com/en/20150730-uk-cameron-under-fire-calling-calais -migrants-swarm.

2. Calais Migrant Solidarity, "Deaths at the Calais Border," https://calaismigrantsolidarity .wordpress.com/deaths-at-the-calais-border/.

3. Admir Skodo, "How Immigration Detention Compares around the World," The Conversation, April 22, 2017, https://theconversation.com/how-immigration -detention-compares-around-the-world-76067; European Council on Refugees and Exiles, "France: Systematic Immigration Detention further Undermines Rights," June 7, 2019, www.ecre.org/france-systematic-immigration-detention-further

-undermines-rights/.

4. "UN Backs Calais 'Jungle' Camp Closure but Raises Child Trafficking Concerns," France 24, October 14, 2016, www.france24.com/en/20161014-un-calais-camp -closure-child-trafficking-france-uk-refugees-jungle.

5. Missing Migrants Project, "Missing Migrants: Tracking Deaths along Migratory Routes," International Organization for Migration, https://missingmigrants.iom.int/.

6. UN Migration Agency's Global Migration Data Analysis Centre, "New Study Concludes Europe's Mediterranean Border Remains 'World's Deadliest,'" International Organization for Migration, November 24, 2017, www.iom.int/news/new -study-concludes-europes-mediterranean-border-remains-worlds-deadliest.

7. "Mediterranean 'By Far World's Deadliest Border' for Migrants: IOM," Reuters, November 24, 2017, www.reuters.com/article/us-europe-migrants/mediterranean -by-far-worlds-deadliest-border-for-migrants-iom-idUSKBN1DO1ZY; Eve Conant, "The World's Congested Human Migration Routes in 5 Maps," IOM: UN Migration, September 9, 2015, https://weblog.iom.int/world%E2%80%99s -congested-human-migration-routes-5-maps.

8. Jonathan Clayton and Hereward Holland, "Over One Million Sea Arrivals Reach Europe in 2015," UNHCR, December 30, 2015, www.unhcr.org/news/latest/2015/12 /5683d0b56/million-sea-arrivals-reach-europe-2015.html; "Migrant Deaths: 19,000 in Mediterranean in Past 6 Years," Info Migrants, October 9, 2019, www.infomigrants .net/en/post/20055/migrant-deaths-19-000-in-mediterranean-in-past-6-years.

9. Reece Jones, *Violent Borders: Refugees and the Right to Move* (London and New York: Verso, 2016), 26.

10. Tom Miles and Stephanie Nebehay, "Migrant Deaths in the Sahara Likely Twice Mediterranean Toll: U.N.," Reuters, October 12, 2017, www.reuters.com/article/us -europe-migrants-sahara/migrant-deaths-in-the-sahara-likely-twice-mediterranean -toll-u-n-idUSKBN1CH21Y.

11. Christina Sharpe, *In the Wake: On Blackness and Being* (Durham: Duke University Press, 2016), 16.

12. Kazim Ali, *Resident Alien: On Border-Crossing and the Undocumented Divine* (Ann Arbor: University of Michigan Press, 2015), 122.

13. Sara Ahmed, *The Cultural Politics of Emotion* (London: Routledge, 2013), 30.

14. Clare Hemmings, "Affective Solidarity: Feminist Reflexivity and Political Transformation," *Feminist Theory* 13, no. 2 (2012): 152.

15. Tamara K. Nopper and Mariame Kaba, "Itemizing Atrocity," *Jacobin Magazine*, August 15, 2014, www.jacobinmag.com/2014/08/itemizing-atrocity/.

16. Charlotte Gifford, "The True Cost of the EU's Border Security Boom," World Finance, January 21, 2020, www.worldfinance.com/featured/the-true-cost-of-the-eus -border-security-boom.

17. Daniel Trilling, *Lights in the Distance: Exile and Refuge at the Borders of Europe* (London: Picador, 2019); Jon Stone, "The EU Has Built 1,000km of Border Walls since Fall of Berlin Wall," *Independent*, November 9, 2018, www.independent.co.uk/news /world/europe/eu-border-wall-berlin-migration-human-rights-immigration-borders -a8624706.html.

18. Stephen Scheel, "'The Secret Is to Look Good on Paper': Appropriating Mobility within and against a Machine of Illegalization," in *The Borders of "Europe": Autonomy of Migration, Tactics of Bordering*, Nicholas De Genova, ed. (Durham: Duke University Press, 2017), 43.

19. Ampson Hagan, "The Political Viability of Anti-immigrationism," Africa Is a Country, March 2019, https://africasacountry.com/2019/03/the-political-viability-of-anti -immigrationism.

20. Mark Akkerman, "Expanding the Fortress: The Policies, the Profiteers and the People Shaped by EU's Border Externalization Programme," Transnational Institute, May 2018, www.tni.org/files/publication-downloads/expanding_the_fortress_-_1.6 _may_11.pdf.

21. Akkerman, "Expanding the Fortress.".

22. Wendy Brown, *Walled States, Waning Sovereignty* (New York and Cambridge: Zone Books, 2017), 13.

23. Taish quoted in Lucy Williamson, "Essex Lorry Deaths: Dunkirk Migrants 'All Scared of Lorries,'" BBC News, October 24, 2019, www.bbc.com/news/world -europe-50174534.

24. Sarah Chynoweth, "'More than One Million Pains': Sexual Violence against Men and Boys on the Central Mediterranean Route to Italy," Women's Refugee Commission, March 2019, www.womensrefugeecommission.org/component/zdocs /document?id=1698-libya-italy-report-03-2019-pdf.

25. International Organization for Migration, "Mediterranean Migrant Arrivals Reach 18,364 in 2019; Deaths Reach 508," May 17, 2019, www.iom.int/news/mediterranean -migrant-arrivals-reach-18364-2019-deaths-reach-508.

26. Cynthia Bejarano, Maria Cristina Morales, and Said Saddiki, "Understanding Conquest through a Border Lens," in *Beyond Walls and Cages: Prisons, Borders, and Global Crisis*, Jenna M. Loyd, Matt Mitchelson, and Andrew Burridge, eds. (Athens: University of Georgia Press, 2012), 29.

27. Bejarano et al., "Understanding Conquest," 31.

28. David Moffette, *Governing Irregular Migration: Bordering Culture, Labour, and Security in Spain* (Vancouver: University of British Columbia Press, 2018).

29. "Declaration on the Repression of African Immigrants" quoted in Clara Lecadet, "Europe Confronted by Its Expelled Migrants: The Politics of Expelled Migrants' Associations in Africa," in De Genova, *The Borders of "Europe,"* 149.

30. No Borders Morocco, "Violence, Resistance, and Bozas at the Spanish-Moroccan Border," in *Open Borders: In Defense of Free Movement*, Reece Jones, ed. (Athens: University of Georgia Press, 2019), 237.

31. No Borders Morocco, "Violence, Resistance, and Bozas," 231.

32. Médecins Sans Frontières, "Violence, Vulnerability and Migration: Trapped at the Gates of Europe; A Report on the Situation of Sub-Saharan Migrants in an Irregular Situation in Morocco," March 2013, www.msf.org/violence-vulnerability -and-migration-trapped-gates-europe.

33. Médecins Sans Frontières, "Violence, Vulnerability and Migration," 15.

34. No Borders Morocco, "Violence, Resistance, and Bozas," 231–2.

35. Olivia Sundberg Diez, "What You Don't Hear about Spain's Migration Policy," EU Observer, February 23, 2020, https://euobserver.com/opinion/147429.

36. Dale Fuchs, "Canary Islands Fear Disaster as Number of Migrants Soar," *Guardian*, September 4, 2006, www.theguardian.com/world/2006/sep/04/spain.mainsection.

37. Ruben Andersson, *Illegality, Inc.: Clandestine Migration and the Business of Bordering Europe* (Oakland: University of California Press, 2014), 36; "Canaries Migrant Death Toll Soars," BBC News, December 28, 2006, http://news.bbc.co.uk/2/hi/europe/6213495.stm.

38. Ruben Andersson, "Rescued and Caught: The Humanitarian-Security Nexus at Europe's Frontiers," in De Genova, *The Borders of "Europe,"* 78.

39. Zach Campbell, "Europe's Plan to Close its Sea Borders Relies on Libya's Coast Guard Doing Its Dirty Work, Abusing Migrants," The Intercept, November 25, 2017, https://theintercept.com/2017/11/25/libya-coast-guard-europe-refugees/.

40. Andersson, "Rescued and Caught," 64–94.

41. African Civil Society Organizations, "Joint Statement: African Civil Society Condemns the Hunt for Migrants on the Continent," 2016, www.statewatch.org/news/2016/may/eu-africa-ngos-statement.pdf.

42. Benjamin Bathke, "More Than 150 Migrants Scale Fence to Spain's Ceuta Enclave in Morocco," Info Migrants, September 2, 2019, www.infomigrants.net/en/post/19221/more-than-150-migrants-scale-fence-to-spain-s-ceuta-enclave-in-morocco.

43. Jones, *Violent Borders*, 23.

44. Human Rights Watch, "Q&A: Why the EU-Turkey Migration Deal Is No Blueprint," November 14, 2016, www.hrw.org/news/2016/11/14/qa-why-eu-turkey-migration-deal-no-blueprint.

45. Trilling, *Lights in the Distance*, 189.

46. Gabriella Lazaridis and Vasiliki Tsagkroni, "Posing for Legitimacy? Identity and Praxis of Far-Right Populism in Greece," in *The Rise of the Far Right in Europe: Populist Shifts and "Othering,"* Gabriella Lazaridis, Giovanna Campani, and Annie Benveniste, eds. (London: Palgrave Macmillan, 2016), 226.

47. Amnesty International, "'I Want to Decide My Future': Refugee Women in Greece Speak Out," 2018, www.amnesty.org/en/latest/campaigns/2018/10/refugee-women-in-greece/#tendemands.

48. Harriet Grant, "'Moria Is a Hell': New Arrivals Describe Life in a Greek Refugee Camp," *Guardian*, January 17, 2020, www.theguardian.com/global-development/2020/jan/17/moria-is-a-hell-new-arrivals-describe-life-in-a-greek-refugee-camp.

49. Human Rights Watch, "Greece, EU: Move Asylum Seekers to Safety," December 6, 2018, www.hrw.org/news/2018/12/06/greece-eu-move-asylum-seekers-safety; Helena Smith, "Greece Plans to Build Sea Barrier off Lesbos to Deter Migrants," *Guardian*, January 30, 2020, www.theguardian.com/world/2020/jan/30/greece-plans-to-build-sea-barrier-off-lesbos-to-deter-migrants.

50. Amnesty International, "'I Want to Decide My Future.'"

51. UN High Commissioner for Refugees, "Refugee Women and Children Face Heightened Risk of Sexual Violence amid Tensions and Overcrowding at Reception Facilities on Greek Islands," February 9, 2018, www.unhcr.org/news/briefing/2018/2/5a7d67c4b/refugee-women-children-face-heightened-risk-sexual-violence-amid

-tensions.html. Data calculated by author as 28 percent of 622 complaints.

52. Marianna Karakoulaki, "The Invisible Violence of Europe's Refugee Camps," Al Jazeera, October 22, 2019, www.aljazeera.com/indepth/opinion/invisible-violence -europe-refugee-camps-191021185959684.html.

53. Médicins Sans Frontières, *Confronting the Mental Health Emergency on Samos and Lesvos*, October 2017, www.msf.org/sites/msf.org/files/2017_10_mental_health _greece_report_final_low.pdf.

54. "Fire Tears Through Greece Refugee Camp after Coronavirus Protest," Al Jazeera, April 19, 2020, www.aljazeera.com/news/2020/04/fire -tears-greece-refugee-camp-coronavirus-protest-200419104541547.html.

55. Syrian Observatory for Human Rights, "A New Casualty by the Turkish Border Guards in an Attempt to Cross the Border Line," November 17, 2017, www.syriahr.com /en/?p=78799.

56. UN High Commissioner for Human Rights, "Turkey: UN Report Details Extensive Human Rights Violations during Protracted State of Emergency," March 20, 2018, www.ohchr.org/EN/NewsEvents/Pages/DisplayNews.aspx?NewsID=22853&LangID=E.

57. Norwegian Refugee Council, "People Have the Right to Seek Asylum and Should Not Be Pushed Back," March 3, 2020, www.nrc.no/news/2020/march/people-have -the-right-to-seek-asylum-and-should-not-be-pushed-back/.

58. Human Rights Watch, "Greece: Violence against Asylum Seekers at Border," March 17, 2020, www.hrw.org/news/2020/03/17/greece-violence-against-asylum -seekers-border.

59. Human Rights Watch, "Greece: Grant Asylum Access to New Arrivals," March 20, 2020, www.hrw.org/news/2020/03/20/greece-grant-asylum-access-new-arrivals.

60. Médecins Sans Frontières, "Greece, the 'Shield' of Europe, and EU Leaders Push Migrants into Danger," March 11, 2020, https://reliefweb.int/report/greece/greece -shield-europe-and-eu-leaders-push-migrants-danger.

61. Aris Roussinos, "What the Hell Is Happening with Migrants in Greece?," Vice, April 3, 2020, www.vice.com/en_us/article/3a8mny/what-the-hell-is-happening -with-migrants-in-greece; BBC News, "EU to Give Migrants in Greece €2,000 to Go Home," March 12, 2020, www.bbc.com/news/world-europe-51859007.

62. Thema Newsroom, "Tsipras: "Government Was Right to Close the Borders"—He Calls for a Political Leaders Council," Pro Thema News, March 3, 2020, http://en .protothema.gr/tsipras-government-was-right-to-close-the-borders-he-calls-for-a -political-leaders-council/.

63. Natasha King, *No Borders: The Politics of Immigration Control and Resistance* (London: Zed Books, 2016).

64. Maximillian Popp, "An Inside Look at EU's Shameful Immigration Policy," Spiegel Online, September 11, 2014, www.spiegel.de/international/europe/europe-tightens -borders-and-fails-to-protect-people-a-989502-4.html.

65. Hungarian Helsinki Committee, "Asylum-Seekers with Inadmissible Claims Are Denied Food in Transit Zones at Border," August 17, 2018, www.helsinki.hu/wp-content/uploads /Denial-of-food-for-inadmissible-claims-HHC-info-update-17August2018.pdf.

66. Maurizio Albahari, "After the Shipwreck: Mourning and Citizenship in the Mediterranean, Our Sea," *Social Research: An International Quarterly* 83, no. 2 (Summer 2016): 275–94.

67. Hans von der Brelie and Jad Salfiti, "'Western Balkan Route' for Migrants, Refugees Stuck at Borders," Euro News, November 30, 2018, www.euronews.com/2018/11 /30/western-balkan-route-for-migrants-refugees-stuck-at-borders.

68. Daniel McLaughlin, "'Absurdistan': Migrants Face Dangerous Winter in Bosnia," *Irish Times*, September 23, 2019, www.irishtimes.com/news/world/europe/absurdistan -migrants-face-dangerous-winter-in-bosnia-1.4027923; Lorenzo Tondo, "'Blood on the Ground' at Croatia's Borders as Brutal Policing Persists," *Guardian*, December 22, 2019, www.theguardian.com/global-development/2019/dec/22/blood-on-the-ground -at-croatia-borders-as-brutal-policing-persists.

69. Amnesty International, *Pushed to the Edge: Violence and Abuse against Refugees and Migrants along the Balkans Route*, 2019, www.amnesty.org/download/Documents /EUR0599642019ENGLISH.PDF.

70. Urs Fruehauf, "EU-Libya Agreements on Refugees and Asylum Seekers: The Need for a Reassessment," *Heinrich Böll Stiftung*, 2011.

71. Nick Squires, "Gaddafi: Europe Will 'Turn Black' Unless EU Pays Libya £4bn a Year," *Telegraph*, August 31, 2010, www.telegraph.co.uk/news/worldnews /africaandindianocean/libya/7973649/Gaddafi-Europe-will-turn-black-unless-EU -pays-Libya-4bn-a-year.html.

72. Zed Nelson, "Lampedusa Boat Tragedy: A Survivor's Story," *Guardian,* March 24, 2014, www.theguardian.com/world/2014/mar/22/lampedusa-boat-tragedy-migrants-africa.

73. Missing Migrants Project, "Missing Migrants: Tracking Deaths Along Migratory Routes," International Organization for Migration, https://missingmigrants.iom.int/.

74. Investigate Europe, "Operation Sophia: Mission Impossible in the Mediterranean," January 2, 2017, www.investigate-europe.eu/operation-sophia-mission-impossible -in-the-mediterranean%E2%80%A8/.

75. Albahari, "After the Shipwreck," 275–94.

76. Bridget Anderson, "Where's the Harm in That? Immigration Enforcement, Trafficking, and the Protection of Migrants' Rights," *American Behavioral Scientist* 56, no. 9 (April 2012): 1241–57.

77. Robyn Maynard, "#Blacksexworkerslivesmatter: White-Washed 'Anti-Slavery' and the Appropriation of Black Suffering," Feminist Wire, September 9, 2015, https:// thefeministwire.com/2015/09/blacksexworkerslivesmatter-white-washed -anti-slavery-and-the-appropriation-of-black-suffering/.

78. "Twisting the 'Lessons of History' to Authorise Unjustifiable Violence: The Mediterranean Crisis," OpenDemocracy, May 20, 2015, www.opendemocracy.net/en/beyond -trafficking-and-slavery/twisting-lessons-of-history-to-excuse-unjustifiable-violence -mediterranean-refugee-c/.

79. Amnesty International, *Punishing Compassion: Solidarity on Trial in Fortress Europe*, March 3, 2020, www.amnesty.org/download/Documents /EUR0118282020ENGLISH.PDF.

80. Sarah Mardini, "I Dragged My Migrant Boat to Safety Now I Face Decades in Jail for

Helping Others," Metro, December 10, 2019, https://metro.co.uk/2019/12/10
/i-dragged-my-migrant-boat-to-safety-now-i-face-decades-in-jail-for-helping
-others-11245438/?ito=cbshare.

81. Anya Edmond-Pettitt and Liz Fekete, "Investigations and Prosecutions for Crimes
of Solidarity Escalate in 2018," Institute of Race Relations, December 6, 2018,
www.irr.org.uk/news/investigations-and-prosecutions-for-crimes-of-solidarity
-escalate-in-2018/.

82. Charles Heller and Lorenzo Pezzani, "Liquid Traces: Investigating the Deaths of
Migrants at the EU's Maritime Frontier," in De Genova, *The Borders of "Europe,"* 97.

83. Lorenzo Tondo, "Matteo Salvini Trial for Kidnapping Authorised by Italian Senate,"
Guardian, February 12, 2020, www.theguardian.com/world/2020/feb/12/matteo
-salvini-trial-for-kidnapping-authorised-by-italian-senate.

84. ANSA, "Migrant Deaths: 19,000 in Mediterranean in Past 6 Years," Info Migrants,
October 9, 2019, www.infomigrants.net/en/post/20055/migrant-deaths-19-000-in
-mediterranean-in-past-6-years.

85. Faras Ghani, "Nearly 1,000 Migrants 'Returned to Libya' this Year," Al Jazeera,
January 14, 2020, www.aljazeera.com/news/2020/01/1000-migrants-returned-libya
-year-200114132748736.html.

86. "Italy Brokers Deal with Libyan Tribes to Curb Migrant Influx," EURACTIV, April
2, 2017, www.euractiv.com/section/politics/news/italy-brokers-deal-with-libyan
-tribes-to-curb-migrant-influx/.

87. Council of the European Union, "Central Mediterranean Route," July 3, 2019, www
.consilium.europa.eu/en/policies/migratory-pressures/central-mediterranean-route/.

88. Displacement Tracking Matrix, "Libya's Migrant Report," International Organization for Migration, July 10, 2019, https://migration.iom.int/reports/libya
-%E2%80%94-migrant-report-25-march%E2%80%94may-2019.

89. United Nations Support Mission in Libya and High Commissioner for Human
Rights, *Desperate and Dangerous: Report on the Human Rights Situation of Migrants
and Refugees in Libya*, December 20, 2018, www.ohchr.org/Documents
/Countries/LY/LibyaMigrationReport.pdf.

90. Sally Harden, "Fear and Despair Engulf Refugees in Libya's 'Market of Human
Beings,'" *Guardian*, April 15, 2019, www.theguardian.com/global-development/2019
/apr/15/fear-and-despair-engulf-refugees-in-libyas-market-of-human-beings.

91. Patrick Wintour, "Libya May Shut Migration Detention Centres after Deadly Air-
strike," *Guardian*, July 4, 2019, www.theguardian.com/world/2019/jul/04/libya
-may-shut-migrant-detention-centres-after-deadly-airstrike.

92. Matina Stevis-Gridneff, "Europe Keeps Asylum Seekers at a Distance, This Time in
Rwanda," *New York Times*, September 8, 2019, www.nytimes.com/2019/09/08
/world/europe/migrants-africa-rwanda.html; Adam Nossiter, "At French Outpost in
African Migrant Hub, Asylum for a Select Few," *New York Times*, February 25, 2018,
www.nytimes.com/2018/02/25/world/africa/france-africa-migrants-asylum-niger.html.

93. IOM Regional Office for West and Central Africa, "IOM Steps Up Response for
Migrants Stranded in Niger amidst COVID-19 Lockdown," April 1, 2020, www.iom
.int/news/iom-steps-response-migrants-stranded-niger-amidst-covid-19-lockdown.

94. Suliman Baldo, *Border Control from Hell: How the EU's Migration Partnership Legitimizes Sudan's "Militia State,"* The Enough Project, April 2017, https://data2 .unhcr.org/fr/documents/download/55954.

95. Fatin Abbas, "Darfur and Development," *The Nation*, March 10, 2005, www.thenation .com/article/darfur-and-development/; Fatin Abbas, "Coming to Terms with Sudan's Legacy of Slavery," African Arguments, January 18, 2018, https://africanarguments.org /2016/01/18/coming-to-terms-with-sudans-legacy-of-slavery-2/.

96. Raven Rakia, "IMF's Involvement Fuels Sudan's Continued Unrest," Truthout, March 25, 2014, https://truthout.org/articles/imfs-involvement-fuels-sudans -continued-unrest/.

97. Jérome Tubiana, Clotilde Warin, and Gaffar Mohammud Saeneen, "Multilateral Damage: The Impact of EU Migration Policies on Central Saharan Routes," Clingendael: Netherlands Institute of International Relations, September 2018, www.clingendael.org /sites/default/files/2018-09/multilateral-damage.pdf.

98. "Open Appeal to the EU's Donald Tusk over Eritrea and Sudan," Eritrea Hub, June 19, 2019, https://eritreahub.org/open-appeal-to-the-eus-donald-tusk-over-eritrea-and-sudan.

99. Lorenzo Tondo, "Nearly 900,000 Asylum Seekers Living in Limbo in EU, Figures Show," *Guardian*, August 25, 2019, www.theguardian.com/world/2019/aug/25/asylum -seekers-limbo-eu-countries.

100. Napuli Langa, "About the Refugee Movement in Kreuzberg/Berlin," *Journal für kritische Migrations-und Grenzregimeforschung* 1, no. 2 (2015): 3.

101. Ida Danewid, "White Innocence in the Black Mediterranean: Hospitality and the Erasure of History," *Third World Quarterly* 38, no. 7 (2017): 1675.

102. Calais Writers, *Voices from the "Jungle": Stories from the Calais Refugee Camp* (London: Pluto Press, 2017), 128.

103. Paul Gilroy, *The Black Atlantic: Modernity and Double Consciousness* (London: Verso Books, 1993), 2.

104. Renisa Mawani, *Across Oceans of Law: The Komagata Maru and Jurisdiction in the Time of Empire* (Durham: Duke University Press, 2018), 86.

105. Gilroy, *The Black Atlantic*, 112.

106. SA Smythe, "The Black Mediterranean and the Politics of the Imagination," *Middle East Report* 286 (Spring 2018), https://merip.org/2018/10/the-black-mediterranean -and-the-politics-of-the-imagination/.

107. "Les Gilets Noirs: We Are in the Airport in France," Detained Voices, May 21, 2019, https://detainedvoices.com/.

108. Thomas Sankara, *We Are Heirs of the World's Revolutions: Speeches from the Burkina Faso Revolution, 1983–87* (New York: Pathfinder, 2007); Thomas Sankara, "Imperialism Is the Arsonist of Our Forests and Savannas," reproduced on Anti-imperialism. org, February 26, 2018, https://anti-imperialism.org/2018/02/26/thomas-sankara -imperialism-is-the-arsonist-of-our-forests-and-savannas/.

109. Mabel Ellen Dove cited in Abayomi Azikiwe, "Pan-Africanism, Women's Rights and Socialist Development," Global Research, August 30, 2016, www.globalresearch .ca/pan-africanism-womens-rights-and-socialist-development/5542994.

110. Julius Kambarage Nyerere, "Capitalism or Socialism? The Rational Choice," *Black*

World 23, no. 5 (March 1974): 45.

111. Walter Rodney, *How Europe Underdeveloped Africa* (London: Bogle-L'Ouverture Publications, 1972), 16–34.

112. Mark Akkerman, *Border Wars: The Arms Dealers Profiting from Europe's Refugee Tragedy*, Transnational Institute and Stop Wapenhandel, July 2016, www.tni.org/files /publication-downloads/border-wars-report-web1207.pdf.

113. Jean Nanga, "The African Continental Free Trade Area: Free Trade and Pan-Africanism," Bilaterals, February 4, 2019, www.bilaterals.org/?the-african-continental-free-trade.

114. Ama Lorenz and Bob Koigi, "EU Accused of Exporting Problem of Overfishing with Mauritania Deal," *Guardian*, June 9, 2016, www.theguardian.com/global -development/2016/jun/09/eu-european-union-accused-exporting-problem -overfishing-mauritania-deal.

115. Patrick Kingsley, "The Small African Region with More Refugees Than All of Europe," *Guardian*, November 26, 2016, www.theguardian.com/world/2016/nov/26/boko -haram-nigeria-famine-hunger-displacement-refugees-climate-change-lake-chad.

116. Tyron P. Woods and P. Khalil Saucier, "Slavery's Afterlife in the Euro-Mediterra- nean Basin," OpenDemocracy, June 19, 2015, www.opendemocracy.net/en/beyond -trafficking-and-slavery/slaverys-afterlife-in-euromediterranean-basin/.

117. Tyron P. Woods and P. Khalil Saucier, "Ex Aqua: The Mediterranean Basin, Africans on the Move, and the Politics of Policing," *Theoria* 61, no. 141 (December 2014): 55.

118. Sohail Daulatzai and Junaid Rana, "Writing the Muslim Left: An Introduction to Throwing Stones," in *With Stones in Our Hands: Writings on Muslims, Racism, and Empire*, Sohail Daulatzai and Junaid Rana, eds. (Minneapolis: University of Minne- sota Press, 2018), xvi.

119. Nesima Aberra, "How Anti-Blackness Is Making the World Ignore African Refu- gees," Everyday Feminism, October 25, 2017, https://everydayfeminism.com/2017 /10/anti-blackness-african-refugees/.

120. Ruben Andersson, "Rescued and Caught: The Humanitarian-Security Nexus at Europe's Frontiers," in De Genova, *The Borders of "Europe,"* 81.

121. Vilna Bashi, "Globalized Anti-Blackness: Transnationalizing Western Immigration Law, Policy, and Practice," *Ethnic and Racial Studies* 27, no. 4 (2004): 584–606.

122. Peo Hansen and Stefan Jonsson, "Building Eurafrica: Reviving Colonialism through European Integration, 1920–1960," in *Echoes of Empire: Memory, Identity and the Legacy of Imperialism*, Kalypso Nicoläidis, Berny Sèbe, and Gabrielle Maas, eds. (London: I.B. Tauris, 2015), 209–26.

123. Achille Mbembe, "The Idea of a Borderless World," Africa Is a Country, November 11, 2018, https://africasacountry.com/2018/11/the-idea-of-a-borderless-world.

Chapter 7

1. Soumaoro Aboubakar, "The Murder of a Trade Unionist," *Jacobin Magazine*, June 10, 2018, www.jacobinmag.com/2018/06/italy-soumayla-sacko-murder-migrant-labor-lega.

2. "Over One-Third of Farmworkers in Italy Are Foreigners," Info Migrants, October 28, 2019, www.infomigrants.net/en/post/20422/over-one-third-of-farmworkers-in

-italy-are-foreigners; Maged Srour, "'Agromafia' Exploits Hundreds of Thousands of Agricultural Workers in Italy," Inter Press Service, July 2018, www.ipsnews.net /2018/07/agromafia-exploits-hundreds-thousands-agricultural-workers-italy/.

3. Asfa-Wossen Asserate, *African Exodus* (London: Haus Publishing, 2018), 153.

4. Martin Khor and Tetteh Hormeku, "The Impact of Globalisation and Liberalisation on Agriculture and Small Farmers in Developing Countries: The Experience of Ghana," *Third World Network*, January 2006.

5. Nicholas De Genova, "Migrant 'Illegality' and Deportability in Everyday Life," *Annual Review of Anthropology* 31 (2002): 439.

6. Thomas Friedman, "Trump Is Wasting Our Immigration Crisis," *New York Times*, April 23, 2019, www.nytimes.com/2019/04/23/opinion/trump-immigration-border -wall.html.

7. Amnesty International, *Exploited Labour: Migrant Workers in Italy's Agricultural Sector*, December 18, 2012, www.amnestyusa.org/files/exploited_labour._italy_migrants _report_web.pdf.

8. Soumaoro, "The Murder of a Trade Unionist."

9. Edward L. Homze, *Foreign Labor in Nazi Germany* (Princeton: Princeton University Press, 2016), 3.

10. Christof Van Mol and Helga de Valk, "Migration and Immigrants in Europe: A Historical and Demographic Perspective," in *Integration Processes and Policies in Europe*, Blanca Garcés-Mascareñas and Rinus Penninx, eds., IMISCOE Research Series (New York: Springer International, 2016), 31–55; Pranay Gupte, "Germany's Guest Workers," *New York Times*, August 19, 1984, www.nytimes.com/1984/08/19 /magazine/germany-s-guest-workers.html.

11. C. Cindy Fan, "The State, the Migrant Labor Regime, and Maiden Workers in China," *Political Geography* 23 (2004): 287.

12. International Labour Migration, "New ILO Figures Show 164 Million People Are Migrant Workers," December 5, 2018, www.ilo.org/global/about-the-ilo/newsroom /news/WCMS_652106/lang--en/index.htm.

13. United Nations General Assembly, Resolution 73/195, *Global Compact for Safe, Orderly and Regular Migration*, December 19, 2018, www.un.org/en/ga/search/view _doc.asp?symbol=A/RES/73/195.

14. "The $78 Trillion Free Lunch; If Borders Were Open," *The Economist*, July 15, 2017, www.economist.com/the-world-if/2017/07/13/a-world-of-free-movement-would -be-78-trillion-richer.

15. Kerry Preibisch, "Migrant Workers and Changing Work-place Regimes in Contemporary Agricultural Production in Canada," *International Journal of Agriculture and Food* 19, no. 1, (2011): 62–82.

16. Preibisch, "Migrant Workers and Changing Work-place Regimes," 66.

17. Tanya Maria Golash-Boza, *Deported: Immigrant Policing, Disposable Labor and Global Capitalism* (New York: New York University Press, 2015), vii–viii.

18. Justin Akers Chacón and Mike Davis, *No One Is Illegal: Fighting Racism and State Violence on the U.S.–Mexico Border* (Chicago: Haymarket Books, 2006), 140.

19. Cindy Hahamovitch, *No Man's Land: Jamaican Guestworkers in America and the Glob-

al History of Deportable Labor (Princeton: Princeton University Press, 2011), 6.

20. Cindy Hahamovitch, "'The Worst Job in the World': Reform, Revolution, and the Secret Rebellion in Florida's Cane Fields," *Journal of Peasant Studies* 35, no. 4 (2008): 770–800, https://doi.org/10.1080/03066150802682029.

21. Marie Brenner, "In the Kingdom of Big Sugar," *Vanity Fair*, January 5, 2011, www.vanityfair.com/news/2001/02/floridas-fanjuls-200102.

22. David Bacon, *Illegal People: How Globalization Creates Migration and Criminalizes Immigrants* (Boston: Beacon Press, 2009), 95; Hahamovitch, *No Man's Land*, 213.

23. Mayra Reiter, "Farmworker Justice Update: 11/13/19," Farmworker Justice, November 14, 2019, www.farmworkerjustice.org/fj-blog/2019/11/farmworker-justice-update -11-13-19; Iris Figueroa, "H-2A Program Growing at Unprecedented Rate; Worker Protections at Risk," Farmworker Justice, October 30, 2018, www.farmworkerjustice.org /fj-blog/2018/10/h-2a-program-growing-unprecedented-rate-worker-protections-risk.

24. Levi Pulkkinen, "Guest Farmworkers Find Their Voices in Washington State," *High Country News*, October 24, 2018, www.hcn.org/articles/justice-long-silent-guest -farmworkers-find-their-voices-in-washington-state.

25. Jeremy Scahill, *Blackwater: The Rise of the World's Most Powerful Mercenary Army* (New York: Nation Books, 2008), 47.

26. Sarah Stillman, "The Invisible Army," *New Yorker*, June 6, 2011, www.newyorker .com/magazine/2011/06/06/the-invisible-army.

27. Scahill, *Blackwater*, 289.

28. Bonnie Barron, "Slain Laborers' Families Barred from Suing KBR," Courthouse News Service, January 20, 2014, www.courthousenews.com/Slain-Laborers-Families -Barred-From-Suing-KBR/.

29. Amnesty International, *Trapped: The Exploitation of Migrant Workers in Malaysia*, 2010, www.amnesty.org/download/Documents/36000/asa280022010en.pdf; Ernst Spaan and Ton van Naerssen, "Migration Decision-Making and Migration Industry in the Indonesia-Malaysia Corridor," *Journal of Ethnic and Migration Studies* 44, no. 4 (2018): 680–95; Seth Mydans, "A Growing Source of Fear for Migrants in Malaysia," *New York Times*, December 10, 2007, www.nytimes.com/2007/12/10 /world/asia/10malaysia.html.

30. Human Rights Watch, "Malaysia: Disband Abusive Volunteer Corps," May 9, 2007, www.hrw.org/news/2007/05/09/malaysia-disband-abusive-volunteer-corps; Blanca Garcés-Mascareñas, *Labour Migration in Malaysia and Spain: Markets, Citizenship and Rights* (Amsterdam: Amsterdam University Press, 2012), 100.

31. Daniel Costa and Philip Martin, *Temporary Labor Migration Programs*, Economic Policy Institute, August 1, 2018, www.epi.org/publication/temporary-labor -migration-programs-governance-migrant-worker-rights-and-recommendations -for-the-u-n-global-compact-for-migration/.

32. Radhika Mongia, *Indian Migration and Empire* (Durham: Duke University Press, 2018).

33. Gaiutra Bahadur, *Coolie Woman: The Odyssey of Indenture* (Chicago: University of Chicago Press, 2014).

34. David McNally, *Another World Is Possible* (Winnipeg: Arbeiter Ring, 2006), 190.

35. International Labour Office, "Toward a Fair Deal for Migrant Workers in the Global Economy," 2004, www.ilo.org/public/english/standards/relm/ilc/ilc92/pdf/rep-vi.pdf.

36. Ohnee Kwon, "We Are Workers: South Korea's Migrant 'Machines'," *Left Voice*, August 17, 2015, www.leftvoice.org/We-are-Workers-South-Korea-s-Migrant-Machines.

37. Susan Ferguson and David McNally, "Precarious Migrants: Gender, Race and the Social Reproduction of a Global Working Class," *Socialist Register* 51 (2014): 3.

38. Chacón and Davis, *No One Is Illegal*, 90.

39. Here I follow David Harvey's reasoning that contradictions in capitalism are resolved through geographic restructuring to maintain capital accumulation. See David Harvey, *The Limits to Capital* (London and New York: Verso, 2006), and Harvey, "Globalization and the 'Spatial Fix,'" *Geographische Revue* (2001): 23–30.

40. Brenna Bhandar, *Colonial Lives of Property: Law, Land, and Racial Regimes of Ownership* (Durham: Duke University Press, 2018), 13.

41. Sandro Mezzadra and Brett Neilson, *Border as Method, or, the Multiplication of Labor* (Durham: Duke University Press, 2013).

42. Brett Story, *Prison Land: Mapping Carceral Power across Neoliberal America* (Minneapolis: University of Minnesota Press, 2019), 4.

43. Amnesty International, *"Their Home Is My Prison": Exploitation of Migrant Domestic Workers in Lebanon*, April 24, 2019, www.amnesty.org/download /Documents/MDE1800222019ENGLISH.pdf.

44. Fred Moten, *Stolen Life* (Durham: Duke University Press, 2018), 87.

45. Raj Patel, *The Value of Nothing* (Toronto: Harper Perennial, 2011), 68.

46. Gus Wezerek and Kristen R. Ghodsee, "Women's Unpaid Labor Is Worth $10,900,000,000,000," *New York Times*, March 5, 2020, www.nytimes.com/interactive /2020/03/04/opinion/women-unpaid-labor.html.

47. Maria Mies, *Patriarchy and Accumulation on a World Scale: Women in the International Division of Labour* (London: Zed Books, 1998), 116.

48. Patricia Hill Collins, *Black Feminist Thought: Knowledge, Consciousness, and the Politics of Empowerment* (New York: Routledge, 2000), 47.

49. "The International Wages for Housework Campaign," Freedom Archives, https://freedomarchives.org/Documents/Finder/DOC500_scans/500.020.Wages .for.Housework.pdf.

50. Ella Baker and Marvel Cooke, "Bronx Slave Market," *The Crisis* 42, no. 11 (November 1, 1930): 330–32.

51. Claudia Jones, *An End to the Neglect of the Problems of the Negro Woman!* (National Women's Commission, 1949), republished on New Frame, www.newframe.com/from -the-archive-an-end-to-the-neglect-of-the-problems-of-the-negro-woman/.

52. Jones, *An End to the Neglect*.

53. Jones, *An End to the Neglect*.

54. Association of Black Women Historians, "An Open Statement to the Fans of The Help," August 12, 2011, http://abwh.org/2011/08/12/an-open-statement-to-the -fans-of-the-help/.

55. Eileen Boris and Premilla Nadasen, "Domestic Workers Organize!" *Journal of Labor and Society* 11, no. 4 (December 2008): 413–37.

56. Premilla Nadasen, *Household Workers Unite: The Untold Story of African American Women Who Built a Movement* (Boston: Beacon Press, 2015), 4.

57. International Labour Organization, "Who Are Domestic Workers?" www.ilo.org /global/docs/WCMS_209773/lang--en/index.htm; Maria Gallotti, "Migrant Domestic Workers across the World: Global and Regional Estimates," International Labour Organization, 2016, www.ilo.org/wcmsp5/groups/public/---ed_protect /---protrav/---migrant/documents/briefingnote/wcms_490162.pdf.

58. Gallotti, "Migrant Domestic Workers."

59. Arlie Hochschild, "Global Care Chains and Emotional Surplus Value," in *On the Edge: Globalization and the New Millennium,* Tony Giddens and Will Hutton, eds. (London: Sage Publishers, 2000), 130–46.

60. Walden Bello, *The Anti-Development State: The Political Economy of Permanent Crisis in the Philippines* (London: Zed Books, 2006), 11; Aurora Almendral, "Why 10 Million Filipinos Endure Hardship Abroad as Overseas Workers," *National Geographic,* December 2018, www.nationalgeographic.com/magazine/2018/12/filipino-workers -return-from-overseas-philippines-celebrates/; Ligaya Lindio-McGovern, "Labor Export in the Context of Globalization: The Experience of Filipino Domestic Workers in Rome," *International Sociology* 18, no. 3 (September 2003): 513–34.

61. E. San Juan Jr., *US Imperialism and Revolution in the Philippines* (London: Palgrave Macmillan, 2008), 4.

62. Walden Bello, "How the Marcos-World Bank Partnership Brought PH Economy to Its Knees," Rappler, April 2, 2019, www.rappler.com/thought-leaders/227198-analysis -how-marcos-world-bank-partnership-brought-philippine-economy-to-knees; Eduardo C. Tadem, "Philippines: The Marcos Debt," Committee for the Abolition of Illegitimate Debt, November 5, 2018, www.cadtm.org/Philippines-The-Marcos-debt.

63. Mike Davis, *Planet of Slums* (London and New York: Verso, 2006), 73.

64. International League of Peoples' Struggle, "International Day against Trafficking: Labor Export Policy Is State-Sponsored Human Trafficking," December 12, 2013, https://ilps.info/en/2013/12/12/international-day-against-trafficking-labor-export -policy-is-state-sponsored-human-trafficking/.

65. Silvia Federici, "Reproduction and Feminist Struggle," in *Women, Development, and Labor of Reproduction: Struggles and Movements,* Mariarosa Dalla Costa and Giovanni F. Dalla Costa, eds. (Trenton: Africa World Press, 1999), 47–66.

66. Bridget Anderson, *Doing the Dirty Work?: The Global Politics of Domestic Labour* (London: Zed Books, 2000), 2.

67. Geraldine Pratt and Migrante BC, "Organizing Filipina Domestic Workers in Vancouver, Canada: Gendered Geographies and Community Mobilization," *Political Power and Social Theory* 35 (2018): 104.

Chapter 8

1. Abdulhadi Khalaf, Omar AlShehabi, and Adam Hanieh, eds., *Transit States: Labour, Migration and Citizenship in the Gulf* (London: Pluto Press, 2015).

2. Gulf Labour Markets and Migration Programme, "Percentage of Nationals and Foreign Nationals in GCC Countries' Populations," April 2017, https://gulfmigration.org

/media/graphs/Graph1_09_05_2017.pdf; Abdoulaye Diop, Trevor Johnston, and Kien Trung Le, "Migration Policies across the GCC: Challenges in Reforming the *Kafala*," in *Migration to the Gulf: Policies in Sending and Receiving Countries,* Philippe Fargues and Nasra M. Shah, eds. (Cambridge: GLMM Programme, Gulf Research Center, 2018), 36.

3. Adam Hanieh, *Lineages of Revolt: Issues of Contemporary Capitalism in the Middle East* (Chicago: Haymarket Books, 2013), 130.

4. Françoise De Bel-Air, "Demography, Migration and Labour Market in Saudi Arabia," *GLMM: Gulf Labour Markets, Migration and Population* 5 (2018): 4; Adam Taylor, "Indonesia Says It Had No Warning Saudi Arabia Would Be Executing Maid," *Washington Post,* October 31, 2018, www.washingtonpost.com/world/2018 /10/31/indonesia-says-it-had-no-warning-saudi-arabia-would-be-executing-maid/.

5. Human Rights Watch, *"As If I Am Not Human": Abuses against Asian Domestic Workers in Saudi Arabia,* July 7, 2008, www.hrw.org/report/2008/07/07/if-i-am-not -human/abuses-against-asian-domestic-workers-saudi-arabia.

6. Annie Kelly and Hazel Thompson, "The Vanished: The Filipino Domestic Workers Who Disappear behind Closed Doors," *Guardian,* October 24, 2015, www.theguardian .com/global-development/2015/oct/24/the-vanished-filipino-domestic-workers -working-abroad; Migrante International, "Matrix of Cases," April 22, 2015, https:// migranteinternationaldotorg.files.wordpress.com/2015/04/matrix-of-cases.pdf.

7. Omar AlShehabi, "Policing Labour in Empire: The Modern Origins of the Kafala Sponsorship System in the Gulf Arab States," *British Journal of Middle Eastern Studies* (2019): 1–20.

8. Andrew M. Gardner, *City of Strangers: Gulf Migration and the Indian Community in Bahrain* (Ithaca: Cornell University Press, 2010), 58.

9. Migrant Forum in Asia, "Reform of the Kafala (Sponsorship) System: Responding to Emerging and Critical Issues," Policy Brief No. 2 to the International Labour Organization, www.ilo.org/dyn/migpractice/docs/132/PB2.pdf.

10. AlShehabi, "Policing Labour in Empire."

11. AlShehabi, "Policing Labour in Empire," 19–20.

12. Adam Hanieh, "Temporary Migrant Labour and the Spatial Structuring of Class in the Gulf Cooperation Council," *Spectrum: Journal of Global Studies* 2, no. 1 (2010): 67–88.

13. Gilbert Achcar, *The People Want: A Radical Exploration of the Arab Uprising* (Berkeley: University of California Press, 2013).

14. Abdulhadi Khalaf, "The Politics of Migration," in Khalaf et al., *Transit States,* 52.

15. Hanieh, "Temporary Migrant Labour," 78.

16. Jill Crystal, *Kuwait: The Transformation of an Oil State* (London: Routledge, 1992).

17. Andrzej Kapiszewski, "Arab Labour Migration to the GCC States," in *Arab Migration in a Globalized World* (Geneva: International Organization for Migration, 2004), 123.

18. Hanieh, *Lineages of Revolt,* 144.

19. Rafeef Ziadah, "Circulating Power: Humanitarian Logistics, Militarism, and the United Arab Emirates," *Antipode* 51, no. 5 (2019): 1684–1702.

20. Jane Kinninmont, "Citizenship in the Gulf," in *The Gulf States and the Arab Uprisings,*

Ana Achague, ed. (Spain: FRIDE and the Gulf Research Center), 49.

21. Jill Crystal, *Oil and Politics in the Gulf: Rulers and Merchants in Kuwait and Qatar* (Cambridge: Cambridge University Press, 1995).

22. De Bel-Air, "Demography, Migration and Labour Market in Saudi Arabia," 5.

23. Adam Coogle, *Detained, Beaten, Deported: Saudi Abuses against Migrants during Mass Expulsions*, Human Rights Watch, May 10, 2015, www.hrw.org/report/2015/05 /10/detained-beaten-deported/saudi-abuses-against-migrants-during-mass-expulsions.

24. Coogle, *Detained, Beaten, Deported*; International Organization for Migration, "Ethiopian Diaspora Continues its Support to IOM for Migrants Returning Home from Saudi Arabia," February 18, 2015, https://ethiopia.iom.int/ethiopian-diaspora -continues-its-support-iom-migrants-returning-home-saudi-arabia.

25. Human Rights Watch, "Saudi Arabia: Events of 2018," *World Report 2019*, www. hrw.org/world-report /2019/country-chapters/saudi-arabia.

26. AlShehabi, "Policing Labour in Empire."

27. Hanieh, *Lineages of Revolt*, 131.

28. International Labour Organization, "Labour Migration: Facts and Figures in Arab States," www.ilo.org/beirut/areasofwork/labour-migration/lang--en/index.htm.

29. Hadi Ghaemi, *Building Towers, Cheating Workers: Exploitation of Migrant Construction Workers in the United Arab Emirates*, Human Rights Watch, November 11, 2006, www.hrw.org/report/2006/11/11/building-towers-cheating-workers /exploitation-migrant-construction-workers-united.

30. Human Rights Watch, *"The Island of Happiness": Exploitation of Migrant Workers on Saadiyat Island, Abu Dhabi*, May 2009, www.refworld.org/pdfid/4a125f4b2.pdf.

31. Human Rights Watch, *Migrant Workers' Rights on Saadiyat Island in the United Arab Emirates: 2015 Progress Report*, February 10, 2015, www.hrw.org/report/2015/02/10 /migrant-workers-rights-saadiyat-island-united-arab-emirates/2015-progress-report.

32. International Trade Union Confederation, *The Case against Qatar*, March 2014, www. ituc-csi.org/IMG/pdf/the_case_against_qatar_en_web170314.pdf.

33. Pete Pattison, "Revealed: Qatar's World Cup 'Slaves,'" *Guardian*, September 25, 2013, www.theguardian.com/world/2013/sep/25/revealed-qatars-world-cup-slaves.

34. Robert Booth, "Qatar World Cup Construction 'Will Leave 4,000 Migrant Workers Dead,'" *Guardian*, September 26, 2013, www.theguardian.com/global-development /2013/sep/26/qatar-world-cup-migrant-workers-dead; Pattison, "Revealed."

35. Amnesty International UK, "Qatar's Lifting of Travel Restrictions for Many Migrant Workers Welcomed," September 5, 2018, www.amnesty.org.uk/press-releases/qatars -lifting-travel-restrictions-many-migrant-workers-welcomed.

36. Amnesty International, "Qatar: Migrant Workers Illegally Expelled During COVID-19 Pandemic," April 15, 2020, www.amnesty.org/en/latest/news/2020/04 /qatar-migrant-workers-illegally-expelled-during-covid19-pandemic/.

37. Pete Pattisson and Roshan Sedhai, "Covid-19 Lockdown Turns Qatar's Largest Migrant Camp into 'Virtual Prison,'" *Guardian*, March 20, 2020, www.theguardian .com/global-development/2020/mar/20/covid-19-lockdown-turns-qatars-largest -migrant-camp-into-virtual-prison.

38. Priyanka Motaparthy, "Understanding Kafala: An Archaic Law at Cross Purposes with Modern Development," Migrant-Rights.org, March 11, 2015, www.migrant-rights.org/2015/03/understanding-kafala-an-archaic -law-at-cross-purposes-with-modern-development/.

39. Bina Fernandez and Marine de Regt, "Making a Home in the World: Migrant Domestic Workers in the Middle East," in *Migrant Domestic Workers in the Middle East: The Home and the World,* Bina Fernandez and Marine de Regt, eds. (London: Palgrave Macmillan, 2014), 10.

40. Rothna Begum, *"I Already Bought You": Abuse and Exploitation of Female Migrant Domestic Workers in the United Arab Emirates,* Human Rights Watch, October 22, 2014, www.hrw.org/report/2014/10/22/i-already-bought-you/abuse-and-exploitation -female-migrant-domestic-workers-united.

41. Cited in Hanieh, *Lineages of Revolt,* 131.

42. Amnesty International, *"My Sleep Is My Break": Exploitation of Migrant Domestic Workers in Qatar,* April 2014, www.amnesty.org/download/Documents/8000 /mde220042014en.pdf.

43. "Indonesia Protests Saudi Execution of Domestic Worker," Al Jazeera, October 31, 2018, www.aljazeera.com/news/2018/10/indonesia-protests-saudi-execution -domestic-worker-181031094812124.html.

44. Preeti Kannan, "Arabtec Workers in UAE Strike over Wage Dispute," *National* (UAE), May 20, 2013, www.thenational.ae/uae/arabtec-workers-in-uae-strike-over -wage-dispute-1.257878.

45. Aimee Bahng, *Migrant Futures: Decolonizing Speculation in Financial Times* (Durham: Duke University Press, 2017), 17.

Chapter 9

1. *O.P.T. v. Presteve Foods Ltd.,* Human Rights Tribunal of Ontario, April 22, 2015, 2015 HRTO 675 (CanLII).

2. *O.P.T. v. Presteve Foods Ltd.*

3. Government of Canada, "Temporary Residents: Temporary Foreign Worker Program (TFWP) and International Mobility Program (IMP) Work Permit Holders– Monthly IRCC Updates," Immigration, Refugees and Citizenship Canada, https:// open.canada.ca/data/en/dataset/360024f2-17e9-4558-bfc1-3616485d65b9.

4. Nandita Sharma, *Home Economics: Nationalism and the Making of "Migrant Workers" in Canada* (Toronto: University of Toronto Press, 2006), 108.

5. Sofia Rodriguez, "Third Ontario Migrant Worker Dies of COVID-19," CBC News, June 21, 2020, www.cbc.ca/news/canada/london/third-ontario-migrant-worker-dies -of-covid-19-1.5621487.

6. Nicholas Keung, "Inquest Sought into Migrant Farmer Deaths," *Star,* September 22, 2010, www.thestar.com/news/investigations/2010/09/22/inquest_sought_into _migrant_farm_worker_deaths.html.

7. Alberta Federation of Labour, "Alberta Hit with 800 Complaints from Foreign Workers: Accommodation, Unfair Wage Deductions Cited," April 1, 2008, www.afl.org

/alberta_hit_with_800_complaints_from_foreign_workers_accommodation_unfair
_wage_deductions_cited.

8. Elena Propokenk and Feng Hou, "How Temporary Were Canada's Temporary For-
    eign Workers?" Statistics Canada, January 29, 2018, https://www150.statcan.gc.ca
    /n1/pub/11f0019m/11f0019m2018402-eng.htm.

9. Sharma, *Home Economics*, 145.

10. Chris Ramsaroop quoted in Rosa Marchitelli, "Migrant Worker Program Called
    'Worse than Slavery' After Injured Participants Sent Home Without Treatment,"
    CBC News, May 16, 2016, www.cbc.ca/news/canada/jamaican-farm-worker-sent
    -home-in-a-casket-1.3577643.

11. Sara Mojtehedzadeh, "Snakes, Rats, Bedbugs, Abuse: Complaints Filed by Mexican
    Migrant Workers Expose Underside of Canada's Seasonal Agriculture Program,"
    Star Vancouver, October 14, 2019, www.thestar.com/news/canada/2019/10/14
    /snakes-rats-bedbugs-abuse-complaints-filed-by-mexican-migrant-workers-expose
    -underside-of-canadas-seasonal-agriculture-program.html.

12. Syed Hussan, "Testimony of Syed Hussan, Coordinator, Migrant Workers Alliance
    for Change," Citizenship and Immigration Committee of Canada, February 28, 2019,
    https://openparliament.ca/committees/immigration/42-1/147/syed-hussan-1/only/.

13. Anthony Fenton, "Responsibility to Protect?," *Briarpatch Magazine*, January 1, 2013,
    https://briarpatchmagazine.com/articles/view/responsibility-to-protect.

14. CBC, "Legacy of Hate," www.cbc.ca/history/EPISCONTENTSE1EP11CH3PA3LE
    .html.

15. Jenna L. Hennebry and Kerry Preibisch, "A Model for Managed Migration?
    Re-examining Best Practices in Canada's Seasonal Agricultural Worker Program,"
    International Migration (February 2012).

16. Christina Sharpe, *In the Wake: On Blackness and Being* (Durham: Duke University
    Press, 2016), 14.

17. Irving Andre, "The Genesis and Persistence of the Commonwealth Caribbean Sea-
    sonal Agricultural Workers Program in Canada," *Osgoode Hall Law Journal* 28, no. 28
    (Summer 2019): 243–301.

18. Andre, "Genesis and Persistence."

19. Robyn Maynard, *Policing Black Lives: State Violence in Canada from Slavery to the
    Present* (Halifax: Fernwood, 2017), 69.

20. Dionne Brand, *No Burden to Carry: Narratives of Black Working Women in Ontario
    1920s to 1950s* (Toronto: Women's Press, 1991), 15.

21. Katherine McKittrick, *Demonic Grounds: Black Women and the Cartographies of Strug-
    gle* (Minneapolis: University of Minnesota Press, 2006), 9.

22. Rinaldo Walcott, *Black like Who?* (Toronto: Insomniac Press, 2003), 23, 41.

23. Jodi A. Byrd, *The Transit of Empire: Indigenous Critiques of Colonialism* (Minneapolis:
    University of Minnesota Press, 2011), xxvi, 24.

24. Glen Sean Coulthard, *Red Skin, White Masks: Rejecting Colonial Politics of Recognition*
    (Minneapolis: University of Minnesota Press, 2014), 13.

25. Chelsea Vowel, *Indigenous Writes: A Guide to First Nations, Métis, and Inuit Issues in
    Canada* (Winnipeg: HighWater Press, 2016), 260–61.

26. Arthur Manuel and Ronald M. Derrickson, *Unsettling Canada: A National Wake-up Call* (Toronto: Between the Lines, 2015).

27. Janet Dench, "A Hundred Years of Immigration to Canada 1900–1999 (Part 2)," Canadian Council for Refugees, https://ccrweb.ca/en/hundred-years-immigration-canada -part-2.

28. Sunera Thobani, *Exalted Subjects* (Toronto: University of Toronto Press, 2007), 154.

29. Thobani, *Exalted Subjects*, 157.

30. Ryan Maloney, "Immigration Survey Shows 'Clear Measure of Racial Discrimination': EKOS Pollster," Huffington Post, April 16, 2019, www.huffingtonpost.ca /2019/04/16/immigration-non-white-immigrants-canada_a_23712911/.

31. Shannon Carranco and Jon Milton, "Canada's New Far Right: A Trove of Private Chat Room Messages Reveals an Extremist Subculture," *Globe and Mail*, April 27, 2019, www.theglobeandmail.com/canada/article-canadas-new-far-right-a-trove-of -private-chat-room-messages-reveals/.

32. Sedef Arat-Koç, "From 'Mothers of the Nation' to Migrant Workers" in *Not One of the Family: Foreign Domestic Workers in Canada*, Abigail B. Bakan and Daiva Stasiulis, eds. (Toronto: University of Toronto Press, 1997), 79.

33. Catherine Dauvergne, *The New Politics of Immigration and the End of Settler Societies* (Cambridge: Cambridge University Press, 2016), 129.

34. Kerry Preibisch, "Migrant Workers and Changing Work-Place Regimes in Contemporary Agricultural Production in Canada," *International Journal of Agriculture and Food* 19, no. 1 (2011): 63.

35. Preibisch, "Migrant Workers and Changing Work-Place Regimes," 77.

36. Aaron M. Orkin et al., "Medical Repatriation of Migrant Farm Workers in Ontario: A Descriptive Analysis," *CMAJ Open* 2, no. 3 (2014): 192–98.

37. Marcia Barrett quoted in Marchitelli, "Migrant Worker Program."

38. Alex Hemingway and David Macdonald, "Whose Wealth Is It Anyway? BC's Top 10 Billionaires and the Rest of Us," Policy Note, December 12, 2018, www.policynote.ca /bc-billionaires/.

39. Sophia Harris, "Canada's Top CEOs Earn 200 Times an Average Worker's Salary: Report," CBC News, January 2, 2018, www.cbc.ca/news/business/ceo-income -pay-canadian-worker-1.4462496.

40. Samir Amin, *Eurocentrism* (New York: Monthly Review Press, 2009), 7–8.

41. Mexican Agricultural Workers of the Golden Eagle Group Farm, "Letter of Concern from the Mexican Agricultural Workers of the Golden Eagle Group Farm, Pitt Meadows," Justicia for Migrant Workers, April 7, 2006, www.justicia4migrantworkers .org/bc/pdf/GE_Worker_Letter_En.pdf.

42. Maple Ridge-Pitt Meadows News, "Aquilini Fines Upheld," January 20, 2012, www.mapleridgenews.com/news/aquilini-fines-upheld/.

43. Ash Kelly and Hana Mae Nassar, "Guatemalan Workers Accuse Management of Harassment at Aquilini Blueberry Farm," News 1130, May 28, 2019, www.citynews1130 .com/2019/05/28/guatemalan-workers-accuse-aquilini-farm/; Paisley Woodward and Belle Puri, "Guatemalan Workers Allege Poor Conditions at Aquilini Berry Farm," CBC News, May 28, 2019, www.cbc.ca/news/canada/british-columbia/aquilini

-farm-workers-allege-poor-conditions-1.5152875.

44. Care Givers' Action Centre and Migrant Workers Alliance for Change, *Care Worker Voices for Landed Status and Fairness,* November 2018, http://migrantrights.ca/wp -content/uploads/2018/11/Care-Worker-Voices-for-Landed-Status-and-Fariness.pdf.

45. Care Givers' Action Centre and Migrant Workers Alliance for Change, *Care Worker Voices.*

46. Arat-Koç, "From 'Mothers of the Nation,'" 57.

47. Arat-Koç, "From 'Mothers of the Nation,'" 55.

48. Audrey Macklin, "Foreign Domestic Worker: Surrogate Housewife or Mail Order Servant?" *McGill Law Journal* 37 no. 3 (1992): 681–760.

49. Immigration official quoted in Arat-Koç, "From 'Mothers of the Nation,'" 76.

50. Audrey Macklin, "On the Inside Looking In: Foreign Domestic Workers in Canada," in *Maid in the Market: Women's Paid Domestic Labour,* Wenona Giles and Sedef Arat-Koç, eds. (Halifax: Fernwood, 1994), 17.

51. Macklin, "Foreign Domestic Worker," 691.

52. Macklin, "Foreign Domestic Worker," 681–760.

53. Ethel Tungohan, "Debunking Notions of Migrant 'Victimhood': A Critical Assessment of Temporary Labour Migration Programs and Filipina Migrant Activism in Canada," in *Disturbing Invisibility: Filipinos in Canada,* Roland Sintos Coloma et al., (Toronto: University of Toronto Press, 2012), 167.

54. Abigail B. Bakan and Daiva Stasiulis, "Foreign Domestic Worker Policy in Canada and the Social Boundaries of Modern Citizenship," *Science and Society* 58, no. 1 (Spring 1994): 7–33.

55. Elsa Galerand, Martin Gallié, and Jeanne Ollivier Gobeil, "Domestic Labour and Exploitation: The Case of the Live-In Caregiver Program in Canada (LCP)," *SAC-PINAY Research Report,* January 2015, www.mcgill.ca/lldrl/labour-law-and-development -research-laboratory; "Submission for the Universal Periodic Review of Canada," Submitted to the United Nations Office of the High Commissioner for Human Rights by PINAY The Filipino Women's Organization in Quebec, October 9, 2012, https:// lib.ohchr.org/HRBodies/UPR/Documents/Session16/CA/PINAY_UPR_CAN_ S16_2013_Filipinowomensorganization_E.pdf.

56. Macklin, "On the Inside Looking In," 13.

57. Migrant Rights Network, "Migrant Care Workers Claim Partial Victory, Continue to Demand Land Statuses on Arrival," June 15, 2019, https://migrantrights.ca/migrant -care-workers-claim-partial-victory-continue-to-demand-landed-status-on-arrival/.

Chapter 10

1. Weiyi Cai and Simone Landon, "Attack by White Extremists Are Growing. So Are Their Connections," *New York Times,* April 3, 2019, www.nytimes.com/interactive /2019/04/03/world/white-extremist-terrorism-christchurch.html.

2. Suketu Mehta, "Immigration Panic: How the West Fell for Manufactured Rage," *Guardian,* August 27, 2019, www.theguardian.com/uk-news/2019/aug/27/immigration -panic-how-the-west-fell-for-manufactured-rage; Julie Bosman, Kate Taylor, and Tim Aragno, "A Common Trait among Mass Killers: Hatred toward Women," *New York*

Times, August 10, 2019, www.nytimes.com/2019/08/10/us/mass-shootings-misogyny
-dayton.html.

3. Aleksandar Hemon, "Fascism Is Not an Idea to Be Debated, It's a Set of Actions to
    Fight," Literary Hub, November 1, 2018, https://lithub.com/fascism-is-not-an-idea
    -to-be-debated-its-a-set-of-actions-to-fight/.

4. Paul Gilroy, "Never Again: Refusing Race and Salvaging the Human," Holberg
    Lecture, May 31, 2019, www.holbergprisen.no/en/news/holberg-prize/2019-holberg
    -lecture-laureate-paul-gilroy.

5. Goldie Osuri and Ather Zia, "'Till the Soldiers Return the Keys': Unyielding Resis-
    tance in Palestine and Kashmir," Mondoweiss, August 15, 2019, https://mondoweiss
    .net/2019/08/unyielding-resistance-palestine/.

6. Reece Jones, *Border Walls: Security and the War on Terror in the United States, India and
    Israel* (London: Zed Books, 2012), 1.

7. Harsha Panduranga, "The Muslim Ban: A Family Separation Policy," Brennan Center
    for Justice, June 26, 2019, www.brennancenter.org/blog/muslim-ban-family
    -separation-policy; "Israel Approves 2,300 New Homes for Settlers in West Bank:
    NGO," Al Jazeera, August 6, 2019, www.aljazeera.com/news/2019/08/israel-approves
    -2300-homes-settlers-west-bank-ngo-190806161537292.html.

8. Eric K. Ward, "Skin in the Game: How Antisemitism Animates White National-
    ism," Political Research Associates, June 29, 2017, www.politicalresearch.org/2017
    /06/29/skin-in-the-game-how-antisemitism-animates-white-nationalism.

9. Wendy Elisheva Somerson, "Anti-Semitism and Zionism Have Formed a Brutal
    Alliance," Truthout, July 26, 2019, https://truthout.org/articles/anti-semitism-and
    -zionism-have-formed-a-brutal-alliance/.

10. Somerson, "Anti-Semitism and Zionism."

11. Ali Abunimah, "Why Won't Israel Lobby Groups Condemn Trump's Anti-Semi-
    tism?" Electronic Intifada, August 21, 2019, https://electronicintifada.net/blogs/ali
    -abunimah/why-wont-israel-lobby-groups-condemn-trumps-anti-semitism.

12. "Savitri Devi: The Mystical Fascist Being Resurrected by the Alt-Right," BBC News,
    October 29, 2017, www.bbc.com/news/magazine-41757047.

13. Justin Rowlatt, "Why India's Hindu Nationalists Are Shedding Their Shorts," BBC
    News, November 5, 2015, www.bbc.com/news/world-asia-india-34718691.

14. Documentation of the Oppressed Database, http://dotodatabase.com/, accessed
    April 23, 2020; Jayshree Bajoria, *Violent Cow Protection in India*, Human Rights
    Watch, February 18, 2019, www.hrw.org/report/2019/02/18/violent
    -cow-protection-india/vigilante-groups-attack-minorities.

15. Dexter Filkins, "Blood and Soil in Narendra Modi's India," *New Yorker*, December 2,
    2019, www.newyorker.com/magazine/2019/12/09/blood-and-soil-in-narendra
    -modis-india.

16. Rana Ayyub, "Reclaiming India from the Fascists," interview by Meara Sharma, *Adi
    Magazine*, Spring 2020, https://adimagazine.com/articles/rana-ayyub-reclaiming
    -india-from-the-fascists/; Sameer Yasir and Billy Perrigo, "'Hate Is Being Preached
    Openly against Us.' After Delhi Riots, Muslims in India Fear What's Next," *Time
    Magazine*, March 3, 2020, https://time.com/5794354/delhi-riots-muslims-india/;

Rana Ayyub, "Narendra Modi Looks the Other Way as New Delhi Burns," *Time Magazine*, February 28, 2020, https://time.com/5791759/narendra-modi-india-delhi -riots-violence-muslim/.

17. Apoorvanand, "How the Coronavirus Outbreak in India Was Blamed on Muslims," Al Jazeera, April 18, 2020, www.aljazeera.com/indepth/opinion/coronavirus-outbreak -india-blamed-muslims-200418143252362.html.

18. B. R. Ambedkar, *Annihilation of Caste* (New Delhi: Arnold, 1990).

19. Shreehari Paliath, "Income Inequality in India: Top 10% Upper Caste Households Own 60% Wealth," *Business Standard*, January 14, 2019, www.business-standard.com /article/current-affairs/income-inequality-in-india-top-10-upper-caste-households -own-60-wealth-119011400105_1.html.

20. M. Zwick-Maitreyi et al., *Caste in the United States: A Survey of Caste among South Asian Americans*, Equality Labs, 2018, https://static1.squarespace.com/static /58347d04bebafbb1e66df84c/t/5d9b4f9afbaef569c0a5c132/1570459664518/Caste _report_2018.pdf.

21. Jean-Yves Camus and Nicolas Lebourg, *Far-Right Politics in Europe* (London: Belknap Press of Harvard University Press, 2017), 167.

22. The Campaign to Stop Funding Hate, "The Foreign Exchange of Hate: IDRF and the American Funding of Hindutva," http://stopfundinghate.org/sacw/index.html.

23. Arundhati Roy, "Walking with the Comrades," *Outlook*, March 29, 2010, www.outlookindia.com/magazine/story/walking-with-the-comrades/264738.

24. Michael Safi, "How Love and a Taste of Honey Brought One Indian Woman's 16- Year Hunger Strike to an End," *Guardian*, November 11, 2018, www.theguardian.com /world/2018/nov/11/irom-sharmila-love-story-worlds-longest-hunger-strike.

25. Jaskaran Kaur and Sukhman Dhami, "Protecting the Killers: A Policy of Impunity in Punjab, India," Human Rights Watch, October 2007, www.hrw.org/reports/2007 /india1007/india1007webwcover.pdf; Romesh Silva, Jasmine Marwaha, and Jeff Klingner, *Violent Deaths and Enforced Disappearances during the Counterinsurgency in Punjab, India*, Benetech's Human Rights Data Analysis Group and Ensaaf, January, 2009, https://ensaaf.org/wp-content/uploads/2018/08/ViolentDeathsReport.pdf.

26. Citizens for Justice and Peace, "Cornered Citizens Tribunal: An Inquiry into the Carnage in Gujarat," 2002, www.sabrang.com/tribunal/.

27. Jess Franklin, "Globalizing the War on Indigenous People: Bolsonaro and Modi," CounterPunch, January 24, 2020, www.counterpunch.org/2020/01/24/globalizing -the-war-on-indigenous-people-bolsonaro-and-modi/.

28. Forum against War on People, "24 April Meeting: Indian State's War on People and the Assault on Democratic Voices," Counter Currents, April 20, 2010, www .countercurrents.org/wop200410.htm.

29. Smita Gupta, "A Shiver Runs through It," *Outlook*, February 22, 2010, www .outlookindia.com/magazine/story/a-shiver-runs-through-it/264255.

30. Azad Essa, "India's Annexation of Kashmir Is Straight Out of the Israeli Playbook," Middle East Eye, August 7, 2019, www.middleeasteye.net/opinion/indias-annexation -kashmir-straight-out-israeli-playbook.

31. BDS Movement, "Solidarity and Unity in Opposing Global Militarization: BNC

Statement on Kashmir," August 13, 2019, www.bdsmovement.net/news/solidarity-and-unity-opposing-global-militarization-bnc-statement-kashmir.

32. Nitasha Kaul, "India's Obsession with Kashmir: Democracy, Gender, (Anti-) Nationalism," *Feminist Review* 119 (2018): 131.

33. "Indian Forces Killed 95,238 Kashmiris since January 1989: Report," Kashmir Global, October 10, 2018, https://kashmirglobal.com/2018/12/10/indian-forces-killed-95238-kashmiris-since-january-1989-report.html; Cathy Scott-Clark, "The Mass Graves of Kashmir," *Guardian*, July 9, 2012, www.theguardian.com/world/2012/jul/09/mass-graves-of-kashmir.

34. Mohamad Junaid, "Disobedient Bodies, Defiant Objects: Occupation, Necropolitics, and the Resistance in Kashmir," The Funambulist, January 2019.

35. Reece Jones, *Violent Borders: Refugees and the Right to Move* (London and New York: Verso, 2016).

36. Jones, *Violent Borders*.

37. Odhikar, "Human Rights Violation by Indian Border Security Force (BSF) against Bangladeshi Citizens 2000-2018," January 2019, http://odhikar.org/wp-content/uploads/2019/01/Statistics_Border_2000-2018.pdf.

38. C. R. Abrar, "Killings at the Bangladesh-India Border," *Daily Star*, January 17, 2020, www.thedailystar.net/opinion/human-rights/news/killings-the-bangladesh-india-border-1855045.

39. Rizwana Shamshad, "Politics and the India-Bangladesh Border Fence," Monash Asia Institute, Monash University, July 1, 2006, http://citeseerx.ist.psu.edu/viewdoc/download?doi=10.1.1.534.6328&rep=rep1&type=pdf.

40. Kate Lamb, "Thousands Dead: The Philippine President, the Death Squad Allegations and a Brutal Drugs War," *Guardian*, April 2, 2017, www.theguardian.com/world/2017/apr/02/philippines-president-duterte-drugs-war-death-squads; David T. Johnson and Jon Fernquest, "Governing through Killing: The War on Drugs in the Philippines," *Asian Journal of Law and Society* 5, no. 2 (November 2018): 359–90.

41. Davinci Maru, "CHR Chief: Drug War Deaths Could Be as High as 27,000," ABS-CBN News, December 5, 2018, https://news.abs-cbn.com/focus/12/05/18/chr-chief-drug-war-deaths-could-be-as-high-as-27000; Amnesty International, "Philippines: UN Investigation Urgently Needed into Duterte Administration's Murderous 'War on Drugs,'" July 8, 2019, www.amnesty.org/en/latest/news/2019/07/philippines-un-investigation-urgently-needed-duterte-war-drugs/.

42. Johnson and Fernquest, "Governing through Killing," 359–90; Amnesty International, *"They Just Kill": Ongoing Extrajudicial Executions and Other Violations in the Philippines' "War on Drugs,"* 2019, www.amnesty.org/download/Documents/ASA3505782019ENGLISH.PDF.

43. Sheila Coronel, Mariel Padilla, and David Mora, "The Uncounted Dead of Duterte's Drug War," *The Atlantic*, August 19, 2019, www.theatlantic.com/international/archive/2019/08/philippines-dead-rodrigo-duterte-drug-war/595978/.

44. "Philippine President Rodrigo Duterte Compares Himself to Hitler," CBS News, September 30, 2016, www.cbsnews.com/news/philippine-president-rodrigo-duterte-compares-himself-to-hitler/.

45. Johnson and Fernquest, "Governing through Killing," 359–90.

46. Oliver Holmes, "Philippines President Rodrigo Duterte Says He Personally Killed Criminals," *Guardian*, December 14, 2016, www.theguardian.com/world/2016/dec /14/philippines-president-rodrigo-duterte-personally-killed-criminals.

47. "Transcript of Call Between President Trump and Philippine President Duterte," *Washington Post*, https://apps.washingtonpost.com/g/documents/politics/transcript -of-call-between-president-trump-and-philippine-president-duterte/2446/.

48. Lynzy Billing, "Duterte's Response to the Coronavirus: 'Shoot Them Dead,'" *Foreign Policy*, April 16, 2020, https://foreignpolicy.com/2020/04/16/duterte-philippines -coronavirus-response-shoot-them-dead/.

49. KARAPATAN, *2018 Karapatan Year-End Report on the Human Rights Situation in the Philippines: Duterte's Blueprint for a Dictatorship*, 2019.

50. Arnold P. Alamon, *Wars of Extinction: Discrimination and the Lumad Struggle in Mindanao* (Illigan City: Rural Missionaries of the Philippines Northern Mindanao Sub-Region Incorporated, 2017), 4.

51. Bong S. Sarmiento, "Rodrigo Duterte's Killing Season Now Opens Fire on Lumads and the Left," Asia Pacific Report, August 19, 2018, https://asiapacificreport.nz/2018 /08/19/rodrigo-dutertes-killing-season-now-opens-fire-on-lumads-and-the-left/.

52. Amee Chew, "It's Time to End U.S. Military Aid to the Philippines," Foreign Policy in Focus, April 8, 2019, https://fpif.org/its-time-to-end-u-s-military-aid-to-the -philippines/.

53. KARAPATAN, *2018 Karapatan Year-End Report*.

54. "Enemies of the State? How Governments and Businesses Silence Land and Environmental Defenders," Global Witness, July 30, 2019, www.globalwitness.org/en /campaigns/environmental-activists/enemies-state/.

55. Amazon Watch, *Complicity in Destruction II: How Northern Consumers and Financiers Enable Bolsonaro's Assault in the Brazilian Amazon*, 2019, https:// amazonwatch.org/assets/files/2019-complicity-in-destruction-2.pdf.

56. Jake Spring, "Brazil's Deforestation Climbs 67% through July as Government Attacks Data," Reuters, August 5, 2019, www.reuters.com/article/us-brazil-environment /brazil-deforestation-climbs-67-through-july-as-government-attacks-data -idUSKCN1UV26N; Jordan Davidson, "Amazon Deforestation Rate Hits 3 Football Fields Per Minute, Data Confirms," EcoWatch, July 26, 2019, www.ecowatch.com /amazon-deforestation-unrecoverable-tipping-point-2639358982.html?rebelltitem =1#rebelltitem1; "Amazon Fires Increase by 84% in one Year–Space Agency," BBC News, August 21, 2019, www.bbc.com/news/world-latin-america-49415973.

57. Survival International, "What Brazil's President, Jair Bolsonaro, Has Said about Brazil's Indigenous Peoples," www.survivalinternational.org/articles/3540-Bolsonaro; Amazon Watch, *Complicity in Destruction II*.

58. Alexander Zaitchik, "Rainforest on Fire: On the Front Lines of Bolsonaro's War on the Amazon, Brazil's Forest Communities Fight against Climate Catastrophe," The Intercept, July 6, 2019, https://theintercept.com/2019/07/06/brazil-amazon -rainforest-indigenous-conservation-agribusiness-ranching/.

59. Sônia Guajara quoted in Christian Poirier, "Indigenous Women Mobilize to Resist

Bolsonaro," Amazon Watch, August 14, 2019, https://amazonwatch.org/news/2019/0814-indigenous-women-mobilize-to-resist-bolsonaro.

60. Sean Purdy, "Here's What Jair Bolsonaro Thinks," *Jacobin Magazine*, October 28, 2018, www.jacobinmag.com/2018/10/jair-bolsonaro-quotes-brazil-election.

61. Vincent Bevins, "The Dirty Problems with Operation Car Wash," *The Atlantic*, August 21, 2019, www.theatlantic.com/international/archive/2019/08/anti-corruption-crusades-paved-way-bolsonaro/596449/.

62. Survival International, "What Brazil's President."

63. Eli Stokols and Noah Bierman, "Trump Embraces Brazil's Bolsonaro, Another Brash President Enmeshed in Scandal," *Los Angeles Times*, March 19, 2019, www.latimes.com/politics/la-na-pol-trump-bolsonaro-brazil-press-conference-20190319-story.html.

64. Luciane Rocha, "Echoing Marielle Franco, Brazil's Black Women Speak Out against Violence," The Conversation, April 18, 2018, https://theconversation.com/echoing-marielle-franco-brazils-black-women-speak-out-against-violence-93993.

65. "Rio Violence: Police Killings Reach Record High in 2019," BBC News, January 23, 2020, www.bbc.com/news/world-latin-america-51220364.

66. Tom Phillips, "Bolsonaro in Spotlight after Photo with Marielle Franco Murder Suspect Surfaces," *Guardian*, March 13, 2019, www.theguardian.com/world/2019/mar/13/jair-bolsonaro-paramilitaries-marielle-franco-suspects.

67. Jonathan Wheatley, "Rio De Janeiro's Militias: A Parallel Power in Bolsonaro's Brazil," *Financial Times*, March 25, 2019, www.ft.com/content/bdd61718-4b10-11e9-bbc9-6917dce3dc62.

68. Rocha, "Echoing Marielle Franco."

69. Daniel Trilling, "Golden Dawn: The Rise and Fall of Greece's Neo-Nazis," *Guardian*, March 3, 2020, www.theguardian.com/news/2020/mar/03/golden-dawn-the-rise-and-fall-of-greece-neo-nazi-trial; Patrick Strickland, "When Prosecuting Far-Right Violence Fails," *The New Republic*, October 30, 2018, https://newrepublic.com/article/151947/prosecuting-far-right-violence-fails.

70. Rosa Vasilaki, "How Greece Became Europe's 'Shield' against Refugees," *Jacobin Magazine*, March 10, 2020, https://jacobinmag.com/2020/03/greece-refugees-european-union-migrants-turkey-border; Helena Smith, "Greece Plans to Build Sea Barrier Off Lesbos to Deter Migrants," *Guardian*, January 30, 2020, www.theguardian.com/world/2020/jan/30/greece-plans-to-build-sea-barrier-off-lesbos-to-deter-migrants.

71. Richard Orange, "Mette Frederiksen: The Anti-immigration Left Leader Set to Win Power in Denmark," *Guardian,* May 11, 2019, www.theguardian.com/world/2019/may/11/denmark-election-matte-frederiksen-leftwing-immigration.

72. Alexander C. Kaufman, "Austria's New Anti-immigrant Green Government Stokes Fears of Climate 'Nightmare,'" Huffington Post, January 18, 2020, www.huffingtonpost.ca/entry/austria-greens-conservatives-climate_n_5e19011ec5b6640ec3d4598b?ri18n=true.

73. Gabriella Elgenius and Jens Rydgren, "Frames of Nostalgia and Belonging: The Resurgence of Ethno-Nationalism in Sweden," *European Societies* 21, no. 4 (2019): 583–602.

74. Andrea L. P. Pirro, *The Populist Radical Right in Central and Eastern Europe: Ideology,*

Impact, and Electoral Performance (New York: Routledge, 2015), 15.

75. Marine Le Pen: 10 Things to Know," *TRT World*, May 4, 2017, www.trtworld.com/europe/marine-le-pen-10-things-to-know-6769; Lucy Middleton, "Priti Patel Vows to End Freedom of Movement 'For Once and For All,'" Metro, October 1, 2019, https://metro.co.uk/2019/10/01/priti-patel-vows-end-freedom-movement-10844424/.

76. Lorenzo Tondo, "Salvini Attacks Italy PM Over Coronavirus and Links to Rescue Ship," *Guardian*, February 24, 2020, www.theguardian.com/world/2020/feb/24/salvini-attacks-italy-pm-over-coronavirus-and-links-to-rescue-ship; Gabriella Lazaridis and Vasiliki Tsagkroni, "Posing for Legitimacy? Identity and Praxis of Far-Right Populism in Greece," in *The Rise of the Far Right in Europe: Populist Shifts and "Othering*," Gabriella Lazaridis, Giovanna Campani, and Annie Benveniste, eds. (London: Palgrave Macmillan, 2016), 208.

77. Birgit Sauer and Edma Ajanovic, "Hegemonic Discourse of Difference and Inequality: Right-Wing Organisations in Austria," in Lazaridis, Campani, and Benveniste, *The Rise of the Far Right in Europe*, 83.

78. Farid Hafez, Reinhard Heinisch, and Eric Miklin, "The New Right: Austria's Freedom Party and Changing Perceptions of Islam," Brookings, July 24, 2019, www.brookings.edu/research/the-new-right-austrias-freedom-party-and-changing-perceptions-of-islam/.

79. Pirro, *The Populist Radical Right*.

80. Milica Stojanovic, "Serbian Anti-migrant Protest Condemned as 'Disgrace,'" Balkan Insight, March 9, 2020, https://balkaninsight.com/2020/03/09/serbian-anti-migrant-protest-condemned-as-disgrace/.

81. Agnieszka Dudzińska and Michał Kotnarowski, "Imaginary Muslims: How the Polish Right Frames Islam," Brookings, July 24, 2019, www.brookings.edu/research/imaginary-muslims-how-polands-populists-frame-islam/.

82. "Polish President and PM Set to Join Fascist March in Warsaw," Freedom News, November 10, 2018, https://freedomnews.org.uk/polish-president-and-pm-set-to-join-fascist-march-in-warsaw/.

83. Barbora Černušáková, "The Roma People's Hungarian Hell," Politico, January 25, 2017, www.politico.eu/article/the-roma-peoples-hungarian-hell/.

84. Colin Woodard, "Hungary's Anti-Roma Militia Grows," *Christian Science Monitor*, February 13, 2008, www.csmonitor.com/World/Europe/2008/0213/p07s02-woeu.html.

85. Vanessa Barker, "Nordic Exceptionalism Revisited: Explaining the Paradox of a Janus-Faced Penal Regime," *Theoretical Criminology* 17, no. 1 (December 2012): 5–25.

86. Birte Siim and Susi Meret, "Right-Wing Populism in Denmark: People, Nation and Welfare in the Construction of the 'Other,'" in Lazaridis, Campani, and Benveniste, *The Rise of the Far Right in Europe*, 115.

87. Camus and Lebourg, *Far-Right Politics*, 191.

88. Edward Said, *Covering Islam: How the Media and the Experts Determine How We See the Rest of the World* (New York: Pantheon, 1981), xv.

89. Edward W. Said, *Orientalism* (London: Penguin Books, 1978), 95, 122.

90. Saba Mahmood, *Politics of Piety: The Islamic Revival and the Feminist Subject* (Prince-

ton: Princeton University Press, 2012), 189.

91. Sohail Daulatzai and Junaid Rana, "Writing the Muslim Left: An Introduction to Throwing Stones," in *With Stones in Our Hands: Writings on Muslims, Racism, and Empire*, Sohail Daulatzai and Junaid Rana, eds. (Minneapolis: University of Minnesota Press, 2018), xi.

92. Sherene Razack, *Looking White People in the Eye: Gender, Race, and Culture in Courtrooms and Classrooms* (Toronto: University of Toronto Press, 1998), 120.

93. Judith Butler, *Gender Trouble: Feminism and the Subversion of Identity* (New York: Routledge, 2006), 125.

94. Sara R. Farris, *In the Name of Women's Rights: The Rise of Femonationalism* (Durham: Duke University Press, 2017).

95. Jeffrey Gedmin, "Right-Wing Populism in Germany: Muslims and Minorities after the 2015 Refugee Crisis," Brookings, July 24, 2019, www.brookings.edu/research/right-wing-populism-in-germany-muslims-and-minorities-after-the-2015-refugee-crisis/.

96. Daulatzai and Rana, "Writing the Muslim Left," x.

97. Hillary Clinton quoted in Patrick Wintour, "Hillary Clinton: Europe Must Curb Immigration to Stop Rightwing Populists," *Guardian*, November 22, 2018, www.theguardian.com/world/2018/nov/22/hillary-clinton-europe-must-curb-immigration-stop-populists-trump-brexit.

98. Aditya Chakrabortty, "Integrate, Migrants Are Told. But Can They Ever Be Good Enough for the Likes of Blair?" *Guardian,* April 24, 2019, www.theguardian.com/commentisfree/2019/apr/24/migrants-tony-blair-british-racism-victims.

99. Saleha Begum quoted in Annie Gowen, "India's Crackdown on Illegal Immigration Could Leave 4 Million People Stateless," *Washington Post*, July 30, 2018.

100. Amnesty International, *Between Fear and Hatred: Surviving Migration Detention in Assam*, 2018, https://amnesty.org.in/assam-detention-centres/.

101. Zeid Ra'ad Al Hussein, "Darker and More Dangerous: High Commissioner Updates the Human Rights Council on Human Rights Issues in 40 Countries," UN High Commissioner for Human Rights, September 11, 2017, www.ohchr.org/EN/NewsEvents/Pages/DisplayNews.aspx?NewsID=22041&LangID=E; United Nations Human Rights Council, "Report of the Detailed Findings of the Independent Fact-Finding Mission on Myanmar," September 17, 2018, www.ohchr.org/Documents/HRBodies/HRCouncil/FFM-Myanmar/A_HRC_39_CRP.2.pdf.

102. United Nations Human Rights Council, "Independent Fact-Finding Mission on Myanmar."

103. Outlook Web Bureau, "Rohingyas Issue Is Similar to India's Kashmir Issue, Says Myanmar's Suu Kyi," *Outlook*, September 7, 2017, www.outlookindia.com/website/story/myanmars-rohingyas-issue-is-similar-to-indias-kashmir-issue-says-myanmars-suu-ky/301375.

104. Aida Alami, "Between Hate, Hope, and Help: Haitians in the Dominican Republic," *New York Review of Books*, August 13, 2018, www.nybooks.com/daily/2018/08/13/between-hope-hate-help-haitians-in-the-dominican-republic/; Human Rights Watch, "Haiti: Stateless People Trapped in Poverty," November 29, 2016, www.hrw.org/news/2016/11/29/haiti-stateless-people-trapped-poverty.

105. Silvio Torres-Saillant, *Introduction to Dominican Blackness*, CUNY Dominican Studies Institute, 2010, www.ccny.cuny.edu/sites/default/files/dsi/upload/Introduction_to_Dominican_Blackness_Web.pdf.

106. Cited in Americas Watch, National Coalition for Haitian Refugees, and Caribbean Rights, *Haitian Sugar Cane Cutters in the Dominican Republic* (New York: Human Rights Watch, 1989), 6.

107. Torres-Saillant, *Introduction to Dominican Blackness*.

108. Jenna M. Loyd and Alison Mountz, *Boats, Borders and Bases* (Oakland: University of California Press, 2018), 225.

109. Lorgia García-Peña, *The Borders of Dominicanidad: Race, Nation, and Archives of Contradiction* (Durham: Duke University Press, 2016).

110. J. Michael Dash, *The Other America: Caribbean Literature in a New World Context* (Charlottesville: University of Virginia Press, 1998), 164.

111. Jane Kinninmont, "Citizenship in the Gulf," in *The Gulf States and the Arab Uprisings*, Ana Achague, ed. (Cordoba: FRIDE and the Gulf Research Center), 47–58.

112. Priyanka Motoparthy, *Prisoners of the Past: Kuwaiti Bidoon and the Burden of Statelessness*, Human Rights Watch, June 13, 2011, www.hrw.org/report/2011/06/13/prisoners-past/kuwaiti-Bidoon-and-burden-statelessness.

113. Atossa Araxia Abrahamian, "Who Loses When a Country Puts Citizenship Up for Sale?" *New York Times*, January 5, 2018, www.nytimes.com/2018/01/05/opinion/sunday/united-arab-emirates-comorans-citizenship.html.

114. Ahmed Abdelkhaleq quoted in Atossa Araxia Abrahamian, "Kuwait Offers Stateless Group Citizenship–From Comoros," Al Jazeera, November 10, 2018, http://america.aljazeera.com/articles/2014/11/10/kuwait-statelesscitizenshipcomoros.html.

115. Abrahamian, "Who Loses When a Country Puts Citizenship Up for Sale?"

116. Mahmood Mamdani, *Define and Rule: Native as Political Identity* (Cambridge: Harvard University Press, 2012).

117. William C. Anderson and Zoé Samudzi, *As Black as Resistance: Finding the Conditions for Liberation* (Oakland: AK Press, 2018), 94.

118. Erica Violet Lee, "Twelve Thousand Moons," Moontime Warrior, June 1, 2017, https://moontimewarrior.com/2017/06/01/twelve-thousand-moons/.

Chapter 11

1. Christopher Mathias, "Go Back to Your Country, They Said," Huffington Post, November 4, 2019, www.huffpost.com/feature/go-back-to-your-country.

2. Keeanga-Yamahtta Taylor, *From #BlackLivesMatter to Black Liberation* (Chicago: Haymarket Books, 2016), 34.

3. Himani Bannerji, *The Dark Side of the Nation: Essays on Multiculturalism, Nationalism, and Gender* (Toronto: Canadian Scholars' Press, 2000), 120.

4. Mahmood Mamdani, "Good Muslim, Bad Muslim: A Political Perspective on Culture and Terrorism," *American Anthropologist* 104, no. 3 (September 2002): 766–75.

5. Elizabeth A. Povinelli, *The Cunning of Recognition: Indigenous Alterities and the Mak-*

ing of Australian Multiculturalism (Durham: Duke University Press, 2002), 6.

6. Ghassan Hage, *White Nation: Fantasies of White Supremacy in a Multicultural Society* (New York: Routledge, 2000), 18.

7. Jean-Yves Camus and Nicolas Lebourg, *Far-Right Politics in Europe* (London: Belknap Press of Harvard University Press, 2017), 194.

8. Bill Fletcher Jr., "Quick Reflections on the November 2016 Election," November 9, 2016, http://billfletcherjr.com/2016/quick-reflections-november-2016-election/.

9. Rachel Kaadzi Ghansah, "A Most American Terrorist: The Making of Dylann Roof," *GQ*, August 21, 2017, www.gq.com/story/dylann-roof-making-of-an-american-terrorist.

10. Listen Chen and Ivan Drury, "The Dead End of Homeless Nationalism: From Refugee Camps to Tent Cities, Displaced Peoples Unite,"The Volcano, September 9, 2019, http://thevolcano.org/2019/09/09/the-dead-end-of-homeless-nationalism -from-refugee-camps-to-tent-cities-displaced-peoples-unite/.

11. David R. Roediger, *The Wages of Whiteness: Race and the Making of the American Working Class*, rev. ed. (London: Verso, 2007).

12. Camus and Lebourg, *Far-Right Politics*, 101.

13. Cheryl I. Harris, "Whiteness as Property," *Harvard Law Review* 106, no. 8 (June 1993), 1707–91.

14. Lou Cornum, "Burial Ground Acknowledgements,"The New Inquiry, October 14, 2019, https://thenewinquiry.com/burial-ground-acknowledgements/.

15. Bureau of Labor Statistics, "Fastest Growing Occupations," September 4, 2019, www.bls.gov/ooh/fastest-growing.htm; Campbell Robertson and Robert Gebeloff, "How Millions of Women Became the Most Essential Workers in America," *New York Times*, April 18, 2020, www.nytimes.com/2020/04/18/us/coronavirus-women -essential-workers.html#click=https://t.co/oaw9tHAwiE.

16. Robin D. G. Kelley, *Yo' Mama's Disfunktional!: Fighting the Culture Wars in Urban America* (Boston: Beacon Press, 1997), 109.

17. Seraj Assi, "Why Kibbutzism Isn't Socialism," *Jacobin Magazine*, August 20, 2016, www.jacobinmag.com/2016/10/kibbutz-labor-zionism-bernie-sanders-ben-gurion.

18. Rosa Vasilaki, "How Greece Became Europe's "Shield" against Refugees," *Jacobin Magazine*, March 10, 2020, https://jacobinmag.com/2020/03/greece-refugees -european-union-migrants-turkey-border.

19. Frantz Fanon, *The Wretched of the Earth* (New York: Grove Press, 2004), 179.

20. Donald Trump quoted in Josh Boak, "AP Fact Check: Trump Plays on Immigration Myths," PBS, February 8, 2019, www.pbs.org/newshour/politics/ap-fact-check -trump-plays-on-immigration-myths.

21. Caroline Mortimer, "Brexit Campaign Was Largely Funded by Five of UK's Richest Businessmen," *Independent*, April 24, 2017, www.independent.co.uk/news/uk/politics /brexit-leave-eu-campaign-arron-banks-jeremy-hosking-five-uk-richest-businessmen -peter-hargreaves-a7699046.html.

22. Matthew Goodwin and Catlin Milazzo, "Taking Back Control? Investigating the Role of Immigration in the 2016 Vote for Brexit," *British Journal of Politics and International Relations* 19, no. 3 (June 2017): 450–64.

23. Gabriella Elgenius and Jens Rydgren, "Frames of Nostalgia and Belonging: The

Resurgence of Ethno-nationalism in Sweden," *European Societies* 21, no. 4 (2019): 583–602.

24. Anna Krasteva, "The Post-Communist Rise of National Populism: Bulgarian Paradoxes," in *The Rise of the Far Right in Europe: Populist Shifts and "Othering,"* Gabriella Lazaridis, Giovanna Campani, and Annie Benveniste, eds. (London: Palgrave Macmillan, 2016), 161–200.

25. Peter James Hudson, *Bankers and Empire: How Wall Street Colonized the Caribbean* (Chicago: University of Chicago Press, 2017), 274.

26. Kornel Chang, "Circulating Race and Empire: Transnational Labor Activism and the Politics of Anti-Asian Agitation in the Anglo-American Pacific World, 1880–1910," *Journal of American History* (December 2009): 679.

27. Chris Carlsson, "The Workingmen's Party and The Denis Kearney Agitation," Found SF, 1995, www.foundsf.org/index.php?title=The_Workingmen%E2%80%99s_Party_%26_The_Denis_Kearney_Agitation; Kevin Starr, "Endangered Dreams: The Great Depression in California," *Washington Post*, 1996, www.washingtonpost.com/wp-srv/style/longterm/books/chap1/endanger.htm.

28. Sandro Mezzadra and Brett Neilson, *Border as Method, or, the Multiplication of Labor* (Durham: Duke University Press, 2013), 281.

29. Lauren Berlant, "National Brands / National Body: Imitation of Life" in *Comparative American Identities: Race, Sex, and Nationality in the Modern Text,* Hortense Spillers, ed. (New York: Routledge, 1991), 113.

30. Justin Akers Chacón, "The Only Way Out of the Crisis Is to Fight for Open Borders," *Spectre*, April 28, 2020, https://spectrejournal.com/the-only-way-out-of-the-crisis-is-to-fight-for-open-borders/.

31. Romain Felli, "Managing Climate Insecurity by Ensuring Continuous Capital Accumulation: 'Climate Refugees' and 'Climate Migrants,'" *Critical Review of International Social and Political Philosophy* 17, no. 5 (June 2014): 349.

32. William Allen et al., "Who Counts in Crises? The New Geopolitics of International Migration and Refugee Governance," *Geopolitics* 23, no. 1 (2018): 217–43.

33. Atilio A. Boron, *Empire and Imperialism: A Critical Reading of Michael Hardt and Antonio Negri* (London: Zed Books, 2005), 46.

34. Lisa Lowe, *Immigrant Acts* (Durham: Duke University Press, 1996), 27–28.

35. Beth Gardiner, "White Supremacy Goes Green," *New York Times*, February 28, 2020, www.nytimes.com/2020/02/28/opinion/sunday/far-right-climate-change.html; Alexander C. Kaufman, "The El Paso Manifesto: Where Racism and Eco-facism Meet," *Mother Jones*, August 5, 2019, www.motherjones.com/environment/2019/08/the-el-paso-manifesto-where-racism-and-eco-facism-meet/.

36. Aude Mazoue, "Le Pen's National Rally Goes Green in Bid for European Election Votes," France 24, April 20, 2019, www.france24.com/en/20190420-le-pen-national-rally-front-environment-european-elections-france.

37. Keston Perry, "What Is Really behind the Crisis in Haiti?," Al Jazeera, September 30, 2019, www.aljazeera.com/amp/indepth/opinion/crisis-haiti-190927092336787.html.

38. Todd Miller, *Storming the Wall: Climate Change, Migration, and Homeland Security* (San Francisco: City Lights Books, 2017).

39. Peter Schwartz and Doug Randall, "An Abrupt Climate Change Scenario and Its Implications for United States National Security," October 2003, https://eesc .columbia.edu/courses/v1003/readings/Pentagon.pdf.

40. Julian Brave NoiseCat, "The Environment Movement Needs to Reckon with Its Racist History," Vice, September 13, 2019, www.vice.com/en_ca/article/bjwvn8/the -environmental-movement-needs-to-reckon-with-its-racist-history.

41. Shelagh Whitley et al., "G7 Fossil Fuel Subsidy Scorecard: Tracking the Phase-Out of Fiscal Support and Public Finance for Oil, Gas and Coal," ODI, June 2018, www.odi.org/publications/11131-g7-fossil-fuel-subsidy-scorecard.

42. Tess Riley, "Just 100 Companies Responsible for 71% of Global Emissions, Study Says," *Guardian,* July 10, 2017, www.theguardian.com/sustainable-business/2017/jul /10/100-fossil-fuel-companies-investors-responsible-71-global-emissions-cdp-study -climate-change; Oxfam, "Extreme Carbon Inequality," December 2, 2015, https:// www-cdn.oxfam.org/s3fs-public/file_attachments/mb-extreme-carbon-inequality -021215-en.pdf.

43. Oliver Belcher et al., "Hidden Carbon Costs of the "Everywhere War": Logistics, Geopolitical Ecology, and the Carbon Boot-Print of the US Military," *Transactions of the Institute of British Geographers* (June 2019): 1–16.

44. Jonathan Watts, "Human Society Under Urgent Threat from Loss of Earth's Natural Life," *Guardian*, May 6, 2019, www.theguardian.com/environment/2019/may/06 /human-society-under-urgent-threat-loss-earth-natural-life-un-report.

45. Baher Kamal, "Indigenous Peoples Lands Guard 80 Per Cent of World's Biodiversity," Inter Press Service News Agency, February 9, 2017, www.ipsnews.net/2017/02 /indigenous-peoples-lands-guard-80-per-cent-of-worlds-biodiversity/.

46. Eriel Deranger, "First Nations Target Trudeau's Climate Plan with Indigenous Climate Action," National Observer (Canada), April 27, 2016, www.nationalobserver .com/2016/04/27/opinion/first-nations-target-trudeaus-climate-plan-indigenous -climate-action.

47. Jonathan Watts, "Environmental Activist Murders Double in 15 Years," *Guardian*, August 5, 2019, www.theguardian.com/environment/2019/aug/05/environmental -activist-murders-double; Nina Lakhani, "More Than 300 Human Rights Activists Were Killed in 2019, Report Reveals," *Guardian*, January 14, 2020, www.theguardian .com/law/2020/jan/14/300-human-rights-activists-killed-2019-report.

Conclusion

1. Wu Ming Foundation, "Migrant Partisans: The Internationalist Resistance against Italian Fascism," Libcom, July 3, 2019, https://libcom.org/history/migrant-partisans -internationalist-resistance-against-italian-fascism.

2. Leanne Betasamosake Simpson, *As We Have Always Done: Indigenous Freedom through Radical Resistance* (Minneapolis: University of Minnesota Press, 2017), 10.

3. Adom Getachew, *Worldmaking after Empire: The Rise and Fall of Self-Determination* (Princeton: Princeton University Press, 2019), 2.

4. Frank Jacobs, "'The West' Is, in Fact, the World's Biggest Gated Community," Big

Think, October 12, 2019, https://bigthink.com/strange-maps/walled-world.

5.   Toni Morrison, "Home," in *The House that Race Built*, Wahneema Lubiano, ed. (New York: Vintage, 1998), 12.

Index

About the Author

Harsha Walia is the award-winning author of *Undoing Border Imperialism* (2013). Trained in the law, she has been a community organizer in migrant justice, anticapitalist, feminist, abolitionist and anti-imperialist movements, including No One Is Illegal, for two decades.